Days Out UK, London and South East England

Published by Best Guides Ltd
P O Box 427
Northampton
NN2 7YJ
T +44 (0) 1604 711994
F +44 (0) 1604 722446
Email mail@daysoutuk.com
Web www.daysoutuk.com

ISBN 1 901 258 37 8
A catalogue record for this book is
available from the British Library

GW00641041

Credits

Editor
Alyson Spark
Editorial Assistant
Leanne Pinnock
Events Data co-ordinator
Leanne Allen
Database Programming
David White
Administration
Kathleen Eele
Publisher
Martin Spark

Photography
Front and back cover:
Tony Stone Images. All English
Heritage and National Trust properties with a picture are copyright to
their respective libraries and are
used with permission.

Printed and bound
in Italy by LEGOPRINT

Every effort has been made to
ensure that the information
published is as accurate as
possible prior to publication. A full
programme of verification directly
with the listed attractions has been
carried out, however Best Guides
Ltd cannot be held responsible for
any errors or omissions or changes
that may have occurred or for the
consequences of reliance on the
information published. We
suggest that you telephone in
advance before attending any
special events to ensure that they
are still on or the dates have not
been changed.

London & South East

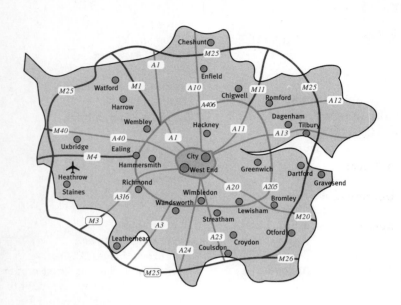

*Note: Further coupons for this area
and other areas are available upon
application.
Please call 0800 316 8900*

London & South East

Kent

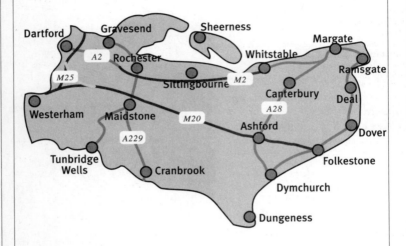

Dartford Gravesend Sheerness Margate
A2 Rochester Whitstable Ramsgate
M25 Sittingbourne M2 Canterbury Deal
Westerham Maidstone M20 A28
Ashford Dover
A229 Tunbridge Wells Folkestone
Cranbrook Dymchurch
Dungeness

Kent

Abbeys

Bayham Old Abbey

Bayham Abbey Lamberhurst Tunbridge Wells Kent TN3 8BG

[off B2169 2m W in East Sussex. BR: Frant 4m. Bus: 0800 696 996]

Tel: 01892 890381

Ruins of a house of 'white' canons, founded in 1208, in an 18th century landscaped setting. The Georgian House (Dower House) is also open to the public.

All year 1 Apr-1 Nov daily 10.00-18.00 (dusk in Oct). 2 Nov-31 Mar Sat-Sun 10.00-16.00.
A£2.00 C£1.00 Concessions£1.50

↓*special events*

▶ **Medieval Monastic Entertainers**
6/5/00-7/5/00
From Noon. Play authentic medieval games, learn about cures, folklore and early machinery, plus a unique guided tour

▶ **Scarecrow Workshops**
22/7/00-23/7/00
From Noon. The opportunity for younger visitors to make miniature scarecrows to take home

▶ **Childrens' Fun Workshop**
5/8/00-6/8/00
From Noon. Hands on fun for all children in idyllic surroundings. Bring a picnic and stay all day!

▶ **Two Gentlemen of Verona**
19/8/00-19/8/00
At 19.45. Shakespeare's classic romantic comedy, full of charming comic characters

▶ **Bayham Abbey Sheepdog Demonstrations**
27/8/00-28/8/00
From Noon. Enjoy displays of sheepdogs, sheep and geese

▶ **Childrens' Medieval Games and Stories**
2/9/00-3/9/00
From Noon. Hands on fun for all children in idyllic surroundings. Bring a picnic and stay all day!

▶ **Music of the Georgian Age**
9/9/00-10/9/00
From Noon. Delightful 18th century music played on authentic copies of period instruments

▶ **Medieval Falconry**
23/9/00-24/9/00
From Noon. Magnificent medieval birds of prey flying free

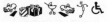

Minster Abbey

Church Street Minster Ramsgate Kent CT12 4HF

[2m from BR Station parallel to High Street]

Tel: 01843 821254

One of the first nunneries in England was built on this site in the 7th century. The Saxon house, one of the few remaining stone Saxon houses in existence, dating from 1027 was rebuilt in later centuries, but is still a religious community and is run by Benedictine nuns. The nuns of the old abbey and the cloisters are open to the public.

All year 1 May-end Sept Mon-Fri 11.00-12.00 & 14.00-16.30, Sat 11.00-12.00, Oct-Apr Mon-Sat 11.00-12.00. Closed Sun

Admission Free

St Augustine's Abbey

Longport Canterbury Kent CT1 1TF

[0.25m E of Cathedral Close. Pay & Display car park opposite abbey entrance in Longport. Bus: from surrounding areas. BR: Canterbury E & W both 0.75m]

Tel: 01227 767345 Fax: 01227 767345

Founded in 598, this is one of the earliest Monastic sites in England. There are remarkable remains of the original 6th century churches, the Norman Church and Medieval Monastery. A new museum and interpretation centre offers interactive audio guides and video displays plus a collection of over 150 important and unique artefacts discovered on site.

1 Apr-31 Oct daily 10.00-18.00 dusk in Oct. 1 Nov-31 Mar daily 10.00-16.00. Closed 24-26 Dec
A£2.50 C£1.30 Concessions£1.90

↓*special events*

▶ **Medieval Monastic Entertainers**
30/4/00-1/5/00
Authentic medieval games, cures, folklore and early machinery, plus a unique guided tour

▶ **Canterbury Tales**
2/7/00-30/7/00
At 13.30 and 15.00. Three of Chaucer's best (and bawdiest!) stories on 2, 9, 16, 23 & 30 July

▶ **Children's Festival**
19/8/00-20/8/00
Fun for all the family including puppet theatre, drama workshops, storytelling, juggling and a magic nature trail

▶ **Medieval Music**
27/8/00-28/8/00
Enjoy melodies and dance tunes dating back to the 12th century

▶ **Life in the Age of St Augustine**
23/9/00-24/9/00
Living history from the year 597AD. With crafts, cookery, medicine and religion

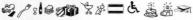

Kent

Agriculture / Working Farms

Hop Farm Country Park

Maidstone Road Paddock Wood Tonbridge Kent TN12 6PY

[on the A228. 20mins fron J5 M25 & 15mins from J4 M20]

Tel: 01622 871577 Fax: 01622 872630

The largest collection of Victorian Oast Houses in the World, housing the Hop Story Museum, Pottery Workshop and Shire Horse Centre. Children's Indoor Play Centre. Animal Village and Nature Trail. Fully licensed Restaurant and Café. A Great Family Day Out!

All year Mar-Oct daily 10.00-18.00. Nov-Feb daily 10.00-16.00. Closed 25 & 26 Dec
Last Admission: Summer 17.00 Winter 15.00
A£4.50 C(5-15)&OAPs&Students£3.00

Parsonage Farm

Rural Heritage Centre North Elham Canterbury Kent CT4 6UY

[.5m from Elham on Elham Valley Road. From Canterbury take A2 towards Dover, turn-off signed Barham.. Plenty of on site parking.]

Tel: 01303 840356/840766 Fax: 01303 840183

Family-run working farm with traditional breeds of farm animals, such as pigs, cattle, chickens, ducks and geese together with many breeds of sheep. The centuries old farmhouse contains exhibits illustrating the history of the farm. Old farm implements and displays of wool processing. Nature trail. Picnic and play area.

8 Apr-30 Sept Tue-Sun 10.30-17.00. Closed Mon
A£3.40 C£2.00

Animal Attractions

South of England Rare Breeds Centre
Woodchurch Ashford Kent TN26 3RJ
[J10 M20 9m, on B2067 between Hamstreet /

Tenterden follow brown tourist signs. Plenty of on site parking available]

Tel: 01233 861493 Fax: 01233 861457
www.rarebreeds.org.uk

A fun family day out with rare farm animals, many to touch. Children's Barn where children can play with young animals, also regular 'Meet the Animals' sessions. You can see the reconstruction of an historic Georgian farmstead, enjoy farm rides, woodland walks, toddler's sandpit and paddling pool, adventure playground. Low price children's menus in 'The Granary'.

All year Summer: daily 10.30-17.30, Winter: Tue-Sun 10.30-16.30. Closed 24 & 25 Dec
A£3.50 C(3-15)£1.90 OAPs£3.00. Group rates: A£2.75 C£1.50

discount offer: Up to Two Adults At Group Rate (£2.75)

↓ *special events*

▶ **Pudding Day**
6/2/00-3/12/00

1st Sunday of every month: 6 Feb, 5 Mar, 2 Apr, 7 May, 4 June, 2 July, 6 Aug, 3 Sept, 1 Oct, 5 Nov & 3 Dec. British puds, served with steaming custard, cream or ice cream

▶ **Half Term - Half Price**
19/2/00-27/2/00

▶ **Easter Fun**
23/4/00-24/4/00

Lots of activities on an 'Easter' theme, including Bunny Hunt, craft fair and children's entertainment

▶ **Real Ale Festival**
27/5/00-27/5/00

Annual CAMRA Beer festival with over 30 real ales, ciders and perry. Morris Dancing, music, games and fun

▶ **Piggy Picnics**
28/5/00-29/5/00

Piglet racing, piggy obstacle course, piggy bathtime, craft fair and a children's competition

▶ **Classic Car Rally**
25/6/00-25/6/00

6th Annual Car Rally - cars, bikes, coaches, lorries and bicycles from yesteryear. Bouncy castle, children's roundabout, arena concourse, competitions, beer tent and BBQ

▶ **A World of Difference**
24/7/00-6/8/00

Magical multi-sensory festival - explore the indoor exhibition and (from 31/7 to 6/8) the inflatable maze - full of light and colour

▶ **Rare Breeds Show and Country Fair**
20/8/00-20/8/00

Show of Rare and Minority Breeds, country craft displays, children's entertainment, local produce, trailer rides, beer tent, BBQ. See horses, dogs, birds of prey, rats, reptiles and ferrets!

▶ **Transport Extravaganza**
27/8/00-28/8/00

Lots of old cars and classic transport plus arena entertainment, funfair, crafts and food

► **Half Term - Half Price!**
21/10/00-29/10/00
Half Price Offer - children paying full entry price can bring one adult at half normal price

► **Christmas Gift Market**
18/11/00-19/11/00
Two day market with lovely local crafts, gifts and seasonal entertainment. (Santa's Stable open both days 11.00-15.00, extra charge)

► **Carols in the Barn**
10/12/00-17/12/00
Dec 10 and 17 only, traditional carols in a traditional setting. Hythe Town Band (Dec 10) and Hythe Salvation Army Band (Dec 17), start 14.30-15.00. Admission Free half an hour before start time

Archaeology

Lullingstone Roman Villa
Lullingstone Lane Eynsford Kent DA4 0JA
[J3 M25 0.5m SW of Eynsford off A225, follow A20 towards Brands Hatch]
Tel: 01732 778000
The excavation of this roman villa in 1949 uncovered one of the most exciting archaeological finds of the century. Here you can see some of the most remarkable villa remains in Britain, including wonderful mosaic tiled floors, wall painting and the ruins of one of the earliest Christian chapels in Britain. Audio tape tour included in price.
27 Mar-31 Oct daily 10.00-18.00 or dusk if sooner. 1 Nov-26 Mar daily 10.00-16.00. Closed 24-26 Dec
Last Admission: 30mins before closing
A£2.50 C£1.90 OAPs&UB40 £1.30

↓*special events*

► **Bones, Skulls, Teeth & Diseases**
15/4/00-16/4/00
Renowed expert Trevor Anderson explains the fascinating facts discovered from medieval skeletons

► **Easter Activities**
22/4/00-22/4/00
Fun for children includng egg painting, colouring competition and Easter Bonnet making

► **Meet the Romans**
27/5/00-1/6/00
Meet a Roman couple living at the Villa and enjoy period activities including face painting and music

► **The Last Romans**
1/7/00-2/7/00
Meet soldiers and a horseman of the type that defended Britain after the departure of Rome's Legions

► **Roman Storytelling**
8/7/00-9/7/00
Enthralling Roman stories to enjoy

► **Roman Mosaics**
15/7/00-16/7/00
An insight into Roman domestic design, with the opportunity to create a mosaic

► **Roman Pottery-making**
22/7/00-23/7/00
Watch a Roman potter in action

► **Meet A Roman Soldier**
29/7/00-30/7/00
Marcus and Agrippina host a variety of activities for younger visitors

► **Jewellery and Mosaic-making**
5/8/00-6/8/00
Make your own Roman and Celtic artefacts

► **Puppet Making Workshops**
12/8/00-13/8/00
The opportunity for younger visitors to make a puppet and take part in a puppet show

► **A Roman Kitchen**
19/8/00-20/8/00
A look at Roman cuisine with the chance to taste some authentic Roman recipes

► **A Roman and his British Wife**
27/8/00-28/8/00
Fascinating talks and displays of Romano-British life

► **Meet A Roman Soldier**
21/10/00-29/10/00
See entry for 29 July

Arts, Crafts & Textiles

Canterbury Royal Museum Art Gallery and Buffs Regimental Museum
High Street Canterbury Kent CT1 2RA
[off A2 London / Dover road in Canterbury centre signposted]
Tel: 01227 452747 Fax: 01227 455047
The city's picture collection including the TS Cooper Gallery - England's leading Victorian animal painter; the Gallery also displays fine archaeological objects and decorative arts resulting from close links with Europe over the centuries. Regular art events are held in the Special Exhibitions Gallery. Also housed here is the Buffs Regimental Museum.
All year Mon-Sat 10.00-17.00. Closed Good Fri and Christmas period
Admission Free

Metropole Arts Centre
The Leas Folkestone Kent CT20 2LS
Tel: 01303 255070
Art exhibitions, chamber/jazz/piano recitals, lectures, workshops, children's events.

Birmingham

From Apr Mon-Sat 10.00 17.00 Sun 14.30-17.00
Admission to exhibitions free

Tunbridge Wells Museum and Art Gallery
Civic Centre Mount Pleasant Royal Tunbridge Wells Kent TN1 1JN
[off A264, brown pedestrian signs, next to the Town Hall]
Tel: 01892 526121/554171 Fax: 01892 534227
www.tunbridgewells.gov.uk
The museum displays local and natural history, archaeology, toys and dolls, and domestic and agricultural bygones. There is a fine display of Tunbridge ware. The art gallery has regularly changing exhibitions which include showings of the Ashton Bequest of Victorian oil paintings.
All year Mon-Sat 09.30-17.00. Closed Bank Hol & Easter Sat
Admission Free

↓ special events
▶ **Arts and Crafts 2000**
4/3/00-18/3/00
Annual arts and craft show by local residents
▶ **The Age of Steam**
16/3/00-16/3/00
George Holland describes his experiences as a local engine driver in the age of steam, starts 20.00
▶ **The Embroiderers' Guild**
27/3/00-8/4/00
Embroidery and textiles by the Tunbridge Wells and District Branch
▶ **Art Out East**
13/4/00-29/4/00
Multicultural, functional and decorative art and craft from East London
▶ **Women in Focus**
5/5/00-3/6/00
Portrait photographer Derek Tamea pays tribute to the leading women of today. Talk on May 5 at 19.15
▶ **Beyond Blue**
30/6/00-12/7/00

Contemporary, colourful and exciting pictures and 3D works by Elizabeth Major and Bill Hudson
▶ **The Perfect Lady 1780-1820**
14/7/00-14/7/00
Lee Ault demonstrates fashion and social attitudes of the Georgian period at 19.15, in the council chamber. Call for details
▶ **Tunbridge Wells on Paper and Canvas**
18/7/00-31/7/00
Views of old Tunbridge Wells in water-colours, oils, engravings, drawings and pastels
▶ **The Ashton Bequest of Victorian Oil Paintings**
3/8/00-16/8/00
Landscapes, genre scenes and still lifes of the 1860s and 1870s from reserve collections
▶ **A Travelling Naturalist's Art**
19/8/00-4/9/00
Wildlife and landscapes in oil and water-colour by Robert Davison
▶ **People, Places and Things**
7/9/00-23/9/00
Bryan Senior's acrylic streets, still lifes, figures landscapes, flowers and more. Talk by Bryan on Sept 12 at 19.15
▶ **Studies in Still Life**
28/9/00-7/10/00
Fruit and flower still lifes in oil and water-colour by Billy Showell
▶ **Annual General Meeting**
3/10/00-3/10/00
19.15 in the art gallery
▶ **Kent Potters Association**
11/10/00-24/10/00
Sculpture, domestic wares and raku, functional and decorative
▶ **The Architect Artists**
28/10/00-15/11/00
Herbert Morel and colleagues show their landscapes and streetscapes. Talk on Oct 31 at 19.15
▶ **New Creations**
18/11/00-5/12/00
Four artists create their own arts and crafts show in all media
▶ **Martin Bedford's New Landscapes**
8/12/00-3/1/01
Landscape abstractions in paint

Birds, Butterflies & Bees

MacFarlan's Butterfly Centre
Canterbury Road Swingfield Dover Kent CT15 7HX
[on junction of A260 with Elham-Lydden road]
Tel: 01303 844244
A tropical greenhouse garden with scores of colourful free-flying butterflies from all over the world among exotic plants such as

bougainvillea, oleander and banana. The temperate section houses British butterflies.
Easter-5 Oct daily 10.00-17.00
A£2.00 C£1.25 OAPs£1.50 Family Ticket £5.50

Wingham Wildlife Park
Rusham Road Shatterling Canterbury Kent CT3 1JL
[A257 between Canterbury and Sandwich]
Tel: 01227 720836 Fax: 01227 722452
A fascinating day out for the whole family. Wander around the landscaped gardens and walk through aviary to see our collection of birds and animals including: llamas, meerkats, otters, prarie dogs, wallabies, parrots, ducks, peafowl, emus and rheas. Then enjoy a snack in the tea-room and a browse through the gift shop.
All year daily 10.00-18.00, dusk in Winter months
Last Admission: 14.30
discount offer: One Free Child With Two Full Paying Adults

Country Parks & Estates

Knole
Knole Sevenoaks Kent TN15 0RP
[off M25 London Orbital at S end of Sevenoaks town just E of A225. BR: Sevenoaks]
Tel: 01732 450608 infoline Fax: 01732 465528
Tour 13 magnificent state rooms in one of the great treasure houses of England. Find exquisite silver furniture, fragile tapestries, rare carpets and other unique furniture including the first 'Knole' settee, state beds and even an early royal loo! Newly restored garden gates and railings; conserved curtains and counterpane on Lady Betty Germain's bed. Study a remarkable collection of historical portraits by masters such as Sir Joshua Reynolds, Van Dyck and Gainsborough. Uncover Knole's intriguing history of connections with the famous: Archbishops of Canterbury, Henry VIII, Elizabeth I, the Sackville family, Dukes of Dorset, Vita Sackville-West and Virginia Woolf whose novel Orlando is set at the house. Enjoy throughout the year the extensive deer park owned by Lord Sackville and visit the displays in the Bewhouse Tea Room. Dogs in park only on lead, do not feed the deer.
House: 27 Mar-31 Oct Wed-Sat 12.00-16.00, Sun, Bank Hol Mon & Good Fri 11.00-17.00.
Garden: May-Sept first Wed in each month only.
Last Admission: House: 15.30, 16.00
£5.00 C£2.50 Family Ticket £12.50. Pre-booked

Groups £4.00. Parking (NT members free) £2.50. Garden: A£1.00 C£0.50. Special Offer: Concessions for NT members on BR London Charing Cross to Knole combined train/bus admission ticket call 0345 484950

↓ *special events*
▶ **Recital by Amabile**
10/6/00-10/6/00
With readings by Gregory Warren Wilson.
Tickets £11.00, starts at 19.30
▶ **Classical guitar with Julian Bream**
9/9/00-9/9/00
At 19.30, tickets £15.00

Festivals & Shows

Biggin Hill Battle Of Britain Open Day
(Air Displays Int Ltd) Biggin Hill Airport Biggin Hill Westerham Kent TN16 3BN
[J4 M25. Bus service available from BR: Bromley South]
Tel: 01959 540959 Fax: 01959 575969
www.airdisplaysint.co.uk
One of the great British summertime events of the year and one of the biggest outside events held inside the M25. International flying display with top teams and pilots. Unique mixture of modern, military, vintage and civilian aircraft. The many family attractions combined with excellent value for family tickets make this event very popular with families as well as enthusiasts. Disabled facilities and privileged viewing areas.
Sept 17 2000, gates open 08.00, flying commences 12.00-16.00
Provisional Ticket Prices: Advance A£11.00 C£4.00 Family (car + 5 occupants max 3 adults) £24.00. Gate A£14.00 C£5.00 Family (car + 5 occupants max 3 adults) £30.00

Biggin Hill International Air Fair 2000
Air Displays Int Ltd Biggin Hill Airport Biggin Hill Westerham Kent TN16 3BN
[J4 M25. Shuttle bus service available from BR:

Kent

Bromley South]
Tel: 01959 540959 Fax: 01959 575969
www.airdisplaysint.co.uk
One of the great British summertime events of the year and one of the biggest outside events held inside the M25. World famous 7 hour international flying display with top teams and pilots. Unique mixture of modern, military, vintage and civilian aircraft. The many family attractions combined with excellent value for family tickets make this event very popular with families as well as enthusiasts. Disabled facilities and privileged viewing area.
June 3-4 2000. Gates open 08.00, flying commences 11.00-18.00 each day
Queuing Times: possible
Advance tickets - Provisional: A£10.00 C(5-15)£4.00 Family Ticket (Car+5 people)£20.00. Car Park £Free. Gate Prices: A£12.50 C(5-15)£4.50 Family Ticket (Car+5 people)£25.00. Car Park £Free

Celebrity Connections Festival
Festival Office: Town Clerk's Office Pierremont Hall Broadstairs Kent CT10 1JX
Tel: 01843 868718 Fax: 01843 866048
www.broadstairs.gov.uk
Celebrity Connections is a mixed Festival. It applauds famous people who have lived in or visited Broadstairs or St. Peter's, with talks, walks, concerts, film, theatre, music, children's clubs etc. Many famous people have graced our lovely town, and the Town Council proudly showcases a choice of celebrities each year.
Oct 26-28 2000. Please call to confirm dates
Prices vary according to the events/concert you choose, please call Festival Office for details

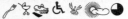

Herne Bay Festival
Herne Bay Kent *[M2 from London and A299 taking Herne Bay turn off after Whitstable]*
Tel: 01227 742690 Fax: 01227 742731
Two weeks of family fun, almost all events are free, including Herne bay carnival and regatta.
Aug 5-20 2000
Admission Free

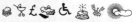

Herne Bay Heavy Horse Day
Events office William Street Herne Bay Kent CT6 5NX
[A2 to A299 signposted to Herne Bay]
Tel: 01227 742690 Fax: 01227 742731
This parade provides a unique oppurtunity to combine a day out at the seaside with the chance to see vintage transport from an age when "horse power" had real meaning.

June 4 2000
Free

Hever 2000
The Lakeside Theatre Hever Castle Hever Edenbridge Kent TN8 7NG
[situated 3m S/E of Edenbridge off B2026 between Seveoaks and East Grinstead. J5 or 6 of M25. Plenty of on site parking.]
Tel: 01732 866114 Box Office Fax: 01732 866796
Since it opened in the early eighties, the Lakeside Theatre has become one of the most popular outdoor venues in the south-east, attracting many thousands every summer, many of whom return year after year. Situated in the beautiful Italian Garden of Hever Castle in Kent, overlooking the lake, it offers the perfect setting for a pre-show picnic with family and friends. The tiered and covered seating make for an unusually initmate audiotrium to enjoy the programme of music, opera and drama which comprises the Summer Festival.
June 22-Aug 27 2000, Wed-Sun, all performances commences 20.00. Gates open for Picnic at 18.30
A£11.50-£18.00. Group rates 10+ 10%

↓*special events*
► **La Boheme**
22/6/00-24/6/00
Performed by Beaufort Opera.
► **The Tempest**
30/6/00-15/7/00
William Shakespeare's play performed by the Kent Repertory Company
► **Classic Jazz**
16/7/00-16/7/00
Humphrey Lyttelton with Stacey Kent.
► **Great Composers**
21/7/00-21/7/00
The Primavera Chamber Orchestra, musical and artistic director Paul Manley.
► **The Best of Gilbert & Sullivan**
22/7/00-22/7/00
Including 'Trial by Jury', performed by Opera Options.
► **Opera Classics**
23/7/00-23/7/00
Popular excerpts and arias from the greatest classical operas performed by the London Opera Players.
► **The Mikado**
25/7/00-30/7/00
Performed by Opera Options. A traditional production of Gilbert & Sullivan's much loved operetta.
► **Private Lives**
4/8/00-19/8/00
Noel Coward's well known play performed by The Kent Repertory Company.

► **Hello Dora**
20/8/00-20/8/00
An evening with Dora Bryan and her celebrated 'one woman' show.

► **The Merry Widow**
24/8/00-26/8/00
Two dates: 24 & 26 Aug. By Franz Lehar - performed by Court Opera Productions.

► **Hey Mr Hammerstein**
25/8/00-27/8/00
Two dates: 25 & 27 Aug. A musical celebration of the career of Oscar Hammerstein, performed by Court Opera Productions.

Kent Beer Festival 2000
Merton Farm Merton Lane Canterbury Kent CT2
[leave A2 at J for Canterbury. Take Hythe turning off ring road. Follow RAC signs to festival]
Tel: 01227 463478 Fax: 01227 463478
This is the 26th Kent Beer Festival held in a huge barn in a Kentish farmyard will feature the usual range of over 100 real ales and ciders from home and abroad. Food stalls, souvenir glasses and entertainment. The festival is run by volunteer members of the Campaign for Real Ale (CAMRA). Free festival programme available.
July 20-22 2000. Thur: 18.30-23.00, Fri: 12.00-16.00 & 18.30-23.00, Sat: 11.30-16.30 & 18.30-23.00
Thur: A£2.00, CAMRA members Free, Fri: Lunchtime free, evening A£4.00 in advance, Sat: A£2.00 each session (free after 21.00). C£Free

Kent County Showground
Detling Hill Detling Maidstone Kent ME14 3JF
[off A249 Link Rd between M20 and M2]
Tel: 01622 630975 Fax: 01622 630978
County showground holding many special events. See Special Events

↓*special events*

► **Kent County Show 2000**
13/7/00-15/7/00
Kent's premier agricultural show featuring over 500 trade stands, livestock, equestrian events, demonstrations and other related attractions. Cheaper if pre paid 01622 630975

► **Detling Transport and Country Festival 2000**
12/8/00-13/8/00

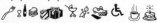

Shepway Festival
The Leas Folkestone Kent CT20
[Folkestone, signposted from J13 M20, A20, A259 & A2]
Tel: 01303 852321 Fax: 01303 852502
www.kents-garden-coast.co.uk

Many events on the days leading up to 3rd September when there will be a major Air show.
Aug 26-Sept 3 2000
Admission free for most events.

Kent

Bay Museum and Pines Gardens
Beach Road St. Margarets Bay Dover Kent CT15 6DZ
[opposite the Pines garden]
Tel: 01304 852764
The Museum contains artefacts collected by the late Fred Cleary CBE, and was created by the Trustees in rememberance of the founder of the St. Margrets Bay Trust. Professionally laid out, the Bay Museum has many items of local, worldwide and maritime interest for both adults and children including special exhibitions and video. There are superb walks North and South along the cliff to Kingsdown and Dover with panoramic views of the channel and the French Coast. The beach and foreshaw are just 100 yards down the hill.
29-31 Mar 14.00-17.00, 3-5 May 14.00-17.00, 24 May-7 Sept Wed-Sun 14.00-17.00
Museum: A£0.65 C£0.35 Garden: A£1.15 C£0.35

Dover Museum
Market Square Dover Kent CT16 1PB
[adjacent to White Cliffs Experience in Market Square]
Tel: 01304 201066 Fax: 01304 241186
www.doveruk.com/museum/
New three-floor museum in the centre of Dover. History and archaeology of Dover on two floors with models and original objects including Roman, Saxon and medieval archaeology, Cinque Ports objects, portrait of Elizabeth I, Victorian and war items. Special exhibition gallery of temporary displays. The Dover Bronze Age Boat, believed to be the world's oldest seagoing boat is now on display in its superb gallery setting.
All year daily 10.00-17.30. Closed 25-26 Dec
A£1.70 C&OAPs£0.90. Local Resident Concession 50% discount
discount offer: Two For The Price Of One

↓*special events*

► **Rocks and Rex**
19/2/00-2/5/00
The Dover Geology and Fossil Show

► **The Fossil Roadshow**
18/3/00-19/3/00
An expert panel identify your rocks and fossils and answer any geology queries. Plus a chance

to see and handle fossils and dinosaurs. Open 10.00-17.00

▶ **Belt Bosses**
22/4/00-22/4/00
Bronze Age Boat Gallery from 10.00-16.30

▶ **Bronze Age Boat Event**
22/4/00-24/4/00
Learn about the Bronze Age by participating in a range of hands-on activities at the Bronze Age Boat Gallery

▶ **'Highlights of the Millennia'**
13/5/00-29/10/00
A look at the definitive eras of the last 2000 years inluding the Roman, Saxon, Tudor and the Second World War periods.

▶ **Roman Mosaics**
30/5/00-30/5/00
Homes of the Millennium exhibition

▶ **Saxon Copper Jewellery**
17/6/00-17/6/00
Homes of the Millennium exhibition from 10.00-16.30

▶ **Tudor Woodblock Printing**
22/7/00-24/10/00
Held on July 22 and Oct 24 only. Homes of the Millennium exhibition, 10.00-16.30

▶ **Victorian Clay Tiles**
30/8/00-30/8/00
Homes of the Millennium exhibition, 10.00-16.30

▶ **World War II Rag Rugs**
23/9/00-23/9/00
Homes of the Millennium exhibition, 10.00-16.30

▶ **Miniature Bronze Age Pots**
18/11/00-18/11/00
In the Bronze Age Boat Gallery, 10.00-16.30

▶ **Victorian Christmas Decorations**
9/12/00-9/12/00
Mezzanine at the Museum, 10.00-16.30

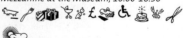

Guildhall Museum
High Street Rochester Kent ME1 1PY
[buses pass through Corporation Street and stop a few yards from the door. Served by open-topped bus during summer holiday weeks. BR: Rochester 1m, Strood 1m or Chatham 2m]
Tel: 01634 848717 Fax: 01634 832919
The Guildhall Museum is located in Rochester High Street very near to Rochester Bridge. It contains many important and varied items of interest from Pre-history to Victorian times. The Museum is housed in two buildings, one dating from 1687 and the other from 1909. The Museum has several hands-on features, coin-minting, brass rubbing and a flintlock musket. Two panoramic cameras located high in the tower atop the 1909 building, provide the opportunity to "City watch." An evocative

feature is the interpretation of life on one of the infamous prison hulks that were the miserable homes of many convicts and prisoners-of-war. Walk down through the decks and see the cramped and insanitary conditions forced upon these luckless individuals.
All year daily 10.00-17.30. Closed a few days over Christmas
Admission Free, Donations Box

Herne Bay Museum And Gallery
William Street Herne Bay Kent CT6 5EW
[A299]
Tel: 01227 367368 Fax: 01227 742560
Displays about the seaside town and its story, and about Reculver Roman Fort nearby. Regular art exhibitions and events held in the gallery.
All year Mon-Sat 10.00-16.00, also Sun July & Aug 13.00-16.00
Admission Free

Museum of Kent Life
Lock Lane Sandling Maidstone Kent ME14 3AU
[J6 M20 then A229 to Maidstone]
Tel: 01622 763936 Fax: 01622 662024
This award-winning 40 acre open air museum reflects changing times and lives in the 'Garden of England' over the last century. The UK's last working oast house plus barn, granary, hoppers huts, and wagon store house featuring fascinating exhibitions including the 'Darling Buds of May.' Special events see Guide.
1 Mar-6 Nov daily 10.00-17.30. Other times for pre-booked groups only
Last Admission: 16.30
A£4.20 C&OAPs£2.70 Family Ticket £12.00 School Pupils £2.00. Group rates: A£3.80 C&OAPs£2.45

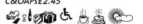

Old Town Hall Museum
Market Place Margate Kent CT9 1ER
[signposted from town and seafront]
Tel: 01843 231213 Fax: 01843 582359
Margate's development as a seaside resort; also old Court Room and Victorian Police cells. Reg Charity No: 288702.
All year Apr-Sept daily 10.00-17.00. Oct-Mar Mon-Fri 09.30-16.30
Last Admission: 30mins before closing
A£1.00 C&OAPs£0.50
discount offer: One Child Free When Accompanied By A Full Paying Adult

Ramsgate Museum
Guildford Lawn Ramsgate Kent CT11 9AY

[well signposted in Ramsgate Town Centre]

Tel: 01843 593532 Fax: 01843 852692

The museum tells the story of Ramsgate in days gone by with paintings and photographs of Royal Harbour, churches, breweries, pubs, shops, Ramsgate personalities and holiday souvenirs. On the first floor, Ramsgate Library Gallery has been constructed to provide a continuous, high quality programme of exhibitions and related events, covering all aspects of the visual arts. The Gallery is funded by Kent County Council.

All year Mon-Thur 09.30-18.00, Fri 09.30-19.00, Sat 09.30-17.00. Closed Bank Hol

Last Admission: Mon-Thur 17.45, Fri 18.45, Sat 16.45

Admission Free

Tenterden and District Museum

Station Road Tenterden Kent TN30 6HN

[off High Street - A28]

Tel: 01580 764310

The buildings and history of Tenterden and Cinque Ports and the Weald of Kent are featured at this local history museum. There are corporation records and insignia as well as exhibits on local trades, agriculture and hop growing. Also on display is the Tenterden Tapestry. New Victorian room and collection of local postcards.

Mar Sat-Sun 14.00-16.30. Apr-Oct Sat-Thur 14.00-16.45. Summer school hol Sat-Thur, late July-Aug 11.00-16.45

A£0.75 C£0.25 OAPs£0.50

Food & Drink

Biddenden Vineyards
Little Whatmans Gribble Bridge Lane

Biddenden Kent TN27 8DH

[off A262, between Biddenden and Tenterden. Plenty of on site parking]

Tel: 01580 291726 Fax: 01580 291933

The present vineyard was established in 1969 and now covers 22 acres. Visitors are welcome to stroll around the vineyard and to taste wines, ciders and apple juice available at the shop. Tea and coffee available. Guided tours for pre-booked groups.

All year Mar-Dec Mon-Sat 10.00-17.00, Sun & Bank Hol 11.00-17.00. Jan-Feb Mon-Sat 10.00-17.00. Closed Sun, also closed Dec 24 from 12.00 -1 Jan incl. Guided tours for pre-booked groups - call for details

Admission and Tastings £Free

discount offer: 10% Discount On All Shop Purchases

↓*special events*

► **Easter Bunny Hunt**

23/4/00-23/4/00

From 11.00 you can hunt for the Easter Bunny and meet the owls from Hawkhurst Owl Sanctuary

► **Special Christmas Promotion**

25/11/00-17/12/00

Free mince pies, mulled cider special offers and a Free Prize Draw every weekend - on following dates: Sat & Sun 25 & 26 Nov, Sat & Sun 2 & 3, 9 & 10, 16 & 17 Dec

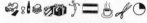

Tenterden Vineyard Park

Small Hythe Tenterden Kent TN30 7NG

[from Tenterden High Street (A28), turn L at the William Caxton Public House onto the B2082 towards Rye, Tenterden Vineyard Park 2m on, on the R. Plenty of parking on site]

Tel: 01580 763033 Fax: 01580 765333

www.chapeldownwines.co.uk/tenterden-vineyardpark

Tenterden Vineyard Park in home to Chapel Down Wines, the leading producer of quality red, white and sparkling wines in the UK. Superb visitor facilities for individuals and groups, free wine tastings. Guided Tours of the winery, daily during June-Sept and weekends only May and Oct.

All year Jan& Feb Mon-Sat 10.00-17.00 Mar-Dec daily 10.00-17.00. Grapevine Café Easter-Oct daily 10.00-17.00

Last Admission: 17.00

Admission £Free. Guided Tours: A£3.50 C£2.00 OAPs£3.00. Group rates available

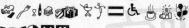

Kent

Kent

Gardens & Horticulture

Bedgebury National Pinetum
Park Lane Goudhurst Cranbrook Kent TN17 2SL
[1.5m N of Cranbrook off A21 onto B2079]
Tel: 01580 211044 Fax: 01580 212423
http://www.forestry.gov.uk
Set in landscaped grounds, Bedgebury houses
the world's most important collection of
Conifers. The combination of magnificent
trees, lakes, Rhododendrons, wildflowers and a
multitude of wildlife, offers visitors a learning
experience and the chance to unwind in a
beautiful and tranquil environment.
Apr-Dec daily 10.00-17.00
A£3.00 C£1.50 OAPs£2.50

Brogdale World of Fruit
Brogdale Road Faversham Kent ME13 8XZ
*[J6 M2, A251 to Faversham, turn L on A2
towards Sittingbourne, 1st L after school]*
Tel: 01795 535286 Fax: 01795 531710
Come and see the largest collection of traditional and new varieties of fruit and plants in
the world, grown in 150 acres of beautiful
orchards. Regular guided tours lasting approximately one hour. A wide range of plant and
fruit for sale in the Plant Centre.

All year daily 09.30-17.30
*Admission Free. Tour prices: A£2.50 C(under
16)£1.50 Concessions£2.00*

Doddington Place Gardens
Church Lane Doddington Sittingbourne Kent
ME9 0BB
*[off A2 at Teynham and Ospringe, also signpost-
ed on A20 at Lenham]*
Tel: 01795 886101
Landscaped gardens in the grounds of a
Victorian country house (not open) with good
views over surrounding parkland and countryside. Edwardian rock garden and formal garden, rhododendrons and azaleas in a woodland setting, fine trees, yew hedges and a
recently built folly.
*May-Aug Sun 14.00-18.00, Wed and Bank Hol
Mon 11.00-18.00. Groups at other times, by
prior arrangement*
*A£3.50 C£0.50. Group rate £2.50. Coaches by
prior arrangement only*

Emmetts Garden
Ide Hill Sevenoaks Kent TN14 6AY
*[4m from M25 J5. 1.5m S of A25 on Sundridge /
Ide Hill road. 1.5m N of Ide Hill off B2042. BR:
Sevenoaks / Penshurst]*
Tel: 01732 868381/750367
Enjoy wonderful views across the Weald of
Kent from this peaceful garden, one of the
highest spots in the county. Follow the mean-
dering paths among rare trees and shrubs
planted by Victorian gardener William
Robinson. Wander around the pretty rock garden and Italianate rose garden or follow the
hillside woodland walk. Come and enjoy the
plants in all seasons - daffodils and bluebells
in Spring, roses in Summer, and glowing
colours in Autumn. And don't forget to look
out for the highest tree-top in Kent!
Wheelchair availab le for access to parts of the
garden. Dogs on leads only.
*27 Mar-30 May Wed-Sun & Bank Hol Mon
11.00-17.30. 2 June-31 Oct Wed, Sat-Sun &
Bank Hol Mon 11.00-17.30. Stable Tearoom and
Shop: As Garden 11.30-16.30*
Last Admission: 16.30
*A£3.00 C£1.50 Family Ticket £7.50. Pre-booked
Groups £2.20*
↓ *special events*
▶ **Bluebell Tour**
2/5/00-2/5/00
Tickets £6.00, starts at 18.30
▶ **Rhododendrons etc**
23/5/00-23/5/00
19.00, tickets £6.00

► **The Blues Band**
29/7/00-29/7/00
Open air concert at 19.30, tickets £13.00
► **Autumn Colours**
17/10/00-17/10/00
Starts at 14.00, a tour of the garden in its "autumn glory". Tickets £6.00

Goodnestone Park Gardens
Nr Wingham Canterbury Kent CT3 1PL
[8m SE of Canterbury 4m E of A2 0.25m SE of B2046 S of A257. BR: Adisham 2m. Plenty of parking on site]
Tel: 01304 840107 Fax: 01304 840107
The garden is approximately 14 acres with many fine trees, a woodland garden and the walled garden with a large collection of old roses and herbaceous plants. Jane Austen was a frequent visitor, her brother Edward having married a daughter of the house. The garden is continually being extended, with new plantings all the time. Member of the Historic Houses Association.
Gardens only: Mon Wed Thur Fri & Sun Mar-Oct 11.00-17.00, Sun Mar-Oct House open by appointment for parties of not over 20. 1999 Times: Mar-Oct Mon, Wed-Sat 11.00-17.00 Sun 12.00-18.00
A£3.00 C(0-12)£0.30 OAPs£2.50 Family Ticket (A2+C2)£4.50 Wheelchair users £1.00. Groups rates 20+ £2.50. Guided Tours £3.50
↓ *special events*
► **Ceramics Exhibition**
7/4/00-9/4/00
► **Garden Lectures**
9/5/00-18/7/00
Held on May 9, June 18 and July 18 only
► **Garden Opera**
11/8/00-11/8/00
► **Hardy Plant Society Sale**
19/8/00-20/8/00

Great Comp Garden
Comp Lane Platt Sevenoaks Kent TN15 8QS
[2m E off B2016]
Tel: 01732 882669/886154

A beautiful seven-acre garden created since 1957 by Mr and Mrs Cameron for low maintenance and year-round interest. There is a plantsmans' collection of trees, shrubs, heathers and herbaceous plants in a setting of fine lawns and grass paths. Planting styles vary from woodland and informal walks to terraces and forms paths, with ruins and ornaments
Daily Apr-Oct 11.00-18.00
A£2.50 C5£1.00 Annual ticket A£7.50 OAPs£5.00

Groombridge Place Gardens and The Enchanted Forest
Groombridge Place Groombridge Tunbridge Wells Kent TN3 9QG
[off A264 on B2100]
Tel: 01892 863999 Fax: 01892 863996
www.groombridgeplace.com
"Groombridge Place is wonderful because it's so different" is what our visitors say! Experience the history, mystery and excitement for yourself. Relax in the stunning formal gardens and enjoy the sheer magic of the Enchanted Forest. Take a canal boat cruise to the Forest, children love the "Dark Walk" and the Groms' Village and everyone is thrilled by the Romany Camp, the Giant Rabbits, the pig racing and the Birds of Prey. let your imagination run wild and you'll discover the best day out in the South East. Please call the venue to confirm dates for the following special events.
12 April-29 Oct daily 09.00-18.00
Last Admission: 17.00
A£7.50 C&OAPs£6.50 (price review in July)
↓ *special events*
► **Millennium Easter Extravaganza**
23/4/00-24/4/00
► **The Robin Hood Legend Live on...**
30/4/00-1/5/00
► **Bank Holiday Family Fun**
28/5/00-29/5/00
► **11th London to Brighton Classic Car Run**

Kent

4/6/00-4/6/00

Route Two: Starts Crystal Place, London. Check point 1. Groombridge Gardens, Kent, Check Point 2. Michelham Priory, Sussex. Finishing at Maderia Drive, Brighton. No charge to visitors at the Start and Finish points

▶ **Take to the Skies**
18/6/00-18/6/00
Hot air balloons and kites
▶ **Living Heritage Craft Fair**
8/7/00-9/7/00
▶ **Wings, Wheels and Steam 2000**
6/8/00-6/8/00
▶ **Scarecrows, Shires and Sheepdogs**
27/8/00-28/8/00
▶ **King Henry V and The Battle of Agincourt**
3/9/00-3/9/00
▶ **Millennium Kent Hot Air Balloon Classic**
10/9/00-10/9/00
▶ **MG Car Club**
17/9/00-17/9/00
South East centre autumn gathering
▶ **Living Heritage Craft Fair**
7/10/00-8/10/00
▶ **Nearly Hallowe'en Adventure**
28/10/00-28/10/00
▶ **Firework Spectacular**
4/11/00-4/11/00

Marle Place Gardens

Marle Place Road Brenchley Tonbridge Kent TN12 7HS

[off B2162 1m S of Horsmonden 1.5m NW of Lamerhurst follow brown and white tourist signs from Brenchley Village]

Tel: 01892 722304 Fax: 01892 724099

Marle Place is a romantic privately owned Wealden Garden of 10 acres close to Scotney and Sissinghurst Castles. A plantsman's garden with many interesting trees and shrubs. Featuring a Victorian gazebo and herb garden. Walled, fragrant garden and ornamental ponds. Yew hedges and herbaceous border. Architecturally important listed, 17th century house.

1 Apr-31 Oct daily 09.30-17.30
Last Admission: 17.00
A£3.00 Groups by arrangement

Mount Ephraim Gardens

Staple Street Hernhill Faversham Kent ME13 9TX

[1m off M2 A2 or A299]

Tel: 01227 751496 Fax: 01227 750940

8 acres of superb gardens set in the heart of family run orchards. The gardens offer an attractive balance of formal and informal with herbaceous border, a Topiary, a Japanese rock garden, water garden, rose terraces and a lake. Vineyard and orchard trails to follow. Tea is served in the Tea Rooms and the new Tea Terrace. Lunches served on Bank Holiday Sundays and Mondays. Craft centre and gift shop. Member of the Historic Houses Association. Dogs on leads allowed.

Gardens: Apr-Sept Mon, Wed, Thur, Sat & Sun 13.00-18.00. Craft Centre: Sun 14.00-18.00 only A£3.00 C£1.00. Group rates £2.50

discount offer: £1.00 Off Entrance For Adults. Valid Until 30 Sept 2000

↓*special events*

▶ **NCCPG Spring Plant Fair**
9/4/00-9/4/00
National Council for the Conservation of Plants and Gardens. For further details call 01227 751496
▶ **Pat a Lamb**
30/4/00-1/5/00
Display of young lambs amid wonderful orchard blossom. For details call 01227 751496
▶ **Millennium Garden Festival**
28/5/00-29/5/00
Wine, craft, plants, farm strawberries, live music, homemade food, gardening demonstrations, children's entertainment and folk dancing. For details call 01227 751496
▶ **Outdoor Shakespeare "A Midsummer Nights Dream"**
14/6/00-24/6/00
Picnic in the gardens Glyndebourne Style then watch Shakespeare. No performance on June 18 (Sun). For details call 01227 751496
▶ **Royal Philharmonic Orchestra**
22/7/00-22/7/00
Popular Classical Concert in the gardens with fireworks. For details call 01227 751496
▶ **Mount Ephraims's Apple Sunday**
9/9/00-9/9/00

Kent

A celebration of English Apples. For details call
01227 751496

Owl House Gardens
Mount Pleasant Lamberhurst Tunbridge Wells
Kent TN3 8LY
[1m NE off A21. Plenty parking on site]
Tel: 01892 890230 Fax: 01892 891290
The Owl House is a small, timber-framed 16th-century house, a former haunt of wool smugglers. Surrounding it are 13 acres of gardens with spring flowers, azaleas, rhododendrons, roses, shrubs and ornamental fruit trees. The sweeping lawns lead to lovely woodlands of oak and birch, and sunken water gardens. Dogs must be on leads
All year daily 11.00-18.00. Closed 25-26 Dec & 1 Jan
A£4.00 C£1.00. Group rates 10% discount

Scotney Castle Garden
Lamberhurst Tunbridge Wells Kent TN3 8JN
[1m S of Lamberhurst on A21. BR: Wadhurst 5m]
Tel: 01892 891081 Fax: 01892 890110
One of England's most romantic gardens, surrounding the ruins of a 14th century moated castle. Rhododendrons. azaleas, water lilies and wisteria flower in profusion. Woodland and estate walks. Strong companion is necessary for disabled visitors. The fax number given is for the National Trust Regional Office.
Garden: 27 Mar-31 Oct Wed-Fri 11.00-18.00, Sat & Sun 14.00-18.00, Bank Hol Mon 12.00-18.00. Castle: May-12 Sept. Closed Good Fri.
Last Admission: 17.00 or dusk
A£4.00 C£2.00 Family Ticket £10.00. Pre-booked Groups 15+ £3.00

↓*special events*
► **Rhododendrons and Ghent Azaleas**
23/5/00-23/5/00
A Garden tour at 14.00. Tickets £6.00
► **Tosca**
6/7/00-8/7/00
Open air opera on July 6 and 8 only. Commences at 19.30, tickets £20.00
► **Barber of Seville**
7/7/00-7/7/00
Open air opera, starts at 19.30, tickets £20.00
► **Gala Concert**
9/7/00-9/7/00
Arias from the well-known operas at 19.30. Tickets £20.00
► **Autumn Colour**
3/10/00-3/10/00
A Garden tour at 14.00, tickets £6.00

Sissinghurst Castle Garden
Biddenden Road Sissinghurst Cranbrook Kent
TN17 2AB
[1m E of village]
Tel: 01580 712850 infoline Fax: 01580 713911
The Tudor mansion of Sissinghurst Castle was bought in a neglected state in 1930 by Sir Harold Nicholson and his wife, the writer Vita Sackville-West. They set about restoring the house and gardens and the gardens now rank among the most attractive and popular in England. Due to limited capacity of the garden, timed tickets are in operation and visitors may have to wait before admission. Daily visitor numbers are restricted: visitors may still visit the Oast House exhibition, woodland and lake walks, restaurant and shop. No tripods or easels in the garden. Admission restricted to 2 wheelchairs at any one time due to narrow and uneven paths. Not an ideal venue for children, no pushchairs admitted, baby carriers are available. No children's games in the garden please. Coffee, lunches, teas in Granary Restaurant
1 Apr-15 Oct Tue-Fri 13.00-18.30, Sat Sun & Good Fri 10.00-17.30. Granary Restaurant: Tue-Fri 12.00-17.30, Sat, Sun & Good Fri 10.00-17.00 for Christmas opening contact for details 01580 713097. 1999 Times: 27 Mar-15 Oct Tue-Fri 13.00-18.30, Sat Sun & Good Fri 10.00-17.30. Granary Restaurant: Tue-Fri 12.00-17.30, Sat, Sun & Good Fri 10.00-17.00 for Christmas opening contact for details 01580 713097.
Last Admission: 30mins before closing
Queuing Times: Timed Tickets
A£6.00 C£3.00

↓*special events*
► **Countryside Capers**
16/8/00-30/8/00
Aug 16 and 30 only. Pond dipping and more in the grounds at 14.00. Tickets £3.50
► **Guided Walk with the Warden**
14/9/00-14/9/00
Commences at 14.00

Sprivers Garden
Lamberhurst Road Horsmonden Tonbridge
Kent TN12 8DR
[2m N of Lamberhusrt on B2162. BR: Paddock Wood]
Tel: 01892 890651 Fax: 01892 890110
This garden includes flowering and foliage shrubs, herbaceous borders, old walls and spring and summer bedding. It is administered and largely maintained on the Trust's behalf by the tenant. No toilet facilities
3 dates in 1999 ONLY: May,June & July 14.00-17.30, not confirmed before publication please call for actual dates

Last Admission: 17.00
£1.00 C£0.50. No reduction for Groups. Parking
limited, only 1 space for coaches

Stoneacre
Otham Maidstone Kent ME15 8RS
*[at N end of Otham village, 3m SE of
Maidstone, 1m S of A20. BR: Bearsted]*
Tel: 01622 862871 Fax: 01622 862157
A half-timbered mainly late 15th century yeoman's house, with great hall and crownpost,
surrounded by a lovely and newly-restored
cottage-style garden. The property is administered and largely maintained in the Trust's
behalf by the tenant. Car park 100 metres narrow drive coach parties to be set down at road
junction.
*1 Apr-31 Oct Wed & Sat 14.00-18.00. 1999
Times: 27 Mar-30 Oct Wed & Sat 14.00-18.00
Last Admission: 17.00*
A£2.50 C£1.25

Yalding Organic Gardens
Benover Road Yalding Maidstone Kent ME18
6EX
*[6m S-W of Maidstone. 0.5m S of Yalding on
B2162. Plenty of on site parking available]*
Tel: 01622 814650 Fax: 01622 814650
www.hdra.org.uk
Beautiful, highly acclaimed gardens that take
you on a fascinating tour through gardening
history. Guided tours, organic café, gift shop
and plant sales. Totally organic!
*May-Sept Wed-Sun and weekends in Apr & Oct
Last Admission: 16.35*
A£3.00 C(under 16)£Free (accompanied)

Guided Tours

Canterbury Guild of Guides
Arnett House Hawkes Lane Canterbury Kent
CT1 2NU
*[Tickets and assembly area at Visitor
Information Centre St. Margaret's Street next to
Canterbury Tales]*
**Tel: 01227 459779/762760 Fax: 01227
459779/762760**
The City's story from Roman times takes
shape; and among the stories of famous his-
torical and literary figures, a ghost may
appear - particularly on Friday evenings...
booked tours for groups are available usually
lasting one and a half hours. Languages avail-
able: French, German, Italian, Dutch,
Portuguese and Spanish.
Walks from Visitor Information Centre: 11 Apr-

31 Oct daily 14.00. 1 July-31 Aug Mon-Sat
11.30. May Bank Hol 11.30 & 14.00
A£3.50 OAPs&Students&C(14+)£3.00 Family
Ticket (A2+C3(0-14)£8.50. Group Rates: A£3.00
OAPs&Students&C(12+)£2.50 Primary C(5-
12)£2.00 Minimum Group charge£38.00

Heritage & Industrial

Canterbury Heritage Museum
Stour Street Canterbury Kent CT1 2RA
*[off A2 London-Dover road in Canterbury centre
signposed]*
Tel: 01227 452747 Fax: 01227 455047
An award-winning museum in a breath-taking
medieval building on the river bank close to
the Cathedral, shops and other attractions. The
tour starts in Roman times and continues up
to the present day. Some of the most exciting
of the city's treasures are shown: the
Canterbury Cross, Anglo-Saxon gold, and
Viking finds. Disabled access on ground floor
only.
visitor comments: Superb museum of local
history - one of the best I have ever visited.
*All year Mon-Sat 10.30-17.00 & Sun June-Oct
13.30-17.00. Closed Good Fri and Christmas
period
Last Admission: 16.00*
A£2.30 C(5-18)£1.15 OAPs&Students£1.50
Family Ticket £5.15. Groups(10+) 10% discount.
Educational Ticket £0.35. Residents Ticket £0.50

Chantry Heritage Centre
Riverside Leisure Area Gravesend Kent DA12
2BH
*[signposted from A226 in Gravesend town cen-
tre]*
Tel: 01474 321520
Seven hundred year old building housing col-
lections of local interest including finds from
the roman town at Springhead and
Pocahontas display.
*Easter-Nov Tue, Wed, Thur & Fri 13.00-16.00,
Sat & Sun 10.00-16.00, Nov-Easter Fri, Sat &
Sun 10.00-16.00*
A£1.50 Concessions£0.75. Parties by arrange-
ment

Dungeness Power Stations' Visitor
Centre
Dungeness Romney Marsh Kent TN29 9PP
*[B2075 at Lydd J10 M20 follow signs for
Brenzett and Lydd]*
Tel: 01797 321815 Fax: 01797 321844
www.bnfl.com
The 'A' and 'B' power stations at Dungeness
make an extraordinary sight in a landscape of

shingle, fishing boats and owner-built houses. There is a high-tech information centre, with 'hands-on' interactive videos and many other displays and models including an environmental exhibition which depicts Dungeness from the Ice Age through to today. Disabled access in the visitor centre only, not on the tour.

Information centre: Easter-Oct daily, Oct-Easter Sun-Fri Regular Tours of A & B power stations available. No children under 5 allowed on tour
Last Admission: 14.45
Admission Free, Tours Free

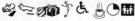

Fleur de Lis Heritage Centre

13 Preston Street Faversham Kent ME13 8NS
[off M2 at Faversham exit to A2. Near Central car-park]

Tel: 01795 534542

Http://www.faversham.org

A thousand years of history and architecture in Faversham are shown in award-winning displays, an audio-visual programme, and a working vintage telephone exchange in this 16th-century building (a former coaching inn). There is a Tourist Information Centre and a bookshop. The Centre, run by 100% voluntary effort, hopes to expand, and all profits go towards its expansion scheme.

All year daily 10.00-16.00, Sun 10.00-13.00.
Guided town tours: Apr-Oct Sat 10.30
Last Admission: 15.30 (Sun 12.30)
A£1.50 OAPs£1.00 Concessions£0.50. Guided town tour £1.00

discount offer: Two For The Price Of One (Excludes Tour)

Great Maytham Hall and The Secret Garden

Rolvenden Kent TN17 4NE
[0.5m S of Rolvenden village on road to Rolvenden Layne BR: Headcorn 10m Staplehurst 10m]

Tel: 01580 241346

Built in 1910 by Sir Edwin Lutyens.
May-Sept Wed & Thur 14.00-17.00
Last Admission: 16.30
A£3.50 C£2.00

Historical

Belmont

Belmont Park Throwley Faversham Kent ME13 0HH
[4m SSW of Faversham 1.5m W of A251 follow brown signs from Badlesmere.
BR: Faversham]

Tel: 01795 890202

Belmont was built in the late 18th century to the design of Samuel Wyatt, in a splendid elevated position with commanding views over the attractive and unspoilt countryside. It has been the seat of the Harris family since it was acquired in 1801. There is a fine collection of clocks.

Easter Sun-end Sept Sat Sun & Bank Hol Mon 14.00-17.00. Groups (minimum 20) by prior arrangement only Tue and Thur
Last Admission: 16.30
Mansion, Grounds & Clock Museum: A£5.00 C£2.50 Group rate A£4.50

Black Charles

Underriver Sevenoaks Kent TN15 0RY
[3m S of Sevenoaks off A21 1m E in the village of Underriver]

Tel: 01732 833036

Charming 14th century home of John de Blakecherl and his family. A small house with beautiful panelling, fireplaces and many other interesting features.

Open to groups by appointment (minimum of 10)
£3.50

Charles Dickens Centre

Eastgate House High Street Rochester Kent ME1 1EW
[buses pass long the A2 -Corporation Street- and stop a few yards from the door. Served by open-topped bus during summer holiday weeks. BR: Rochester 0.5m, Strood 1.5m or Chatham 1.5m. Taxi ranks at stations]

Tel: 01634 844176 Fax: 01634 827980

The Charles Dickens Centre is housed in a fine Elizabethan building that Dickens knew well. Here are recreated scenes from some of the authors most well known books, Mr Pickwick addresses the Pickwick club, Marley's ghost will come and go, Miss Haversham maintains her lonely vigil and Squeers whacks the school desk to jolt his nervous class into continuing their spelling tests.

All year daily 10.00-17.30. Closed Christmas
Last Admission: 16.45
A£3.50 C&OAPs&Students£2.50 Family Ticket £9.50.

Chartwell

Mapleton Road Westerham Kent TN16 1PS
[2m S of Westerham, fork left off B2026 after 1.5m. BR: Edenbridge / Edenbridge Town / Sevenoaks]

Tel: 01732 866368 infoline Fax: 01732 868193

Home of Sir Winston Churchill from 1924 until the end of his life. The rooms, left as they were

Kent

in his lifetime, evoke his career and interests, with pictures, maps, documents and personal mementoes. Two rooms are given over to a museum of his many gifts and uniforms. Terraced gardens descend towards the lake. New for this year the Chartwell Explorer Bus offering all-inclusive tickets from London, and a new leaflet on the countryside walks between Chartwell and Emmetts Garden.

visitor comments: A beautiful house and garden to see - all year long.

27 Mar-31 Oct Wed-Sun, Bank Hol Mon & Good Fri 11.00-17.00. Additionally Tue in July & Aug 11.00-17.00.

Last Admission: 16.30

Queuing Times: Timed ticket possible delays

House, garden & studio: A£5.50 C£2.75 Family Ticket £13.75. Garden & studio only: A£2.75. Coaches and groups by appointment.

↓ *special events*

► **Music, Memories and Moonlight**

17/6/00-17/6/00

An evening with the Herb Miller Orchestra, starts 19.30, tickets £17.50

► **Churchill's Garden - A Guided Tour**

5/7/00-19/7/00

Held on July 5 and 19 only. Tour begins at 18.00, tickets £6.00

► **"Tails" of Chartwell**

11/8/00-22/8/00

Held on Aug 11 and 22 only. A storytelling event at 14.00, tickets £3.50

Chiddingstone Castle

Chiddingstone Edenbridge Kent TN8 7AD

[off B2027 at Bough Beech]

Tel: 01892 870347

The 'castle' is a 17th-century house, almost completely rebuilt in the castle style c1800 by William Atkinson. It contains Stewart and Jacobite paintings and other relics, Egyptian and Oriental antiquities and a fine collection of Japanese lacquer and swords. The interior has recently been refurbished with extra rooms open to visitors.

Apr-May, Easter & Spring Bank Hol 11.30-17.30, June-Sept Wed-Fri 14.00-17.30 Sun & Bank Hol 11.30-17.30 Other times for parties by arrangement. Castle may be closed at short notice for private functions

Last Admission: 17.00

A£4.00 C(under 5)£Free (5-15)£2.00 accompanied by adult

Cobham Hall

Cobham Gravesend Kent DA12 3BL

[adjacent to A2 / M2 between Gravesend / Rochester. 8m from J2 M25. 27m from London]

Tel: 01474 823371 Fax: 01474 822995/824171

Cobham Hall is an outstandingly beautiful, red brick mansion in Elizabethan, Jacobean, Carolian and 18th century styles. This former home of the Earls of Darnley is set in 150 acres of parkland. The Gothic Dairy and some of the classical garden buildings are being renovated. Independent international boarding and day school. The grounds yield many delights for the lover of nature, especially in Spring, when the gardens and woods are resplendent with daffodils, narcissi and a myriad of rare bulbs. The House is open for Guided Tours each day from 13.00-16.00 with delicious cream teas available in the dining room.

Mar & Apr Wed, Sun & Easter Weekend 14.00-17.00, July-Aug Wed & Sun 14.00-17.00

Last Admission: 16.00

A3.50 C&OAPs£2.50

discount offer: £1.00 Off Admission to House/Garden. Valid until 29 Aug

Conduit House

Canterbury Kent CT

[access very difficult 5-10mins walk from St Augustine's Abbey within the new St Martin's Heights housing estate]

Tel: 01732 778000

The Conduit House is the monastic waterworks which supplied nearby St Augustine's Abbey.

By appointment please call

Admission Free

Deal Castle

Victoria Road Deal Kent CT14 7BA

[SW of Deal town centre]

Tel: 01304 372762

www.english-heritage.org.uk

Crouching low and menacing, the huge, rounded bastions of this austere fort, built by Henry VIII, once carried 119 guns. Designed to resemble a Tudor Rose, Deal Castle is one of three artillery forts on the Kent coast built to counter the threat of invasion during the mid-16th century. Today the castle still appears exactly as it was originally intended to look: powerful and virtually impregnable. Its remarkable coastal position affords breathtaking views out to sea. It is a fascinating castle to explore, with long, dark passages, battlements and a massive basement with an exciting exhibition.

27 Mar-31 Oct daily 10.00-18.00 (dusk in Oct). 1 Nov-26 Mar Wed-Sun 10.00-16.00. Closed 24-26 Dec.
A£3.00 C£1.50 Concessions£2.30

↓ *special events*

▶ **1940**
23/4/00-24/4/00
Meet members of the "Dad's Army" who defended Deal in 1940

▶ **King Henry's Mercenaries**
6/5/00-7/5/00
From Noon. Meet colourful German mercenaries of 1546 in garrison at the castle

▶ **Civil War Music and Dance**
28/5/00-29/5/00
From Noon. Courtly music and stately dance from the mid 17th century

▶ **Captaine Staffage's Cornucopia of ye Curious**
10/6/00-11/6/00
From Noon. Laugh and groan in equal measures as 17th century travelling players put on an hilarious show!

▶ **Schoole of Defence**
1/7/00-2/7/00
Soldiers and gentlemen duel for honour and glory

▶ **Puppet Making Workshops**
8/7/00-9/7/00
From Noon. The opportunity for younger visitors to make a puppet and take part in a puppet show

▶ **Passage to the New World, 1650**
15/7/00-16/7/00
From Noon. Find out why you should take ship to help found a new colony on Long Island, New England

▶ **Tudor Music**
22/7/00-23/7/00
From Noon. Lively music played on many instruments, with the opportunity to join in!

▶ **Recruiting for Wellington**
29/7/00-30/7/00
From Noon. Redcoat soldiers in camp, with living history displays, drill and musket-firing

▶ **The History Man**
5/8/00-6/8/00
From Noon. Enjoy unusual guided tours with the presenter of the BBC's History Man programmes

▶ **Tudor Printing**
12/8/00-13/8/00
From Noon. Tudor Printing Children can use wood blocks to print their own 1588 Armada newsheet

▶ **Traditional Song**
19/8/00-20/8/00
From Noon. A performance of delightful unaccompanied song

▶ **Tudor Living History**
27/8/00-28/8/00
From Noon. 16th century living history, sciences and entertainments

▶ **Soldiers from the Sea**
21/10/00-22/10/00
From Noon. Naval warfare from the Romans to the 20th century, with talks and demonstrations

▶ **Meet Father Christmas**
2/12/00-17/12/00
Meet Santa on 2, 3, 9, 10, 16 & 17 Dec

Dover Castle and Secret Wartime Tunnels
Dover Castle Dover Kent CT16 1HU
[on E side of Dover]
Tel: 01304 211067
www.english-heritage.org.uk
Discover 2000 years of history from the Iron Age to World War II. take the atmospheric tour deep underground in the secret wartime tunnels. See the reconstruction of preparations for Henry VIII's visit in the medieval Keep. Experience life under siege in 1216 in the fabulous sound and light presentation.
visitor comments: Really good value for money. Interesting and educational, very lifelike. Great views.
All year 1 Apr-30 Sept daily 10.00-18.00. 1 Oct-31 Oct daily 10.00-17.00. 1 Nov-31 Mar daily 10.00-16.00. Closed 24-26 Dec
Last Admission: 1 hour before closure
A£6.90 C£3.50 Family Ticket £17.30 Concessions£5.20

↓ *special events*

Kent

► Castle Characters

19/2/00-31/8/00

From 11.00. Meet colourful costumed characters and uniformed soldiers from Dover Castle's past. On 19-27 Feb, 21-24 Apr,   30 Apr-1 May & 1-31 Aug

► The Imperial Roman Army

30/4/00-1/5/00

At 12.30 & 15.00. Superbly armoured legionaries and auxiliaries 100AD on parade

► Castle Characters

27/5/00-4/6/00

From 11.00 Meet the 1940's inhabitants of the secret wartime tunnels

► Their Finest House - Dover, 1940

28/5/00-29/5/00

From Noon. The castle as it might have looked in 1940 the time of the "Miracle of Dunkirk", with military vehicles, checkpoints, "Dads Army" volunteers and much more

► Archery Tournament

22/7/00-23/7/00

From 11.00. The annual medieval "Archer of the Kingdom" festival. With combat, weapons displays and market traders

► Firepower Through The Ages

5/8/00-6/8/00

From Noon. Fearsome artillery weapons from the Romans to World War II. Earplugs not provided!

► Preparing for War, 1483

27/8/00-28/8/00

From Noon. 15th century soldiers recreating preparations for the invasion of France

► The Ghosts of Dover Castle

21/10/00-29/10/00

From 11.00.Meet the Castle's resident ghosts!

► A Medieval Siege

28/10/00-29/10/00

From 11.00.Witness an exciting 15th century siege, featuring archery, cannon-fire and dramatic assaults on the inner bailey

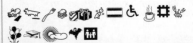

Dover Old Town Gaol

Dover Town Hall Biggin Street Dover Kent CT16 1DL
[M20 A2 signposted in Dover town]
Tel: 01304 201200 Fax: 01304 201200
High-tech animation, audio-visual techniques and 'talking heads' take visitors back to Victorian England to experience the horrors of life behind bars, listening, as they walk through the reconstructed courtroom, exercise yard, and cells, to the stories of the felons and their jailers. You can even try the prisoner's beds.
All year Tue-Sat 10.00-16.30, Sun 14.00-16.3. Closed Mon & Tue Oct-May call 01304 202723 for further information
Last Admission: 16.30
A£3.50 C&OAPs£2.10 (1999 prices)
discount offer: Two For The Price Of One

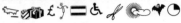

Dymchurch Martello Tower

Dymchurch Kent TN
[access from High Street, not from seafront]
Tel: 01732 778000
One of the many artillery towers which formed part of a chain of strongholds intended to resist an invasion by Napoleon. It is fully restored, with an original 24-pounder gun on the roof.
10-13 Apr & 2-4 May 14.00-17.30. 9 May-11 July Weekends & Bank Hol Mon 14.00-17.30. 18 July-31 Aug daily 14.00-17.30. 1-30 Sept Sat-Sun 14.00-17.30
A£1.00 C£0.50 Concessions£0.80

Eynsford Castle

Eynsford Kent *[M25 then M20 then off A225 in Eynsford]*
The walls of this castle at 30ft high, come as a surprise in the pretty little village. The castle was begun in the 11th century by William de Eynsford, who later retired to become a monk. Also to be seen are the remains of the castle hall and ditch.
All year 1 Mar-30 Sept daily 10.00-18.00. 1 Oct-28 Feb 10.00-16.00
Admission Free

Fort Amherst

Dock Road Chatham Kent ME4 4UB
[A231 from Chatham to Gillingham]
Tel: 01634 847747 Fax: 01634 847747
Fort Amherst is the finest Georgian fortress in the country, comprising a large gatehouse, tunnel complex, ditches, magazines, barracks and Civil Defence exhibition. The park-like set-

Kent

ting within the fortifications, together with an 1815 re-enactment most summer Sundays, provides a fascinating visit for all the family.
Daily 10.30-16.30, closed 25 Dec
Last Admission: 15.30
A£4.00 C(5+)£2.00 OAPs&Students£2.00 Family Ticket(2A+2C) £10.00

Gad's Hill Place

Gravesend Road Higham Rochester Kent ME3 7PA
[on A226 3m from Rochester 4m from Gravesend Station: Higham]
Tel: 01474 822366
Grade I listed building built in 1780 Home of Charles Dickens from 1857-1870. Fully restored conservatory. Now licensed for civil weddings.
1st Sun in month Easter-Oct and Bank Hol Sun 14.00-17.00. During Rochester Dickens Festivals (June and Dec) 11.00-16.00. At other times by arrangement
Last Admission: 16.00
A£2.50 C£1.50. Groups by arrangement

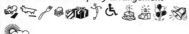

Godinton House

Ashford Kent TN23 3BW
[1.5m W of Ashford off Maidstone Road at Potter's Corner A20
Station: Ashford 2m]
The existing house belongs mostly to Jacobean times. The interior of Godinton contains a wealth of very fine panelling and carving, particularly in the Hall and on the Staircase. The house contains interesting portraits and much fine furniture and china. The gardens were originally laid out in the 18th century.
East Sat Sun & Mon June-Sept Sun & Bank Hols only 14.00-17.00
House & Garden £2.00 (C0-16)£1.00 Weekdays by appointment only Parties of 20 or more £1.50

Great Maytham Hall and The Secret Garden

Rolvenden Kent TN17 4NE
[0.5m S of Rolvenden village on road to Rolvenden Layne BR: Headcorn 10m Staplehurst 10m]
Tel: 01580 241346
Built in 1910 by Sir Edwin Lutyens.
May-Sept Wed & Thur 14.00-17.00
Last Admission: 16.30
A£3.50 C£2.00

Hever Castle and Gardens

Hever Castle Hever Edenbridge Kent TN8 7NG
[off J5/6 M25, off B2026. 3m from BR: Victoria London to Edenbridge Town]
Tel: 01732 865224 Fax: 01732 866796
www.HeverCastle.co.uk
South East England Tourist Board Visitor Attraction of the Year Award - 1998. This romantic 13th century moated Castle was the childhood home of Anne Boleyn. In 1903 William Waldorf Astor acquired the Castle and created beautiful gardens. He filled the Castle with wonderful furniture, paintings and tapestries which visitors can see today.
Children will enjoy the costumed figure exhibition of Henry VIII and his six wives, and the Anne Boleyn Books of Hours. The spectacular award winning gardens include topiary, Italian and Tudor Gardens, a 110 metre herbaceous border and a lake. Families will enjoy the yew maze (open May-Oct), the splashing water maze (open April-Oct), the Miniature Model Houses Exhibition and the Adventure Playground.
visitor comments: Excellent children's playground (bring a change of clothes for the water maze!) Somewhere to spend the whole day.
1 Mar-30 Nov daily, Castle: 12.00-18.00. Gardens: 11.00-18.00. Winter months 11.00-16.00
Last Admission: 60mins before closing
Castle & Gardens: A£7.80 C(5-16)£4.20 Under

Kent

5's £Free Family Ticket (A2+C2)£19.80
OAPs£6.60. Gardens only: A£6.10 C(5-16)£4.00
Under 5's £Free Family Ticket (A2+C2)£16.20
OAPs£5.20. Group rates 15+ available on
request

↓ *special events*

▶ **Easter Weekend**
21/4/00-24/4/00
Easter egg trail and local bands in the garden
▶ **May Day Music and Dance**
29/4/00-1/5/00
*A weekend of traditional music and dance fea-
turing local Morris dancers*
▶ **Merrie England Weekend**
27/5/00-29/5/00
A wekend of archery, medieval music and dance
▶ **Rose Festival**
24/6/00-25/6/00
*Featuring specialist nurseries and tours of the
garden*
▶ **Longbow Warfare**
16/7/00-3/9/00
*Demonstrations of the Longbow as a military
weapon on the following dates: 16, 23 & 30
July, 27 & 28 Aug, 2 & 3 Sept*
▶ **Jousting Tournaments**
22/7/00-26/8/00
*Presented by the Knights of Royal England on
the following dates in July 22 & 29, & Aug 5, 6,
12, 13, 19, 20 & 26*
▶ **Patchwork and Quilting Exhibition**
8/9/00-10/9/00
A magnificent display of patchwork quilts

Ightham Mote
Mote Road Ivy Hatch Sevenoaks Kent TN15 0NT
*[6m E of Sevenoaks off A25 and 2.5m S of
Ightham off A227. BR: Borough Green /
Wrotham / Hildenborough / Sevenoaks]*
Tel: 01732 811145 Fax: 01732 811029
Explore 650 years of history in one house!
Cross the walled moat and enter a medieval
and Tudor manor house with rooms dating
from as early as the 1340's. See the courtyard,
the Great Hall and the Robinson Library laid
out as seen in a 1960 edition of Homes and
Gardens magazine. Enjoy the newly restored
Tudor chapel, drawing room and Billiards
room and visit the housekeeper's room and
butler's pantry. Learn in a major exhibition
about the methods and materials used in the
restoration project - the largest of its kind ever
undertaken by the National Trust. Enjoy extensive grounds - gardens, lakes, and woodland
and estate walks.
*28 Mar-31 Oct Mon, Wed-Fri, Sun, Bank Hol
Mon & Good Fri 11.00-17.30. Car Park: All year
dawn-dusk for estate walks*
Last Admission: 16.30

A£5.00 C£2.50 Family Ticket £12.50. Group
rates 15+ £4.00 - no reduction Sun & Bank Hol

↓ *special events*

▶ **Flora and Fauna**
6/5/00-6/5/00
*A guided walk of the garden. Tickets £6.00,
begins at 14.30*
▶ **Romeo and Juliet**
17/6/00-17/6/00
Open air theatre at 18.30. Tickets £9.00
▶ **Music at the Mote**
1/7/00-1/7/00
*Commences at 19.30. Music and songs from the
West End Shows. Tickets £16.00*
▶ **The Emperor's New Clothes**
6/8/00-6/8/00
*Open air theatre for families. Starts at 18.30,
A£8.00 C£4.00*
▶ **Family Fun Day with Treasure Hunt**
24/8/00-24/8/00
Normal opening times and prices

Kit's Coty House and Little Kit's Coty House
Maidstone Kent ME
*[W of A229 N of Maidstone, Bus: Maidstone &
District 101 / 126, BR: Maidstone East /
Gillingham]*
Ruins of two prehistoric burial chambers, tak-
ing their name from the Celtic phrase for
'tomb in the woods'.
All year any reasonable time
Admission Free

⛩

Knights Templar Church
Dover Kent CT
*[on the Western Heights above Dover BR: Dover
Priory 0.75m]*
Standing across the valley from Dover Castle
are the foundations of a small circular 12th
century church.
All year any reasonable time
Admission Free

⛩

Ladham House
Ladham Road Goudhurst Cranbrook Kent TN17
1DB
*[from Goudhurst, up hill past church on right.
Keep on rd for 0.25m until you reach Chequers
Inn on left, turn left - signpost B2079 to
Horsmonden and Marden. Over small cross-
roads then first right signposted Blantyre House
and Curtisden Green. Ladham House is on left
with tall black wrought Iron gates]*
**Tel: 01580 211203/212674 Fax: 01580
212596**
10 acres of rolling lawns, fine specimen trees,
rhododendrons, azaleas, camellias, shrubs and

magnolias. Newly planted arboretum. Spectacular twin mixed borders. Fountain garden and bog garden. Fine view. Reserected Old Rock garden with waterfall. Dogs on leads allowed.

House: by appointment only for private functions. Garden: All year daily (please ring owner first before making journey). Also open 2 & 16 May & 4 Oct for National Gardens Scheme 13.30-17.30 with tea & refreshments supplied on these days only
Gardens: A£2.50 C(under 12)£Free. Guided Tours: A£3.00

Leeds Castle

Maidstone Kent ME17 1PL
[4m at J8 of M20 A20]
Tel: 01622 765400 Fax: 01622 735616
www.leeds-castle.co.uk

The site of a manor of the Saxon royal family in the 9th century, Leeds Castle was described by Lord Conway as 'the loveliest Castle in the world.' Built on two islands in the middle of a lake and set in 500 acres of landscaped parkland, it was converted into a royal palace by Henry VIII and left to the nation by its last private owner, Olive, Lady Baillie, in 1975. The Lady Baillie Garden, opened in Spring 1999, is in memory of someone who spent so much of her life restoring the Castle and filling it with treasures. Other attractions include the Woodland Walk and Duckery, a unique Dog Collar Museum, exotic bird Aviary, Maze and Underground Grotto, Victorian Greenhouses, shops and restaurants. Full programme of special events.

visitor comments: A lovely castle - fantastic maze and beautiful gardens with small lakes and rivers.

All year, Mar-Oct daily Park & Gardens: 10.00-17.00, Castle: 11.00-17.30. Nov-Feb daily, Park: 10.00-15.00, Castle: 10.15-15.30 Closed 25 Dec, 24 June and 1 July
Last Admission: Stated closing times
Castle & Park: A£9.50 C(5-15)£6.00 Family Ticket £26.00 OAPs&Students£7.50. Park & Gardens: A£7.50 C(5-15)£4.50 Family Ticket £21.00 OAPs&Students£6.00

↓ special events

▶ **Greenhouse Weekend**
8/4/00-9/4/00
Top advice from the Castle's professional plantsmen

▶ **Celebration of Easter**
22/4/00-24/4/00
Fun for the young and not-so-young, face painting, Punch and Judy, Circus Workshops and plenty of refreshments

▶ **Woodland Walk's Festival of English Food and Wine**
13/5/00-14/5/00
Samplings, talks, celebrity cooks, Morris Dancing and a jazz band add to the colourful atmosphere

▶ **Half Term Amazing Mazes**
27/5/00-4/6/00
Mazes of all shapes and sizes will be appearing throughout the Castle's beautiful grounds

▶ **Leeds Castle Open Air Concerts**
24/6/00-1/7/00
Carl Davis will conduct the Royal Liverpool Philharmonic Orchestra. Gates open at 16.00 - entertainment from 17.30. Concert begins at 20.00. Advance tickets sales only from the box office from 1 Feb Tel: 01622 880008. Book early to avoid disappointment

▶ **Kent Children's Promenade Concert**
28/6/00-28/6/00
A wonderful event by children for children. Children must be accompanied by an adult, and adults must be accompanied by a child! Gates open at 16.30. Concert commences at 18.00-19.30

▶ **Festival of Summer Floral Art**
20/7/00-23/7/00
A riot of colour and scent will enhance the splendid Castle rooms

▶ **Great Leeds Castle Balloon and Vintage Car Weekend**
9/9/00-10/9/00
With up to 30 hot air balloons, Tiger Moth displays, a cavalcade of vintage cars, veteran bicycles, Champagne and much more, there is plenty for all

▶ **Autumn Gold - A Festival of Flowers and Produce**
18/10/00-22/10/00
The Castle's magnificent interior is filled with exotic flower displays and presentations of produce from the Garden of England.

▶ **Half Term Fun - Halloween Week**
23/10/00-27/10/00
Children can learn all about the traditions of Halloween.

▶ **Grand Firework Spectacular**
4/11/00-4/11/00
Gates open at 17.00, extra entertainment from 17.30, with the display scheduled for 19.30. Call for further details after 1 Oct

▶ **Christmas at the Castle**

10/12/00-24/12/00
During December the Castle is traditionally decorated with trees, garlands and swags, lunchtime carols. Dates to be confirmed

Lullingstone Castle
Lullingstone Park Eynsford Dartford Kent DA4 0JA
[M25 sliproad to Brands Hatch, A20 / A225 0.5m South Eynsford station]
Tel: 01322 862114 Fax: 01322 862115
In house, Queen Anne State rooms, family portraits, armour. Tearooms in 15th century brick gatehouse. Church of Norman origin, herb garden, flower borders. Member of the Historic Houses Association.
Apr-June Sun & Bank Hol 14.00-18.00. July-Sept Sat, Sun & Bank Hol 14.00-18.00. Thur & Fri by arrangement
Last Admission: 17.30
House & Gardens: A£3.75 C£1.50 & OAPs£3.00. Group Rates 10%

Maidstone Museum and Bentlif Art Gallery
St. Faiths Street Maidstone Kent ME14 1LH
[close to County Hall behind the Army & Navy]
Tel: 01622 754497 Fax: 01622 602193
www.museum.maidstone.gov.uk
Set in an Elizabethan manor house which has been much extended over the years, this museum houses a surprising and outstanding collection of fine and applied arts, including oil paintings and watercolours, furniture, Roman, Anglo-Saxon and Medieval archeology, ceramics, costumes and a collection of

Japanese art and artefacts. Please apply for details of temporary exhibitions, workshops etc. Photography allowed by prior consent. Disabled access limited.
All year Mon-Sat 10.00-17.15, Sun 11.00-16.00. Closed 25-26 Dec
Last Admission: 17.00
Admission Free
↓*special events*
► **Magic People**
11/3/00-11/3/00
Where do tales of fairies and elves come from?
► **On the FRAC track - Crossing the Century**
25/3/00-7/5/00
Contemporary art work from Fonds Regional d'Art Contemporain (FRAC) Nord-Pas de Calais
► **Springtime**
8/4/00-8/4/00
Make your own creepy crawlies
► **Fairytales and Fantasy**
19/5/00-18/6/00
Exhibition of illustrations from the golden age of children's books.
► **Quilt Art - 'Poetic Licence'**
8/7/00-20/8/00
Exhibition of contemporary quilts with workshops.
► **Millennium Geologists**
16/9/00-16/9/00
Roadshow of fascinating fossils, strange shells and rocks
► **Embroiderers Guild**
23/9/00-29/10/00
One of the largest exhibitions of embroidery and textiles
► **Helen Sears/Photo Works**
6/11/00-3/12/00
Contemporary photography with a concurrent exhibition at Maidstone Library Gallery
► **Kent Field Club Annual Exhibition**
9/12/00-9/12/00
Kent wildlife and natural habitats with stalls and outdoor activities
► **Portrait Exhibition featuring Joan La Dell**
15/12/00-31/12/00
The concept of portrait painting including the relationship between the artist and sitter

Maison Dieu
Ospringe Kent ME
[in Ospringe on A2 0.5m W of Faversham (20mins walk)]
Tel: 01795 534542
This forerunner of today's hospitals remains largely as it was in 16th century with exposed beams and an overhanging upper storey. It contains an exhibition about Ospringe in Roman times.
11 Apr-31 Oct Weekends & Bank Hol 14.00-

17.00. For further details contact The Faversham Society on 01795 534542. Keykeeper in Winter.
A£1.80 C£0.50

Milton Chantry
Gravesend Kent ME
[E of Gravesend off A226]
Tel: 01474 321520
A small 14th century building which housed the chapel of the leper hospital and the chantry of the de Valance and Montechais families. It later became a tavern and in 1780 part of a fort.
Wed,Thur, Fri, Sat, Sun & Bank Hol 10.00-16.00 . Closed 1 Jan-28 Feb. For school parties and for exhibition opening telephone 01474 321520
A£1.50 C&Concessions£0.75

New College of Cobham
The Street Cobham Gravesend Kent DA12 3BX
[4m W of Rochester 4m SE of Gravesend 1.5m from junction Shorne-Cobham (A2) In Cobham rear of Church of Mary Magdalene Station: Sole St (1m)]
Tel: 01474 814280
Almshouses based on medieval chantry built 1362, part reuilt 1598. Originally endowed by Sir John de Cobham and descendants.
Apr-Sept Fri-Wed 10.00-19.00, Oct-Mar Mon, Tues, Wed, Sat & Sun 10.00-16.00
Admission Free

New Tavern Fort
Riverside Leisure Area Gravesend Kent DA12 1DD
[signed from A226 in Gravesend town centre]
Tel: 01474 337600
A guardian of the Thames against foreign invasion over 200 years it now welcomes visitors. Many of the emplacements have been re-armed and the underground magazines are open during summer weekends.
May-Sept Sat & Sun 10.00-17.00 Bank Hol 14.00-17.00
A£1.20 C&OAPs£0.60 Family Ticket £2.75

Old Soar Manor
Old Soar Road Plaxtol Sevenoaks Kent TN15 0QX
[2m S of Borough Green A25 approached via A227 and Plaxtol. Narrow lane unsuitable for coaches. BR: Borough Green / Wrotham]
Tel: 01732 810378
The solar block of late 13th century knight's dwelling. Exhibition on Manor and surrounding areas. No toilet facilities.
1 Apr-30 Sept daily 10.00-18.00. 1999 Times: 27 Mar-30 Sept daily 10.00-18.00

Admission Free

Owletts
The Street Cobham Gravesend Kent DA12 3AP
[1m S of A2 at W end of village at junction of roads from Dartford / Sole Street. BR: Sole Street]
Tel: 01892 890651 Fax: 01892 890110
A modest red-brick Charles II house with contemporary staircase and plasterwork ceiling, and small pleasure and kitchen gardens. Former home of the architect Sir Herbert Baker. The property is now administered and largely maintained on the Trust's behalf by the tenant. Groups by pre-arrangement. The fax number given is for the National Trust Regional Office.
1 Apr-30 Sept Wed & Thur only 14.00-17.00. 1999 Times: 31 Mar-30 Sept Wed & Thur only 14.00-17.00
Last Admission: 16.30
A£2.00 C£1.00

Penshurst Place and Gardens
Penshurst Tonbridge Kent TN11 8DG
[BR: Tonbridge]
Tel: 01892 870307 Fax: 01892 870866
www.penshurstplace.com
The original manor house was built by Sir John de Pulteney between 1340 and 1345 and is perfectly preserved. Successive owners enlarged it during the 15th, 16th and 17th centuries, and the great variety of architectural styles creates an elaborate and dramatic backdrop for the extensive collections of English, French and Italian furniture, tapestries and paintings.
Weekends only from 4 March. Daily from 1 April-31 Oct. Grounds: 10.30-18.00 House: 12.00-17.00 Shop and Plant Centre: 10.30-18.00
Last Admission: 17.00
House & Grounds: A£6.00 C(5-16)£4.00 Family Ticket £16.00 OAPs&Students&UB40£5.50 Adult Party (20+)£5.30. Grounds only: A£4.50 C(5-16)£3.50 Family Ticket £13.00 OAPs&Students&UB40£4.00. Garden Season Ticket £22.00. Pre-booked Guided House Tours:

A£6.00 C(5-16)£3.20, Garden Tours: A£6.50 C(5-16)£4.00

↓ *special events*

▶ **ARMADA!**
1/4/00-2/4/00
Penshurst Place in 1588

▶ **Easter at Penshurst**
23/4/00-24/4/00
An activity trail and tractor trailer rides

▶ **Craft Fair**
29/4/00-1/5/00
Leading showcase for crafts in the South East

▶ **Treasure Island**
14/5/00-13/8/00
Mrs Humphreys Productions in the Stage Garden held on May 14 and Aug 13 only

▶ **Classic Car Show**
28/5/00-29/5/00
Hundreds of classic cars on display. Open 10.00-17.00. A£5.00 C(5-16)£1.00 OAPs£4.00

▶ **Wind in the Willows**
18/6/00-18/6/00
Mrs Humphreys Productions in the Stage Garden

▶ **Sunday Falconry Displays**
2/7/00-27/8/00
July 2, 9, 16, 23, 20, Aug 6, 13, 20, 27 only. Static and flying displays of magnificent birds of prey

▶ **Jazz in the Barons Hall**
11/8/00-11/8/00
Black Cat jazz with Tina May

▶ **A Midsummer Night's Dream**
20/8/00-20/8/00
Theatre Set-up presents this Shakespearean classic in the Barons Hall

▶ **Weald of Kent Craft Show**
8/9/00-10/9/00
The leading craft showcase in the South East

▶ **Half-term Fun**
23/10/00-27/10/00
Activity trail and house quiz to amuse younger visitors

Quebec House

Quebec Square Westerham Kent TN16 1TD
[off A25]
Tel: 01892 890651 Fax: 01892 890110
Westerham was the birthplace of General Wolfe who spent his childhood in the multi-gabled, square brick house now renamed Quebec House. The house probably dates from the 16th Century but was extended and altered in th 17th Century. It contains a Wolfe museum and an exhibition on Wolfe and the Quebec campaign. The fax number given is for the National Trust Regional Office.
28 Mar-31 Oct Sun & Tue only 14.00-18.00
Last Admission: 17.30
A£2.50 C£1.25. Group rates £1.80

↓ *special events*

▶ **The Regency Duo - Mozart and Haydn**
25/5/00-25/5/00
Held at 15.00 (£10.00) and 19.30 (£12.00)

▶ **The English Bach**
12/10/00-12/10/00
Presented by Oliver Davies at 15.00 (£10.00) and 19.30 (£12.00)

Quex House and Gardens, Powell-Cotton Museum

Quex Park Birchington Kent CT7 0BH
[in Birchington 0.5m S of Birchington Square, SW of Margate, 13m E of Canterbury. Signposted. BR: Birchington. Plenty of on site parking.]
Tel: 01843 842168 Fax: 01843 846661
Quex House was built as a Regency gentleman's Country residence and grew to become the Victorian mansion we see today. Still home to Powell-Cotton family, it has a mellow atmosphere, many of the rooms appearing much as they did during Major Powell-Cotton's lifetime and complimented by flowers from the walled gardens at Quex. There are some splendid pieces of oriental and period furniture, fine rugs and porcelain, as well as family portraits and an extensive collection of silver, clocks and memorabilia. The polished mahogany cases displaying Major Powell-Cotton's treasures give Quex Museum its authentic quality, so often lacking in modern visitor attractions. There are eight galleries in all - three of them built by the Major himself - containing an amazing variety of items from the animal dioramas to striking tribal art, weapons, carvings and costumes, as well as valuable collections of European and Chinese porcelain and local archaeology. What began as one man's museum has been painstakingly cared for and added to by members of the Powell-Cotton family and now offers visitors an exciting insight into discoveries of a great Victorian Explorer. Member of the Historic Houses Association.
Gardens, Museum & Restaurant: Mar, Nov-Dec

Sun only 11.00-17.00, Apr-Oct Tue-Thur, Sun &
Bank Hol 11.00-18.00, Quex House 14.30-18.00
Last Admission: 17.00
Summer: A£3.50 C&OAPs £2.80. Winter: A£2.50
C&OAPs£1.80

Richborough Roman Fort
Richborough Sandwich Kent CT13 9JW
[1.5m N of Sandwich off A257]
Tel: 01304 612013
www.english-heritage.org.uk
Now landlocked in the Kent countryside,
Richborough Castle once stood on the coast,
the bridgehead from which the Romans
launched their invasion in AD43. The foundations of the great monumental archway built
to mark the conquest of Britain, can still be
seen. The museum contains finds from the
site.
All year 1 Apr-1 Nov daily 10.00-18.00 (dusk in
Oct). 2-30 Nov Wed-Sun 10.00-16.00. 1 Dec-28
Feb Sat-Sun 10.00-16.00. 1-31 Mar Wed-Sun
10.00-16.00
A£2.50 C£1.30 Concessions£1.90

↓special events
► **Medieval Archery**
15/4/00-16/4/00
Meet bowmen of the 12th century. With crusaders, crafts and cookery
► **Archaeological Artist in Residence**
20/5/00-21/5/00
Handle museum objects and learn the techniques of logging, measuring and taking rub-
bings from items discovered at archaeological
digs
► **Bones, Skulls, Teeth & Diseases**
27/5/00-29/5/00
The fascinating facts discovered from medieval
skeletons
► **Medieval Falconry**
3/6/00-4/6/00
Magnificent medieval birds of prey flying free
► **Shakespeare's Romans**
17/6/00-18/6/00
Fun for all the family with a light-hearted re-
working of five Shakespearean tales
► **Roman Festival**
29/7/00-30/7/00
Sample receipes, mosaic-making, 1st century
legionaries on parade and practicing battle tac-
tics, exciting skirmish as soldiers and horsemen
beat off savage Saxon raiders
► **Wind in the Willows**
27/8/00-28/7/00
Meet Toad, Ratty, Mole and Badger in this
enchanting children's fantasy

Riverhill House Gardens
Riverhill Sevenoaks Kent TN15 0RR
[2m south of Sevenoaks on the A225]
Tel: 01732 458802/452557
Small Ragstone house built in 1714 and home
of the Rogers family since 1840. Spectacular
hillside garden woodland walks and sheltered
terraces. Listed garden of historic interest.
Apr, May & June Sun and Bank hol weekends
1998 daily, 24 May-1 June 12.00 18.00
A£2.50 C£0.50 Pre-Booked Parties 20+ £3.50
includes guided tour of house

Rochester Castle
The Keep Rochester Kent ME1 1SX
[J1 M2 J2 M25, by Rochester Bridge A2]
Tel: 01634 402276
No one can miss the great square keep as it
towers above the River Medway, a daunting
reminder of the history of the City. The Castle
is well known as one of the best preserved and
finest examples of Norman architecture in
England, measuring 113 feet high, 70 feet
square, with walls 11-13 feet thick. The Keep is
one of the tallest in the country; visitors may
wind their way up the spiral staircase leading
to the battlements and take in the superb
panoramic views of the City and the surrounding countryside.
All year daily Apr-Sept 10.00-18.00, Oct-Mar
10.00-16.00. Closed 25-27 Dec & 1 Jan
Last Admission: 60mins before closing
A£3.50 Concessions£2.50

Roman Painted House
New Street Dover Kent CT17 9AJ
[M2 & M20 meet at Dover, town centre location
with own small car parking other parking signposted nearby]
Tel: 01304 203279
Five rooms of a Roman hotel built 1,800 years
ago, now famous for its unique, well-preserved Bacchic frescos. The Roman underfloor
heating system and part of a late-Roman
defensive wall are also on view. There are
extensive displays on Roman Dover with video
and commentary. Foreign language commentaries are available.
Apr-Sept Tue-Sun 10.00-18.00 & Bank Hol Mon.
Closed Mon. Groups at other times by prior
arrangement
Last Admission: 30mins before closing
A£2.00 C&OAPs£0.80

Shell Grotto
Grotto Hill Margate Kent CT9 2BU
[Grotto Hill is situated off Dane Road in central
Margate]

Tel: 01843 220008 Fax: 01843 220008

Accidentally discovered in 1835 by schoolboys digging in the fields adjacent to their school, the Grotto's origin is still a mystery. Millions of shells have been used to decorate the 2,000 sq ft of winding passages with exquisite mosaic designs. For the first twenty years of it being open to the public it was lit by oil lamps and has passed through gas lighting to modern day electric light. Much of the original colour has faded but, taking that it has been on view for 150 years, it is still in a very good state of preservation. As to its origin we think it is a form of pagan workship of the continuity of life!

visitor comments: Unique and unexplained history, excellent.

Apr-Oct daily 10.00-16.00, 10.00-17.00 in high season

Last Admission: 15mins before closing

A£1.80 C£0.90 OAPs£1.80 School & Group rates 10% discount

Squerryes Court

Squerryes Westerham Kent TN16 1SJ

[J5 or J6 M52 0.5m W of Westerham, signposted from A25. Plenty of on site parking.]

Tel: 01959 562345/563118 Fax: 01959 565949

This beautiful 1681 manor house, has been the family home of the Wardes since 1731. It contains many fine Italian, 17th and 18th century Dutch and English pictures, as well as furniture, porcelain and tapestries. Also featured are items related to General James Wolfe of Quebec, a lovely 18th Century landscaped garden, a lake, a dovecot and a restored formal garden. Please note ONLY the three downstairs rooms pf the house are suitable for wheelchairs, and pushchairs access is for the garden only. Dogs are allowed on a lead in the garden only. Member of the Historic Houses Association.

1 Apr-30 Sept Wed, Sat, Sun & Bank Hol Mon, Garden: 12.00-17.30. House: 13.30-17.30. Pre-booked groups of 20+ welcome any day

Last Admission: 17.00

House & Grounds: A£4.20 C£2.50 OAPs£3.80 Grounds: A£2.50 C£1.50 OAPs£2.20

discount offer: Two For The Price Of One. Valid Until 1 Apr-30 Sept 2000

↓ *special events*

▶ **National Garden Scheme**

8/7/00-9/7/00

Times: Grounds 12.00 House13.30-17.30. Last entry 17.00

▶ **Festival Of Flowers 2000**

14/7/00-16/7/00

Presented by Sevenoaks Flower Club. Donations to Cancer Research Campaign. Time: 11.00-

17.30

St Augustine's Cross

Ebbsfleet Minster Kent CT

[2m E of Minster off B29048, BR: Minster 2m, Bus: 01 Ramsgate / Canterbury]

19th century cross, in Celtic design, marking the traditional site of St Augustine's landing in 597.

All year any reasonable time

Admission Free

St Leonard's Tower

West Malling Kent ME

[on unclassified road W of A228]

Tel: 01732 870872

An early and particularly fine example of a Norman tower keep, built 1080 century by Gundulf, Bishop of Rochester.

External viewing any reasonable time.

Telephone for internal viewing

Admission Free

Sutton Valence Castle

Maidstone Kent ME

[5m SE of Maidstone in Sutton Valence village on A274, BR: Headcorn 4m, Bus: Maidstone & District / Nu-Venture, Chalkwell 12 Maidstone / Tenterden]

The ruins of a 12th century stone keep built to monitor the important medieval route across the Weald from Rye to Maidstone.

All year any reasonable time

Admission Free

Temple Manor

Strood Rochester Kent ME

[in Strood (Rochester) off A228]

Tel: 01634 827980

The 13th century manor house of the Knights Templar with added 17th century extensions. It was built to provide lodgings for members of this Order on their way to and from the crusades. Temple Manor is in Strood, set on the opposite side of the river Medway to Rochester Castle. The building is of simple design and consists of two levels, an undercroft and a large hall in which visitors would await audience with the Templars. The undercroft and most of the outer walls are original and retain many of their early features. The extensions are open for view and show quite clearly how the house was added and developed over the centuries. It was in occupation well into this century and last used as a farmhouse.

Easter-end Sept & Good Fri, Sat & Sun & Bank Hol.Mon, 10.00-18.00. At other times by prior arrangement call Commerical Office Mon-Fri:

01634 827980
Last Admission: 17.30
Admission Free

Tonbridge Castle

Castle Street Tonbridge Kent TN9 1BG
[in town centre off High Street. BR: Tonbridge main line / Charing Cross]
Tel: 01732 770929 Fax: 01732 770449
Reputedly England's finest example of the layout of a Norman Motte and Bailey Castle with 13th century Gatehouse set in landscaped gardens overlooking the River Medway. The site is clearly interpreted for your enjoyment.
Venue now closed until Sept 2000
Last Admission: 1 hour before closing
A£3.45 C£1.70 Family Ticket £8.00

Town Hall

King Street Fordwich Canterbury Kent CT2 0DP
[off A28 signposted from A28 in Sturry]
Tel: 01227 710756 Fax: 01227 710756
The timber-framed Tudor town hall and courtroom is thought to be the oldest and smallest in England. It overlooks the River Stour, peaceful now but hectic in the Middle Ages, because Fordwich was the port for Canterbury. The old town jail can also be visited.
Easter & June-Sept Sun 14.00-16.00 & Wed in July-Aug 14.00-16.00
Last Admission: 16.00
A£0.50 C£0.10

Tudor Yeoman's House

Sole Street Cobham Gravesend Kent DA12 3AX
[1m SW of Cobham on W side of B2009 just N of Sole Street Station. BR: Sole Street]
Tel: 01892 890651 Fax: 01892 890110
A 15th century yeoman's house of timber construction. The property is administered and maintained on the Trust's behalf by the tenant. No toilet facilities.
Main Hall only, by written application to the Regional Office
£0.50. No reduction for children or Groups

Upnor Castle

High Street Upper Upnor Rochester Kent ME2 4XG
[on unclassified road off A228. Car parking is central in the Village and visitors should then walk the 200 yards following the sign to the Castle entrance overlooking the river]
Tel: 01634 827980
Upnor Castle, is set in the village of Upper Upnor on the banks of the river Medway. This attractive turreted Castle is backed by rolling wooded hills and fronted by a water battery jutting out into the river Medway. It survives as an impressive reminder of stirring and troubled times. Built in the year 1559 as a gun fort on the orders of Queen Elizabeth I to defend warships at anchor in the reaches of the Medway and Chatham Dockyard, Upnor saw action when in 1667 the Dutch, under the command of Admiral de Ruyter, sailed into the river to wreak havoc among the British fleet. Soon after this the Castle was converted into a gunpowder store (Magazine) and at one time it stored more powder than the Tower of London. If you like to sketch, draw or paint, Upnor Castle is for you, whether it be the buildings or the shore line, river birds, boats or trees.
Apr 1-Sept 30 daily 10.00-18.00. For other times call the Seasonal Custodian 01634 718742 or central office out of season 01634 827980
Last Admission: 17.30
A£3.50 C£2.50 Concessions£2.50 Family Ticket (A2+C2)£9.50

Walmer Castle

Kingsdown Road Walmer Deal Kent CT14 7LJ
[on coast S of Walmer on A258, J13 M20 or from M2 to Deal. Limited parking on site]
Tel: 01304 364288 Fax: 01304 364826
www.english-heritage.org.uk
Walmer Castle was built by Henry VIII, designed to withstand the mightiest bombardment. It is the official residence of the Lord Warden of the Cinque Ports, a post once held by the Duke of Wellington who died here. Wellington's famous boots can be seen. The castle is still used today by HM the Queen Mother in her official capacity as Warden of the Cinque Ports. A garden has been created to mark her 95th birthday.
1 Apr-30 Sept daily 10.00-18.00, 1 Oct-31 Oct daily 10.00-17.00, 1 Nov-31 Dec Wed-Sun 10.00-16.00. Closed 24-26 Dec. Closed Jan & Feb 2001. 1 Mar-31 Mar Wed-Sun 10.00-16.00. Closed when Lord Warden is in residence
A£4.50 C£2.30 Concessions£3.40 Personal stereo tour included in admission price, also available for the partially sighted, those with learning difficulties, and in French & German. RHS members free

↓ *special events*
► **Life Below Stairs**
15/4/00-28/8/00
Servant's gossip and tales, 15-24 Apr, 17/18 June, 29/30 July & 27/28 Aug
► **Garden Tours**
16/4/00-26/8/00
A look at the history and development of the Lord Warden's Gardens on 16 Apr, 7 May, 18 June, 13 & 26 Aug

► **Garden Tour**
21/4/00-21/4/00
Spring flowers at Walmer

► **Easter Egg Hunt**
22/4/00-22/4/00
Egg Hunt for C(under 5) from 13.00-14.00, with an Easter Trail competition from 13.00-16.00 for C(5+)

► **Garden Tour**
24/4/00-24/4/00
See entry for 21 April

► **Regency Murder Mystery**
30/4/00-1/5/00
A murder to solve, plots, sword fights and tight breeches!

► **Fantastical Fairy Tales!**
20/5/00-21/5/00
21st century versions of your favourite fairy tales, as told by the villainous Grimey Brothers!

► **Flower Festival**
23/6/00-25/6/00
Enjoy beautiful blooms and wonderful arrays of period flower arrangements. Not to be missed!

► **Garden Tour**
25/6/00-25/6/00
The Herbacous border in summer

► **More Fairy Tales...**
2/7/00-2/7/00
...from the Enchanted Garden   Back by popular demand! Prepare yourself for a new magical adventure in the enchanted gardens...from the Enchanted Garden Back by popular demand! Prepare yourself for a new magical adventure in the enchanted gardens, on 28/ 29 May, 4, 11, June, 2, 9 July, 3, & 10 Sept

► **The Roaring Twenties!**
22/7/00-23/7/00
Enjoy a Brideshead Revisited-style garden party. Play croquet, listen to the gramophone, even learn to Fox-trot!

► **Garden Tour**
30/7/00-30/7/00
See entry for 25 June

► **The Wednesday Tour**
2/8/00-2/8/00
Looking at the history and development of the gardens

► **The Bard and the Blade**
5/8/00-6/8/00
Shakespearean dialogue and dramatic duels with sword and dagger

► **The Wednesday Tour**
9/8/00-9/8/00
See entry for 2 August

► **The Wednesday Tour**
16/8/00-16/8/00
See entry for 2 August

► **The Wednesday Tour**
23/8/00-23/8/00
See entry for 2 August

► **Captain Hook!**
16/9/00-17/9/00
The magical adventures of Peter Pan, Captain Hook and of course, the crocodile!

► **The Approach of Autumn**
24/9/00-24/9/00
A look at how the gardens prepare for the onset of winter

Western Heights
Dover Kent CT
[above Dover town on W side of harbour]
Tel: 01304 241806
Parts of moat of 19th century fort built to fend off a French invasion. Now incorporated into White Cliffs Countryside Project.
All year any reasonable time
Admission Free

Wool House
Wells Street Loose Maidstone Kent ME15 0EH
[3m SE of Maidstone 1/4m W of the Cranbrook road A229 BR: Maidstone East / Maidstone West]
Tel: 01892 890651
A 15th century half-timbered house, thought to have been used for the cleaning of wool. The house is administered and largely maintained on the Trust's behalf by the tenant. No toilet facilities.
Apr-Sept by written application to tenant
£0.50. No reduction for children or parties

Landmarks

Gateway To The White Cliffs
Langdon Cliffs Dover Kent CT16 1HJ
Tel: 01304 202756
New for 1999! The gateway to Britain, the White Cliffs of Dover are internationally famous. The Visitor Centre has spectacular views and introduces the visitor to five miles of coast and countryside through imaginative display and interpretation.
OPENS Easter 1999. Visitor Centre: 1 Apr-31 Oct daily 10.00-17.00. 1 Nov-24 Mar 2000 daily 11.00-16.00. Closed 25 Dec. Car Park: daily 09.00-18.00 (later in summer)
Parking: Mon-Fri £1.20, Sat-Sun £1.50 (NT Members Free) Coaches £5.00

Living History Museums

Canterbury Roman Museum
Butchery Lane Longmarket Canterbury Kent

CT1 2RA
[off A2 London / Dover road in Canterbury centre signposted]
Tel: 01227 785575 Fax: 01227 455047
Underground, at the level of the Roman town, you will find this famous Roman house with its mosaic floors. Following the discoveries of archaeologists, you walk through a fascinating reconstruction of Roman buildings, including a market place with stallholders wares of the period. Displays reveal a wealth of objects rescued by excavations. In the 'touch the past' area you can handle artefacts and take part in archaeological discovery.
All year Mon-Sat 10.00-17.00, Sun June-Oct 13.30-17.00. Closed Good Fri & Christmas period
Last Admission: 16.00
A£2.30 C(5-18)£1.15 Family Ticket £5.15 OAPs& Students£1.50. Group rates10+ 10% discount. Educational Ticket £0.35. Residents Ticket £0.50

Canterbury Tales
St. Margaret's Street Canterbury Kent CT1 2TG
[main routes into Canterbury are M2/A2. Located just off the pedestrianised High Street]
Tel: 01227 454888 Fax: 01227 765584
www.heritageattractions.co.uk/
Join us in 2000 as we celebrate 600 years of Chaucer's Canterbury Tales. Step back in time to join Chaucer's famous band of pilgrims on their journey to the shrine of St Thomas Becket in Canterbury Cathedral. Hear their tales of love, greed, chivalry and intrigue and experience life in the 14th century, complete with authentic sights, sounds and smells. Foreign language commentaries are available.
visitor comments: Good layout. Interesting and fun for all ages. Headphones available in 5 languages.
All year Mar, June, Sept & Oct daily 09.30-17.30, July-Aug daily 09.00-17.30, Nov-Feb Sun-Fri 10.00-16.30, Sat 09.30-17.30.
A£5.50 C(5-16)£4.60 Family Ticket £17.50 OAPs&Students£4.60
discount offer: One Child Free With Each Full Paying Adult

Maritime

Dolphin Sailing Barge Museum
Crown Quay Lane Sittingbourne Kent ME10 3SN
[J5 M2 or J7 M20 then N on A2 signposted in Sittingbourne]
Tel: 01795 423215
The museum is dedicated to presenting the history of the Thames spritsail sailing barge, many of which were built along the banks of Milton Creek. Tools of the trade, photographs of many barges and associated artefacts can be seen at the barge yard along with the sailing barge Cambria and others in for repair.
Easter-Oct Sun & Bank Hol 11.00-17.00. Other times by arrangement
Last Admission: 30mins before closing
A£1.50 C&OAPs&UB40£0.75

Dover Transport Museum
Alfred Road Dover Kent CT16 2AD
Tel: 01304 822409
Large display boards listing all rescues, ships assisted, lives saved etc. from 1864 to 1960. Model of former lifeboat, Faithful Forester.
Easter-end Oct Sun 11.00-17.00, 31 May-31 Oct Thur-Fri 14.00-17.00. Pre-booked groups at any time
Admission Free

Maritime Museum
Clock House Pier Yard Royal Harbour Ramsgate Kent CT11 8LS
[follow all signposts to Ramsgate Harbour]
Tel: 01843 587765 Fax: 01843 587765
Various aspects of the maritime heritage of East Kent includes engravings, prints, ships and other models, fishing and shipbuilding implements, navigational instruments, artefacts from shipwrecks of the Goodwin Sands, RNLI memorabilia and solar meridian line. Adjacent floating exhibits in the museum's historic ship collection. No dogs at all, the Harbour is a restricted area for all animals. Reg Charity No: 288702.
All year Apr-Sept daily 10.00-17.00. Oct-Mar Mon-Fri 10.00-16.30
Last Admission: 16.00
A£1.50 C&OAPs£0.75 Family Ticket £4.00
discount offer: One Child Free When Accompanied By A Full Paying Adult
↓ *special events*
► **Set 2000**
17/3/00-26/3/00
A Science, Engineering and Technology project. Results Mar 25 at the Royal Harbour
► **International Maritime Conference 'It's About Time!'**
28/4/00-1/5/00
Guest speakers address issues of local and national interest and importance. Call for details
► **Ramsgate Museum Exhibition**
1/5/00-31/5/00
Artefacts retrieved from the Man of War Stirling Castle wrecked on the Goodwin Sands in the 1703 Great Storm

Kent

► **'Cobbs Dynasty'**
1/5/00-31/5/00
The story of a local family's brewing and bank-
ing business. Held at the Margate Museum

► **Dunkirk Little Ships**
5/6/00-5/6/00
A flotilla from The Association of Dunkirk Little
Ships return to Ramsgate Harbour from their
60th Anniversary pilgrimage to France.

► **250th Harbour Birthday Party for Children**
16/6/00-16/6/00
At the Harbour from 12.30

► **Maritime Festival**
1/7/00-2/7/00
Ships to visit, shore based displays, steam vehi-
cles, traction engines, fairground, refreshments,
vintage and classic cars, 10.00-18.00 at the
Royal Harbour

► **Children's Open Day - Maritime Museum**
27/7/00-27/7/00
Family event with competitions, prizes, displays
and activities, from 10.00-16.00 around the
Museum and Pier Yard

► **250th Anniversary of Harbour Celebrations**
5/8/00-6/8/00
Ramsgate Costumed Walks Group provide guid-
ed celebration walks with famous characters.
Sat-Sun, 18.00 from the Harbour

► **Children's Open Day - Margate Museum**
26/8/00-26/8/00
Family fun, 10.00-16.00 in and around the Old
Town Hall Museum and Tudor House, Margate

► **Trips on Dunkirk Little Ships**
1/9/00-30/9/00
Due to run twice a week, times to be advised
when tides are known, from the Royal Harbour

► **Open Days**
18/10/00-21/10/00
Free entry from 10.00-20.00 at Ramsgate
Maritime and Margate Old Town Hall Museum

► **Fireworks and Illuminated Vessels**
5/11/00-5/11/00
At Ramsgate Harbour, times to be advised

► **Festive Celebrations**
9/12/00-9/12/00
Sailors Church at 14.30 with the Ramsgate
Costumed Walks Group. Christmas carols and
seasonal refreshments also

Old Lighthouse

Dungeness Road Dungeness Romney Marsh
Kent TN29 9NB
[Dungeness Point]

Tel: 01797 321300 Fax: 01303 242049

Lighthouse constructed in 1901 - operating
1904. Now redundant due to the construction
of the Power Station wish obscured the Sector
Light - Climb the 169 steps view the great lens
- step out onto the balcony. On a clear day you
can see France!

Mar, Apr, May & Oct weekend only 10.30-17.00.

June-last weekend Sept daily 10.30-17.00

Last Admission: 17.30

A£2.20 C(0-16)&OAPs£1.20 Family Ticket
(A2+C3(0-16)£5.60 Student£1.50

South Foreland Lighthouse

St Margaret's-at-Cliffe Dover Kent *[at St*
Margaret's-at-Cliff. BR: Martin Mill]

**Tel: 01304 852463/202756 Fax: 01892
890110**

A distinctive landmark on the White Cliffs of
Dover with views to France. The lighthouse
was built in 1843 and used by Marconi for first
radio communications as an aid to navigation
in 1989. Tower, information room and spiral
stairs to balcony around the light are open.

4 Apr-25 Oct Sat, Sun & Bank Hol Mon 14.00-
17.30. 1999 Times: 27 Mar-31 Oct Sat, Sun &
Bank Hol Mon 12.30-17.30. Also 29 Mar-4 Apr,
31 May-4 June, 26 July-3 Sept, 26-29 Oct Mon-
Fri 12.30-17.30

Last Admission: 17.00 or dusk if sooner

A£1.50 C£0.75. Parking at St Margaret's village
or NT car park at Langdon Cliffs 2m £1.20

Whitstable Museum And Gallery

Oxford Street Whitstable Kent CT5 1DB

[in town centre close to the Theatre, Library and
St Mary's Hall, and in walkding distance of the
car parks and railway station]

Tel: 01227 276998 Fax: 01227 772379

Displays of Whistable's seafaring traditions;
oysters, diving and wrecks. Maritime art
gallery and natural history displays. There are
shows featuring work by people from the area,
opportunities to be part of the national exhibition network, and major contributions to
the town's festivals. The Gallery's commitment
to local topics brings fascinating celebrations
of wildlife and the town's link with the sea.
Events related to the exhibitions are arranged
regularly, and also include workshops with
practising artists for schools and colleges.

All year 10.30-13.00 & 14.00-16.00. Closed Wed,
Sun, Good Fri & Christmas week

Admission Free

World Naval Base, Chatham
Chatham Kent ME4 4TZ
[J1 or J3 M2 or from J6 M20 follow signs for Chatham and then Brown Anchor. BR: Chatham. Plenty of parking on site]
Tel: 01634 823800 Fax: 01634 823801
www.worldnavalbase.org.uk
World Naval Base, Chatham is Europe's most exciting maritime heritage destination. The 80 acre site dates back over 400 years and was once one of Britain's most important naval bases. Battle Ships! displays three powerful fighting ships - H.M.S. Cavalier, Britain's last remaining W.W.II destroyer, the spy submarine Ocelot and the last Victorian sloop, Gannet. Guided tours around the destroyer and submarine reveal what life was like for those on board and are included in the price. The Wooden Walls animatronic gallery allows visitors to walk through the Royal Dockyard of 1758 and discover how Britain's wooden warships were built. Lifeboat! tells the heroic story of the R.N.L.I. with an exciting display of 15 full size lifeboats, film and artefacts. In the Ropery craftsmen still use traditional techniques to make the rope that still rigs the world's grandest sailing ships. The Kent Police Museum, a brewery, craft workshops, licensed restaurants and gift shops are also on site.
27 Mar-29 Oct daily 10.00-18.00. Feb, Mar & Nov only Wed, Sat & Sun 10.00-16.00
Last Admission: 60mins before closing
A£8.50 C(5-16)£5.50 Family Ticket (A2+C2)£22.50 Concessions£6.50

Military & Defence Museums

Kent and Sharpshooters Museum
Hever Castle Hever Edenbridge Kent TN8 7NG
[J5/6 M25. Follow signs to Hever Castle]
Tel: 01732 865224 Fax: 01732 866796
The Kent and Sharpshooters Museum is housed in the Gate House of Hever Castle. It is open on days when the castle is open but has to close on busy days due to congestion. It houses many interesting artefacts linked to the regiment.
1 Mar-30 Nov daily (except on busy days) 12.00-18.00
Museum: Admission Free. Castle & Gardens: A£6.50 C(5-16)£3.30 Family Ticket £16.30 OAPs£5.70.

Kent Battle of Britain Museum
Aerodrome Road Hawkinge Folkestone Kent CT18 7AG
[on A260 in Hawkinge]
Tel: 01303 893140
Once a Battle of Britain Station, today it houses the largest collection of authentic relics and related memorabilia of British and German aircraft involved in the fighting. Also shown are British and German uniforms and equipment, and full-size replicas of the Hurricane, Spitfire and Me 109 used in Battle of Britain films. No photography or recording permitted.
Easter-Sept daily 10.00-17.00, Oct daily 11.00-16.00
Last Admission: 60mins before closing
A£3.00 C£1.50 OAPs£2.50 Parties 20+ 10% discount

Princess of Wales's Royal Regiment and the Queen's Regiment Museum
Inner Bailey Dover Castle Dover Kent CT16 1HU
[M20 follow signs to Dover Castle]
Tel: 01304 240121 Fax: 01304 240121
Trace the fascinating story of The Princess of Wales's Royal Regiment from its beginnings in 1572 to present day. Walk through life-like displays and discover what it was like being a soldier or marine. Discover the history of the Victoria Cross first awarded at the end of the Crimean War in 1856.
All year daily, Summer: 10.00-18.00 Winter: 10.00-16.00
Admission to Dover Castle includes visit to Museum A£6.25 C£3.25 Concessions£4.75 nominal fee for photograph taken with A Drum Major in ceremonial dress

Royal Engineers Museum
Prince Arthur Road Gillingham Kent ME4 4UG
[off B2004]
Tel: 01634 406397 Fax: 01634 822371
The prize-winning museum tells the story of Britain's soldier engineers - the Sappers - and their work around the world in peace and war from 1066 to the present day. It is a treasure trove of the unexpected ranging from Wellington's battlemap of Waterloo to a Harrier Jump jet. The magnificent medal displays include 24 Victoria crosses and the

Kent

Kent

regalia of Field Marshal Lord Kitchener.
Something for everyone.

All year Mon-Thur 10.00-17.00, Sat-Sun 11.30-17.00, Bank Hol Mon 11.30-17.00. Closed Good Fri, 25-26 Dec & 1 Jan

A£3.50 C&OAPs&UB40s£2.00 Family Ticket £9.00. Guided Tour £5.00. Group rate 15+ 30% discount

discount offer: One Child Free With One Full Paying Adult

↓*special events*

► The Anglo-Boer War

2/10/99-2/5/02

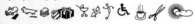

Mills – Water & Wind

Crabble Corn Mill

Lower Road River Dover Kent CT17 0UY
[off A256 between Dover / Whitfield on A2]
Tel: 01304 823292 Fax: 01304 826040
www.invmed.demon.co.uk

Visit this beautifully restored Georgian watermill, built 1812. Now fully working, producing traditionally stoneground wholemeal flour from Kentish organic wheat (organic flour on sale). Tour the whole mill, see regular demonstrations of it working. Cafe serves 'Kentish Fare' local produce, including home-baking with mill's flour. Gallery with exhibitions of local artists. Riverside gardens being developed.

1 April-30 Sept daily 11.00-17.00. Winter opening Sundays only 11.00-17.00. Closed 25 Dec-31 Jan. Pre-booked tours any day or evening

A£2.00 C£1.00 Family Ticket £5.00 OAPs£1.50

discount offer: 50p Off Adult Ticket or £1.00 Off Family Ticket

Willesborough Windmill

Windmill Trust Mill Lane Willesborough Ashford Kent TN24 0GQ
[2m E of Ashford town centre just off A292]
Tel: 01233 661866

Willesborough Windmill built in 1869 has now been restored as a working smock mill. Visitors can view the turn-of-the-century miller's cottage, enjoy guided tours of the mill.

Easter-end Sept Sat Sun & Bank Hol 14.00-17.00
A£1.00 C&OAPs£0.50, Group rates available on application

Music & Theatre Museums

Finchcocks

Finchcocks Museum Riseden Goudhurst Kent TN17 1HH
[M20 then A28 off A262 or A21 London / Hastings road then A262]
Tel: 01580 211702 Fax: 01580 211007
www.argonet.co.uk/finchcocks

This fine early Georgian house stands in a spacious park with a beautiful garden, and contains an outstanding collection of keyboard instruments from the 17th century onwards. They have been restored to playing condition, and there are musical tours on all open days and private visits. Visually handicapped visitors may touch the instruments as well as hear them. Special events include Fairs (30-31 May & 8-11 October). Music Festival weekends in September.

Easter-Sept Sun & Bank Hol Mon 14.00-18.00, Aug Wed, Thur & Sun 14.00-18.00. Private groups by appointment Apr-Oct

A£6.00 C£4.00. Group visits £6.00. Evening £7.00-£8.00

Smallhythe Place

Smallhythe Road Tenterden Kent TN30 7NG
[3m S of Tenterden on B2082]
Tel: 01580 762334

Once a Tudor harbour master's house, this half timbered, 16th Century building became Dame Ellen Terry's last home. It is now a museum of Ellen Terry memorabilia. The barn has been made into a theatre and is open most days courtesy of the Barn Theatre Company. Charming cottage garden, including Ellen Terry's rose garden.

27 Mar-31 Oct Mon-Wed, Sat, Sun, Bank Hol Mon & Good Fri 13.30-18.00
Last Admission: 17.00
A£3.00 C£1.50 Family Ticket £7.50

↓*special events*

► Theatre of Flowers

17/6/00-18/6/00

Held in the Barn Theatre at 13.30-17.30, tickets £2.00

► The Importance of being Earnest

27/7/00-5/8/00

Held on July 27-30 and Aug 3-5 only

► Treasure Hunt

8/8/00-8/8/00

Tickets £2.00, 11.00-16.00

Natural History Museums

Folkestone Museum and Sassoon Gallery

Folkestone Library 2 Grace Hill Folkestone Kent CT20 1HD

[J13 M20 follow signs to Town Centre upstairs first floor of Folkestone Library]

Tel: 01303 850123 Fax: 01303 242907

The Sassoon Gallery shows a programme of temporary exhibitions of contemporary art and craft. Music and drama events are also occasionally held. The Museum holds a permanent collection of art, and also has displays on Folkestone's history, archaeology, fossils, and natural history.

All year Mon-Sat 09.30-17.00. Closed Sun & Bank Hol

Admission Free

On the Water

Paddle Steamer Kingswear Castle

The Historic Dockyard Chatham Kent ME4 4TQ

[BR: Chatham]

Tel: 01634 827648 Fax: 01634 827648

A unique part of Britain's maritime heritage, the award-winning, coal-fired paddle-steamer Kingswear Castle offers morning, afternoon, evening and day cruises from Chatham and Rochester and is available for private hire. Sail back into history amid a splendour of gleaming brass and wood panelling. Watch the steam engine turning the paddles.

May-Sept

£3.95-£19.95 - according to length of cruise chosen

Palaces

Archbishops' Palace and Solar Restaurant and Tearooms

Mill Street Maidstone Kent ME15 6YE

[in town centre]

Tel: 01622 663006 Fax: 01622 682451

Located in the oldest quarter of Maidstone overlooking the River Medway, the 14th-century Palace has recently been restored to its former glory.

All year daily 10.30-17.00. Closed 25 & 26 Dec

Admission Free

Places of Worship incl Cathedrals

Aylesford Priory

The Friars Aylesford Kent ME20 7BX

[J6 M20 A229 from M2 follow the Friars signs all the way]

Tel: 01622 717272 Fax: 01622 715575

Built in the 13th and 14th centuries and then closed down in the Reformation, the priory has been restored and is now a house of prayer, guesthouse, conference centre and a place of pilgrimage and retreat. It has fine cloisters, and displays sculpture and ceramics by modern artists, also a pottery and upholsterers workshop.

All year daily 09.00-dusk. Gift & book shop May-Sept 10.00-17.00, Oct-Apr 10.00-16.00. Guided tours of the pirory by arrangement Donations

Canterbury Cathedral

Cathedral House The Precincts Canterbury Kent CT1 2EH

[in Canterbury town centre. Parking is not permitted within The Precincts except for a certain very limited provision for disabled drivers, by prior arrangement]

Tel: 01227 762862 Fax: 01227 865222

Permits for individual, personal photography in the Cathedral can be obtained at the Welcome Centre of the Cathedral Gift Stall. Audio-visual presentation lasts 14mins and runs regularly throughout the day in the Theodore (at the North-West corner of the Great Cloister) from mid February to 31 October. Ancient ghosts tread the flagstones: Archbishop Simon Sudbury, killed in 1381 by Wat Tyler is supposed to haunt the tower named after him for the doubtful reason that his head is buried in Suffolk and his torso within the walls of Canterbury. Another ghost is that of an unknown monk seen by several visitors in the last few years. When a member of the choir school attached to the cathedral was walking round the cloisters one evening and saw the figure of the man approaching her, silently with his head bowed in contemplation or prayer. She merely glanced at him, thinking he was a member of the religious orders who carry out pilgrimage to the holy spot, and passed by. As the figure drew level, she suddenly felt extremely cold and turning to see the monk suddenly vanish.

General Visiting: Mon-Sat Easter-30 Sept 08.45-19.00, 1 Oct-Easter 08.45-17.00. The Crypt all year daily 10.00-16.30. Sun all year 12.30-14.30, Crypt 16.30-17.30. Guided Tours: Mon-Sat call for full details. For information on Church Services call above number

Last Admission: 30mins before closing
A£3.00 C&Concessions £2.00 C(0-4)£Free.
Guided Tours: A£3.00 OAPs&Students£2.00
Accompanied C£1.20 Groups upto 9 £30.00
School Groups each £0.50. Audio Visual: A£1.00
OAPs&Students£0.70 Accompanied C£0.50
School Groups each £0.50. Audio Tours:
A&OAPs£Students£2.70 Accompanied
C&Students Groups 10+ £1.70 School Groups
each £1.00. Toilets £0.20

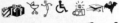

Faversham Stone Chapel

Faversham Kent ME
[1.5m W of Faversham on A2, Bus: 333
Maidstone / Faversham]
The remains of a small medieval church incorporating part of a 4th century Romano-British
pagan mausoleum. Under local management
agreement with the Faversham Society
visitor comments: No parking nearby.
All year any reasonable time
Admission Free

Horne's Place Chapel

Appledore Kent [1.5m N of Appledore]
Tel: 0831 218680
This 14th century domestic chapel was once
attached to the manor house. The house and
chapel are privately owned and visitors are
requested to respect the owner's privacy.
By appointment only for further details contact
01304 211067
Admission Free

Rochester Cathedral

High Street Rochester Kent ME1 1JY
Tel: 01634 401301 Fax: 01634 401410
**www.net-west.co.uk/webs.rochester-
cathedral**
Rochester Cathedral offers a warm welcome to
all visitors. A place of prayer and pilgrimage
for nearly 1400 years, the Cathedral is open
throughout the year. Whether you come as a
worshipper or a tourist, you will enjoy the
delights of its Norman and Early English architecture. The Cathedral Tea Rooms offer refreshment with home-made cakes and light lunches. The Cathedral Shops sell a variety of religious gifts and souvenirs. A chair lift, level
access and a specially adapted toilet means
that the Cathedral is accessible for those in
wheelchairs.
All year daily, call for details
Admission Free but donations are welcomed.
Guided tours: £2.00 per person, must be booked
in advance.

St John's Commandery

Swingfield Kent [2m NE of Densole off A260]
Tel: 01304 211067
A medieval chapel, converted into a farmhouse
in the 16th century. It has a fine moulded plas-
ter ceiling and a remarkable timber roof.
By appointment only for internal viewing.
External viewing any reasonable time
Admission Free

St John's Jerusalem

Main Road Sutton at Hone Dartford Kent DA4
9HQ
[3m S of Dartford at Sutton-at-Hone on E side
of A225. BR: Farningham Road]
Tel: 01892 890651 Fax: 01892 890110
A National Trust Property. A large garden,
moated by the River Darent. The house is the
former chapel of a Knights Hospitaller
Commandery, since converted into a private
residence. The east end of the chapel which is
open to view, was retained for family worship,
but was later converted into a billiard room.
Former Chapel & Garden only: 31 Mar-27 Oct
Wed 14.00-18.00
Last Admission: 17.30
A£1.00 C£0.50

Police, Prisons & Dungeons

West Gate Museum

St Peter's Street Canterbury Kent CT1 2RA
[off A2 London / Dover road, in Canterbury cen-
tre signposted]
Tel: 01227 452747 Fax: 01227 455047
Panoramic views from the battlements; prison
cells; replica armour to try on.
All year Mon-Sat 11.00-12.30 &13.30-15.30.
Closed Good Fri & Christmas week
A£1.00 C(5-18)£0.50 Family Ticket £2.30
OAPs&Students£0.65. Group rates 10+ 10% dis-
count. Educational Ticket £0.15. Residents Ticket
£0.30

Railways

Kent and East Sussex Steam Railway

Tenterden Town Station Tenterden Kent TN30
6HE
[on the A28 main road between Ashford and
Hastings]
Tel: 01580 765155
There are engines and carriages dating from
Victorian times waiting to take you for a ride
through 7 miles of beautiful countryside on

this charming rural railway. Refreshment Rooms, Video Theatre, Letterpress Printworks, Gift Shop, Museum, Play Area, Luxury Dining Cars, Dinners, Lunches and Teas, booking essential.

visitor comments: Enjoyable day for 2-100 year olds! A rather different way to enjoy a family roast Sunday Lunch

14-22 Feb, Mar Sun only, Apr-Oct weekends & school hol, June & Sept daily except Mon & Fri, July & Aug daily, Dec Santa Specials at weekends, 10.30-16.20
Last Admission: 16.20
A£6.50 C£3.25 Family Ticket £17.50 Concessions £5.60 School Parties £4.00 Group Rates £5.60

Romney Hythe and Dymchurch Railway
New Romney Station Littlestone Road New Romney Kent TN28 8PL
[J11 M20 signposted, Hythe station, other stations on A259. Plenty parking places]
Tel: 01797 362353/363256 Fax: 01797 363591
www.rhdr.demon.co.uk
The world's smallest public railway has its headquarters here. The concept of two enthusiasts coincided with Southern Railway's plans for expansion, and so the thirteen-and-a-half mile stretch of 15 inch gauge railway came into being, running from Hythe through New Romney and Dymchurch to Dungeness Lighthouse. Picnic areas available (indoor and outdoor). Visit can be anything from 1 hour to a full day.
visitor comments: Not to be missed. Stations are well kept, clean and tidy. A excellent train journey, with stops for tea.
Regular services Easter-Sept daily also weekends in Mar & Oct and October half-term daily
Fares depend on length of journey, C£half-price, discount for pre-booked parties of 15+. OAP concessions available
discount offer: One Adult or Child Travels Free with One Adult Paying Full Rate All Stations Return Ticket. Valid For One Person Per Coupon, Per Day. Not Valid Special Events or Bank Holidays

Sittingbourne and Kemsley Light Railway
Kemsley Down Station Mill Way Sittingbourne Kent ME
[near BR: Sittingbourne]
Tel: 01634 852672
Exhibition of railways in Kent, including many pictures of former Bowater industrial Railway (paper mills).
Easter-Oct Sun 13.30-16.30, All Bank Hol and Wed & Sat in Aug
A£2.60 C(3-13)£1.30 Family Ticket (A2+C4)£7.00 OAPs£1.80, group bookings on application

RNLI Stations

Dover Lifeboat Station
Dover Kent CT
(1837) Thames, Western Docks.
Visits not suitable, prior arrangement can be made but care must be taken as the lifeboat is inside the dock area.
Admission Free

Dungeness Lifeboat Station
Dungeness Kent TN
(1826) Mersey, between Pilot Inn and Lighthouse.
Easter-Sep Parties only by appointment
Admission Free

Littlestone-on-Sea Lifeboat Station
Littlestone-On-Sea Kent TN
[off the A259 in Littlestone]
(1966) Atlantic 21, The Foreshore, Coast Drive, Greatstone.
Most weekends
Admission Free

Margate Lifeboat Station
Margate Kent CT
(1860) Mersey and Inflatable 'D', The Rendezvous.
Easter-Sept
Admission Free

Walmer Lifeboat Station
Walmer Kent CT
(1856) Atlantic 21 and Inflatable 'D', in boathouse, seafront.
All year each Sun morning, Parties by appointment in writing only
Admission Free

Kent

Kent

Roman Era

Reculver Towers and Roman Fort
Reculver Herne Bay Kent CT6 6SU
[3m E of Herne Bay]
Tel: 01227 740676
The Roman Regulbium was one of the forts
built during the 3rd century to defend the
Saxon Shore. The fort was in good condition
until the 18th century, when erosion of the
cliffs on which it stands caused part of the
walls to collapse into the sea below. An
Information Centre run by the Kent Wildlife
Trust is nearby.
*All year any reasonable time, exterior viewing
only*
Admission Free

Richborough Roman Amphitheatre
Sandwich Kent CT
*[J7 M2 onto A2, BR: Sandwich 1.75m, 1.25m N
of Sandwich off A257]*
Tel: 01304 612013
Remains associated with the nearby 3rd centu-
ry fort.
Phone for details
Admission Free

Social History Museums

Draper's Museum Of Bygones
4 High Street Rochester Kent ME1 1PT
Tel: 01634 830647 Fax: 01634 404436
Enter a bygone world packed with memories
at Draper's Museum of Bygones. The home to
thousands of nostalgic exhibits from the last
one hundred years shown in 16 old shop sets
and displays on three floors. For all the family
to enjoy.
*All year Mon-Sat 10.00-17.00, Sun 12.00-17.00
A£2.50 C£1.25 Family Ticket £6.00
OAPs&Students£1.75. Group rates 10+ call for
details*

Spectator Sports

Brands Hatch
Brands Hatch Road Fawkham Longfield Kent
DA3 8NG
*[situated on the A20 London-Maidstone road nr
West Kingsdown, 3m from J3 off M25 follow
brown tourist signs]*
**Tel: 020 7344 4444 T/Master Fax: 01474
874766**
www.brands-hatch.co.uk
A disabled viewing area on the outside of

Clearways and Paddock Hill grandstand, plus
facilities in the John Foulston Centre, Kentagon
and Hailwoods. Tickets available in advance by
calling 0870 60 60 611. For prices note the
Price Grade on each event and refer to the list
of prices.
*Open for race meetings, see special events for
details*
*Queuing Times: possible on big race days
PRICE GRADES: AA - Gate Price £33.00 - Advance
£28.00 - Two Day Pass £33.00, Three Day Pass
£35.00 - Qualifying £8/£15.00 - C£2.00 -
Program £5.00 - Seating BH £15.00. Grade A -
Gate Price £22.00 - Advance £20.00 - Two Day
Pass £26.00 - Qualifying £11.00 - C£1.00 -
Program £3.00 - Seating BH £10.00 - South
Bank £5.00 - Group rates £95.00. Grade B - Gate
Price £22.00 - Advance £20.00 - Two Day Pass
£26.00 - Qualifying £11.00 - C£1.00 - Program
£1.00 - Seating BH £8.00 - South Bank £4.00 -
Group rates £100.00. Grade C - Gate Price
£16.00 - Advance £12.00 - Two Day Pass £17.00
- Qualifying £8.00 - C£Free - Program £tba -
Seating BH £Free - South Bank £3.00. Grade D -
Gate Price £11.00 - Advance £9.00 - Two Day
Pass £13.00 - Qualifying £6.00 - C£Free -
Program £tba - Seating BH £Free - South Bank
£2.00. Grade E - Gate Price £10.00 - Advance
£8.00 - Two Day Pass £11.00 - Qualifying £5.00
- C£Free - Program £tba - Seating BH £Free -
South Bank £2.00. Season Ticket £210.00.
Discounts for Club Members on ALL advance
tickets*

↓ *special events*
▶ **Champion of Brands £1 Day (BMCRC)**
5/3/00-5/3/00
*Featuring: Super Sidecar, Supersport 600,
Supersport 400, Powerbike and more - Indy
Circuit. Price Grade: £1 Day*
▶ **MRO Bike Championship (MRO)**
12/3/00-12/3/00
*Featuring: Supersport 600 & 400, 750cc, 125cc,
Powerbike, Super Sidecar, 250cc Aprilia, Suzuki
1200 Bandit Shootout - Indy Circuit. Price
Grade: D*
▶ **Motoring News Spring Festival (BRSCC)**
19/3/00-19/3/00
*Featuring: Spring Formula Ford Festival, ARP
Formula 3, Ford Saloons, Ford Si, Legends x2,
Mod Prod Saloon, Super Coupé - Indy Circuit.
Price Grade: D*
▶ **British Superbike Championship (BARC)**
25/3/00-26/3/00
*Featuring: Superbike x2, 125cc, 250cc,
Supersport, Superstock - Indy Circuit. Price
Grade: B*
▶ **BOSS Spring Raceday (BRSCC)**
2/4/00-2/4/00
*Featuring: BOSS Formula, Porche 924, Kent
County Formula, MG Midgets, Formula Saloons,
VW Challenge, and more - Indy Circuit. Price
Grade: D*

▶ **British Touring Car Championship (TOCA)**
8/4/00-9/4/00
Featuring: British Touring Cars x2, Formula Fiesta, Formula Renault, Renault Clio, Lotus Elise, plus support - Grand Prix Circuit. Price Grade: A

▶ **750 Spectacular (750 M/C)**
15/4/00-16/4/00
Featuring: 750 Formula, Sports 2000, Formula 4, Formula VEE x2, 750 Trophy, Kit Cars, Roadsports, Hot Hatch, and more - Indy Car. Price Grade: D

▶ **Easter Champion Of Brands (BMRC)**
23/4/00-24/4/00
See entry for 5 March, Price Grade: D

▶ **Grand Nationals (BRSCC)**
30/4/00-1/5/00
Featuring: TVR Tuscans x3, Euro Palmer Audi x2, Classic F1 Cars, Kent Country Formula Ford, Mighty Minis, and more - Indy Curcuit. Price Grade: C

▶ **British Sportscar Raceday (MGCC)**
7/5/00-7/5/00
Championships organised by the MG Car Club - Indy Circuit. Price Grade: D

▶ **Classic Festival (BARC)**
13/5/00-14/5/00
Featuring: Pre '66 Classic and Historic aloons, Pre '74 Post Historic Touring Cars, and more - Indy Circuit. Price Grade: D

▶ **Champion of Brands GP Weekend (BMCRC)**
28/5/00-29/5/00
See entry for 5 March, - Grand Prix Circuit. Price Grade: D

▶ **Powertour (BRDC)**
3/6/00-4/6/00
Featuring: British GT, British Formula 3, National Saloons plus support - Grand Prix Circuit. Price Grade: B

▶ **Eurocar Extravaganza (NRSCC)**
25/6/00-25/6/00
Featuring: Eurocar V8 x2, Eurocar V6 x2, Legends x2, Pick-ups x2, Euro Formula First - Indy Circuit. Price Grade: D

▶ **Historic Superprix (HSCC)**
1/7/00-2/7/00
Featuring: Pre '66 Grand Prix Cars, RJB Thundersports, Classic Formula 3, Derek Bell Trophy, and more - Indy Circuit. Price Grade: D

▶ **Midsummer Astons (AMCC)**
8/7/00-9/7/00
Featuring (Sat): Thoroughbred Sports Cars, AMOC Formula Jnrs, Post '65 Sports v Saloon, Pre '65 Sports & Saloon, JXS/E Type Challenge, TR Register, Enduro Part 1. (Sun): Group C, Ferrari Maranello, Intermarque, Angol-American, Porsche Classic, Auston Healeys, Pre-war Sports/Feltham Astons, Aston Martin Champ, Enduro Part 2, Indy Circuit. Price Grade: D

▶ **Midsummer BOSS Formula (BRSCC)**
22/7/00-23/7/00
Featuring: BOSS Formula, Formula Renault, Kent County Formula Ford x2, Marcos Mantis x2, Formula Saloons x2, International Saloons, South Eastern Sports & Saloonsand more - Indy Circuit. Price Grade: D

▶ **World Superbike Championship (FIM)**
4/8/00-6/8/00
Featuring: World Superbike x2, World Supersport, European Superstock, Sidecar World Cup - Grand Prix Circuit. Price Grade: AA

▶ **Caterham Festival**
19/8/00-20/8/00
Caterham Superlight, Caterham Roadsport, Caterham Graduate, Caterham Scholarship, Indy Circuit. Price Grade: D

▶ **British Touring Car Championship**
27/8/00-28/8/00
See entry for 8 April

▶ **Champion of Brands Raceday (BMRC)**
2/9/00-2/9/00
See the entry for 5 March, Indy Circuit

▶ **MRO Bike Championships (MRO)**
3/9/00-3/9/00
See entry for 4 March

▶ **Grand Nationals (BRSCC)**
9/9/00-10/9/00
Featuring: Euro Palmer Audi x2, TVR Tuscan x3, Kent County Formula Ford, Porsche Cup, Classic F1 Cars - Grand Prix Circuit. Price Grade: C

▶ **British Superbike Championship (BARC)**
23/9/00-24/9/00
Featuring: British Superbike x2, British 125cc, British 250cc, British Supersport, British Superstock - Grand Prix Circuit. Price Grade: B

▶ **BOSS Autumn Spectacular (BMCRC)**
30/9/00-1/10/00
Featuring: BOSS Formula, Legends x2, Alfas, Auto Italia, Fiats, Porsche Classic, Porsche 924, 2CV x2, Ginettas, Westfields - Indy Circuit. Price Grade: D

▶ **Champion of Brands Finals Day**
8/10/00-8/10/00
See entry for 5 March, Indy Circuit

▶ **Formula Ford Eurocup Finals (BRSCC)**
15/10/00-15/10/00
Featuring: Formula Ford Eurocup, Ford Saloons, Ford Si, Kent County Formula Ford, International Formulas Ford, Open Sports Cars, Road Saloons - Indy Circuit. Price Grade: D

▶ **Formula Ford Festival and World Cup (BRSCC)**
21/10/00-22/10/00
Zetec Formula Ford drivers from championships all over the world compete to win the most coverted title of the year. Includes: Super Classic Formula Ford, Sports 2000, Formula Ford Trophy, CARS Historic Formula Ford, Classic Formula Ford, T-Cars x2, Radical Bi-Duro x2, Indy Circuit. Price Grade: C

▶ **Winter Series (BRSCC)**
5/11/00-5/11/00
Programme to be confirmed. Call for details or see the website - Indy Circuit. Price Grade: D

► **Winter Series (BRSCC)**
19/11/00-19/11/00
See entry for 5 November

► **Winter Series (BRSCC)**
26/11/00-26/11/00
See entry for 5 November

Folkestone Racecourse
Westenhanger Folkestone Kent *[just off J11 M20 and close to Folkestone town. Trains from Cahring Cross go directly to Westenhanger station which is adjacent to the course. Plenty of on site parking]*
Tel: 01342 834800 Fax: 01342 835874
Folkestone Racecourse is the only racecourse in Kent. Folkestone celebrated its centenary in 1998. Ideally placed close to the channel tunnel and just off junction 11 of the M20, the pretty little course holds meetings on the flat and national hunt in the winter months. Boxes are avaiable for private use and the members restaurant overlooks the course. Sponsorship and corportate hospitatlity are not as expensive as you think and racegoers will enjoy a delightful day at the races, close to the action and the horses in the parade ring.
See fixture dates below
Members and Granstand £12.00 C(under 16)£Free

discount offer: £2.00 discount per person, on production of voucher

↓ *special events*
► **March Fixtures**
17/3/00-20/3/00
National Hunt on Mar 17 and 20 only
► **April Fixture**
18/4/00-18/4/00
Flat Racing on Apr 18 only
► **May Fixtures**
5/5/00-17/5/00
National Hunt on May 5 and 17 (eve, United Hunts Meeting) only
► **June Fixtures**
7/6/00-30/6/00
National Hunt on June 7 60's and 70's Night and June 30 only
► **July Fixtures**
13/7/00-31/7/00

Flat Racing on July 13 Caribbean Day and July 31 Family Fun Day
► **August Fixtures**
18/8/00-24/8/00
Flat Racing on Aug 18 Clowns and Magic Day and Aug 24 Kent Headline Day
► **October Fixture**
2/10/00-2/10/00
National Hunt on Oct 2 only
► **November Fixtures**
8/11/00-27/11/00
National Hunt on Nov 8 and 27 only
► **December Fixtures**
15/12/00-19/12/00
National Hunt on Dec 15 and 19 only

Lydden International Motor Racing Circuit
Wootton Canterbury Kent CT4 6RX
[7 miles south east of Canterbury off main A2 London Dover]
Tel: 01304 830557 Fax: 01304 831715
A motor racing circuit operated by the British Motor Cycle Racing Club. It hold events throughout the year see Special Events for details.
Varies depending on event

Theme & Adventure Parks

Dreamland Fun Park
Marine Terrace Margate Kent CT9 1XG
[off the M2, A28 to Margate]
Tel: 01843 227011 Fax: 01843 298667
The South East's largest seaside amusement park. A mix of traditional and new family attractions opposite Margate's sandy beach.

Easter-late Oct daily 10.00-18.00, 10.00-22.00 during peak season. Opening Times under review

A£12.00 C£8.00. Prices under review

discount offer: One Child Wristband Free With Every Full Paying Adult Wristband

White Cliffs Experience

Market Square Dover Kent CT16 1PB

[signposted on entry to Dover town centre for vehicles and from BR]

Tel: 01304 214566/210101 Fax: 01304 212057

www.dover.gov.uk/tourism/wce/wce-home.htm

Roman Encounters is an exciting hands-on experience where you can visit a Roman street, have a go at making a mosaic or building a Roman road. Enjoy a visit to our Magical Mechanical Theatre, our acclaimed 1940's Dover Street and Gromet's Challenge - our indoor playground for children. All this, plus a FREE visit to Dover Museum - where The Dover Bronze Age Boat, believed to be the world's oldest seagoing boat is now on display in its superb gallery setting.

visitor comments: Interesting presentation of historic facts for all ages.

All year 1 Apr-31 Oct daily 10.00-17.00, Nov-Mar 10.00-15.00

Last Admission: Apr-Oct: 17.00 Nov-Mar: 15.00

Full Visit: A£5.95 C(4-14)&UB40s£4.15 Family Ticket (A2+C2)£18.95 (up to 3 additional chil-

dren)£3.50 OAPs&Students£4.80. Group discount: A£5.20 C(4-14)&UB40s£3.50 OAPs&Students£4.00. Travel Trade: A£4.20 C(4-14)&UB40s£3.15 OAPs&Students£3.70. School parties: UK children aged (5-18)£3.25 , Overseas (5-18)£3.60, One adult FREE per 10 children, additional adults same rate as children. Language Schools Students £3.60, One adult FREE per 10 students

discount offer: One Child Free With One Full Paying Adult

↓ special events

► **Fascinating Food Quiz**
19/2/00-27/2/00

► **Be a Deteggtive**
12/4/00-25/4/00

Solve our puzzle going back 2000 years in our family quiz. On Apr 23 and 24, children will be rewarded with Easter eggs

► **Easter Card Workshop**
13/4/00-14/4/00

Children can make their own Easter card, we supply the materials

► **Pavement Picasso**
27/5/00-27/5/00

11.00-13.00, the theme is 2000 Years of History. Free to enter, all materials provided and prizes for all entrants

► **Commemorative Events**
27/5/00-1/6/00

For the 60th Anniversary of the Dunkirk Evacuation

► **Highlights of the Millennia Quiz**
27/5/00-4/6/00

A quiz to accompany the exhibition in Dover Museum

► **Food through the Millennia**
1/6/00-2/6/00

Sample food and drink from Roman Britain and Britain during rationing

► **Roman Festival for Schools**
20/6/00-23/6/00

Children participate in a range of Roman related activities - mainly outdoors if dry. A visual spectacle!

► **A Slice of Life in Roman Britain**
24/6/00-24/6/00

Experience and learn about domestic life and life as a Roman soldier. Students from the Academy at South Kent College will be creating Roman hair styles and battle wounds from 10.30-16.00

► **Battle of Britain, July 2000 60 Years**
8/7/00-9/7/00

► **Invasion!**
26/7/00-3/9/00

Successful 43 AD. Unsuccessful 1940. A quiz for the family

► **Roman Food and Drink**
4/8/00-6/8/00

Sample the delights of this fascinating period of history

Kent

▶ **Ration Book Fare**
22/8/00-23/8/00
Food and drink from the 1940s
▶ **Animals through the Millennia**
21/10/00-29/10/00
The role of animals through the centuries
▶ **Preparing for Christmas**
2/12/00-3/12/00
Make decorations to take home
▶ **Winter Traditions**
21/12/00-7/1/01
A quiz for the family

Tourist & Visitor Information Centres

Ashford Tourist Information Centre
18 The Churchyard Ashford Kent TN23 1QG
Tel: 01233 629165
2 Feb-31 Mar Mon-Sat 09.30-17.00, 1 Apr-31 Oct Mon-Sat 09.30-17.30, 1 Nov-31 Dec Mon-Sat 09.30-17.00, Closed Bank Hol

Broadstairs Tourist Information Centre
6B High Street Broadstairs Kent CT10 1LH
Tel: 01843 862242 Fax: 01843 865650
Jan 2-Dec 31 Mon-Sat 09.00-17.00, Apr 1-Oct 1 Sun 10.00-16.00

Canterbury Visitor Information Centre
34 St. Margarets Street Canterbury Kent CT1 2TG
[follow signposts]
Tel: 01227 766567 Fax: 01227 459840
www.canterbury.co.uk
Tourist Information Centre supplying: Local and National Accommodation Bookings; Local Theatre and Festival Bookings; Holiday Information Service; Guided Tours.
All year Mon-Sat 09.30-17.00, also Sun in Summer 10.00-16.00
Admission Free

Cheriton Tourist Information Centre
St Martin's Plain Cheriton High Street Folkestone Kent CT19 4QD
Tel: 01303 270547

Clacket Lane Tourist Information Centre
Clacket Lane Services Westerham Kent TN16 2ER
[J5-6 westbound M25]
Tel: 01959 565615 Fax: 01959 565617
Tourist Information Centre supplying: Accommodation Booking; Maps; Guides; Sightseeing Tour Booking; Tourist Information; Ferry, Shuttle and Eurostar Booking; Traffic Information; Directions/Route Finding; Fax and Photocopying Services
2 Jan-31 Dec Mon-Sun 09.00-17.00

Clacket Lane Tourist Information Centre
Motorway Services (eastbound) Westerham Kent TN16 2ER
[J5-6 M25]
Tel: 01959 565063 Fax: 01959 565064
Tourist Information Centre supplying: Accommodation; Maps and Guides; Ferry Bookings; Eurotunnel Bookings; Euro Star; Route Planning.
2 Jan-31 Dec Mon-Sun 09.00-17.00
Admission Free

Cranbrook Tourist Information Centre
Vestry Hall Stone Street Cranbrook Kent TN17 3HA
Tel: 01580 712538
1 Apr-4 Oct Moon-Fri 09.30-17.30 Sat 10.00-16.30

Deal Tourist Information Centre
Town Hall High Street Deal Kent CT14 6BB
Tel: 01304 369576
2 Jan-31 Dec Mon-Fri 09.00-17.00, 1 July-31 Aug Sat 09.00-13.00, Closed 12.30-13.30

Dover Tourist Information Centre
Townwall Street Dover Kent CT16 1JR
Tel: 01304 205108 Fax: 01304 225498
www.doveruk.com
Daily 09.00 - 18.00

Faversham Tourist Information Centre
Fleur de Lis Heritage Centre 13 Preston Street Faversham Kent ME13 8NS
[3 mins from M2; 4 mins walk from BR: Faversham]
Tel: 01795 534542
Tourist Information Centre supplies: Accommodation Booking; Guides; Souvenirs; Books and Picture Postcards on sale - very wide range. Run by Voluntary effort for the good of the area.
2 Jan-31 Dec Mon-Sat 10.00-16.00, 1 Apr-30 Sept Sun 10.00-16.00, Bank Hol 10.00-16.00
Admission Free

Folkestone Tourist Information Centre
Harbour Street Folkestone Kent CT20 1QN
Tel: 01303 258594

Kent

2 Jan-Easter Mon-Sat 09.00-17.30 Sun 10.00-16.00, Easter-30 June Mon-Sun 09.00-17.30, 1 July-4 Sept Mon-Sun 09.00-18.00, 2 Oct-31 Dec Mon-Sat 09.00-17.30, Closed for lunch 13.00-14.00

Herne Bay Visitor Information Centre
12 William Street Herne Bay Kent CT6 5EJ
Tel: 01227 361911 Fax: 01227 361911
2 Jan-30 June Mon-Sat 10.00-16.00, 1 July-31 Aug Mon-Sun 10.00-17.00, 1 Sept-24 Dec Mon-Sat 10.00-16.00

Hythe Tourist Information Centre
En Route Travel Red Lion Square Hythe Kent CT21 5AU
Tel: 01303 267799
28 Mar-30 Sept Mon-Sun 09.00-17.00 Closed for lunch 13.30-14.30

Maidstone Tourist Information Centre
The Gatehouse Palace Gardens Maidstone Kent ME15 6YE
Tel: 01622 602169 Fax: 01622 673581
Tourist Information Centre, voted South East England Tourist Board TIC of the Year 1997, supplying: Accommodation Bookings; BABA Local Guide Books; Souvenirs; Excursion Bookings; Hoverspeed Agents; Audio Walking Tours for Hire; National Express and Eurolines Agent
Apr-Oct Mon-Sat 09.30-17.00, Sun 10.00-16.00. Nov-Apr Mon-Fri 08.30-17.00, Sat 09.30-15.00
Admission Free

Maidstone Tourist Information Centre
J8 M20 Motorway Service Area Hollingbourne Kent ME17 1SS
[J8, M20]
Tel: 01622 602169
Tourist Information Centre on M20, First Motorway Service Area after Channel Ports and Tunnel, supplying Local Information; Route Planning; Bureau de Change; Accommodation Bookings; Guide Books.
All year daily 08.30-18.30. Closed 25-26 Dec
↓ special events
▶ Kent Dolls House and Miniatures Fair
23/4/00-23/4/00
Venue: Great Danes Hotel, Hollingbourne, Maidstone, take M20, off at J8, follow signposts. Open: 10.30-16.30. 110 stands of everything you can think of from the world on miniatures, in a friendly and easilt accessible venue. Refreshments, huge car park and FREE prize draw. A£2.50 Accompanied C£Free OAPs£2.00
▶ Kent Dolls House and Miniatures Fair

17/9/00-17/9/00
See entry for 23 April

Margate Tourist Information Centre
22 High Street Margate Kent CT9 1DS
Tel: 01843 220241 Fax: 01843 230099
2 Jan-31 Dec Mon-Sat 0.900-17.00, 1 Apr-1 Oct Sun 10.00-16.00

New Romney Tourist Information Centre
Town Hall House 35 High Street New Romney Kent TN28 8BT
Tel: 01797 364044
28 Mar-28 Sept Mon-Sun 09.00-17.00, Bank Hol 09.00-17.00 Closed for lunch 12.30-13.30

Ramsgate Tourist Information Centre
19-21 Harbour Street Ramsgate Kent CT11 8HA
Tel: 01843 583333 Fax: 01843 591086
2 Jan-31 Dec Mon-Sat 09.00-17.00 Sun 10.00-16.00

Rochester Tourist Information Centre
95 High Street Rochester Kent ME1 1LX
Tel: 01634 843666
2 Jan-31 Dec Mon-Fri 09.30-17.00 Sat 10.00-17.00 Sun 10.30-17.00
↓ special events
▶ Spring Art Focus
28/4/00-28/5/00
Music, dance, drama and the opportunity for children to develop their creative skills
▶ Sweeps Festival
29/4/00-1/5/00
The traditional waking of 'Jack in the Green'. Folk Music, Chimney Sweeps and dancing in the streets
▶ Horticulture Festival
7/5/00-28/5/00
May 5, 14, 21 and 28, Cozenton Nursery, Rainham. Afternoons of horticulture and entertainment
▶ Navy Days
27/5/00-29/5/00
Action on land, sea and air, creating one of Europe's biggest military spectaculars
▶ Dickens Festival
2/6/00-4/6/00
Watch Dickens' colourful characters come to life and mingle with people dressed in period costume
▶ Celebrating Medway
15/7/00-16/7/00
Water based activities, street entertainment, stalls and a spectacular Medway pageant around Chatham
▶ Medway Concerts
20/7/00-29/7/00

July 20-22 and 27-29 only. Feast of shows ranging from pop to classical in Gillingham and Rochester

▶ **Dickensian Christmas**
2/12/00-3/12/00
Victorian High Street glows with the sights and sounds of pre-christmas 100 years ago, snow guaranteed!

Sevenoaks Tourist Information Centre
Buckhurst Lane Sevenoaks Kent TN13 1LQ
Tel: 01732 450305 Fax: 01732 461959
1 Jan-31 Mar Mon-Sat 09.30-16.30, 1 Apr-31 Oct Mon-Sat 09.30-17.00, 1 Nov-31 Dec Mon-Sat 9.30-16.30, Bank Hol 10.00-13.00 Closed for lunch Jan-Mar & Oct-Dec

Tenterden Tourist Information Centre
Town Hall High Street Tenterden Kent TN30 6AN
Tel: 01580 763572
1 Apr-25 Oct Mon-Sat 09.30-17.00, Closed for lunch 13.30-14.00

Tonbridge Tourist Information Centre
Castle Street Tonbridge Kent TN9 1BG
Tel: 01732 770929 Fax: 01732 770449
Tourist Information Centre supplying: Accommodation Booking Service; Theatre Bookings; THA Membership; Books, Map & Guides; Holiday Information Service; Civil Marriages in the Town Hall
2 Jan-31 Dec Mon-Fri 08.30-17.00, Sat 09.00-16.00, Sun 10.30-16.00. 1 Apr-30 Sept Sat 09.00-17.00, Sun 10.30-17.00. 1 Oct-31 Dec Sat 09.00-16.00, Sun 10.30-16.00
Admission Free

Tunbridge Wells Tourist Information Centre
The Old Fish Market The Pantiles Tunbridge Wells Kent TN2 5TN
Tel: 01892 515675
2 Jan-31 May Mon-Sat 09.00-17.00, 4 May-28 Sept Sun 10.00-17.00, 1 June-31 Aug Mon-Sun 09.00-18.00, 1 Sept-30 Sept Mon-Sun 09.00-17.00, 1 Oct-31 Dec Mon-Sat 09.00-17.00 Sun 10.00-16.00

Whitstable Tourist Information Centre
7 Oxford Street Whitstable Kent CT5 1DB
Tel: 01227 275482
www.canterbury.co.uk
2 Jan-30 June Mon-Sat 10.00-16.00, 1 July-31 Aug Mon-Sat 10.00-17.00, 1 Sept-24 Dec Mon-Sat 10.00-16.00

Toy & Childhood Museums

Romney Toy And Model Museum
The Station 2 Littlestone Road Littlestone New Romney Kent TN28 8PL
[0.5m off A259 at New Romney station]
Tel: 01797 362353 Fax: 01797 363591
www.rhdr.demon.co.uk
A fascinating collection of old, and not so old, toys and models. The centrepiece is one of the largest operating model railways in the country with up to 30 trains in operation at any one time.
Easter-end Sept daily 10.00-17.00
A£0.80 C£0.40

Transport Museums

C M Booth Collection of Historic Vehicles
63-67 High Street Rolvenden Cranbrook Kent TN17 4LP
[based in Falstaff Antiques. On A28 6m from Cranbrook, 3m from Tenterden]
Tel: 01580 241234
The collection is made up of historic vehicles and other items of interest connected with transport. The main feature is the unique collection of three-wheel Morgan cars, dating from 1913. Also here is the only known Humber Tri-car of 1904; and items include a 1929 Morris van, a 1936 Bampton caravan, motorcycles and bicycles.
All year Mon-Sat 10.00-18.00
A£1.50 C£0.75

Eurotunnel Education Service
Administration Building Cheriton Parc Folkestone Kent CT19 4QS
Tel: 01303 288700 Fax: 01303 288742
Visits, Tours and Conferences in the UK and France. These services are available ONLY for groups in own coach or minibus. Please contact us with your brief. We can then advise on the options and itinerary best suited to the requirements of your group. Passports essential and visas as appropriate for non-EU citizens. Exhibition Visit: Bilingual information panels, construction models, viewing tower and video show give a comprehensive overview of the Channel Tunnel in our exhibition at the Centre d'Affaires, which overlooks the terminal at Calais. Visit lasts minimum 60 minutes. Colour worksheets are available in

French or English for education groups. Conferences: A presentation tailored to your professional or curriculum area of interest. The development of Eurotunnel, the owner and operator of the Channel Tunnel, together with a background on the history and construction of the tunnel, can provide the basis for more detailed study needs. Maximum group numbers 120. UK Tour of the Terminal: A 45 minute guided tour of the Eurotunnel terminal at Folkestone gives an insight into the complexity of the engineering tasks related to this major transport terminal and an understanding of the operation of the Eurotunnel transport service. Site visits for specialists: An opportunity to visit the operational heart of Eurotunnel transport services. Restricted to adults and groups of 15 and subject to operational restrictions, these visits may be available to groups with a specialist interest in rail operations and/or engineering systems. Presentation included. Passports are required for access to site. An information pack on the history, construction and operation of the Channel Tunnel is available on receipt of cheque or postal order. Photography allowed with permission.

Open for group bookings only. Reservations are essential for all visits
Exhibition Visit: £3.00 per person (exc. vat & discount). Conferences: from £15.00 per person. UK Terminal Tour: £2.50 per person. Site visits for specialists: from £25.00 per person. Conferences - as for France: from £15.00 per person. Information Pack £2.00. Cheques should be made payable to: The Channel Tunnel Group Limited. Prices for all services are exclusive of Eurotunnel shuttle fares, unless otherwise stated. For coach ticket sales please tel: 01303 272770. For all other Eurotunnel shuttle fares please tel: 0990 35 35 35.

discount offer: 10% Discount On All Group Bookings

Tyrwhitt Drake Museum of Carriages
Mill Street Maidstone Kent ME15 6YE
[close to River Medway & Archbishops Palace well signposted.]
Tel: 01622 663006 Fax: 01622 682451
A wide array of horse-drawn carriages and vehicles are displayed in these late-medieval stables, which are interesting in themselves. The exhibits include state, official and private carriages, and some are on loan from royal collections. Viewed as one of the finest collections in Europe
visitor comments: Amazing collection. Strong royal connection.
Mar-Oct daily 10.30-17.15, Nov-Feb 12.30-16.30. Closed 25-26 Dec
Last Admission: 45 mins before closing

A£1.50 C(0-5)£Free C&OAPs£1.00 Family Ticket £4.00 Disabled free - carer half-price.
Concession rates available telephone for details.

Victorian Era

Dickens House Museum
Victoria Parade Broadstairs Kent CT10 1QS
[on main seafront at Broadstairs]
Tel: 01843 862853
The house was immortalised by Charles Dickens in David Copperfield as the home of the hero's aunt, Betsy Trotwood. Dickens' letters and possessions are shown, with local and Dickensian prints, costumes and general Victoriana. The parlour is furnished as described in the novel.
Apr-mid Oct daily 14.00-17.00
Last Admission: 16.45
A£1.50 C£0.50 Groups please pre-book.

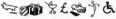

Wildlife & Safari Parks

Druidstone Wildlife Park
Honey Hill Blean Canterbury Kent CT2 9JR
[on the A290. Plenty of parking available on site]
Tel: 01227 765168 Fax: 01227 768860
A garden park with woodland walk, adventure playground and under 5's play area. Wallabies, deer, owls and parrots are among the animals and birds that make this park their home. New for 2000, squirrel monkeys.
April-end Oct daily 10.00-17.30. Nov 10.00-16.30
Last Admission: 16.45

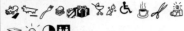

Kent

A£3.50 C£2.50 OAPs£3.00

discount offer: Two For The price Of One.
Valid Until 30 Nov 2000

Howletts Wild Animal Park

Bekesbourne Lane Bekesbourne Canterbury
Kent CT4 5EL
[signposted off A2 3m S of Canterbury]
**Tel: 0891 800 605 Info Line Fax: 01227
721853**
www.howletts.co.uk

Howletts is one of John Aspinall's wild animal
parks and has the world's largest breeding
gorilla colony in captivity. It also has tigers,
small cats, free-running deer and antelope,
snow leopards, bison, ratel, the UK's most successful herd of breeding African elephants,
and many endangered species of monkeys all
housed in natural enclosures. Many new animals and enclosures for 1999.

visitor comments: Wonderful, friendly park
with healthy, clean and content looking animals.

*All year daily 10.00-17.00 or dusk in Winter.
Closed 25 Dec*
Last Admission: Summer 17.00 Winter 15.30
*A£8.90 C(under 4's)£Free C(4-14)&OAPs£6.90
Family Ticket £26.00*

discount offer: £2.00 Off Adult or Child
Admission When Accompanied By A Full
Paying Adult

Port Lympne Wild Animal Park

Aldington Road Lympne Hythe Kent CT21 4PD
*[J11 M20. Park is 5mins away signposted from
this juction]*
Tel: 01303 264647 Fax: 01303 264944

John Aspinall's 300-acre wild animal park
houses hundreds of rare animals: Black rhinos,
Indian elephants, wolves, bison, black and
snow leopards, Siberian and Indian tigers,
gorillas and monkeys. The mansion designed
by Sir Herbert Baker is surrounded by 15 acres
of spectacular gardens. The Spencer Roberts
mural room depicts over 300 animals and
birds from South East Asia. Many new animals
and enclosures for 1999.

visitor comments: Very clean. Take a picnic
and enjoy the wonderful scenic views.

*All year daily 10.00-17.00. Winter closing 15.30.
Closed 25 Dec*
Last Admission: Summer 17.00 Winter 15.30
*A£8.90 C(under 4)£Free C(4-14)&OAPs£6.90
Family Ticket £26.00*

London

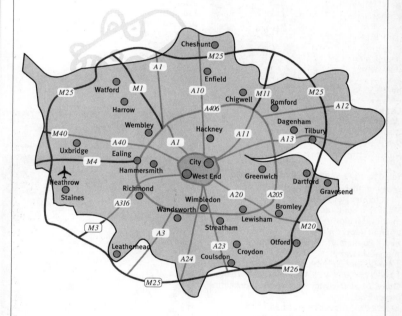

Cheshunt
M25
A1
Enfield
Watford *M1*
M25
A10
Harrow
Chigwell *M11* Romford *M25* *A12*
Wembley
A406
Dagenham
M40 Hackney *A11* Tilbury
A40 *A1* *A13*
Uxbridge Ealing
M4 City
Hammersmith West End Greenwich
Neathrow Dartford
Richmond *A20* *A205* Gravesend
Staines Wimbledon
A316 Wandsworth Bromley
M3 Lewisham *M20*
A3 Streatham
Leatherhead *A23* Otford
A24 Coulsdon Croydon *M26*
M25

London

Abbeys

Chapter House And Pyx Chamber of Westminster Abbey

East Cloisters Westminster Abbey London SW1P 3PE

[Tube: Westminster, east side of the Abbey cloister]

Tel: 020 7222 5897 Fax: 020 7222 0960
www.english-heritage.org.uk

The Chapter House was built in 1250 by Royal Masons. It contains some of the finest medieval sculpture to be seen and still has its original floor of glazed tiles. The tiled floor can now be seen in its former glory due to recent specialist cleaning.

1 Apr-30 Sept daily 09.30-17.00. 1-31 Oct daily 10.00-17.00. 1 Nov-31 Mar daily 10.00-16.00. Closed 24-26 Dec. May be closed at short notice on state occasions
A£2.50 C(0-5)£Free C(5-16)£1.30 Concessions£1.90. EH Members £Free

↓ *special events*

▶ **Medieval Life**
20/5/00-21/5/00
From Noon. Calligraphy, spinning and weaving, games and crafts

▶ **Medieval Life**
17/6/00-18/6/00
See entry for 20 May

▶ **Music of the Normans and Angevins**
30/9/00-1/10/00
From Noon. Music played on authentic copies of period instruments by this ever-popular duo

Westminster Abbey

Broad Sanctuary London SW1P 3PA
[Tube: St James's Par]
Tel: 020 7222 5152 Fax: 020 7233 2072

Westminster Abbey is primarily a working church. It has been at the heart of English history for nearly 1000 years, being the setting for every coronation since 1066. The Abbey is a 'Royal Peculiar' and unlike other churches is under the jurisdiction of a Dean and Chapter subject only to the Sovereign. In 1932 a Benedictine monk was seen floating some distance from the floor, disappearing through a wall opposite the south transept. There is another spirit which frequents the deanery. Two monks are known to have been killed in the abbey, one during a robbery in 1303, the other in King Richard IIs time when, a lunatic attacked and murdered one of the attendant brothers.

Abbey: All year Mon-Fri 09.00-16.45, Sat 09.00-14.45 & 15.45-17.45. Cloisters: All year daily 08.00-18.00
Last Admission: Abbey: 60mins before closing
Abbey: A£5.00 C(0-16)£2.00
OAPs&Students£3.00. Cloisters: Admission Free

Agriculture / Working Farms

Freightliners Farm

Sheringham Road London N7 8PF
[Holloway Road (A1), off Liverpool Road. BR/Tube: Highbury / Islington. Tube: Caledonian / Holloway Road]
Tel: 020 7609 0467 Fax: 020 7609 9934

Freightliners Farm is a model of a working farm in the heart of Islington. It's a great place to get away from the bustle of city life and make contact with the farming world. Take the opportunity to buy one of our many delicious eggs, honey and healthy produce. We also sell compost, hay, straw and animal feed. With many different types of animal from old and rare breeds to newly born chicks, piglets or lambs there is much to see for all the family. We have an education worker who runs school programmes relating to the National Curriculum. Classroom is available for hire for meetings and children's parties, call for details.

All year Tue-Sun 09.00-13.00 then 14.00-17.00
Admission Free

↓ *special events*

▶ **Freightliners Farm Open Day**
29/5/00-29/5/00
Sheep shearing, pony and donkey rides and lots of other activities. 11.00-17.00

Hackney City Farm

1a Goldsmiths Row London E2 8QA
[junction of Hackney Road / Goldsmiths Row BR: Cambridge Heath]
Tel: 020 7729 6381
A thriving city farm with sheep, pigs, calves, chickens, ducks, geese etc... Farm café, gardens, textile classes, pottery classes, play schemes, film and tv. Feeding times 08.30 and 16.30.
All year Tue-Sun 10.00-16.30. Closed Mon
Last Admission: 16.00
Admission Free

Vauxhall City Farm

24 St Oswald's Place (entrance in Tyers Street) London SE11 5JE
[BR/Tube: Vauxhall]
Tel: 020 7582 4204
Two thirds of an acre of derelict land, transformed in 1977 by volunteers into a working farm. The animals are all friendly and used to being petted by visitors large and small. Bella the pig and Jacko the donkey are the favourites. A wide range of talks on Vauxhall City Farm is offered, plus lots of hands-on-work with the animals. Donkey rides, pony-care classes and milking demonstrations are also available on request. Registered Charity No. 281512. Many events are organised for fundraising, call for further programme details.
All year Sat, Sun, Tue, Wed, Thur 10.30-16.30
Closed for 10 days over Christmas.
Admission Free - donations welcome. Guided

Tours: Schools & Groups Talk Tour: C£1.00. Milking Demonstrations: C£0.50. Spinning Demonstrations: C£0.50. Min charge per group £5.00. Classroom available

Battersea Dogs' Home and Bell Mead Kennels

4 Battersea Park Road London SW8 4AA
[BR: Battersea Park. Tube: Vauxhall. Bus: 137]
Tel: 020 7622 3626 Fax: 020 7622 6451
www.dogshome.org
In 1860, Mrs Tealby, concerned by the number of animals roaming the streets of London, opened the Temporary Home for Lost and Starving Dogs' in Holloway. In 1871, the Home moved to its present site in Battersea, and was renamed Battersea Dogs' Home. The Home has remained here ever since, carrying out the same high ideals set by the Founder. Taking in stray and lost dogs, they are held for the statutory 7 days, to give their original owners a chance to claim them. Battersea then goes about finding new loving homes for any of the unclaimed dogs.
All year 6 days a week. Mon, Tue, Wed & Fri 10.30-16.15, Sat & Sun 10.30-15.15. Closed Thur. Bell Mead: all year Mon-Sat 10.00-12.00 & 14.00-16.00, Sun 09.30-12.00
Admission £0.50

College Farm

45 Fitzalan Road Finchley London N3 3PG
[North Circular/Finchley Road intersection. M1 J2, A1 North Circular intersection. Tube: Finchley Central]
Tel: 020 8349 0690 Fax: 020 8346 9988
College farm has a variety of farm animals housed in historic farm buildings. Art Gallery and cream teas on Sunday afternoons.
All year daily, Summer: 10.00-18.00, Winter 10.00-17.00
A£1.50 C(0-3)£Free C£0.75 OAPs£1.25

Kentish Town City Farm

1 Cressfield Close Grafton Road London NW5 4BN
[Tube: Chalk Farm / Kentish Town. BR: Kentish Town / Gospel Oak]
Tel: 0171 916 5421
Lots of pigs and sheep to see, as well as a wide range of farm activities for children and plenty of hands-on-demonstrations
All year Tue-Sun 09.00-18.00
Admission Free

Mudchute Community Farm

151 Manchester Road Isle of Dogs London E14

London

London

[DLR: Crossharbour Station, 5min walk]
Tel: 020 7515 5901 Fax: 020 7538 9530
Mudchute Community Farm boasts 17 acres of farmland housing pigs, sheep, goats, rabbits, chickens, geese and ducks, plus a llama! Lots of hands-on activities are on offer, in addition to an education centre for children, containing all the information on animal care. The riding stables have special facilities for those with disabilities.
All year Mon-Sun 09.00-17.00
Admission Free

Newham City Farm
King George Avenue Custom House London E16 3HR
[end of A406 intersection with A13, turn R to City, turn L into Tollgate Rd, bear R into Stansfeld Rd, Farm is on the right. BR: DLR Royal Albert Tube: Plaistow]
Tel: 020 7476 1170 Fax: 020 7474 4960
We are an inner city farm and visitor centre enabling visitors to get close to animals and the environment and find out information about them. Guided tours are available but need to be pre-booked. We also have special event days and activities. Animals include rare and minority breeds of cattle, sheep, pigs, goats and poultry. We also have a shire horse.
All year Tue-Sun Summer: 10.00-17.00. Winter: 10.00-16.00
Last Admission: 10mins before closing
Admission Free. School groups must pre-book £0.50 per head in Borough, £0.75 per head outside Borough

Spitalfields Farm
Weaver Street London E1 6HJ
[Tube: Whitechapel / Aldgate East]
Tel: 020 7247 8762
This farm houses a range of farm animals, including pigs, ducks and sheep. The farm offers a range of activities during school holidays, including drama workshops, animal care, painting, drawing and pottery classes for all ages with a qualified expert.
All year Tue-Sun 10.30-17.00
Admission Free but donations welcome

Stepney Stepping Stones Farm
Stepney Way London E1 3DG
[Tube: Stepney Green]
Tel: 020 7790 8204
An urban farm with educational and recreational facilities. Cows, sheep, goats, pigs, donkeys. Smaller animals that can be seen and enjoyed by the children. Scraps of food are welcome please ask before feeding to the animals. Tuck shop, wide selection of home produced jams, chutneys, pickles, honey and souvenirs. Classroom have games and books for visiting children to enjoy whilst parents have a cup of tea. Most of the site is wheelchair and pushchair accessible and dogs must be kept on a lead, no bicycles, limited on site parking. Impromptu special events throughout the year call for details.
All year Summer: Tue-Sun & Bank Hol 09.30-18.00. Winter Tue-Sun & Bank Hol 09.30-dusk
Admission Free - donations welcome. Pre-booked guided tours for groups £0.45 each

Surrey Docks Farm
Rotherhithe Street Rotherhithe London SE16 1EY
[S end of Rotherhithe. Bus: P11, 10min walk from Surrey Quays Shopping Centre]
Tel: 020 7231 1010 Fax: 020 7237 6525
Surrey Docks farm is a special place for schools to visit, children are always really inspired to learn at first hand and experience the direct contact with the animals. The farm aims to use the direct experiences as a basis for delivering many elements of the national curriculum. Special talks and demonstrations can be booked at extra cost, on topics such as Goats and Milk, Bees and Honey, Eggs and Feathers and Sheep and Wool. Sample packs are available, as well as a Sensory Trail and other trails. The farm has a central animal yard, where visitors can meet the animals; goats, sheep, a cow, pigs and poultry. The farm has lovely gardens, including vegetable, herb, dye garden and orchard.
All year Tue-Sun 10.00-17.00. Closed for lunch 13.00-14.00 weekends & School Hol. Closed Fri during School Hol
Last Admission: 17.00
School parties £1.50 per head. Bookings: Daphne Ferrigan

Archaeology

Petrie Museum of Egyptian Archaeology
University College London Gower Street London WC1E 6BT
[Tube: Euston Square / Russell Square / Goodge Street / Euston. At the south end of University College London, opposite Malet Street]
Tel: 020 7504 2884 Fax: 020 7504 2886
The Museum holds one of the largest and most inspiring collections of Egyptian archaeology outside Egypt. The display illustrates life in the Nile Valley from prehistory through Pharaonic to Roman and Islamic times. Most of the objects on display were excavated or bought in Egypt by William Petrie.

Tue-Fri 13.00-17.00 Sat 10.00-13.00 closed at Christmas and Easter
Admission free, donations requested

Arts, Crafts & Textiles

A & J Speelman Ltd
129 Mount Street London W1Y 5HA
Tel: 020 7499 5126 Fax: 020 7355 3391
Specialising in top quality Chinese works of art, Tibetan bronzes, Japanese works of art and South East Asian sculpture.
Please call for details
Admission Free

Agnew's
43 Old Bond Street London W1X 4BA
[Tube: Green Park]
Tel: 020 7629 6176 Fax: 020 7629 4359
www.agnewsgallery.com
If you happen to be shopping for Old Masters then Thomas Agnew and Son's Ltd is the place to visit. They have a worldwide reputation for exhibiting some of the finest Old Master paintings and drawings, and many works pass through their hands on their way to famous art galleries and museums.
All year Mon-Fri 09.30-17.30, Thur 09.30-18.30. Closed Bank Hol
Admission Free except for some loan exhibitions

Alchemy Gallery
157 Farringdon Road London EC1R 3AD
[Tube: Farringdon]
Tel: 020 7278 56666 Fax: 020 7278 96666
Photographic and contemporary art exhbition venue.
All year Mon-Fri 09.30-18.00
Admission Free

Alexander Götz
35 Connaught Square London W2 2HL
Tel: 020 7724 4435 Fax: 020 7262 9891
Specialising in ancient works of art from South and South East Asia, particularly sculpture and occasionally jewellery in stone, bronze, silver and gold.
Please call for details

Anthony d'Offay Gallery
9 21 23 & 24 Dering Street Off New Bond Street London W1R 9AA
[off New Bond Street. Tube: Bond Street / Oxford Circus]
Tel: 020 7499 4100 Fax: 020 7493 4443
www.doffay.com
Postwar international art: Carl Andre, Georg Baselitz, Joseph Beuys, Fransesco Clemente, Gilbert & George, Richard Hamilton, Howard Hodgkin, Jasper Johns, Ellsworth Kelly, Anselm Kiefer, Willem de Kooning, Jeff Koons, Roy Lichtenstein, Richard Long, Bruce Nauman, Mario Merz, Tatsuo Miyajima, Reinhard Mucha, Sigmar Polke & Gerhard Richter, Ed Ruscha, Kiki Smith, Cy Twombly, Andy Warhol, Rachel Whiteread.
All year Mon-Fri 10.00-17.30, Sat 10.00-13.00. Closed Sun
Admission Free

Apsley House, The Wellington Museum
Hyde Park Corner London W1V 9AF
[Tube: Hyde Park Corner]
Tel: 020 7499 5676 Fax: 020 7493 6576
The refurbished London residence of the Duke of Wellington; the Iron Duke's palace which houses his famous collection of paintings, porcelain, silver, order and decorations. Paintings by artists including Goya, Velasquez, Rubens and Brueghel. In the Basement see the two new displays: the Duke's Death and Funeral and Medals and Memorabilia; also see the new video of a personal tour of the House and collections by the eighth Duke who lives there with his family in private apartments.
All year Tue-Sun & Bank Hol Mon 11.00-17.00. Closed Good Fri, May Day, 24-26 Dec & 1 Jan Last Admission: 16.30
A£4.50 Concessions£3.00 C£Free. Pre-booked

London

London

Group rates £2.50. Price includes sound guide
discount offer: Two For The Price Of One

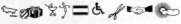

Architecture Foundation

The Economist Bldg 30 Bury Street London
SW1Y 6AU
*[Tube: Green Park / Piccadilly. Bus: 8 / 9 / 14 /
19 / 38]*
Tel: 020 7839 9389 Fax: 020 7839 9380
www.architecturefoundation.org.uk
The Architecture Foundation is a registered
charity established in 1991. It aims to promote good contemporary design and architecture in the built environment and to encourage public understanding of city-wide issues.
The Foundation believes that bringing architecture and urban issues to as wide an audience as possible at both local and national
level is the first important step to improving
the places where we live and work. The
Foundation's events have attracted more than
a million people in Britain and abroad. All
events are free. London Interactive is a multi-
layered digital plan of London generated from
aerial photography providing information
about contemporary urban design and the
Foundation's work past, present and future.
Developed by Hayes Davidson, the leading
exponents of architectural imaging, London
Interactive has been open for free public use
since 25th November 1997.
All year Tue-Sun 12.00-18.00
*Admission Free. For Membership details please
call the above number*

Asian Art Gallery

8 Duke Street St James's London SW1Y 6BN
Tel: 020 7930 0204 Fax: 020 7930 8588
With Christopher Cruckner specialising in
Chinese and Tibetan works of art and Malcolm
Fairley on the Japanese side, the Asian Art
Gallery covers a whole range of disclipines
which is evident in the outstanding works
shown. An important group of paintings,
palace furninshings and works of art made by
imperial command, including a 'national trea-
sure' - a Chinese thanka.
Call for details
Admission Free

Association Gallery

81 Leonard Street London EC2A 4QS
[Tube: Old Street]
Tel: 020 7739 6669 Fax: 020 7739 8707
www.aophoto.co.uk
The Association Gallery features purely photographic exhibitions on a variety of topics. It
exists to act as a showcase for the work of its

members who are professional photographers
in the fields on advertising, fashion and editorial photography. Contemporary British photography of the highest professional standards. The superb new building features
increased office space, meeting rooms and an
impressive new gallery space.
*Re-Opens after moving on the 11 Sept 98. All
year Mon-Fri 09.30-18.00. Closed Christmas &
New Year and all Bank Hol Sat 12.00-16.00*
Admission Free

Axia East Christian and Islamic Art

121 Ledbury Road London W11 2AQ
Tel: 020 7727 9724 Fax: 020 7229 1272
Established in London in 1974 and open by
appointment only, Axia focuses on two over-
lapping areas, on the Islamic side specialising
in textiles, metalwork and other precious
objects, while on the Christian side they are
leading specialists in early icons and Byzantine
works of art.
By Appointment only
Admission Free

Bankside Gallery

48 Hopton Street London SE1 9JH
*[BR: Waterloo. Tube: Blackfriars Southwark.
Buses: 45 / 59 / 63 / 149 / 172 / P11. There are
some parking meters behind the Gallery, and
the nearest car park is in Coin Street (off
Stamford Street)]*
Tel: 020 7928 7521 Fax: 020 7928 2820
Home of the Royal Watercolour Society and the
Royal Society of Painter-Printmakers. Holds
regular exhibitions of contemporary water-
colours and prints. Well stocked bookshop and
artist's supplies. Has special art-related
events including artists talks, workshops, tours
and courses.
*During exhibitions: Tue 10.00-20.00, Wed-Fri
10.00-17.00, Sat 13.00-17.00, Sun 13.00-17.00.
Closed Mon*
Last Admission: 16.45
Queuing Times: minimal
*A£3.50 Concessions£2.00 Friends£Free.
Admission to Society exhibitions includes a free
catalogue*

Barbican Art Gallery

Level 3 Gallery Floor Barbican Centre Silk
Street London EC2Y 8DS
*[the Barbican Centre is well signposted & has 4
car parks, 2 off Beech Street & 2 off Silk Street.
Call Box Office for Disabled Parking Permit.
Tube: Barbican / Moorgate / St. Paul's /
Liverpool Street / Bank / Mansion House. BR:
Liverpool Street / Farringdon / Blackfriars / City
Thameslink / Barbican / Moorgate. Rail savings*

available through the Theatre and Concert Travel Club call 01727 841115]
Tel: 020 7588 9023 24hr info Fax: 020 7628 0364
www.barbican.org.uk
One of Britain's leading art venues, the Gallery offers a diverse program of temporary shows. Call for current details. NCP paying car park in Barbican Centre & Aldersgate Street. Free parking for people with disabilities.
All year Mon, Thur-Sat 10.00-18.45, Tue 10.00-17.45, Wed 10.00-19.45, Sun & Bank Hol 12.00-18.45
A£5.00 Concessions£3.00 Family Ticket (A2+C3)£12.00. Reduced admission after 17.00 Mon-Fri inclusive £3.00. Season tickets for each exhibition available. Group bookings: (10+) should be made at least 2 weeks in advance on 0181 638 8891. Education programme information call 0171 638 4141 x7640

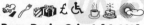

Barry Davies Oriental Art Ltd
1 Davies Street London W1Y 1LL
Tel: 020 7408 0207 Fax: 020 7493 3422
One of London's principal dealers in Japanese art for over 20 years with one of the largest galleries dedicated to this field in the world, Barry Davies specialises in netsuke with examples by all the major artists, as well as 17th and 18th century porcelain including Nabeshima and Kakiemon and Imari ware. He also features cloisonné enamels by the great Imperial Court artists and carries an extensive stock on lacquer, metalwork, okimono, textiles and screens, swords and sword fittings.
Call for details
Admission Free

Beagle Gallery
303 Westbourne Grove London W11 2QA
Tel: 020 7229 9524 Fax: 020 7792 0333
Specialising in Chinese domestic furniture and works of art, the gallery has a permanent display of 18th and 19th century Chinese softwood furniture with an emphasis on the simple lines of Ming designs. Also on display are Indian sculptures, Tibetan bronzes and Chinese works of art and scholars' objects.
Call for details
Admission Free

Ben Janssens Oriental Art Ltd
5 St. James's Chambers 2 Ryder Street London SW1Y 6QA
Tel: 020 7835 1600 Fax: 020 7373 5187
Dealing by appointment only, Ben Janssens specialises in antique works of art from China and Japan.

Please call for details
Admission Free

Ben Uri Art Society and Gallery
126 Albert Street London NW1 7NE
Tel: 0207 482 1234 Fax: 0207 482 1414
www.benuri.ort.org
The aim of the Society is to promote Jewish art as part of the Jewish cultural heritage. The gallery provides a showcase for exhibitions of contemporary art by Jewish artists, as well as for the Society's own permanent collection of over 700 works by artists including Bomberg, Auerbach, Gertler, Epstein and Kitaj.
By appointment only
Admission Free

Bonhams
Montpelier Street London SW7 1HH
Tel: 020 7393 3900 Fax: 020 7393 3905
Bonhams will hold an auction of Far Eastern Ceramics and Works of Art on Friday 20 November comprising a selection of fine Chinese export porcelain, Qing dynasty lacquers, bronzes and snuff bottles; Japanese Edo and Meji period ceramics, inro, netsuke, lacquer and swords. Of special interest are two gilt copper Tibetan sculptures - figures of Padmapani and Vajrapani.
Call for details
Admission Free

British Museum
Great Russell Street London WC1B 3DG
[Tube: Holborn / Tottenham Court Road / Russell Square]
Tel: 020 7636 1555 Fax: 020 7323 8118
www.british-museum.ac.uk
Founded in 1753, this is the world's oldest museum. Two and a half miles of galleries display the national collection of antiquities, prints and drawings. The Museum departments are: Greek and Roman, Egyptian, Prehistoric and Romano-British, Western Asiatic, Oriental, Japanese, Coins, Medals and Bank Notes, Medieval and Later, Prints and Drawings and Ethnography. The Mexican Gallery from Olmec to Aztec: Prehispanic Art and Culture from Mexico. Among the famous exhibits are the Elgin Marbles, Lindow Man, the Rosetta Stone, and Egyptian Mummies. The British Library Reading Rooms have moved to St Pancras. As part of the Millennium Commission for development projects the renovation of the Great Court will be open to the public for the first time in 150 years creating a dramatic new public space. People will be able to meet and enjoy themselves close to one of

the world's greatest cultural resources.
All year Mon-Fri 10.00.17.00, Sun 12.00-18.00
Admission Free. A charge may be made for
Temporary Exhibitions

↓ *special events*
► **Prints and Drawings Exhibitions**
1/12/99-1/4/00
► **Divine Rule**
1/12/99-1/5/00
► **Prints and Drawings Exhibitions**
1/6/00-1/9/00
► **Prints and Drawings Exhibitions**
1/10/00-1/12/00
► **Inaugural Exhibition**
1/11/00-30/11/00
► **Prints and Drawings Exhibition**
1/12/00-1/3/01
► **Prints and Drawings Exhibition**
1/6/01-1/9/01
► **Exhibition for Japan Festival**
1/9/01-1/12/01
► **Prints and Drawings Exhibition**
1/10/01-1/11/01

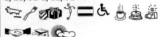

Christie's
8 King Street St James's London SW1Y 6QT
Tel: 020 7839 9060 Fax: 020 7839 7026
Call for details
Admission Free

↓ *special events*
► **Gala Charity Auction**
4/5/00-4/5/00
All proceeds will benefit Fairbridge, a leading UK
youth charity. Auction at 19.00. Viewing May 2-
4 09.00-16.30

Christie's South Kensington
85 Old Brompton Road London SW7 3LD
Tel: 020 7321 3121 Fax: 020 7321 3321
Call for details
Admission Free

Christopher Cooke
Taybridge House, 3 Taybridge Road London
SW11 5PR
Tel: 020 7350 0504 Fax: 020 7978 5461
Christopher Cooke sells 17th and 18th century
Chinese furniture and is also the leading
restorer of Chinese furniture.
Call for details
Admission Free

Cohen and Cohen
101b Kensington Church Street London W8
17LN

Tel: 020 7727 7677 Fax: 020 7229 9653
Specialising in Chinese export porcelain, in
particular armorial services, European subjects, famille verte, tobacco leaf and unusual
blue and white pieces dating from circa 1650
to circa 1800.
Call for details
Admission Free

Contemporary Applied Arts
2 Percy Street London W1P 9FA
[Tube: Goodge Street / Tottenham Court Road]
Tel: 020 7436 2344 Fax: 020 7436 2446
Contemporary Applied Arts is a professional
association of craftspeople whose aims
include making available the best contemporary craftwork to the public and collectors. The
gallery holds several exhibitions a year, from
solo and small group shows to large mixed
exhibitions. The basement shop has a constantly changing display including ceramics,
glass, furniture, jewellery, textiles, wood and
metal.
All year Mon-Sat 10.30-17.30. Closed Sun Bank
Hol & 25 Dec-5 Jan
Admission Free

Courtauld Institute Gallery
Somerset House Strand London WC2R 0RN
[Tube: Temple / Embankment]
Tel: 020 7848 2526 Fax: 020 7873 2589
www.courtauld.ac.uk
The Courtauld Gallery is housed in Somerset
House on the Strand. It holds an important
collection of European paintings from the
Renaissance to the 20th century, and one of
the finest collections of Impressionist and
Post-Impressionist paintings in the country.
Having moved from Woburn Square in March
and opened at Somerset House in 1990 the
galleries contain the superb collection of
paintings begun by Samuel Courtauld in the
1920s and 1930s and presented to the
University of London in memory of his wife.
All year daily Mon-Sat 10.00-18.00, Sun & Bank
Hol 12.00-18.00
Last Admission: 17.15
A£4.00 C£Free OAP&Students£2.00

Danart
75 St. Mary's Mansions St. Marys Terrace
London W2 1SY
Tel: 020 7724 9687 Fax: 020 7724 6228
Specialising in South East Asian gold jewellery,
hold and silver statuettes and votive objects.
Call for details
Admission Free

Design Museum

Butler's Wharf 28 Shad Thames London SE1 2YD

[Tube: London Bridge / Tower Hill]

Tel: 020 7403 6933 Fax: 020 7378 6540

www.designmuseum.org

The world's first museum dedicated to the study of 20th-century design. This stylish museum enables visitors of all ages to rediscover one hundred years of design, view state-of-the-art innovations from around the world and enjoy an extensive programme of special exhibitions on design and architecture.

All year daily 11.30-18.00. Closed Christmas Day

Last Admission: 17.30

Queuing Times: minimal

A£5.50 C&Concessions£4.00 Family Ticket (2A+2C) £12.00 Students £4.50

discount offer: One Child Free With Each Full Paying Adult

↓*special events*

► **Bauhaus Dessau**

10/2/00-4/6/00

The Bauhaus has profoundly influenced the architecture, design and craftmanship of modern times

► **Buckminster Fuller**

1/6/00-1/10/00

This exhibition will provide the first opportunity in this country to assess the vast range of his creative output.

► **Five Designs of Mr Brunel**

1/10/00-1/4/01

A look at a selection of the work of Isambard Kingdom Brunel

► **Luis Barragan**

1/3/01-1/7/01

The celebrated architect whose work has stretched far beyond his native Mexico

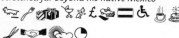

Dulwich Picture Gallery

College Road Dulwich London SE21 7AD

[just off A205 South Circular. BR: Victoria / West Dulwich]

Tel: 020 8693 5254 Fax: 020 8766 0090

The oldest public picture gallery in England is also one of the most beautiful. Housed in a building designed by Sir John Soane in 1811, displaying a fine cross-section of Old Masters. The Gallery will be closed from 1st Jan 1999 to May 2000 this is due to the award of a £5 million grant from the Heritage Lottery Fund. The money will go towards restoring and refurbishing the original gallery and a new building is to be constructed which will house lecture theatres, workshops and a café. England's oldest public art gallery reopens following a £9m refurbishment and extension. Development project includes facilities such as a lecture hall, practical art room and cafe. Reopens with an exhibition entitled 'Soane's Favourite Subject: The Story of the Dulwich Picture Gallery'.

All year Tue-Fri 10.00-17.00, Sat 11.00-17.00, Sun 14.00-17.00, Bank Hol Mon 11.00-17.00. Closed Mon. Guided tours Sat & Sun 15.00. The Gallery will be closed in 1999 for refurbishment and new building

Last Admission: 16.45

A£3.00 C(0-16)&Disabled&UB40s£Free OAPs&Students£1.50. Free to all on Fridays. Guided Tours: £4.00 per head

↓*special events*

► **'Soane's Favourite Subject: The Story of the Dulwich Picture Gallery'.**

1/5/00-31/5/00

Eskenazi Limited

10 Clifford Street London W1X 1RB

Tel: 020 7493 5464 Fax: 020 7499 3136

Eskenazi Limited is a family run firm which has been dealing in oriental art since 1925 and has until now held 49 specialist exhibitions.

Please call for details

Admission Free

↓*special events*

► **Masterpieces from ancient China**

5/6/00-8/7/00

Exhibition focusing on just ten bronzes dating from the Shang dynasty, circa 12th century BC to the Western Han dynasty, 1st century BC.

Estorick Collection of Modern Italian Art

39a Canonbury Square London N1 2AN

[Buses: 271 to door. 4, 19, 30, 48 to Upper Street / Canonbury Lane. Tube: Highbury / Islington. Limited parking on site]

Tel: 020 7704 9522 Fax: 020 7704 9531

The permanent collection shows powerful images by early 20th century Italian Futurists including Balla, Boccioni, Carrà, Severini and

Russolo. There are also works by such figurative artists as Modigliani, Sironi and Campigli and the metaphysical painter de Chirico. An exciting programme of temporary exhibitions and events is scheduled for 2000. Credit cards are only accepted for shop purchases. Disabled access is limited to two floors and we have limited Orange Badge holders parking on site.
All year Wed-Sat 11.00-18.00. Sun 12.00-17.00. Closed Good Fri. Shop & Café: Gallery hours. Library: By appointment only, call for details. Guided Tours available for groups of 10+ Last Admission: Wes-Sat 17.30, Sun 16.30 A£3.50 C(under 16)£Free Concessions£2.50 includes exhibition and permanent collection. Café shop and garden free
discount offer: Two For The Price Of One

↓*special events*
▶ **The Art of Noises featuring Derek Shiel**
2/2/00-5/3/00
An exhilarating exhibition featuring twelve sound sculptures. Derek will be in Gallery 1, Wed-Fri 11.00-18.00, Sat 14.00-18.00 and Sun 13.00-17.00
▶ **Sculpted Sound**
1/3/00-1/3/00
Flautist Nicky Heinen and percussionist Trevor Taylor in concert with Derek Shiel
▶ **Primo Conti: A Futurist Prodigy (1900-1988)**
15/3/00-21/5/00
Exhibition of 15 paintings, 34 drawings and related archive material. A rare opportunity to see the work of the only 'child Futurist'.
▶ **Fortunato Depero (1892-1960)**
4/10/00-22/12/00
A leading figure in Italian Futurism, Depero celebrated technology and sought to break down traditional divisions between the arts.

Flowers East
199-205 Richmond Road London E8 3NJ
[BR: Hackney Central. Tube: Bethnal Green. Bus: 106 / 253. Limited parking on site]
Tel: 020 8985 3333 Fax: 020 8985 0067
Angela Flowers Gallery opened in Soho in 1970 with the aim of introducing young contemporary British artists and promoting established artists whose excellence deserved greater recognition. In 1988 the gallery moved to Hackney, in London's East End, and became

Flowers East. Since then it has acquired PLC status and expanded into one of the biggest and most important commercial galleries in the country. Flowers East has two large gallery spaces (as well as several smaller ones) and represents more than thirty-five artists, from young newcomers to major international figures. There is also a separate graphics department which publishes and sells limited edition prints by a wide range of contemporary artists. In February 1998 expansion continued overseas with the opening of Flowers West in Santa Monica, California, thus helping to further its artists' careers on the international stage.
All year Tue-Sat 10.00-18.00
Admission Free

Francesca Galloway
21 Cornwall Gardens London SW7 4AW
Tel: 020 7937 3192 Fax: 020 7937 4958
Dealing by appointment only and specialising in Indian miniatures, European, Islamic and early Chinese textiles and Indian trade cloths.
By appointment only, please call
Admission Free

Gerard Hawthorn Ltd
104 Mount Street London W1Y 5HE
Tel: 020 7409 2888 Fax: 020 7409 2777
Specialising in Ming and Qing dynasty Chinese works of art and ceramics and also dealing in Japanese and Korean art.
Please call for details
Admission Free

Gilbert Collection
Somerset House Strand London WC2R 1LN
[by Waterloo Bridge, entrances on Victoria Embankment and Strand]
Tel: 020 7240 4080 Fax: 020 7240 4060
www.gilbert-collection.org.uk
A new museum for the magnificent Gilbert

Collection of decorative arts will open at Somerset House, London, in May. The 18th century building provides 30,000 square feet (2,800 square metres) for the collection. A grant from the Heritage Lottery Fund has provided finance for the project. Sir Arthur Gilbert has formed the collection since the 1960s. His gift of it to the British people in 1996 was one of the most important art bequests ever made. The collections of European silver, gold snuffboxes, and Italian mosaics are pre-eminent in the world. Other displays include furniture, Russian church art and portrait miniatures. Somerset House is already the home of the Courtauld Gallery, which has one of Britain's finest collections of Impressionist and Old Master paintings.

Opens May 2000 Fri-Sat 10.00-18.00, Sun & Bank Hol Mon 12.00-18.00. Closed 24-26 Dec & 1 Jan

Last Admission: 17.15

A£4.00 OAPs, Foreign & p/t Students£3 Disabled & Helpers £2.00. Joint ticket with the Coutauld Gallery A£7.00 OAPs, Foreign & p/t Students£5 C£Free. Mon 10.00-14.00 everyone £Free

Grays Antique Market
58 Davies Street London W1Y 2LP
Tel: 020 7439 2822 Fax: 020 7287 5488
Please call for details
Admission Free

Gregg Baker Oriental Art
132 Kensington Church Street London W8 4BH
Tel: 020 7221 3533 Fax: 020 7221 4410
Dealing primarily in Japanese paper screens and works of art in bronze, wood and ivory from both Japan and China.
Call for details
Admission Free

Hampton Hill Gallery
205 High Street Hampton Hill London Middlesex TW12 1NP
[Tube: Richmond]
Tel: 020 8977 1379 Fax: 020 8977 3876
Watercolours, drawings and prints, 18th-20th century. Framing and restoration service. Approximately four changing exhibitions.
All year Tue-Sat 09.00-17.30
Admission Free

Institute of Contemporary Arts
The Mall London SW1Y 5AH
[Tube: Charing Cross / Piccadilly Circus]

Tel: 020 7930 3647
ICA contains two Galleries with changing art exhibitions of contemporary art by both well known and new artists, 2 cinemas, and a theatre, along with a bookshop, licensed bar and café. There is a programme of talks throughout the year based on a wide range of subjects. The Institute (ICA) was established in 1947 in an effort to offer British artists some of the facilities which were available to United States artists at the Museum of Modern Art in New York. Originally in Dover Street, it has been incongruously situated in part of John Nash's Classical Carlton House Terrace (1833) since 1968.

All year daily Mon 12.00-23.00, Tue-Sat closes 01.00, Sun closes 22.30. Closed Christmas week and Public Hol

Mon-Fri Admission: A£1.50 Concessions£1.00. Weekend: A£2.50 Concessions£1.50

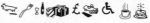

Jacqueline Simcox
54 Linton Street Islington London N1 7AS
Tel: 020 7359 8939 Fax: 020 7359 8939
A private dealer whose visitors are welcomed by appointment, dealing in Asian textiles and works of art and specialising in 17th century and earlier Chinese textiles including silk fabrics from the imperial workshops, religious and secular work in embroidery, tapestry or brocade.
Please call for details
Admission Free

Jill George Gallery Ltd
38 Lexington Street Soho London W1R 3HR
[Tube: Piccadilly Circus / Oxford Circus]
Tel: 020 7439 7319 Fax: 020 7287 0478
Contemporary Art Gallery specialising in paintings, drawings, water colours and limited edition prints by British artists, from the established artist to the recent graduate. Monthly exhibition programme, as well as a selection of originals and prints always on display.
All year Mon-Fri 10.00-18.00, Sat 11.00-17.00

John Eskenazi Ltd
15 Old Bond Street London W1X 4JL
Tel: 020 7409 3001 Fax: 020 7629 2146
Specialising in carpets, textiles, Oriental works of art from South East Asia, India, Tibet and Himalaya.
Please call for details
Admission Free

London

Jorge Welsh Oriental Porcelain and Works of Art

116 Kensington Church Street London W8 4BH

Tel: 020 7229 2140 Fax: 020 7792 3535

Specialising in Chinese ceramics and export porcelain form the neolithic period to the 18th century as well as dealing in Indo-Portuguese and other oriental works of art for the Portuguese market.

Please call for details

Admission Free

Katie Jones

195 Westbourne Grove London W11 2SB

Tel: 020 7243 5600 Fax: 020 7243 4653

The only London dealer specialising in unusual and eclectic objects of Japanese art including the best of traditional folk arts.

Please call for details

Admission Free

Linda Wrigglesworth Chinese Costume and Textiles

34 Brook Street London W1Y 1YA

Tel: 020 7408 0177 Fax: 020 7491 9812

Specialist in Ming and Qing dynasty Chinese costume and textiles as well as Korean and Tibetan textiles, Linda Wrigglesworth is celebrating twenty years in business.

Please call for details

Admission Free

Little Holland House

40 Beeches Avenue Carshalton Surrey SM5 3LW

[on B278 off A232 BR: Carshalton Beeches]

Tel: 020 8770 4781 Fax: 020 8770 4666

An Arts and Crafts style house built in 1902-04 by artist, designer and craftsman Frank Dickinson (1874-1961) who created and furnished his home in line with the theories of William Morris and John Ruskin. The listed interior contains hand-made furniture, metalwork, carvings and paintings by Dickinson.

First Sun in the month plus Bank Hol Sun & Mon 13.30-17.30

Admission Free

Littleton & Hennessy - Oriental Art

London **Tel: 020 7376 4236 Fax: 020 7376 3873**

Richard Littleton and James Hennessy offer a private and personal service by appointment in the field of Chinese ceramics and works of art.

Please call for details

Admission Free

London International Gallery of Children's Art

O2 Centre 255 Finchley Road London NW3 6LU

[on the Finchley Road between Swiss Cottage and Golders Green]

Tel: 020 7435 0903

The London International Gallery of Children's Art (LIGCA) is a registered charity which celebrates the creativity of young people and promotes international understanding through cultural exchange. LIGCA's workshops and school visits encourage the creativity of children and offer a safe and richly diverse place to express themselves. Through shows hung in London and around the world's cultural heritage through the eyes of other children and the chance to discover the connections between their daily lives and the art world.

All year Tue-Thur 16.00-18.00, Fri-Sun 12.00-18.00. Closed Mon

Admission Free but donations are welcomed

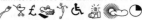

London Silver Vaults

Chancery House 53-64 Chancery Lane London WC2A 1QS

[Bus: 6 / 9 / 11 / 13 /& 15 to Fleet Street end OR 7 / 8 / 22 / 25 & 32 to Holborn end. Tube: Chancery Lane]

Tel: 020 7242 3844

The London Silver Vaults - the world's best kept secret. Silverware for the home; corporate and presentation items; commissions; jewellery; object d'art; repairs and restorations and valuations. There's nothing like the London Silver Vaults anywhere else in the world. A variety of shops provide an unparalleled display of finest silverware, ranging from pre-Georgian pieces to modern works. Open six days a week, there is something for everyone to buy. This includes serious collectors or those just looking for delightful items for the home of some wonderful jewellery and gifts. Silverware can also be commissioned for company presentations and special gifts.

All year Mon-Fri 09.00-17.30, Sat 09.00-13.00

Admission Free

Mall Galleries

The Mall London SW1Y 5BD

[Tube: Charing Cross / Embankment / Piccadilly Circus]

Tel: 020 7930 6844 Fax: 020 9839 7830

www.mallgalleries.org.uk

These galleries are the exhibition venue for eight art society's annual exhibitions including the Royal Society of Portrait Painters. It also hosts a number of, high profile, art competitions, and one man and small group shows.

All year daily 10.00-17.00

London

A £2.50 C&Concessions £1.00

Mallett
141 New Bond Street London W1Y 0BS
[also:
Bourdon House
2 Davies Street
London W!y 1LG]
Tel: 020 7499 7411 Fax: 020 7495 3179
Specialises in Chinese export porcelain, lacquer, paper, paintings and furniture and other works of art.

Martinware Pottery Collection
Southall Library Osterley Park Road Southall London UB2 4BL
[Tube: Ealing Broadway]
Tel: 020 8574 3412
The local library houses the Martinware Pottery which was made by the Martin brothers at their factory in Southall from 1877-1915. Local history material available for sale, ie postcards booklets etc.
All year Tue & Thur 09.30-19.45, Wed & Sat 09.30-17.00
Admission Free

Medici Galleries
7 Grafton Street London W1X 3LA
Tel: 020 7629 5675 Fax: 020 7495 2997
Exhibitions throughout the year, original paintings, ceramics and sculpture by contemporary artists; original prints, limited editions and reproduction prints. Greeting cards, Christmas cards and calendars.
All year Mon-Fri 09.00-17.30. Closed Bank Hol
Admission Free

Michael and Henrietta Spink Ltd
2-5 Old Bond Street London W1X 3TB
Tel: 020 7290 9020 Fax: 020 7629 4256
Dealing by appointment only they specialise in Indian, South-East Asian and Islamic works of art, paintings, sculpture and manuscripts.
Please call for details
Admission Free

Michael Goedhuis Ltd
116 Mount Street London W1Y 5HD
Tel: 020 7629 2228 Fax: 020 7409 3338
Specialising in Chinese and Japanese ancient and contemporary art including archaic and later bronzes and 20th century and contemporary Chinese paintings.
Call for details
Admission Free

Narwhal Inuit Art Gallery
55 Linden Gardens Chiswick London W4 2EH
[Tube: Turnham Green]
Tel: 020 8747 1575 Fax: 020 8742 1268
Narwhal Inuit Art Gallery is a permanent exhibition of Canadian, Russian and Greenlandic Inuit (Eskimo) art. Carvings and graphics since 1955. Plus resource Gallery and educational facilities for schools and colleges. Teachers pack available through NIAFF a registered charity and education foundation.
All year daily by appointment only, please call for appointment.
Admission Free. For large groups a small fee maybe applicable. By appointment only, please call before visiting.

National Gallery
Trafalgar Square London WC2N 5DN
[Tube/BR: Charing Cross. Tube: Leicester Sq / Embankment / Piccadilly Circus. Buses: 3 / 6 / 11 / 11 / 12 / 13 / 15 / 23 / 24 / 29 / 53 / x53 / 77a / 88 / 91 / 94 / 109 / 139 / 159 / 176. A public car park is in Whitcomb St. One parking space for disabled badge holders can be booked through the Chief Warder's Office on 0171 747 2854]
Tel: 020 7839 3321 Fax: 020 7930 4764
www.nationalgallery.org.uk
A neo-classical building opened in 1838. All the great periods of European paintings are represented here although only a selection of British works are included. Particular treasures include Van Dyck's Arnolfini Marriage, Van Gogh's Sunflowers and Constable's Haywain. The Sainsbury Wing houses the early Renaissance works from 1260-1510. The West Wing painting from 1510-1600, the North Wing painting from 1600-1700 and the East Wing painting from 1700-1900. There are exhibitions throughout the year.
visitor comments: Beautiful, an incredible collection.
All year Mon-Sat 10.00-18.00, Sun 14.00-18.00, June-Aug Wed until 20.00. Closed Good Fri, 24-26 Dec & 1 Jan. Guided Tours: Mon-Fri 11.30 & 14.30, Sat 14.00 & 15.30, Wed evenings 18.30. Signed tours for the deaf on the first Sat of each month 11.30. Lunchtime Lectures: Tue-Fri 13.00, Sat 12.00. Films & Special Lectures: Mon 13.00 Admission Free - some major exhibitions charged for. Group bookings of adult parties can be made with special lectures or tours provided.
↓*special events*
► **Primary Pick: Watch this Place**
5/1/00-5/5/00
This display explores how artists have painted places, from real views of towns and buildings to imaginary countryside settings for stories.

► **Family Events**
8/1/00-29/4/00
Starting from 8 January 2000, there will be regular Saturday morning talks, introducing the Collection in a lively and interactive way. Talks will begin at 11.30am in the Education Centre foyer, and last approximately one hour. The sessions are aimed at families with children aged 5 to 11 years, and include a free badge.

► **Painted Illusions**
2/2/00-1/5/00
The Art of Cornelius Gijsbrechts.

► **Seeing Salvation: The Image of Christ**
26/2/00-7/5/00
Sainsbury wing. The exhibition explores how the figure of Christ has been represented in the Western tradition.

► **Encounters: New Art from Old**
14/6/00-17/9/00
Contemporary artists show work inspired by Old Masters. Admission charged.

► **Telling Time**
18/10/00-14/1/01
The exhibition Telling Time will be a Gallery-wide event focusing on the fascinating relationships between time and painting. Admission free.

► **Impression: Painting Quickly in France**
1/11/00-28/1/01
The first exhibition ever to examine how the Impressionists revolutionised the practice of the oil sketch, making it central to their work. Sainsbury Wing, admission charged.

National Portrait Gallery
2 St. Martins Place London WC2H 0HE
[Tube: Charing Cross / Leicester Square. Opposite Church of St Martin-in-the-Fields to the N of Trafalgar Square. Disabled access found at the Orange Street entrance]
Tel: 020 7306 0055 Fax: 020 7306 0056
www.npg.org.uk
A collection of portraits illustrating British history which was first housed in its present accommodation in 1896. The building was designed in the style of an Italian palazzo with a further wing added in 1933. Also displayed are sculptures, miniatures, engravings, photographs and cartoons. Gift shop and Book shop selling a unique range from books to posters and cards. Portrait Café now open.
All year 10.00-18.00, Sun 12.00-18.00. Closed Good Fri, May Day, 24-26 Dec & 1 Jan Admission Free, some exhibitions are charged.
↓ *special events*
► **BP Portrait Award 2000**
1/1/00-24/3/00
Further information: BP Portrait Award Tel 0171 306 0055 Ext 274/245. CLOSING DATE FOR

ENTRIES Friday 24 March 2000.
► **Recent Acquisitions**
15/1/00-31/5/00
Porter Gallery (Room 35) Exciting new commissions and acquisitions for the contemporary collection.

► **Princes of Victorian Bohemia**
28/1/00-14/5/00
Photography Gallery. In the 1860s the painter David Wilkie Wynfield produced a series of strikingly original photographic portraits of his artist contemporaries.

► **Photographs by Snowden**
25/2/00-4/6/00
Wolfson Gallery. The first complete retrospective of Snowdon's photographic work.

► **Defining Features**
14/4/00-17/9/00
Studio Gallery. This wide-ranging and innovative exhibition will include portraits, in all media, of scientists, doctors and technologists from the foundation of the Royal Society to the present day.

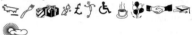

Nicholas Grindley Ltd
13 Old Burlington Street London W1X 1LA
Tel: 020 7437 5449 Fax: 020 7494 2446
Specialising mainly in Chinese furniture together with Chinese scholars' objects, sculpture and works of art.
Call for details
Admission Free

Oliver Hoare
7 Onslow Gardens London SW7 3LY
Tel: 020 7835 1600 Fax: 020 7373 5187
Specialises in Islamic art.

Orleans House Gallery
Riverside Twickenham Middlesex TW1 3DJ
[BR: St. Margarets from Waterloo. Access from Richmond Road A305]
Tel: 020 8892 0221 Fax: 020 8744 0501
www.guidetorichmond.co.uk/orleans.html
Strolling through secluded woodland gardens brings you to a stunning 18th century interior design and challenging exhibitons of fine and applied art. Marble Hill Park and Ham House lie across from the Gallery, or be artistic for an afternoon on a pre-booked workshop. Finish off with great pub grub in this tranquil haven, reached easily from London and the south east by road, rail, or een by boat.
All year Tue-Sat 13.00-17.30, Sun & Bank Hol 14.00-17.30, Oct-Mar 16.30 closing
Admission Free

Paul Champkins

41 Dover Street London W1X 3RB
Tel: 020 7495 4600 Fax: 01235 751658
Specialising in Chinese, Japanese and Korean art, Paul Champkins deals by appointment only. He is one of the few dealers in London specialising in Lorean art.
By Appointment only
Admission Free

Percival David Foundation of Chinese Art

53 Gordon Square Bloomsbury London WC1H 0PD
[Tube: Russell Square / Euston / Euston Square]
Tel: 020 7387 3909 Fax: 020 7383 5163
The First and Second Floor Galleries house permanent displays of ceramics. Special exhibitions are sometimes held in the Ground Floor Gallery. Evening lectures and other events are periodically held for members of the Friends Society, which was established in July 1991.
All year Mon-Fri 10.30-17.00. Closed Christmas-New Year, Easter & all Bank Hol
Last Admission: 5mins before closing
Admission Free - donations welcome. Pre-booked groups

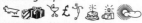

Peter Kemp Antiques

170 Kensington Church Street London W8 4BN
Tel: 020 7229 2988 Fax: 020 7229 2988
Specialists in Oriental porcelain and works of art.

Phillips Auctioneers

101 New Bond Street London W1Y 0AS
Tel: 020 7629 6602 Fax: 020 7409 7133
Specialising in Chinese and Japanese Ceramics and Works of Art.
Please call for details
Admission Free

Photographers' Gallery

5 & 8 Great Newport Street London WC2H 7HY
[Tube: Leicester Square]
Tel: 020 7831 1772 Fax: 020 7836 9704
www.photonet.org.uk
The Photographers' Gallery, the first independent gallery in Britain devoted to photography, was founded in 1971 at No 8 Great Newport Street. This building now houses the Gallery's primary exhibition space and a bookshop. In 1980 the Gallery also moved into No 5 Great Newport Street. Initially rented, the freehold was acquired in 1986 thanks to a successful fundraising campaign. In 1993, both buildings in Great Newport Street underwent

extensive refurbishment, designed by architect Nick England who improved the galleries for displaying photography; made fully accessible visitor facilities especially for those with mobility, hearing and seeing difficulties; redesigned the café and reception areas; and created an eye-catching street frontage. Exhibitions are shown in three galleries presenting a diverse, innovative and changing programme of photographic exhibitions. It also sells Britain's finest selection of original vintage, modern and contemporary photographs and advice on all aspects of print collecting.
All year Mon-Sat 11.00-18.00 Sun 12.00-18.00
Print sales Tue-Sat 12.00-18.00
Admission Free

Priestley & Ferraro

17 King Street London SW1Y 6QU
Tel: 020 7930 6228 Fax: 020 7930 6226
Specialising in all Chinese art from the Song period and earlier with the emphasis on fine early ceramics, sculpture and works of art.
Please call for details
Admission Free

Queen's Gallery

Buckingham Palace Buckingham Palace Road London SW1A 1AA
[Tube: Victoria / St James Park]
Tel: 020 7839 1377 Fax: 020 7839 8168
www.royal.gov.uk
The Queen's Gallery at Buckingham Palace holds a diverse range of exhibitions from the Royal Collection, one of the finest art collections in the world. The Royal Collection has been amassed over the past 300 years by succeeding sovereigns, consorts and other members of the Royal Family, the majority of items were acquired before the end of the reign of King George V. Private Evening Tours at The Queen's Gallery are available exclusively for groups to enjoy these exhibitions. The tours can be arranged for groups (minimum of 15 persons), by appointment and subject to availability, after normal opening hours, between 16.30-17.30. Groups may provide their own speaker or guide if required. Permission is given by the Director of the Royal Collection for arts orientated groups and charities with Royal Patronage to hold private views of these exhibitions at The Queen's Gallery. Regrettably, due to architectural limitations, The Queen's Gallery is inaccessible for wheelchair users.
All year daily 09.30-16.30, during exhibitions except 2 Apr. Closed between exhibitions, see special events. Gallery Shop: 09.30-17.00.
Closing in the autumn for major remodelling and extension and re-open in 2002, the year of

The Queen's Golden Jubilee
Last Admission: 16.00
A£4.00 C(0-17)£2.00 OAPs£3.00. Group Private
Evening Tours: surcharge of £0.50 per person on
standard admission

Robert Hall
15c Clifford Street London W1X 1RF
Tel: 020 7734 4008 Fax: 020 7734 4408
Specialising in Chinese snuff bottles.
Please call for details
Admission Free

Robert Kleiner & Co Ltd
30 Old Bond Street London W1X 4HN
Tel: 020 7629 1814 Fax: 020 7629 1239
Specialist in Chinese works of art, ceramics
and jades and an authority on snuff bottles.
Please call for details
Admission Free

Roger Keverne and Michael Gillingham
120 Mount Street London W1Y 5HB
Tel: 020 7355 1711 Fax: 020 7409 7717
Among their specialities are Chinese jade,
porcelain, enamels and cloisonné as well as
early bronzes and ceramics.
Please call for details
Admission Free

Rossi & Rossi Ltd and Maharukh Desai
91c Jermyn Street London SW1Y 6JB
**Tel: 020 7321 0208/839 4341 Fax: 020 7321
0546**
Anna Marie Rossie who has been dealing with
Asian art for over 25 years and her son Fabio
who joined the business in 1988, specialise in
Indian and Himalayan art. Maharukh Desai
specialises in Indian art including jewellery,
arms and armour, Islamic metalwork, early
Mughal textiles, and Mughal architectural
panels as well as early Indian photographs and
18th-century costumes.
Please call for details
Admission Free

Royal Academy of Arts
Burlington House Piccadilly London W1V 0DS
*[Tube: Piccadilly Circus / Green Park. Buses: 9 /
14 / 19 / 22 / 38]*
Tel: 020 7300 8000 Fax: 020 7300 8011
www.royalacademy.org.uk
The Royal Academy, in the heart of London's
West End, is world famous for its exhibition
programme. Founded in 1768, the Royal
Academy is the oldest fine arts institution in

Britain. Their exhibitions attract more than a
million people each year, putting the Academy
among the top ten attractions for paying visitors in London. The shop, café and restaurant
are open to all, whether visiting an exhibition
or not.
*Daily 10.00-18.00, Fri until 20.30, except Sun in
June-Aug. Closed Good Fri, 25-26 Dec*
Last Admission: 17.30
*Depends on Exhibition, call 020 7413 1717 for
details and to book.*

↓ special events
▶ **1900: Art at the Crossroads**
16/1/00-3/4/00
*Art at the Cross-roads will bring together about
250 paintings and a selection of sculptures.
Those artists who in 1900 were thought of as
avant-garde, or were entirely disregarded but
are now seen as great masters will be seen
alongside those who were acclaimed at the
time. Works by Cezanne, Degas, Gauguin,
Munch, Klimt, Rodin and Toulouse-Lautrec will
be shown.*
▶ **Chardin: 1699 - 1779**
9/3/00-28/5/00
*Sackler Wing. His paintings are incomparable in
their control of tonal harmony, glimmering
light and in the vitality of his use of paint.
Visitors to the exhibition will have the rare pleasure of seeing a large group of his masterpieces
and scholars will have the opportunity to re-
assess his work.*
▶ **Alive**
30/3/00-12/5/00
*An exhibition of work by students from schools
across the UK who have taken part in dynamic
life drawing workshops organised by the
Outreach Programme. This unique scheme is
now celebrating its tenth year.*
▶ **Summer Exhibition 2000**
29/5/00-7/8/00
*The Summer Exhibition was first held in 1769,
the year after the Royal Academy was founded,
and is the oldest, largest and most popular
open exhibition in the world. Any artist may
enter work for selection and talented newcomers can find their work hung alongside that of
artists with an international reputation, including Royal Academicians.*
▶ **Scottish Colourists**
29/6/00-24/9/00
*This exhibition, which will open at the Royal
Academy of Arts and then travel to the Scottish
National Gallery of Modern Art
(Autumn/Winter 2000), will bring together for
the first time up to one hundred of the
Colourists' most important paintings from pri-
vate and public collections.*
▶ **Terry Frost RA**
12/10/00-12/11/00
*The Royal Academy exhibition promises, like
Frost himself, to be full of a celebratory enthusi-*

asm for life itself.
► **The Great Watercolours of JMW Turner**
2/12/00-11/2/01
This exhibition will concentrate upon the large, set-piece drawings, from early works such as the Lambeth view to the final Swiss scenes.
► **Premiums**
11/2/01-24/2/01
These exhibitions provide an excellent platform from which the students can launch their professional careers.
► **French Master Paintings from Baltimore**
1/6/01-1/9/01
This exhibition will bring together 50 masterpieces of the 19th and early 20th century, drawn from two highly important art collections that reflect the exceptional level of taste in Baltimore during this period.

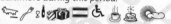

Royal College of Art
Kensington Gore London SW7 2EU
[Tube: South Kensington / High Street Kensington. Next to the Royal Albert Hall]
Tel: 020 7590 4444 Fax: 020 7590 4124
www.rca.ac.uk
Founded in 1837 the Royal College of Art started life as the Government School of Design and in 1992 moved into it's new Stevens building in Kensington Gore. It is an exclusively postgraduate institution that has established and maintained a world wide reputation for work of the highest quality, from the fine arts of painting and sculpture to the design of products for large scale and small scale industries, to the communications media of film, photography and graphics. It's exhibition programme is a great way to sample it's work, past and present.
All year daily 10.00-18.00 - but dependant on individual exhibition - call for fuller details
Most exhibitions are free

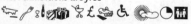

Royal Institute of British Architects Heinz Gallery
21 Portman Square London W1H 9HF
[Tube: Marble Arch / Bond Street]
Tel: 020 7307 3628 Fax: 020 7486 3797
Changing architectural exhibitions throughout most of the year. The Gallery is part of the RIBA Drawings Collection which can be viewed by appointment.
All year Mon-Fri 11.00-17.00, Sat-11.00-14.00. Study Room: Tue-Thur by appointment
Admission Free

Royal Society For The Encouragement of Arts Manufactures and Commerce
8 John Adam Street London WC2N 6EZ

[Tube: Charing Cross / Embankment]
Tel: 020 7930 5115 Fax: 020 7839 5805
Founded in 1754, the RSA moved to its bespoke house designed and built by Robert Adam in 1774. The most interesting features of the Society's premises are its Great Room, a lecture hall, capacity 200, with murals by James Barry and the recently restored vaults.
All year Mon-Fri 10.00-13.00 by prior arrangement
Admission Free

S Marchant & Son
120 Kensington Church Street London W8 4BH
Tel: 020 7229 5319 Fax: 020 7792 8979
Specialising in Ming and Qing imperial porcelain, ancient pottery, transitional porcelain, famille rose, blanc de chine, Chinese jade, furniture, cloisonné and works of art.
Please call for details
Admission Free

Saatchi Gallery
98A Boundry Road London NW8 0RH
[Tube: St John's Wood / Swiss Cottage. Bus: 139 / 31]
Tel: 020 7624 8299/328 8299 Fax: 020 7624 3798
Regularly changing exhibitions of contemporary art by renowned artists such as Andy Warhol and Frank Stella are displayed in a converted warehouse. The Gallery draws from a collection of over two thousand paintings, scultures and installations. Works which are not on display at the Gallery are frequently on loan to museums around the world.
15 Jan-12 Apr Thur-Sun 12.00 18.00
Last Admission: 17.45
Admission £4.00 C(0-12)£Free
Concessions£2.00. Groups 10+ £40.00 School Groups £Free
↓ *special events*
► **Eurovision**
1/1/00-1/4/00

Sam Fogg
35 St. George Street London W1R 9FA
Tel: 020 7495 2333 Fax: 020 7409 3326
Specialising in manuscript and printing from China, Japan, the Himalayas, India and the Middle East.
Please call for details
Admission Free

Serpentine Gallery
Kensington Gardens Kensington London W2 3XA

[Tube: South Kensington / Lancaster Gate]
Tel: 020 7298 1515 Fax: 020 7402 4103
www.serpentinegallery.org
The Serpentine's monthly exhibition programme reflects the achievements of established British artists and major international figures as well as younger and newly emerging artists from Britain and abroad.
All year daily 10.00-18.00
Admission Free

↓*special events*
▶ **Yayoi Kusama**
26/1/00-19/3/00
Paintings, collages, watercolours, films, sculptures and reconstructions of environmental installations. Kusama's vibrating patterned works explore her ongoing obsessions with dots, nets, food and sex.
▶ **The Greenhouse Effect**
4/4/00-21/5/00
International group exhibition exploring the ways in which young artists are reinterpreting the classical subject of nature in art.

Shirley Day Ltd and Anthony Carter
91b Jermyn Street London SW1Y 6JB
Tel: 020 7839 2804 Fax: 020 7839 3334
Specialising in Asian artifacts, Buddhas, jewellery, furniture and textiles.
Call for details
Admission Free

Sir John Soane's Museum
13 Lincoln's Inn Fields London WC2A 3BP
[Tube: Holborn]
Tel: 020 7430 0175 info Fax: 020 7831 3957
The house built in 1812 contains Sir John Soane's splendid collection of antiquities, sculpture, paintings, drawings and books. Included are the Rake's Progress and Election series of paintings by William Hogarth and the Sarcophagus of Seti I dating from 1290BC.
All year Tue-Sat 10.00-17.00, First Tue of month 18.00-21.00. Lecture Tour Sat 14.30 - limited number of tickets sold from 14.00. Closed Bank Hol. Groups must book in advance
Admission free, donations appreciated

Sotheby's
34-35 New Bond Street London W1A 2AA
Tel: 020 7293 5000 Fax: 020 7293 5989
Please call for details
Admission Free

South London Gallery
65 Peckham Road Camberwell London SE5 8UH
[Tube: Oval. Bus: No 36, next to Camberwell

College of Art]
Tel: 020 7703 6120 Fax: 020 7252 4730
The gallery presents a programme of up to eight exhibitions a year of cutting-edge contemporary art, and has established itself as South East London's premier venue for contemporary visual arts.
When exhibitions are in progress only: Tue-Fri 11.00-18.00, Thur 11.00-19.00, Weekends 14.00-18.00
Admission Free

Soviet Carpet and Art Gallery
303-305 Cricklewood Broadway London NW2 6PG
[A5 1m from North Circular Road at Staples Corner. BR: Cricklewood]
Tel: 020 8452 2445 Fax: 020 8450 2642
The largest stock of hand-made rugs and fine art from Russia in the UK. Thousands of Rugs from the Caucasus, Turkmenia, Iran, Pakistan, Turkey, China, Afghanistan at trade prices direct to the public. Specialising in inexpensive paintings, prints, art textiles, ceramics and handicrafts. Many top Russian names represented. Museum-quality paintings at prices 2 to 10 times below gallery prices (including Socialist Realism).
All year Sun 10.30-17.30. Weekdays by appointment only
Admission Free
discount offer: 5% Discount Off All Rugs; 15% Discount Off All Art

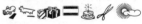

Spink
5 King Street St James's London SW1Y 6QS
Tel: 020 7930 7888 Fax: 020 7839 4853
Founded in 1666, Spink is one of the oldest established dealers in London.
Please call for details
Admission Free

Sydney L Moss Limited
51 Brook Street London W1Y 1AU
Tel: 020 7629 4670 Fax: 020 7491 9278
Specialising in Chinese and Japanese painting and calligraphy, Chinese 'literati' art, scholars' rocks and later bronzes, Japanese netsuke, lacquer and inro.
Please call for details
Admission Free

Tate Britain

Millbank London SW1P 4RG
[Tube: Pimlico]
Tel: 020 7887 8000 Fax: 020 7887 8007
www.tate.org.uk

On 24 March 2000, the Tate Gallery at Millbank will be relaunched as Tate Britain as part of the Tate's ambitious programme of expansion and development. The Tate holds the greatest collection of British art in the world. The new Gallery will show British art from the sixteenth century to the present day in a dynamic series of new displays and exhibitions. In 2000 Tate Britain will celebrate the extraordinary range and quality of the Tate's British collection by displaying its many masterpieces in new, theme-based galleries. In this special year, historic and modern works will hang together in challenging juxtaposition, drawing out new meanings from famous and familiar images.

All year daily 10.00-17.50. Closed 24-26 Dec
Admission Free (excluding special exhibitions)

↓ *special events*

► **The Age of Reynolds and Gainsborough**
1/1/99-1/4/00

► **Hogarth and his Contemporaries**
1/1/99-1/4/00
Focuses on England's first great native painter who dominated British art in the first hald of the 18th century.

► **Ruskin, Turner and the Pre-Raphaelites**
9/3/00-29/5/00
A major exhibition marking the centenary of John Ruskin's death in 1900, and launches a year of international celebrations of his life and work. Admission: £6.50 (concessions £4.50)

► **New Acquisitions in British Art**
23/3/00-28/5/00
In 2000, a suite of rooms will be devoted to showing acquisitions of British art made over the last ten years by artists as diverse as William Hogarth, Thomas Gainsborough, Barbara Hepworth, Damien Hirst and Gillian Wearing.

► **Mona Hatoum**
24/3/00-9/7/00
The celebrated British artist Mona Hatoum has created a spectacular new group of works for the Tate's Duveen Galleries in the first of a new series of annual sculpture exhibitions.

► **Romantic Landscape: The Norwich School of Painters 1803(1833**
24/3/00-17/9/00
Paintings by John Sell Cotman, John Crome, and a host of exceptional works by lesser-known figures. Together with special displays of Turner and Constable, Romantic Landscape will offer the richest display of the great period of British landscape painting seen in London for many years.

► **New British Art 2000**
6/7/00-24/9/00
New British Art 2000 is the first in a series of major exhibitions of contemporary art, to be held every three years at Tate Britain.
Admission: £5.50 (concessions £4.00)

► **Turner Prize 2000**
20/10/00-23/1/01
The Turner Prize is awarded to a British artist under 50, for an outstanding presentation of their work in the last year.

► **William Blake**
9/11/00-11/2/01
This exhibition will take a fresh, bold look at the unique and innovative Romantic British artist and poet, William Blake (1757(1827).
Admission: £7.50 (concessions £5.00)

Tate Modern

25 Sumner Street London SE1
[Tude: Southwark]
Tel: 020 7887 8000 Fax: 020 7887 8007
www.tate.org.uk

Tate Modern will open to the public in the transformed Bankside Power Station on 12 May 2000. It is one of the most significant of all the projects being created for the new Millennium in Britain. Standing at the heart of London, beside the Thames and linked to St Pauls Cathedral by the first new bridge to be built in central London since 1894, Tate Modern will become a symbol of London in the twenty-first century. The new Gallery will take its place among the great modern art museums of the world. It will display the Tate Collection of international twentieth-century

London

art, widely acknowledged to be one of the three or four most important in the world, featuring major works by the most influential artists of this century including Bourgeois, Picasso, Matisse, Mondrian, Duchamp, Dalí, Bacon, Giacometti, Pollock, Rothko and Warhol. It will also be a Gallery for the twenty-first century exhibiting new art as it is created and drawing in new audiences.

Opens 12th May 2000 Sun-Thur 10.00-18.00
Fri-Sat 10.00-22.00
Admission Free (excluding special exhibitions)

↓ *special events*

▶ **The Unilever Series- Louise Bourgeois**
12/5/00-31/10/00
The French-born American sculptor Louise Bourgeois will create the inaugural work which will be unveiled in May 2000 when Tate Modern opens.

▶ **Herzog & de Meuron**
12/5/00-31/12/00
Herzog & de Meuronis work will be celebrated through an exciting new form of exhibition. Their relationship with the building of Sir Giles Gilbert Scott, the original architect of Bankside Power Station, will be explored at ten locations situated throughout the building.

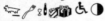

Textile Gallery
12 Queen Street London W1X 7PL
Tel: 020 7499 7979 Fax: 020 7409 2596
Please call for details
Admission Free

Thomas Coram Foundation for Children
40 Brunswick Square London WC1N 1AZ
[Tube: Russell Square / King's Cross. Bus: to Russell Square]
Tel: 020 7520 0300 Fax: 020 7837 8084
London's first Picture Gallery, including works by Hogarth, Gainsborough and Reynolds; musical scores by Handel; furniture and clocks; mementoes from the Founding Hospital (founded 1739).
By special appointment only
A£2.00 Concessions£1.00

Two10 Gallery
The Wellcome Trust 210 Euston Road London NW1 2BE
[BR/Tube: Euston / King's Cross. BR: St Pancras. Tube: Euston Square / Warren Street]
Tel: 020 7611 7211 Fax: 020 7611 8545
www.wellcome.ac.uk
The Two10 Gallery presents temporary exhibitions on the interaction between contemporary medical science and art. Recent exhibitions have included 'Before Birth: the art and

science of life in the womb' and 'Multiplicity: 24 artists look at cloning'.
All year Mon-Fri only 09.00-18.00. No Bank Hol
Admission Free

Victoria and Albert Museum
Cromwell Road South Kensington London SW7 2RL
[Tube: South Kensington. There are two car parks in the area, charges vary but approx £5.00 for up to 2 hours & £9.00 up to 4 hours. Limited meter parking]
Tel: 020 7942 2000 Fax: 020 7942 2266
www.vam.ac.uk
The Victoria and Albert museum holds one of the world's largest and most diverse collections of decorative arts. 146 galleries contain unrivalled collections dating from 3,000 BC to the present day. Furniture, fashion, textiles, paintings, silver, glass, ceramics, sculpture, jewellery, books, prints and photographs illustrate the artistic life of many different cultures from around the world. Superb highlights for any visit should include: the V&A's collection of Italian Renaissance sculpture, the largest outside Italy; paintings and drawings by the 19th-century artist John Constable; the superb Canon Photography Gallery; and the Dress Gallery, covering over four hundred years of European fashionable dress from the mid-16th century to the present day. Re-opening in Feb 2000, The Silver Galleries: Phase Two, showcasing over 1000 extraordinary pieces from the National Collection of Silver. Free family activities on selected days. Guided tours, disabled access, shop, restaurant, Friends society, galleries and rooms available for hire.
visitor comments: Immense. Incredible. You need a whole day. Nice to relax in the Garden.
All year daily 10.00-17.45, Wed (Late View - seasonal) 18.30-21.30. Closed 24-26 Dec
A£5.00 C(0-18)£Free OAPs£3.00*. Free Entry between 16.30-17.45. Free admission for: Disabled and carer, UB40 holders, full time students, Patrons and Friends of the V&A American and International Friends of the V&A.

Senior Citizens will be admitted FREE to the V&A as of the 1 April 2000. Some exhibitions may carry a separate charge in addition to the standard Museum entry.

discount offer: Two For The Price Of One. Valid on Standard Museum Admission (£5) Only. Not Valid for Exhibitions

↓ *special events*

▶ **Mao Zedong at the V and A**
13/10/99-23/4/00
Mao: From Icon to Irony and Fashioning Mao chart the impact of Mao Zedong's 'cult of personality' on Chinese Art and Culture.

▶ **Breathless! Photography and Time**
10/2/00-17/9/00
Exhibition exploring the notion of time and its associated themes of movement, speed, growth and reflection

▶ **Art Nouveau 1890-1914**
6/4/00-30/7/00
A timely reappraisal of this extraordinary style with masterpieces drawn from private and public collections throughout Europe and North America.

▶ **Brand New**
19/10/00-14/1/01
Exhibition examining how brands are constructed and their values communicated in the context of global consumerism

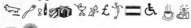

Wallace Collection
Hertford House Manchester Square London W1M 6BN
[Tube: Bond Street. Bus: routes to Selfridges 5mins from Oxford Street]
Tel: 020 7563 9500 Fax: 020 7224 2155

www.wallace-collection.com
A national museum housing one of the finest collections in the country, and acquired principally in the 19th century by the 3rd and 4th Marquesses of Hertford and Sir Richard Wallace, the illegitimate son of the 4th Marquess. The collection is displayed against the opulent backdrop of Hertford House. The superb range of fine and decorative arts includes magnificent 18th century French paintings, furniture and porcelain; old master paintings; princely arms and armour, and opulent displays of gold boxes, sculpture, and Renaissance works of art. In June the Wallace Collection is celebrating its centenary with the opening of new galleries, education facilities and a courtyard restaurant.
All year Mon-Sat 10.00-17.00, Sun 14.00-17.00. Closed 1 May, 24-26 Dec & 1 Jan
Admission Free

Whitechapel Art Gallery
Whitechapel High Street London E1 7QX
[adjacent to Tube: Aldgate East]
Tel: 020 7522 7878/7522 7888 Fax: 020 7377 1685
A purpose-built gallery opened 1901 in the heart of the East End. Organises major exhibitions, generally of modern and contemporary art; no permanent collection. An extensive community education programme for adults and children, public tours, lectures, workshops, audio-visual programmes and studio visits.
All year Tue-Sun 11.00-17.00, Wed 11.00-20.00. Closed Mon and Bank Hol
Most exhibitions are Free

↓ *special events*

▶ **Live in your Head**
4/2/00-2/4/00
Show focusing on the quiet explosion of conceptual and experimental practices which took place during the 60' and 70's.

William Morris Gallery
Lloyd Park Forest Road Walthamstow London E17 4PP
[Tube: Walthamstow Central]
Tel: 020 8527 3782 Fax: 020 8527 7070
www.lbwf.gov.uk/wmg/home.htm
The world's only museum devoted to William Morris, the great Victorian artist-craftsman, is located in his family home (built 1740s). Newly designed displays show the whole range of Morris's work - fabrics, stained glass, wallpapers, tiles and furniture - as well as work by the Art & Crafts Movement he inspired. Limited access for wheelchair users to the

ground floor, where main exhibitions are housed.

All year Tue-Sat 1st Sun in each month 10.00-13.00 & 14.00-17.00. Closed Mon & Bank Hol. Phone for details of Christmas/New Year opening

Admission Free

Woodlands Art Gallery

90 Mycenae Road Blackheath London SE3 7SE

[BR: Westcombe Park. Bus: 53 / 54 / 108 / 202 / 286 / 306/ 380 / 386 all stop at the Royal Standard which is a few minutes walk from gallery]

Tel: 020 8858 5847 Fax: 020 8858 5847

Gallery on the ground floor of John Julius Angerstein's country villa built in 1774, surrounded by pleasant garden.

All year Mon & Tue 11.00-17.00, Thur, Fri & Sat 11.00-17.00, Sun 14.00-17.00. Closed Wed

Last Admission: 17.00

Admission Free

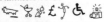

World of Silk

Bourne Road Crayford DA1 4BP

[15mins from J2 M25, 2mins from A2 / M2 Bexley / Bexleyheath]

Tel: 01322 559401 Fax: 01322 550476

A guided tour (which must be pre-booked) will take visitors through the museum which depicts the origins of silk, the printing process, the history of sericulture and the story of the silk routes. Visitors will see craftsmen screen printers, a video presentation and many original wooden blocks, tools, etc.

All year Mon-Fri 09.30-17.00, Sat 09.30-16.30. Closed Sun & Bank Hol

Museum only: A£1.50 Family Ticket £4.00 OAPs&Students£1.00. Guided Tour of Museum & Mill: A£2.50 Family Ticket £8.00 OAPs&Students£2.00

Birds, Butterflies & Bees

London Butterfly House

Syon Park Brentford Middlesex TW8 8JF

[Tube: Gunnersbury then bus 237 or 267. By road off A310]

Tel: 020 8560 0378 Fax: 020 8560 7272
www.butterflies.org.uk

The first live walk through butterfly exhibition situated in the middle of Syon Park - one of London's most popular parks and Stately Homes. An exotic indoor garden full of colourful, free-flying tropical butterflies. Separate displays of leaf cutting ants, spiders, lizards and other creepy crawlies. A wildlife themed gift shop is the perfect place to end your visit.

All year, Apr-Oct daily 10.00-17.30, Oct-Mar daily 10.00-15.30. Closed 25 & 26 Dec

Last Admission: 30mins before closing

A£3.30 C&OAPs£2.00 Family Ticket £7.75. School parties C£1.75

Caverns & Caves

Chislehurst Caves

Old Hill Chislehurst BR7 5NB

[off A222]

Tel: 020 84673264 Fax: 020 82950407

This labyrinth of caves has been called the enigma of Kent. Miles of mysterious caverns and passages hewn out of the chalk over some 4,000 years can be explored with experienced guides to tell the history and legends of the caves.

Daily during school holidays including half terms. All other times Wed-Sun. Tours: hourly from 10.00-16.00. Closed Mon, Tue and 24-25 Dec

Last Admission: 16.00

A£3.00 C&OAPs£1.50. Longer tours Sun & Bank Hol only: A£5.00 C&OAPs£2.50

discount offer: One Free Admission When A Second Admission Of Equal Or Greater Value Is Purchased

Communication Museums

BBC Experience
Broadcasting House Portland Place London
W1A 1AA
[Tube: Oxford Circus / Great Portland St]
Tel: 0870 60 30 304 Booking
www.bbc.co.uk/experience
BBC Experience allows the visitor a unique
opportunity to view the corporations' heritage
including the central role it has played in the
nation's history and culture. A series of interactive displays will allow you to have fun trying out a range of broadcasting activities. You
can become a sports commentator, direct
Eastenders, create a radio play and of course
read the weather. Education officer available
for schools.
All year daily - opening hours vary call for
details
Last Admission: Last Tour: 16.30
Queuing Times: Timed admission
A£6.95 C£4.95 Concessions£5.95 Family
Ticket(2A+2C) £19.95. Ticket will provide entry
for specific times. Pre-booking recommended
during holidays. Groups rates available
↓ *special events*
▶ **The Amazing Art of Gormenghast**
1/1/00-31/12/00
Behind the scenes to the making of BBC's
Gormenghast, an ambitious adaptation of
Mervyn Peake's classic trilogy. Costumes, scenery,
special effects, lighting, props and secrets of the
cast and characters will be on display
▶ **School Workshops**
1/1/00-31/12/00
Workshops are presented by our Education
Officer or a specialist guest presenter on the fol-
lowing themes: Sounds in the Air, Key Stage 2 (7-
11); The Radio and TV Age, Key Stages 2 & 3 (7-
14); The BBC - Voice of the Nation, Key Stages 3
& 4; How to Make Radio Drama, Key Stages 2-4
& post 16 (7-18), Duration 2.5 hours, Cost
£75.00 and Make a Radio Magazine Production.
Average duration is 60mins, Max Group size for
each workshop is 30, the cost £45.00 (unless
otherwise stated). To book any of the above

Workshops call 0870 603 0304

Museum of the Moving Image
South Bank Belvedere Road Waterloo London
SE1 8XT
[Tube: Waterloo]
Tel: 020 7401 2636 24hr Fax: 020 7815 1419
www.bfi.org.uk
The magical world of film and television
comes to life before your eyes at the Museum
of the Moving Image. There you're the star!
You can fly like Superman, read the news, see
Charlie Chaplin's hat and cane, audition for a
Hollywood screen role and meet the cast of
actor guides. Ooh! What A Carry One is an
exhibition celebrating 40 years of great British
comedy from the Carry On team. Delving into
the low budget, high jinks, kiss-me-quick
world of clips, original treasures and memories of farce and fun from the stars of the most
successful and best-loved series of films in
British cinematic history.
All year daily 10.00-18.00. Closed 24-26 Dec.
The Museum will close to the public on 31
August 1999, due to the redevlopment of the
South Bank. access to the museum's collection
of exhibits will continue next year through a
UK-wide touring exhibition and displays to the
public. The plans to create a new cultural com-
plex include a larger British Film Institute cen-
tre, comprising a new, improved Museum of the
Moving Image and National Film Theatre that
will open around 2003.
Last Admission: 17.00
Queuing Times: 30mins maximum
A£6.25 C(under 5)£Free C(5-16)£4.50 Family
Ticket (A2+C2)£17.00 Students£5.25

Costume & Jewellery Museums

Crown Jewels of the Millennium Exhibiton
The Old Royal Naval College Greenwich London
SE10
[BR: from Charing Cross or London Bridge to
Greenwich / Maze Hill]
Tel: 01753 833773 Fax: 01753 833722
This unique museum displays the crown and
court jewels of some 12 countries.
Painstakingly re-created by gem craftsmen
and master jewellers over the last 100 years
the collection consists of over 150 crowns,
tiaras, swords, sceptres, royal & imperial jewels and replicas of famous diamonds, many of
the originals no longer exist. Guided tours
available.

London

London

All year Mon-Sat & Bank Hol 10.00-17.00, Sun 12.00-17.00
A£5.00 C(under 16)£Free if accompanied by an adult Concessions£3.00. Group rates 10+ £3.00. 12 month Season Ticket £10.00. Greenwich residents £Free (proof of residence required)

Fan Museum
12 Crooms Hill Greenwich London SE10 8ER
[BR: Greenwich / Maze Hill / Blackheath, opposite Greenwich Theatre]
Tel: 020 8305 1441 Fax: 020 8293 1889
The world's only Fan Museum with its unsurpassed collections of more than 3,000 fans dating from the 11th century is housed in beautifully restored listed Georgian houses. Changing exhibitions, shop, workshop, study facilities. Orangery and landscaped garden. Special tours and private functions. Fan making classes. Refreshments available by prior arrangement. All programme of exhibitions are listed within the special events section, you can contact the Museum for further details on the above number.
All year Tue-Sat, Summer: 11.00-17.00, Sun 12.00-17.00. Winter: 11.00-16.30, Sun 12.00-16.30
A£3.00 Concessions£2.00

Country Parks & Estates

Aldenham Country Park
Dagger Lane Elstree Borehamwood Hertfordshire WD6 3AT
[signposted from J5 M1, A1(M), A41 & A5. Entrance off Aldenham Road]
Tel: 020 8953 9602 Fax: 020 8953 9602
The park consists of 175 acres of woodland and parkland set around a large reservoir. Attractions include a network of foothpaths, Winnie the Pooh's 100 Acre Wood, a rare breeds farm, lakeside and punt fishing, children's adventure play areas and picnic sites.
Nov-Feb daily 09.00-16.00, Mar, Apr, Sept & Oct 09.00-17.00, May-Aug daily 09.00-18.00. Closed 25 Dec
Admission Free. Parking approx £2.00
↓special events
► Country Craft Fayre
18/8/00-20/8/00
Traditional entertainment and crafts with a Viking theme. Commences 10.00-18.00. Tickets from £1.00-£5.00

Osterley Park
Isleworth Middlesex TW7 4RB

[J3 M4 via Thornbury Road in N side of A4 BR: Syon Lane, Tube: Osterley]
Tel: 020 8568 7714 Fax: 020 8568 7714
A National Trust Property. Completed in 1575, Osterley was transformed by Robert Adam into an elegant 18th century villa for the founders of Child's Bank. Set in 140 hectares of landscape park and farmland. There are ornamental lakes and pleasure grounds with classical garden buildings.
House: 1 Apr-31 Oct Wed-Sun & Bank Hol Mon 13.00-16.30. Grand Stables: Summer Sun afternoons only. Park & Pleasure Grounds: All year daily 09.00-19.30 or sunset if sooner. Prebooked Groups Wed-Sat. Park will close earlier for major events. Car Park closed Good Fri & 25 & 26 Dec
Last Admission: House: 16.00
A£4.10 C£2.05 Family Ticket £10.25. Park & Pleasure grounds: Admission Free. Car Park: £2.50. NT members £Free. Pre-booked Group rates £3.50. Discounts for those arriving by public transport with valid LT travelcard: non members A£1.00 off NT members receive a £1.00 vouch towards guide book or cream tea.

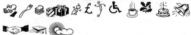

Exhibition & Visitor Centres

Chelsea Old Town Hall
Kings Road London SW3 5EE
[Tube: Sloane Square]
Tel: 020 7361 2220 Fax: 020 7361 3442
Exhibition and Conference centre
Times and dates vary according to events
Price varies according to event
↓special events
► Twentieth Century Modernist Fair
9/3/00-12/3/00
Over 40 dealers offering all things 20th century. Admission £6.00.
► Chelsea Antiques Fair
15/9/00-24/9/00

Earls Court and Olympia Ltd
Earls Court Exhibition Centre Warwick Road London SW5 9TA
[Travelling to the venues: Tube: Piccadilly Line / District Line with underground link from Earls Court Station. Buses: 31 / 74 / C1 & C3 run to Earls Court. 9 / 10 / 27 / 28 and 49 run to Olympia. By Car: Major motorway connections are close to Earls Court Olympia and car parking is available on site and nearby. Parking Reservations: parking can be pre-booked using Mastercard, Visa and Amex on 0800 0568 444]

London

Tel: 020 7385 1200 Fax: 020 7370 8223
www.eco.co.uk

Earls Court Olympia, London's leading exhibition and events venue, provides 60 000sqm of space, plays host to 100 shows and welcomes two million visitors every year. The venue offers a variety of flexible space. Olympia's three exhibition halls are the busiest in London, hosting over 150 events and attracting over one million visitors annually. Olympia combines the finest Victorian architecture with modern facilities and offers easy access for national and international visitors.

Times and dates vary according to events
Queuing Times: Dependant on event
Price varies according to event

↓ *special events*

▶ **National Wedding Show**
2/3/00-5/3/00

▶ **Daily Mail Ideal Home Show Sponsored by Barclays**
16/3/00-9/4/00
The forerunner of home shows in the UK, with over 650 exhibitors.

▶ **The National Needlecraft Show - Spring 2000**
23/3/00-26/3/00
The UK's biggest stitching show.

▶ **London International Dive Show 2000**
25/3/00-26/3/00
Mar 25 09.30-18.00, Mar 26 09.30-17.00, A£8.50 C£2.00, £2.50 advance discount, call 020 8977 9878. Sub-aqua diving equipment, holidays, boats and training courses.

▶ **The Evening Standard Homebuyer Show**
31/3/00-2/4/00
London and the South East's largest residential property exhibition.

▶ **The Evening Standard Homebuying Show**
31/3/00-2/4/00
Mar 31 11.00-18.00, Apr 1 10.00-18.00, Apr 2 10.00-17.00. £5.00 pre booking advisable. A one stop property shop.

▶ **Salute 2000**
1/4/00-1/4/00
A war gaming show dealing primarily with table top games.

▶ **The Cosmopolitan Show 2000**
27/4/00-1/5/00
Open 10.00-18.00, tickets £12.00 in advance (call 0870 902 9022), £14.00 on door. Fashion, beauty, health and fitness, shopping, entertainment, advice and make-overs.

▶ **The Times Spring Crème 2000**
16/5/00-18/5/00
10.00-17.00. Tickets free but pre-booking advisable, call 020 7453 5368. Show for senior secretaries, PAs and office managers

▶ **The Stamp Show 2000**
22/5/00-28/5/00
With stamps for sale, famous collections to admire and activities for children.

▶ **The Summer Fine Art & Antiques Fair**
8/6/00-18/6/00
Buy from 410 international dealers selling a wide choice of fine furniture, paintings, jewellery, silver, ceramics, glass and much more.

▶ **20th Century Antiques Fair**
14/6/00-17/6/00

▶ **The Daily Telegraph House and Garden Fair**
29/6/00-2/7/00
June 29-July 1 10.00-18.00, July 2 10.00-17.00. Ticket prices to be confirmed. Exclusive interiors and gardening fair

▶ **Artists and Illustrators Exhibition 2000**
27/7/00-30/7/00
Open July 27 and 29 10.00-18.00, 28 10.00-20.00 and 30 10.00-16.00. Prices tba

▶ **Autumn Needlecraft 2000**
7/9/00-10/9/00

▶ **Autumn Visit 2000**
15/9/00-16/9/00

▶ **Live 2000**
21/9/00-24/9/00
The consumer-electronics and home entertainment event.

▶ **Discover Dogs in London 2000**
4/11/00-5/11/00
Details to be confirmed

▶ **Careers Live 2000**
8/11/00-9/11/00
Details to be confirmed

▶ **Fine Art and Antiques Fair**
13/11/00-19/11/00
Details to be confirmed

▶ **Online Information Services**
5/12/00-7/12/00

▶ **Olympia Showjumping 2000**
14/12/00-18/12/00
Details to be confirmed

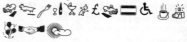

ExCel
Mace Gateway Royal Victoria Dock London E16 1XL *[Tube: Canning Town]*
Tel: 020 7476 0101 Fax: 020 7476 1818
www.excel-london.co.uk

Opening in the Autumn of 2000 this new purpose-built complex is designed to stage Britain's most prestigious events, exhibitions and conferences.

Goethe-Institut London
50 Princes Gate Exhibition Road London SW7 2PH
[Tube: South Kensington]
Tel: 020 7596 4000 Fax: 020 7594 0240
www.goethe.de/gr/lon/enindex.htm

The Goethe-Institut London offers a broad variety of events to present German culture (exhibition, films, lectures and seminars). The

London

Library re-opened on 6th September 1999 after extensive re-organisation and conversion to an on-line lending system.
All year Mon-Fri 10.00-20.00, Sat 09.30-12.30. Closed 7, 14 Mar & Easter Weekend, 9-30 Aug Christmas & New Year
Admission Free. Library Membership fee from Sept A£20.00 Concessions£10.00. Short term membership available - call 0171 596 4044

↓ *special events*
► **Audible Light**
23/1/00-19/3/00
Museum of Modern Art, Tue-Sun 11.00-18.00 and Thur 11.00-21.00. Eight artists use artificial light and sound as a sculptural medium
► **Lothar Götz: Last Orders**
14/2/00-1/4/00
Goethe-Institut Gallery, German artist Lothar Götz will create a new wall based work, inviting the viewer to explore new perspectives

Islington Business Design Centre
52 Upper Street Islington Green London N1 0QH
[Tube: Angel]
Tel: 020 7359 3535 Fax: 020 7226 0590
An Exhibition and Conference centre opened in 1986, formally the Royal Agricultural Halls. As well as hosting many events it is also home to over 100 permanent design showrooms.
dependant on exhibition / event being held
Depends on event

Kensington Town Hall
Hornton Street London W8 7NX
[Tube: High Street Kensington]
Tel: 020 7361 2220 Fax: 0171 361 3442
Exhibition and Conference Centre.
Times and dates vary according to events
Price varies according to event

↓ *special events*
► **Kensington Antiques Fair & Contemporary Art Fair**
11/8/00-13/8/00

RHS Royal Horticultural Halls
80 Vincent Square & Greycoat Street Westminster London SW1P 2PE
[Tube: St James's Park / Pimlico / Victoria]
Tel: 020 78284125/834 4333
www.horticultural-halls.co.uk
The beauty of gardening is that, no matter how experienced you are, there are always new ideas to try and discoveries to make. For thousands of gardeners, the Royal Horticultural Society is the best inspiration of all with its gardens, flower shows and special events. Established in 1804, the Royal

Horticultural Society has been conserving Britain's gardening heritage for nearly 200 years. The Society's flagship garden is Wisley in Surrey, with 26 other beautiful gardens around the country. There are monthly RHS flower shows in Westminster as well as hundreds of talks and demonstrations at RHS Gardens and centres.
Dependent on event
Prices are dependent on event

Wembley Conference and Exhibition Centre
Empire Way Wembley Middlesex HA9 0DW
[M1, M4, M40, A406. Well signposted from all major approach roads. Tube: Wembley Park / Wembley Stadium]
Tel: 020 8902 8833
www.hotelworld.com/wembley
World famous stadium and unique in the history of sport and entertainment. Extensive list of special events. For the latest news on all Wembley events call Wembley Update 0891 600 1966. Calls charged at £0.50 per minute.
Box Office: Mon-Sat 09.00-21.00, Sun 10.00-18.00, tel: 0181 900 0902
Prices vary according to event

Festivals & Shows

Barking Carnival Festival
St Margarets Church Barking Abbey The Broadway Barking Essex *[A13/A1406. Barking Underground & LRT]*
Tel: 020 8227 2620 Fax: 020 8227 2765
10.00-17.00 Musical Concert & Children's Entertainment; Trade area & Children's rides. 19.00-22.00 Twilight Classical Concert featuring The Aminta Chamber Orchestra of London.
May 27 2000 10.00-17.00 and19.00-21.30 for classical concert
Admission Free

Bearfests 2000
Kensington Town Hall Hornton Street Kensington London *[Tube: Kensington High St]*
Tel: 01273 697974 Fax: 01273 626255
All things BEARY!! 150 exhibitors offering 1000s of collectable bears plus bear making fabrics & supplies; bear repairs; books; jewellery. Free festival programme available.
Feb 27, May 21, Aug 27 & Nov 19 2000. BTBA entry at 10.30, public entry 12.00-16.30 A£4.00 C(0-16)£2.00 Family Ticket (A2+C2)£10.00. Tickets available from: Hugglets Publishing 01273 697974

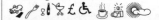

Chinese New Year Festival 2000

Chinatown London *[Tube: Leicester Sq / Piccadilly Circus / Tottenham Court Rd]*
Tel: 020 7734 5161
Stalls selling crafts and delicacies overflow from the main Gerrard St / Newport Place area. Lions and dragons snake their way through the streets, gathering gifts of money and food. Stage for performers in Leicester Square.
6 Feb 2000 First Sun after Chinese New Year
Admission Free

City and Guilds of London Art School 2000

124 Kennington Park Road London SE11 4DJ
[Tube: Kennington]
Tel: 020 7735 2306 Fax: 020 7582 5361
www.cityandguildsartschool.ac.uk
Graduate Show for painting, sculpture, conservation studies, illustration, decorative arts, stone and wood carving and gilding. Work for sale.
June 22-25 2000 10.00-18.45 Thur-Sat and 10.00-17.00 Sun
Last Admission: 18.00 Thur-Sat and 16.30 Sun
Admission Free

City of London Festival

London *[various venues in City]*
Tel: 020 7377 0540 Fax: 020 7377 1972
www.city-of-london-festival.org.uk
The jubilant bells of St Mary-Le-Bow ring out to launch this festival celebrating the best in opera, music, theatre, jazz, poetry and dance. Performances in historic settings throughout the city including Livery Halls, St Pauls Cathedral and the Tower of London.
June 20-13 July 2000
Prices vary according to event. Tickets available from Barbican Box Office: 0171 638 8891

Covent Garden Flower Festival 2000

Covent Garden London *[BR: Charing Cross. Tube: Covent Garden. NCP car parks in the area]*
Tel: 020 7735 1518 Fax: 020 7735 9163
www.vgroup.co.uk
The fourth annual Covent Garden Flower Festival will present eight days of free attractions all set in and around Covent Garden Market in Central London. The Festival is a celebration of the urban gardening experience with displays and activities geared for everyone from the amateur enthusiast to experts and professional urban landscapers. Devised as a free alternative to traditional shows, the Festival is a great day out in Covent Garden.
June 18-25 2000, 11.00-19.00 daily

Admission Free. Tickets for walks and special events available from Festival Office: 020 7735 1518

Dagenham Town Show

Central Park Wood Lane Dagenham Essex *[A13, A127. Dagenham East Underground Station. Plenty of parking on site]*
Tel: 020 8227 2620 Fax: 020 8227 2765
Musical concert, children's rides and entertainment, marquees, displays, 5-a-side football, golf and bowls competition, trade area, animals and horticulture exhibition.
July 8-9 2000 Sat 11.00-19.00 Sun 11.00-22.00
Admission Free

Festival For Life

Blackheath Halls 23 Lee Road Blackheath London SE3
[A2 to Central London, follow signs to Blackheath and concert halls. Trains to Blackheath from Charing Cross or London Bridge]
Tel: 020 7252 4671
The largest event of its kind in South London, featuring performances of T'ai Chi and Egyptian Dancing and demonstrations of complimentary therapies such as shiatsu, aromatherapy, reiki and osteopathy. Stalls will sell books, tarot cards, oils, jewellery and more.
Feb 5-6 and May 6-7 11.00-1900 all days
Last Admission: 18.00
A£3.00 C£Free Concessions available

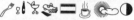

Fleadh 2000

Finsbury Park London N4
[Train, Underground or Bus to Finsbury Park Station, Seven Sisters Road]
Tel: 020 8961 5490 Fax: 020 8961 5743
www.fleadhfestival.com
London's longest running outdoor festival. A feast of musical entertainment.
July 2000 call for details. 12.00-midnight
Last Admission: 22.00
£30.00 in advance (prices to be confirmed)

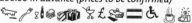

Flora London Marathon 2000

Greenwich London *[Starting points: Charlton Road, St John's Park, Shooters Hill Road. All competitors join up after 3m]*
Tel: 020 7902 0199
www.london-marathon.co.uk
On Sunday, 16 April, the eyes of the world will be on 26.2 miles of the London's streets to watch around 30,000 people take part in the 2000 Flora London Marathon. The race's international status comes from its success in com-

bining elite sport with human endeavour and spirit - there is something for everyone to enjoy whether running or viewing - it's truly the 'people's race'. Its unique character has developed over the past nineteen years. Great attention has been paid to developing every aspect of the event from the elite races through to the carnival entertainment along the course, ensuring that every piece of the jig-saw falls into place on Race Day. The result is one of the world's most exciting and prestigious major annual sports events.

The Flora London Marathon is also world renowned for its success as a charity fundraising event - tens of thousands of runners raise sponsorship for charities of their choice, making their efforts count for worthy causes. In 2000 around 41,500 people will be accepted to run - of these an expected 30,000 will take part on the day. In addition, millions more will be part of the occasion. The Flora London Wheelchair Marathon - is a race organised by the Flora London Marathon in close collaboration with a Flora London Wheelchair Marathon committee and is open to disabled athletes. Many of the world's best wheelchair athletes travel to London to compete.

Apr 16 2000. Start time from 09.30

Grosvenor House Art and Antiques Fair

Grosvenor House Hotel Park Lane London W1A 3AA
[NCP Car Park opposite Grosvenor House. Buses 2 10 16 36 73 74 82 137 137A. Underground Marble Arch, Hyde Park Corner, Green Park. Train, Eurostar from Paris to Waterloo.]
Tel: 020 7399 8100 Fax: 020 7495 8747
www.grosvenor-antiquesfair@msn.com
86 top dealers from all over the world to exhibit £300million of the very finest art and antiques. Anything from antiquities to modern art, pieces are vetted by 140 specialists with prices ranging from a few hundred to over £1million.
Private Preview: June 13 2000 11.00-20.00. To the public June 15 11.00-17.00 June 14,16,19 11.00-20.00 June 17,18,20 11.00-18.00
Last Admission: 2 hours before closing
Queuing Times: possible
Single ticket £16.00 double £27.00 inc. handbook. Concessions available. Final two hours of day £8.00

Hampstead and Highgate Festival

Hampstead London *[Local arts venues, churches and museums. Well serviced by public transport]*
An international festival of the arts set in the historic and culturally rich villages of Hampstead and Highgate. A wealth of con-

certs and events featuring classical music, opera, jazz, film, exhibitions and literature.
May 18-27 2000
Tickets vary according to event.

Harvest Festival of the Pearly Kings and Queens

St. Martin's Place London WC2N4JJ
[Tube: Trafalgar Square, Charing Cross or Leicester Square]
Tel: 020 7930 0089
Dressed in their traditional costumes, a barrow load of cockneys - Pearly Kings, Queens and Princesses from all the London boroughs, gather for a harvest thanksgiving every year. The festival begins with a procession delivering produce to the church. Please call to confirm starting time.
visitor comments: "Pearlies" happy to be photographed before and after service. Thoroughly enjoyed procession and service.
Oct 1 2000. Service begins at 15.00
Admission Free

International Playwriting Festival 2000

At The Warehouse Theatre Dingwall Road Croydon CR0 2NF
[adjacent to East Croydon train station]
Tel: 020 8680 4060 Box Office Fax: 020 8688 6699
www.uk-live.co.uk/warehouse_theatre
The International Playwriting Festival celebrates 15 years of continuous national and international success. With the festival, the Warehouse Theatre has consolidated its role as a powerhouse of new writing. The festival is held in two parts; a competition with entries taken from all over the world, then a series of play readings and the presentation of the best work in November. A unique relationship with Italian partners Premio Candani - Arta Terme offers writers opportunities in Europe. Further details and application forms are available from January. Please send a s.a.e. to: Carolyn Braby Vernon, Festival Administrator at the above address. Closing date for entries is Monday 30 June 2000.
Nov 2000 dates to be confirmed
Prices are dependant on your choice of performance, information will be available from the Box Office

London Film Festival

South Bank Waterloo London SE1
[Cinemas participating include National Film Theatre and Odeon West End Theatre. Tube: Waterloo and Embankment]
Tel: 020 7928 3232 Box Office

www.lff.org.uk

The London Film Festival is one of the largest film festivals in the world. As well as premieres and exclusive screenings showcasing some of the most exciting new talent before anyone else in the UK, the festival runs a number of special events which allow the audience to put questions to the film makers and stars. This is the 44th Festival, last years screened over 150 feature films and played host to some of the hottest Hollywood names.

Nov 2-16 2000
From A£7.20

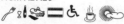

London Lesbian and Gay Film Festival

National Film Theatre South Bank London
[Tube: Waterloo and Embankment]
Tel: 020 928 3232

The National Film Theatre plays host to this key event in the gay calendar. The LLGFF is an annual festival showcasing over 50 features as well as a wide selection of short films.

Mar 30-Apr 13 2000
From A£6.20, OAPs£4.70, Concessions and School Parties £4.70

London Open House

West Hill House 6 Swains Lane London N6 6QU
[various venues in London]
Tel: 0891 600061
www.londonopenhouse.demon.co.uk

Two days celebrating the wealth of the capital's cultural heritage by opening buildings of architectural significance and interest to the public. It forms part of European Heritage Open Days. Every participating building will have a fact sheet and an architect or architectural historian available to offer and interpretation. A complete list is available from the internet site - the areas of London in which buildings are open is listed here for basic assistance. All buildings are opened up by building owners and tenants who have entered into the spirit of the event and generously given up their time. As a visitor, please respect this fact. Please note that London Open House has no direct responsibility for how accessible each building is and for how long its doors are open. Areas: Bexley - Brent - Bromley - Camden City - Ealing - Enfield - Greenwich - Hackney - Hammersmith & Fulham - Haringey - Harrow - Havering - Hillingdon - Islington - Kensington & Chelsea - Lambeth - Newham - Redbridge - Richmond - Southwark - Tower Hamlets - Waltham Forest - Wandsworth - Westminster.

Sept 23-24 2000
Admission Free

Notting Hill Carnival

Notting Hill London *[Tube: Notting Hill Gate / Westbourne Park / Bayswater / Queensway / Holland Park. Bus: 7 / 12 / 18 / 23 / 31 / 36 / 52 / 94 / 302. Special Express route 12X from Notting Hill Gate - Victoria]*
Tel: 020 8964 0544 Fax: 020 8964 0545

As well as the procession of costume soca and steel bands, which winds its way over a route of 3 miles, the area plays host to 45 licensed static sound systems, each playing their own soca, reggae, jazz, soul, hiphop, funk music and hundreds of street stalls.

27-28 Aug 2000.
Admission Free

Ricky Week

Bury Grounds Bury Lane Rickmansworth Hertfordshire WD3
[J18 M25, follow signs to Rickmansworth A412 / A404. BR: Metropolitan line to Rickmansworth]
Tel: 01923 772325

Ricky Week started in 1954 and has been celebrated each year since then. It enables societies/clubs to stage events to boost their funds and give to charity. The Canal Festival is very popular coinciding with "Steam Trains on the Met" organised by the Railway Company.

May 13-21 2000
Various ticket prices dependent on event

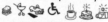

Spitalfields Festival

Christ Church Commercial Street Spitalfields London E1 6LY
[Train/Tube: Liverpool St and Aldgate East. Car parking in Whites Row opposite the church]
Tel: 020 7377 1362 Fax: 020 7247 0494

A World-class festival combining a feast of early music with new commissions from leading British composers, supported by performances from the year-round education and community programme. Many events are free. Walks and talks around the area also.

June 5-23 2000 events at various times
A£Free-£25.00 Concessions £2.00 less, group rates 10% discount

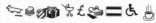

Thames Festival

Barge House Street South Bank London SE1 9PH
[advisable to park and ride in via the Underground or take the bus]
Tel: 0207 9288998 Fax: 0207 9282927
www.thamesfestival.org

The Valentine Ball will be held for 3,000 invitation holders and their guests once again on Friday 11th February 2000 on all seven floors

London

London

of The Café Royal. Please wear evening dress with your personal Valentine Heart, which we will send you with your ball ticket. At midnight, trumpeters from the Household Cavalry will sound a fanfare heralding the start of the sacred rites of St.Valentine. This is a fun competition throughout the evening by which everyone is able to meet anyone else they fancy; it's to collect as many hearts of the opposite sex as you can. You may woo them, exchange them or seduce them, but not snatch, buy or break them. Both the guy and the girl who win most hearts will also win Jeroboams of Champagne. The Cafe' Royal will be offering our guests a selection of light snacks from £3.50 all evening. Additionally, your ball ticket will give you free entrance, after the ball, to Stringfellows nightclub.

Valentine Ball Fri 11th Feb 2000

£45.00 buy a ticket to the Valentine Ball and get a £5 voucher off our next Big Bang Ball- usually October call for details

Folk & Local History Museums

Bexley Museum

Hall Place Bourne Road Bexley Kent DA5 1PQ

[close to A2 Black Prince interchange. BR: Bexley]

Tel: 01322 526574 Fax: 01322 522921

www.earl.org.uk/earl/members/bexley/index.html

The Local History Museum of the Borough of Bexley, housed in a Tudor and Jacobean Mansion set in parkland. Permanent archaeology and natural history displays with temporary exhibition of social history. Local Studies Centre and Visitor Centre. Guided tours of house are available if booked in advance.

All year Mon-Sat 10.00-17.00 dusk in winter. Summer: Sun 14.00-18.00. Gardens open daily. Please call and check times before starting your journey

Hall Place: Admission £Free. Charges made for ticket events

Bromley Museum and Priory Gardens
The Priory Church Hill Orpington BR6 0HH
[J4 M25, A224]
Tel: 01689 873826
www.bromley.gov.uk
The museum is housed in an impressive medieval / post medieval building set in attractive gardens. Find out about the archaeology of the London Borough of Bromley. Learn about Sir John Lubbock, 1st Lord Avebury, the eminent Victorian responsible for giving this country its Bank Holidays. See how people lived before World War II. Guided tours by arrangement. Throughout the year there are changing exhibitions by the Museum and local groups. Gardens and ground floor of museum only is suitable for wheelchairs. Enabling dogs are admitted. For details of the following events, call the venue.
Bromley Museum: All year Mon-Fri 13.00-17.00, Sat 10.00-17.00. 1 Apr-31 Oct Sun 13.00-17.00, Bank Hol 13.00-17.00 Mornings Mon-Fri for educational purposes only. Priory Gardens: All year Mon-Fri 07.30-dusk, Sat Sun & Bank Hol 09.00-dusk
Admission Free

↓ *special events*
► "Simply Dinosaurs"
8/1/00-16/3/00
A touring exhibition by the Dinosaur Society
► Orpington Photographic Society
18/3/00-25/3/00
► "In and Around Bromley a Century Ago"
27/3/00-9/4/00
► "Commemoratives"
11/4/00-26/4/00
With school collaboration
► Orpington Sketch Club Open Exhibition
28/4/00-6/5/00
► Museums and Galleries North
1/5/00-4/6/00
► "The Borough's Churches"
8/5/00-22/6/00
► Botanical Illustration
12/6/00-9/7/00
► "What is a Museum?"
10/7/00-26/7/00
► 2000 years of settlement in the Cray Valley

29/7/00-28/8/00
► St Mary Cray Action Group display
30/8/00-27/9/00
► Bromley's Hall of Fame
29/9/00-29/10/00
► Orpington Sketch Club Members Exhibition
3/11/00-11/11/00

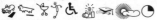

Bruce Castle Museum
Burlington Lane Tottenham Haringey London N17 8NU
[J25 M25 take A10 High Rd turn off into Lordship Lane, Bruce Castle is situated in Church Lane. Tube: Wood Green]
Tel: 020 8808 8772 Fax: 020 8808 4118
The museum houses several permanent exhibitions that delve deep into Haringey's past: A major collection of postal history material formed because of Bruce Castle's historic association with Sir Rowland Hill; Victorian costume and domestic equipment providing a fascinating insight into Victorian life; A reconstruction of a 1930's office giving a view of the workplace during the inter-war period; An original Roman kiln excavated from Highgate and a collection of local photographs, painting and prints. Although not 'officially' haunted it has been said that a large gathering of people in eighteenth century costume, have been seen, though, when approached, the gathering disappears into the walls.
All year Wed-Sun 13.00-17.00. Closed Winter Bank Hol and Good Friday. Groups at other times, by arrangement
Last Admission: 10mins before closing
Admission Free

Bushey Museum and Art Gallery
Rudolph Road Bushey Hertfordshire WD2 3DU
[limited on site parking]
Tel: 020 8420 4057 Fax: 020 8420 4923
www.busheymuseum.org
Permanent displays showing Bushey from the earliest times to the present day, especially social history and local products, plus the Monro Circle, the life of Sir Hubert von Herkomer RA and his Art School and subsequent art schools.
All year Thur-Sun 11.00-16.00. Groups by appointment
Admission Free

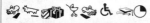

Church Farmhouse Museum
Greyhound Hill London NW4 4JR
[J2 M1, off A41. Tube: Hendon Central]
Tel: 020 8203 2666 Fax: 020 8359 3157
Built about 1660, the oldest surviving dwelling in the Borough of Barnet. Victorian furnished dining room, kitchen and scullery. Programme of changing exhibitions throughout the year featuring social history, decorative arts and local history.
All year Mon-Thur 10.00-12.30 & 13.30-17.00, Sat 10.00-13.00 & 14.00-17.30, Sun 14.00-17.30. Closed Good Fri, 25-26 Dec & 1 Jan
Last Admission: 15mins before closing
Admission Free

Cuming Museum
155-157 Walworth Road London SE17 1RS
[Tube: Elephant & Castle]
Tel: 020 7701 1342 Fax: 020 7703 7415
The museum of Southwark's history. The worldwide collections of the Cuming family combined with the local history of Southwark, with artefatcs from Roman times through to the days of Chaucer, Shakespeare and Dickens to the present day. Special exhibitions on local themes.
All year Tue-Sat 10.00-17.00. Closed Bank Hol. School & adult parties daily by appointment
Admission Free

Dartford Borough Museum
Market Street Dartford Kent DA1 1EU
[in Dartford town centre]
Tel: 01322 343555
The museum is a community local history museum which aims to serve the needs of people living and working in the Borough of Dartford. Exhibitions and services are, where possible, geared to the interests and requirements of the local community. Museum staff work with local schools and special interest groups to facilitate maximum access to the collections. As with all museums, a substantial proportion of the collections is not on permanent display.
All year 12.30-17.30. Sat 09.00-13.00 & 14.00-17.00. Closed Wed. Guided Tours by arrangement
Admission Free

East Surrey Museum
1 Stafford Road Caterham Surrey CR3 6JG
[BR: Caterham Valley]
Tel: 01883 340275
Changing displays of local history, archaeology, natural history, crafts and local artists. A children's 'hands-on' room which contains items topical for children from colouring to
All year Wed & Sat 10.00-17.00, Sun 14.00-17.00
A£0.30 C&OAPs£0.20

London

London

Erith Museum

Erith Library Walnut Tree Road Erith Kent DA8
1RS
[A206 adjacent to Erith Town Hall]
Tel: 01322 526574
Local history, including archaeology, industry
and famous events.
Mon & Wed 14.15-17.15 Sat 14.15-17.00
Admission Free

Forty Hall Museum

Forty Hill Enfield Middlesex EN2 9HA
[close to the junction of M25 and A10]
Tel: 020 8363 8196 Fax: 020 8367 9098
The mansion of Forty Hall was built in 1629 for
Nicholas Raynton, Lord Mayor of London, and
then altered in the 18th century. It has fine
plaster ceilings and collection of 17th & 18th
century furniture, paintings, ceramics and
glass. There are also local history displays and
temporary exhibitions. Set in rolling parkland.
Venue may be closing in March 1999, please
telephone before visiting.
*All year Thur-Sun 11.00-17.00. Venue may be
closing in March 1999, please telephone before
visiting*
Admission Free

Greenwich Borough Museum

232 Plumstead High Street London SE18 1JL
[J10 M25, A206 BR: Plumstead]
Tel: 020 8855 3240 Fax: 020 8316 5754
Local museum of archaeology, history and nat-
ural history. Also temporary exhibitions, chil-
dren's activities and sales point. Schools
Service and Saturday Club. Adult lecture pro-
gramme and workshops.
*All year Mon 14.00-19.00, Tue-Sat 10.00-13.00
& 14.00-17.00. Closed Wed, Sun & Bank Hol*
Admission Free

Hampstead Museum

Burgh House New End Square London NW3 1LT
Tel: 020 7431 0144
1703 house with original panelling and stair-
case. A museum of Hampstead history, old
photographs and water colours. Constable
Room, Allingham collection. Disabled access to
ground floor only.
*All year Wed-Sun 12.00-17.00. Good Fri & Bank
Hol 14.00-17.00*
Admission Free

↓*special events*
▶ **"Theatrical Hampstead"**
4/2/00-30/4/00
*An exhibition focusing on the histories of the-
atres and actors in Hampstead from 1709 to
the present.*

▶ **Idylls and Ideas**
8/3/00-8/3/00
*Slide lecture about the history of open air per-
formances in Hampstead Garden Suburb, 20.00,
tickets A£3.00 and Concessions£2.00*

Harrow Museum and Heritage Centre

Headstone Manor Pinner View Harrow
Middlesex HA2 6PX
*[Tube: Harrow on the Hill on the Metropolitan
Line, bus H14 or H15 to Kodak Sportsground]*
Tel: 020 8861 2626 Fax: 020 8863 6407
Based in listed 16th century timber barn and
medieaval moated house. Purpose of the
museum is to reflect the history of Harrow:
1930's, Victorian, Agriculture and Trades dis-
plays.
*All year Wed-Fri 12.30-17.00, Weekends & Bank
Hol Mon 10.30-17.00, during Winter months
closing at dusk. Pre-booked Groups by arrange-
ment*
Admission Free

Honeywood Heritage Centre

Honeywood Walk Carshalton Surrey SM5 3NX
[by Carshalton Ponds off A232. BR: Carshalton]
Tel: 020 8770 4297 Fax: 020 8770 4777
www.sutton.gov.uk
The history of the borough and its people plus
a programme of exhibitions, presented in a
17th century listed building. Features include
Edwardian Billiard Room, Tudor Gallery and
Art Gallery.
*All year Wed-Fri 10.00-17.00, Sat Sun & Bank
Hol Mon 10.00-17.30*
A£1.20 £0.50
discount offer: Two For The Price Of One

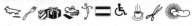

Livesey Museum

682 Old Kent Road London SE15 1JF
[Tube: Elephant & Castle, Bus: 53, 172, 10mins]
Tel: 020 7639 5604 Fax: 020 7277 5384
Southwark's family museum holds a lively programme of hands-on exhibitions for children
up to 12 years, their schools, families and carers. Special workshops which compliment the
exhibitions during school holidays may have
charge a levied, please call venue nearer to the
holiday period for further information. JAN -
August 1999 'Mind Your Language' the show
that explores communication and literacy
through the ages.
*All year Tue-Sat 10.00-17.00, closed during
changing of exhibitions, please call if travelling
some distance*

Admission Free

Museum of Richmond

Old Town Hall Whittaker Avenue Richmond
Surrey TW9 1TP
Tel: 020 8332 1141 Fax: 020 8940 6899
www.lostwax.com/museum.html
This new independent museum deals with
Richmond's rich and colourful history in a live-
ly and informative way. Varied collections,
models, dioramas and audio visual displays.
Lively temporary exhibitions and events.
*All year Tue-Sat 11.00-17.00, Sun May-Oct
13.00-16.00. Closed Bank Hol. Parties welcome
weekday mornings by arrangement*
*A£1.00. Annual pass A£3.00 Concessions£0.50
Annual pass £1.50. Pre-booked school parties
please call*

Public Record Office

Kew Richmond Surrey TW9 4DU
*[Tube: Kew Gardens. Plenty of parking avail-
able]*
Tel: 020 8876 3444 Fax: 020 8392 5266
www.pro.gov.uk
The Public Record Office is the national archive
of England and Wales, and its records cover
almost 1000 years of history. Many of its key
treasurers will be on display in a new
Education and Visitor Centre, opening in April
2000. A full programme of exhibitions and
events is planned for Millennium Year, including themed open days, a poetry festival and

behind-the-scenes tours.
*All year Mon, Wed, Fri & Sat 09.00-17.00, Tue
10.00-19.00, Thur 09.00-19.00*
Admission Free

Ragged School Museum

46-50 Copperfield Road London E3 4RR
[A11 or A13. Tube: Mile End]
Tel: 020 8980 6405 Fax: 020 8983 3481
Once the house of Dr Barnardo's Ragged Day
School set up in the 1880s, this museum
examines the experience of growing up in the
East End during the late victorian period.
Visitors can also experience how victorian chil-
dren were taught in a reconstructed class-
room. There are also displays on local history,
industry and life in the East End.
*All year Wed & Thur 10.00-17.00 & first Sun of
each month 14.00-17.00*
Last Admission: 16.45
Admission Free, donations appreciated

Sherlock Holmes Museum

221b Baker Street London NW1 6XE
[Tube: Baker Street]
Tel: 020 7935 8866 Fax: 020 7738 1269
www.sherlock-holmes.co.uk
This famous address was opened as a museum
in 1990. The first floor rooms contain all the
features familiar to the Holmes enthusiast,
and an authentic Victorian atmosphere has
been maintained throughout the house,
including an attractive old English restaurant,
Hudson's, on the ground floor of the Museum.
Visitors are encouraged to take photographs.
All year daily 09.30-18.00. Closed 25 Dec
*A£5.00 C(0-16)£3.00. Group rates on applica-
tion*

Thurrock Museum

Thameside Complex Orsett Road Grays Essex
RM17 5DX
[centre of Grays Town]
Tel: 01375 382555 Fax: 01375 370806
Local history, agriculture, trades and industries are illustrated, with a display on archaeology from the Stone Age to the Medieval period. Temporary exhibitions are held throughout
the year.
All year Mon-Sat 09.00-17.00. Closed Bank Hol
Admission Free

Upminster Tithe Barn Agricultural and Folk Museum

Hall Lane Upminster Essex *[Tube: Upminster]*
Collection of 12,500 artefacts including agri-

London

cultural implements, craft and farm tools, local bricks and domestic bygones, displayed in 15th century timber and thatched barn.
First full weekend of each month Apr-Oct 14.00-18.00
Admission free. Donations welcome

Valence House Museum and Art Gallery
Becontree Avenue Dagenham Essex RM8 3HT
[Tube: Becontree]
Tel: 020 8595 8404 Fax: 020 8252 8290
Valence House is the home of the Borough's local history museum and art gallery. The earliest parts of the building date from the 1400's. It is the only remaining manor house in Dagenham and is partially surrounded by a moat. In the 14th Century, Valence Manor was held by Aylmer de Valence, Earl Pembroke who gave the building its name. On display are various artifacts illustrating the history of the area. These include Stone Age and Bronze Age tools and Roman pottery. One of the most important industries in Barking from the 14th Century until Victorian times was fishing. Major fishing fleets operated out of the mouth of Barking Creek, and many relics from the period are on display. The history of the massive Becontree Estate which covers much of the Borough is charted in the new Becontree Room. The Museum holds regular events and displays on Saturdays throughout the year, and Guided Tours or Local History talks can be arranged. Please call for an appointment. The O'Leary Gallery opened in 1991, and was named after the charismatic librarian John Gerard O'Leary. It houses temporary exhibitions throughout the year. There is a lovely herb garden in the grounds and a café which opens on Saturdays only. Disabled access to the first floor is difficult.
All year Tue-Fri 09.30-13.00 & 14.00-16.30, Sat 10.00-16.00. Closed Public Hol
Admission Free

Vauxhall St Peter's Heritage Centre
310 Kennington Lane London SE11
[Tube: Vauxhall / Oval]
Tel: 020 7793 0263 Fax: 020 7820 0038
Built on the site of Vauxhall Gardens, St Peter's is a classic Victorian Gothic Church housing Victorian paintings, mosaics and carvings. With various exhibitions on the history of Vauxhall and Charlie Chaplin.
All year Tue-Thur 10.30-16.00. Closed 24 Dec-4 Jan
Admission Free

Vestry House Museum
Vestry Road nr Hoe Street Walthamstow

London E17 9NH
[Tube: Walthamstow Central]
Tel: 020 8509 1917
Local interest museum housed in a former 18th century workhouse. An interesting collection of domestic objects, the most fascinating piece is the Bremer car: Britain's first vehicle driven by an internal combustion engine. Also houses the local studies Library and Archives which are available by appointment only. Guided tours for pre-booked groups.
All year Mon-Fri 10.00-13.00 & 14.00-17.30, Sat 10.00-13.00 & 14.00-17.00. Closed Bank Hol
Admission Free, pre-booked school groups welcome

Wandle Industrial Museum
The Vestry Hall Annexe London Road Mitcham Surrey CR4 3UD
[BR: Mitcham, facing Mitcham cricket green]
Tel: 020 8648 0127
Reflects the life and industries of the River Wandle. Special exhibits on Arthur Liberty, William Morris, Merton Priory, Lord Nelson, Surrey Iron Railway, snuff and tobacco.
All year Wed 13.00-16.00 and first Sun of month 14.00-17.00
A£0.20 Concessions£0.10

Wandsworth Museum
The Courthouse 11 Garratt Lane Wandsworth London SW18 4AQ
Tel: 020 8871 7074/7075 Fax: 020 8871 4602
The story of Wandsworth will be told in a new and exciting way at the new Wandsworth Museum.
All year Tue-Sat 10.00-17.00, Sun 14.00-17.00
Admission Free

Watford Museum
194 High Street Watford Hertfordshire WD1 2HG
[signposted off Ring Road. Next to BR: Watford High Street]
Tel: 01923 232297 Fax: 01923 232297
A good art gallery and a museum specializing in the history of Watford from the earliest times to the present day. There are special features on the local industries of printing and brewing, together with a display on wartime Watford, based on the Dad's Army TV series. Temporary exhibitions take place throughout the year. Victorian section. New modern gallery on Watford since the 19th century.
All year Mon-Fri 10.00-17.00, Sat 10.00-13.00 & 14.00-17.00. Closed Bank Hol
Admission Free

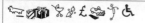

Westminster Abbey Museum

20 Dean's Yard London SW1P 3PA

[Tube: Westminster, East Cloister at Westminster Abbey]

Tel: 020 7222 5152/233 0019 Fax: 020 7233 2072

Museum housed in magnificent Norman Undercroft. The Abbey's famous collection of Royal and other effigies forms the centrepiece of the exhibition. Other items on display include replicas of Coronation regalia and surviving panels of medieval glass.

visitor comments: Beautiful. Go early and avoid the crowds.

All year daily 10.30-16.00

Last Admission: 45mins before closing

A£2.50 C(0-16)£1.30 OAPs&Students£1.90

Wimbledon Society's Museum

Village Club Ridgway Wimbledon London SW19 4QD

[Tube/BR: Wimbledon, at junction of Ridgway / Lingfield Road]

Tel: 020 8296 9914

History and natural history of Wimbledon. Photographic survey mostly 1900-14 containing 2000 prints. Good collection of watercolours and prints.

All year Sat 14.30-17.00

Admission Free

Food & Drink

Bramah Tea and Coffee Museum

Maguire Street Butlers Wharf London SE1 2NQ

[next to the Design Museum by the River Thames. Tube: Tower Hill / London Bridge]

Tel: 020 7378 0222 Fax: 020 7378 0219

The museum charts the 350 year social and commercial history of these favourite beverages, through a glittering array of ceramics, metal, prints and paraphernalia; housed appropriately in Butlers Wharf, the centre of tea warehousing a hundred years ago. The museum has a shop and café selling traditional teas and coffee.

All year daily 10.00-18.00. Closed 25-26 Dec

Last Admission: 17.30

A£3.50 C&Concessions£2.00 Family Ticket £8.00. From 1st Nov 98: A£4.00 C&Concessions£2.50 Family Ticket £9.00

London

Fuller's Griffin Brewery Tours

Chiswick Lane South London W4 2QB

[Tube: Turnham Green / Stamford Brook]

Tel: 020 8996 2063 Fax: 020 8996 2079

www.fullers.co.uk

London's oldest brewery which offers a comprehensive tour of this historic site. The tour will show visitors the brewing process from first to last, demonstrating how traditional methods and the newest technology work together in harmony. No children under 14 years of age. Advance booking is essential for all visitors.

All year Mon, Wed, Thur & Fri 11.00, 12.00, 13.00 & 14.00

£5.00. Discount of 10% for groups of 15+.

Ram Brewery Visitor Centre

The Brewery Tap 68 Wandsworth High Street London SW18 4LB

[on South Circular Rd (A205) and the main A3 Portsmouth Rd. From N of the Thames, cross the river by Putney Bridge or Wandsworth Bridge. NCP Car Park in the Arndale Centre, off Buckhold Road. BR: Wandsworth Town / Clapham Junction. Tube: East Putney. Bus: 28 / 37 / 39 / 44 / 77A / 156 / 170 / 220 / 337]

Tel: 020 8875 7005 Fax: 020 8875 7006

www.youngs.co.uk/

Young's Ram Brewery, in the south London suburb of Wandsworth, is a living and working museum of English brewing through the ages. Traditional draught beer, or real ale as it is now known, has been produced here for more than 400 years by methods that have stood the test of time. The equipment used today to produce some of the world's best known beers is a stunning mixture of ancient and modern. Victorian vessels where beer ferments for a week stand alongside modern stainless steel equipment operated by computerised control panels. There are two magnificent 19th century steam engines - believed to be the oldest of their kind still working on their original site - and two splendid brewing coppers, used for well over a century to boil ale, stout and porter with hops. Young's also has London's last remaining cooperage, where wooden barrels used to be made and are still repaired. Much of the beer is delivered locally by horse-drawn dray, as it has been since the early days. Twenty heavy horses, mainly Shires, share the brewery stables with a ram, goats, a pony and a donkey. A farrier makes all the horses' shoes in the smithy behind the stables.

All year Mon-Sat 10.00-18.00. Full brewery tours last about 1 hour 15 mins. Family tours of stables last about 45 mins. Tours start at 10.00, 12.00, 14.00 & 16.00. Tailor-made packages available for organised groups, company meetings or entertaining. School party visits arranged for stables. Please telephone for further information and to check availability and space on tours (max no. 15-20). Larger groups can be accommodated subject to prior arrangement, £1.00 non-refundable depost per head for groups 10+. Pre-booked evening tours for min of 20 with meal or buffet, ideal starting time 18.00-18.30
Full Brewery Tour: A£5.50 accompaniedC(14-17)£3.00 OAPs£4.50. No children under 14. Prices include beer samples and half pint of beer or a soft drink. Family Stable Tour: A£3.50 accompaniedC(5-18)£2.00 C(0-5)£Free Family Ticket £9.00. Pre-booked groups 10+ £1.00 per head

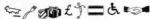

Vinopolis, City of Wine
Bank End / Clink Street London SE1
[Between Southwark Cathedral & Shakespeare's Globe. Coach drop facilities at Southwark Street, SE1. Tube: London Bridge. Buses: 17, 21, 35, 40, 43, 38, 133, 149, 344, 501, 521, P3, P11, N21, N35, N47, N70. NCP Parking: on St Thomas Street and Newcomen Street]
Tel: 0870 444477 Fax: 020 7915 0414
www.evinopolis.com
Built on the site on an old Roman wine store, Vinopolis is the world's largest complex dedicated day and night to wine and all its pleasures and CHILD FREE. At the heart of Vinopolis is the Wine Odyssey, a grand tour through the world's wine cultures. Passing through 20 vast and dramatically themed Wine Odyssey rooms, visitors can learn about every aspect of wine culture and history at their own pace. As a grand finale, visitors enter The Grand Tasting Halls to sample wines from around the world at their leisure. Also houses: Four Restaurants, Wine by the Glass, Champagne Bar, Gift Shopping, Vinopolis Vaults.
All year daily 10.00-17.30. Pre-booked Groups Mon-Sat excluding Bank Hol. Closed Christmas Day
Last Admission: 16.30
A£10.50. Group rates A£8.50 includes: 5 FREE tasting samples, Personal Audio Guide,

Admission to Vinopolis Gallery (one ticket free with every 45 booked). Ticketmaster: 0870 444 4777

Gardens & Horticulture

Capel Manor
Bullsmoor Lane Enfield Middlesex EN1 4RQ
[3mins from J M25 / A10 S turn right at traffic lights. BR: Turkey Street, Liverpool Street line]
Tel: 020 8366 4442 Fax: 01992 717544
Capel Manor is Greater London's only specialist College of Horticulture and Countryside studies with the 30 acres of richly planted and diverse gardens, which surround the Georgian manor. A comprehensive self-guided tour starts from the new visitor's centre.
visitor comments: The Spring Show is lovely with lots of stalls to visit, but take along a picnic lunch. Gardens are attractive and well kept.
All year Mon-Fri daily 10.00-17.30. Weekends Mar-end Oct 10.00-17.30
A£4.00 C(3-16)£2.00 Concessions£3.50. Special rates for coaches, garden tours

Chelsea Physic Garden
66 Royal Hospital Road London SW3 4HS
[entrance in Swan Walk. Tube: Sloane Square]
Tel: 0207 352 5646 Fax: 0207 376 3910
www.cpgarden.demon.co.uk
The second oldest botanic garden in England

was begun in 1673 for the study of plants used in medicine by the Society of Apothecaries. By the late 18th century it was famous throughout Europe for is rare and unusual plants, and it is still used for botanical and medicinal research.

Apr-Oct Wed 12.00-17.00, Sun 14.00-18.00. Also opening during Chelsea Flower Show week & Chelsea Festival week. Groups at other times, by appointment
A&OAPs£4.00 C(5-15)
Students&Unemployed£2.00
discount offer: Two For The Price Of One. Valid Until 29 Oct 2000

↓ special events
▶ **Timely Cures - Pharmaceutical Plants**
9/7/00-3/9/00
Photographic exhibition matched with the launch of a planted pharmaceutical garden
▶ **Summer School - Medicinal Plants**
7/8/00-11/8/00
Collections of herbal, pharmaceutical and essential oil plants, talks and demonstrations. Strictly limited numbers, please book in advance. Recreational course
▶ **Summer School in Medicinal Plants**
14/8/00-18/8/00
Herbal, pharmaceutical and essential oil plants, talks and demonstrations. Strictly limited numbers, please book in advance. Professional course

Kensington Gardens
Kensington London W8
[Tube: Queensway / Lancaster Gate]
This was part of Hyde Park until William III enclosed his palace gardens and even today the two areas are not physically divided. the 'invisible' boundary runs from north to south across the Serpentine Bridge. Kensington Gardens are noted for their tranquility and formality.
All year, any reasonable time
Admission Free

Kew Gardens Royal Botanic Gardens
Kew Richmond Surrey TW9 3AB
[Tube: Kew Gardens. BR: Kew Bridge]
Tel: 020 8940 1171 Fax: 020 8332 5197
www.rbgkew.org.uk
World-famous gardens at Kew began as a 9 acre site laid out by George III's mother Princess Augusta in 1759. Given to the state in 1841 the gardens covered 300 acres by 1904 - their present size. Famous landmarks are the Chinese Pagoda and the Palm House with plants from the tropics. Construction is under way for a Millennium Seed Bank to be completed by October 1999. The Royal Botanic Gardens aims to collect seeds of all British flora by the end of the year 2000 and ten per cent of the world's flowering plants by the

year 2010, 25,000 species in all. They will be stored in freezers inside the research and exhibition centre, near Haywards Heath. Visitors will watch scientists at work, descending in glassed lifts to the vaults protecting the seeds. The bank will make its stocks available for research into the potential medical and industrial properties of plants that are disappearing in the wild.

All year daily Garden: from 09.30 closing times vary according to season, from 16.00 in Winter up to 19.30 in Summer. Conservatories close earlier. Closed 25 Dec & 1 Jan
A£5.00 C(5-16)£2.50 C(0-5)£Free Family Ticket £13.00 Concessions&OAPs££3.50

Morden Hall Park
Morden Hall Road Morden London SM4 5JD
[off A24 and A297 S of Wimbledon N of Sutton]
Tel: 020 8648 1846 Fax: 020 8687 0094
A National Trust Property. A green oasis on the heart of SW London, this former deer park has an extensive network of waterways, a tree-lined avenue, Elizabethan hay meadows and an interesting collection of vernacular buildings. Old estate workshops house a selection of local craftspeople whose work is on view. Riverside walk, Garden Centre, Restaurant and Shop.
Park only open all year in daylight hours
Admission Free

↓ special events
▶ **Springtime at Morden**
16/4/00-16/4/00
Meet at the car park bridge for this 1.5-mile walk, donations wlecome 14.30-15.30
▶ **Countryside and Crafts Come to Town**
29/4/00-1/5/00
Craft Fair with a Viking theme, 10.00-18.00, A£3.50 C£1.50 OAPs£2.50
▶ **Park Trees**
14/5/00-14/5/00
Meet at the car park bridge for this 1.5-mile walk, donations welcome, 14.00-15.30
▶ **Explorer Days**
30/5/00-24/10/00
Activities include river dipping, minibeast hunts and environmental games. Suitable for 5-9 year olds. Booking essential - tickets from Snuff Mill Environmental Centre. Telephone 020 8542 4232 for information, C£3.00, 10.00-12.00 on 30 & 31 May, 1 & 2, 8 & 9, 22 & 23, 29 & 30 Aug & 24 Oct
▶ **Meadows at Morden**
11/6/00-11/6/00
Meet at the car park bridge for this 1.5-mile walk, donations welcome, 14.00-15.30
▶ **Twelfth Night**
15/6/00-18/6/00

London

Performed by Maqama Theatre Company, bring cushions no seats. Tickets from the Southern Region Box Office on 01372 451596 or the National Trust Shop at Morden Hall Park. Performance on Thur is for school parties and other groups of 10+ at £5.00, otherwise: A£7.00 C£5.00, 19.30-22.00

► **Art in the Park**
8/7/00-9/7/00
Exhibition, demonstrations and performances of visual and performing arts by local artists in an open-air arts setting. Plus children's art activities, donations 10.00-16.30

► **Summer Roses**
9/7/00-9/7/00
Meet at the car park bridge for this 1.5-mile walk, donations welcome, 14.00-15.30

► **Puppetry**
28/7/00-28/7/00
Using scrap material children will be making puppets. Suitable for 6-10 year olds, booking essential. Telephone 020 8542 4232 for information, C£4.00 10.00am-12.00 noon or 14.00-16.00

► **Urban Nature Conservation**
13/8/00-13/8/00
Meet at the car park bridge for this 1.5-mile walk, donations welcome, 14.00-15.30

► **Puppetry**
31/8/00-31/8/00
See entry for 28 July

► **Discovering History**
17/9/00-17/9/00
Meet at the car park bridge for this 1.5-mile walk, donations welcome, 14.00-15.30

► **Apple Day**
21/10/00-21/10/00
Taste English Apples in the old Snuff Mill, visit the Orchard then treat yourself with our apple theme menu, donations welcome, 10.00-16.30

Museum of Garden History
5 Lambeth Palace Road Lambeth London SE1 7LB
[Tube: Victoria / Waterloo. Bus: 507 / C10. Just across the Thames is the Palace of Westminster and the Houses of Parliament and a little further on, the Tate Gallery]
Tel: 020 7401 8865 Fax: 020 7401 8869
www.compulink.co.uk/~museumgh
Museum of Garden History is an historic, listed building, previously the Parish Church of St Mary at Lambeth, with an accurately recreated 17th century garden and a permanent exhibition of all aspects of the history of gardens. Tombs of John Tradescants elder and younger the royal gardeners to Charles I & II, Elias Ashmole founder of the Ashmolean Museum and Captain Bligh of the Bounty can be found

in the grounds. There are displays illustrating the history of the Tradescants, Captain Blight and Gertrude Jekyll, the stories of some plant hunters who explored in remote regions to find the delights that we take for granted in our gardens today. A fine collection of historic garden tools including a 17th century watering pot, 18th century dibber, 19th century fern trowl, a 20th century lawn mower and so much more. Set amid the beauty and traquillity of a garden based on a 17th century Knot Garden design, filled with traditional plants. Lectures, courses, concerts, fairs and art exhibitions are regularly held throughout the year.
All year daily Mon-Fri 10.30-16.00, Sun 10.30-17.00. Closed Sat and from second Sun in Dec to first Sun in Mar. The Ark Garden is open Apr-Oct Wed only.
Admission Free, voluntary donations requested

Roof Gardens
99 Kensington High Street London W8 5ED
[Tube: High Street Kensington]
Tel: 020 7937 7994 Fax: 020 7938 2774
Built in 1938, The Roof Gardens was the largest of it's kind in Europe standing 100 feet above Kensington High Street on top of what was then one of London's finest department stores-Derry and Toms. The Gardens were constructed around three themes. The Spanish Garden with it's court of fountains and formal design, the Tudor garden and walk constructed in old red brick and the woodland or English garden, complete with streams, ducks and flamingos. Since then it has flourished as a private members club on Thursday and Saturday evenings and a unique function venue where conferences, product launches and wedding receptions can be organised. Now part of the Virgin empire, visitors are welcome to walk around the gardens when there is no function taking place.
All year daily on non function days
It is free to visit the gardens. To book a function please telephone.

Guided Tours

Angel Walks
26B Canonbury Square Islington London N1 2AL
[meeting places vary with each walk / please see special events for details]
Tel: 020 7226 8333
Your Guide, Peter Powell has lived in Islington for 25 years. He is a local historian and lecturer and worked for many years as a professional actor and singer. He lives in the flat next door to that of George Orwell in Canonbury Square.

This is the tenth year of Angel walks. Other walks available for private parties at times to suit including evenings, (preferably 8 or more persons) are:- Highgate; Hampstead; Joe Orton Walk; Arts Theatres and Pubs of Islington; Clerkenwell; Canonbury and the Alwynes. Lectures on all these subjects for all ages by arrangement. All walks take about 2 hours each.
Call for details
A£4.00 C(0-14)£Free C£3.00

Apples, Actors and Arias Stepping Out London Walk
Embankment Tube London WC2R 2PH
[Tube: Embankment, Villiers Street Exit]
Tel: 020 8881 2933 Answerphon Fax: 020 7405 6036
Explore the streets leading up to the Strand and enter Covent Garden via a hidden court-yard. Learn about the actors, authors and artists who lived here. Stand where Eliza Doolittle sold her flowers and hear the history of the market and theatres.
All year Sun 14.00
A£4.50 Concessions£3.50

Black Taxi Tours of London
7 Durweston Mews London W1H 1PB
[There are pick up points anywhere within zone 1 on the London Underground system]
Tel: 020 72894371/07956 38412 Fax: 020 7224 2833
www.blacktaxitours.co.uk
Visitors who find the hurly burly of bus and coach tours too much to bear can breath a sigh of relief from now on. Black Taxi Tours of London offer a personalised special tour of the city in the comfort of a licensed taxi cab. Taxis pick up guests from their hotel for a two hour tour of London, stopping at the major sights to take photographs. The drivers provide a full commentary, with fascinating anecdotes and the type of traveller's tales that only a sea-soned cab driver would know.
All year day or night pre-booked only, 8.00-23.00
Two hour taxi tour £65 (£70 from April 2000) for up to 5 passengers.

Harrow School Tours
15 London Road Harrow-on-the-Hill Harrow Middlesex HA1 3JJ
[easy reach of M1 / M40 / M4 / M25. Tube: Harrow-on-the-Hill / South Harrow]
Tel: 020 8422 2303 Fax: 020 8422 2303
Fascinating tour of one of Britain's finest pub-lic schools. Three types of tour available.

Limited parking space available. Tea can be arranged in term time for a minimum of 20 people if booked in advance.
Pre-booked guided tours only. Please telephone or write for details
Short Tour: A£3.80 Students&OAPs£3.05 Small Groups £36.00; Standard Tour: A£4.25 Students&OAPs£3.50 Small Parties £40.00; Full Tour: A£4.90 Students&OAPs£4.05 Small Groups £43.00. Organisers and adults accom-panying school parties admitted free. Full Tea: £3.70, Tea & biscuits: £1.75

Historical Walks of London Tours
3 Florence Road South Croydon Surrey CR2 0PQ
[various starting points. Tube: Aldgate; Baker Street; Blackfriars; Farringdon; Green Park; Monument; Russell Square; Sloane Square; Temple; Westminster & Whitechapel]
Tel: 020 8668 4019/5327 Fax: 020 8668 4019
Varied daily programme of themed Historical Walks of London, including Jack the Ripper, Politcal London, The City of London, Pub Walks. Walks last about two hours, no need to book - just turn up at the underground station venue. Private tours can be arranged and meeting places on request. The Week at a Glance: SUNDAY 11.00 The London of Dickens & Shakespeare Tube: Blackfriars; 11.00 The Real London Easterender Tube: Aldgate; 14.30 London Royal & Aristocratic Tube: Green Park; 19.00 Historic Pub Walk - Mayfair Tube: Green Park; 19.00 Jack the Ripper Tube: Whitechapel. MONDAY 11.00 Legal London Tube: Tenple; 14.00 Literary London Tube: Russell Square; 19.30 Graveyards, Ghouls and Ghosts of the Old City Tube: Farringdon. TUESDAY 11.00 The Real London Easterenders Tube: Aldgate; 14.00 Charles Disckens' London Tube: Blackfriars; 19.30 Jack the Ripper Tube: Whitechapel. WEDNESDAY 11.00 Legal London Tube: Temple; 14.30 London Royal & Aristocratic Tube: Green Park; 19.00 London Scandals Historic Pub Walk Tube: Baker Street. THURSDAY 11.00 Inside Some Hidden Interiors of Old London Tube: Temple; 14.30 A Walk in the Footsteps of Sherlock Holmes Tube: Baker Street; 19.30 The Jack the Ripper Whitechapel Murders Tube: Whitechapel; 19.35 Historic Pub Walk Ghosts by Gas Light Tube: Temple. Friday 11.00 Historic Westminster Government & Parliament Tube: Westminster; 14.30 A City in the Blitz & Churchill's Cabinet War Rooms Tube: Westminster; 19.00 An Historic Pub Walk Chelsea Tube: Sloane Square. SATURDAY 11.00 London's Historic Curiosities the Buried City Tube: Blackfriars; 14.30 The City of London a 2000 Year History Tube: Monument; 19.00 Jack the Ripper Tube: Whitechapel.
All year daily 11.00, 14.30 and 19.00. Closed

London

London

24-26 Dec
Last Admission: latest tour 19.35
A£4.50 C(0-14)£Free when accompanied by an
Adult. Concessions&OAPs Groups&School
Parties£3.50

London Guides - The Fourth Dimension

5 Sloane Street London SW1X 9LA
[Tube: Knightsbridge, south exit outside Harvey
Nichols, opposite the Hyde Park Hotel]
Tel: 020 7235 2591
Liz Keay is a registered City of London Guide
with her main tour: Beautiful Belgravia -
Mirror of Power. Belgravia is one of London's
most beautiful and exclusive areas - but only
170 years ago it was The Five Fields, and haunt
of robbers. Buckingham Palace became
London's royal residence in the 1830s and
Belgravia became home to the upper echelons
of society. It's fine buildings and spacious
squares reflect the elegance of their origins.
Further walks available by arrangement
include: Crusaders, Lawyers, Literary London
from Temple to Blackfriars approx 1.3/4 hours
; Heart of the City from Bank (circular walk)
approx 1 hour; Shipping, Empire, Crime from
Liverpool Street (circular walk) approx 1 hour;
Celebrated Citizens of Old London from
Mansion House (ending in Cheapside, nearest
tube St. Paul's) approx 1 hour and The Trial
and Execution of King Charles I from
Westminster
Beautiful Belgravia: all year every Mon at
10.30. NB: Please call to confirm walk is avail-
able before setting out on: 0171 235 2591 or
0171 735 2784 or 0171 837 6520. Other walks
by arrangement please call above numbers for
fuller details
A£4.00 young C£Free C&Concessions£3.00.
Groups 20+ £2.50 each

Original London Walks

P O Box 1708 London NW6 4LW
[meeting points are given with each walk.
Travel Tip: to calculate how long an under-
ground journey in central London will take,
simply allow an average of three minutes
between stations]
Tel: 020 7624 3978/794 1764 Fax: 020 7625
1932
http://london.walks.com/
Cental office for a series of London Guided
Walks, call for full brochure
All year, see individual walks
Prices are dependant on walk chosen. Explorer
Days are priced separately. Discount Walkabout
Card available

Pied Piper Walks

19 Solent Road London NW6 1TP

[starting points will be given upon booking]
Tel: 020 7435 4782
Pied Piper Walks are somewhat unique in that
you can make a group booking (minimum of
5) and choose from their catalogue of 200
walks / themes on a date and time suitable for
you. There are walks suitable for just about
everyone, whether you'd like something for
the children, an historial theme, or even a pub
walk. Just call.
All year for pre-booked groups (min 5)
A£4.00 C£3.00

Stepping Out Guided Walks

32 Elvendon Road London N13 4SJ
[meeting points are given with each walk]
Tel: 020 8881 2933 Fax: 020 7405 6036
www.walklon.ndirect.co.uk
Stepping Out offers walks in a wide variety of
areas. The groups are usually small so you will
be able to see and hear our knowledgeable,
friendly guides. All our guides have recognised
guiding qualifications obtained through the
City University or the London Tourist Board
(Blue Badge). Tours start at or near a convenient transport point where your guide will be
displaying Stepping Out leaflets. Walks take
place in all weathers and regardless of numbers. Stepping Out guides can be booked for
private group walks at times and dates to suit
the group. If travelling by coach, we can
arrange a coach tour with stops for short
walks in areas best explored on foot. In addition to the subjects listed in the special events,
pre-booked tours can be arranged on the following themes: American London, Barbican,
Barnsbury, Broadgate, Children's Secret City,
Docklands, Fleet Street, The Financial City,
Golden Hinde Riverside Walk, Greenwich,
Inside Parliament, Islington, Library London,
Medical London, Oscar Wilde's London,
Primrose Hill, Regents Park, St Paul's Cathedral,
South Kensington, Tate Gallery Highlights,
Tower of London, Westminster Abbey. Away
Days in Bath, Canterbury, Stratford on Avon
and Windsor.
All year, details are available upon request
A£4.50 Concessions£3.50 except the Society of
London Theatre's walk and the Oxford Awayday

Theatre Royal Drury Lane

Catherine Street London WC2B 5JF
[Tube: Covent Garden]
Tel: 020 74945091/info 240535
Tour of the world's largest operational theatre
and home of the hit musical 'Miss Saigon.' Tells
the theatre's history and looks at the Royal
Box, front house, understage and backstage.
Tour conducted by highly knowledgeable and
experienced tour guide. School parties are

very welcome. Refreshements may be booked in advance. Photography is allowed but not of the Stage for Miss Saigon as this has a copyright.

All year Sun-Fri 12.30,14.15 and 16.45, Wed & Sat 11.00 and 13.00

A£7.50 C(0-14)£5.50. Group discounts available, call to book: 0171 494 5454

Theatre Royal Haymarket

Haymarket London SW1Y 4HT

[located opposite Charles II Street. NCP in Whitcomb Street. Coaches may set down outside the theatre with prior arrangement. Tube: Leicester Square / Piccadilly Circus]

Tel: 020 7930 8800 Bookings

In the Hay Market, in the very heart of London's West End, stands the theatre of perfection - Theatre Royal Haymarket. Royal in age, royal in story and truly royal in beauty and atmosphere. Celebrating 275 years - the theatre is ageless. The only Grade I listed Drama Theatre in our great city. The lure of the stage, deep in emotion, home of the finest British Drama, in the footsteps of the most celebrated Actors, street to stage, three centuries of 'pure theatre.' A one hour tour, a chance to explore what has never been seen by the public before. Illegal performances, riots and ghosts, satire and scandal and practical jokes. Parties between 10 & 20 will receive a special reduction. VIP and hospitality packages can be arranged promptly. Please contact Theatre Manager Mark Stradling 0171 930 8890

All year Tours times: Wed 17.30, Thur 12.30 & Sat 15.00

Tour price £12.00 per person.includes a live tour of approximately 60mins, ending pre-performance, and an exclusive souvenir

Walking Tours Jewish London

The Jewish Museum 80 East End Road London N3 2SY

[each walk has a pre-arranged meeting place call for leaflet showing details]

Tel: 020 8349 1143 Fax: 020 8343 2162

The Jewish Museum arranges specialised guided walks of Jewish London, for both groups and individuals. Our guides are experienced, well-informed volunteers with a wealth of knowledge. The Museum offers a wide range of tours of Jewish interest, including: The Jewish East End - Whitechapel, The Jewish East End - Spitalfields, The Jewish City of London, The Jewish West End & Sephardi London. Wherever possible, your guide will arrange for you to enter synagogues, cemetaries and other sites of interest.

Each walk has a pre-arranged date and time call for leaflet showing details

£5.00 £4.00 for Museum Friends. Pre-booked groups of 20-30 persons call for details

Heritage & Industrial

Bank of England Museum

Threadneedle Street London EC2R 8AH

[entrance in Bartholomew Lane. Tube: Bank]

Tel: 020 7601 5545 Fax: 020 7601 5808

www.bankofengland.co.uk

A fascinating insight into the world of banking and money from the Bank of England's foundation in 1694 to the present day. Unique displays of banknotes and gold bars. Experience the worlds of modern technology with the exciting interactive videos, and foreign exchange dealing games.

All year Mon-Fri 10.00-17.00. Closed weekends & Bank Hol

Admission Free

Guide Heritage Centre

17-19 Buckingham Palace Road London SW1W 0PT

[Tube: Victoria. Located in Palace Place on the corner of Palace Street]

Tel: 020 7834 6242 Fax: 020 7630 9052

Experience the interactive world of Guiding. Meet Brown Owl in the roots of her tree, experience life under canvas in Base Camp, find out how the Brownies got their name. Who started Guiding for girls? What is Guiding all about? And what are the challenges in the global world of Guiding today. The answers to all these questions and more can be found at The Guide Heritage Centre.

All year Mon-Sat 09.30-17.00. Closed Bank Hol

£2.50 per person

Kew Bridge Steam Museum

Green Dragon Lane Brentford Middlesex TW8 0EN

[100 yards from the N side of Kew Bridge, next to the tall Victorian Tower. Bus: 65, 237, 267, 391. BR: Kew Bridge. Tube: Gunnersbury / Kew Gardens]

Tel: 020 8568 4757 Fax: 020 8569 9978
www.cre.canon.co.uk/~davide/kbsm

Housed in massive Victorian pumping station. Unique collection of water pumping engines including world's largest working Beam Engine. In steam every weekend. New 'Water for Life' gallery explores the story of London's water. Waterwheel and diesel engine house.

All year daily 11.00-17.00. Closed Good Fri & Christmas week
Weekdays: A£2.80 C(5-15)£1.00
OAPs&Concessions£1.50 Family Ticket £7.00.
Weekends: A£3.80 C(5-15)£2.00
OAPs&Concessions£2.50 Family Ticket £10.50

Markfield Beam Engine and Museum
Markfield Road South Tottenham London N15 4RB
[BR/Tube: Seven Sisters / Tottenham Hale]
Tel: 020 8800 7061

1886 Beam Pumping Engine restored to working order in original building. Steaming certain weekends and by arrangement. Small exhibition to illustrate aspects of public health engineering for which the large pumping engine was developed. Parking on site is limited.

28 Mar-1 Nov Sun only except Easter Sun by prior arrangement on 01763 287331 if venue is unattended
A£3.00 Concessions£2.00 on steam days otherwise voluntary donation

Royal Mint Sovereign Gallery
7 Grosvenor Gardens London SW1W 0BH
[4mins walk from BR: Victoria and 10mins walk from Victoria Coach Station]
Tel: 020 7592 8601 Fax: 020 7592 8634
www.royalmint.com

The new Royal Mint Sovereign Gallery relates the 500-year old history of the famous Gold coin. A unique exhibition incorporating rare and priceless displays. The Gallery also offers for sale souvenir coin sets in gold and silver a perfect memento of your visit to the U.K. or as a gift for a very special occasion such as a Christening, Birthday or Wedding. During 1999 two special commemorative crowns will be issued for the Princess Diana Memorial and for the Millennium.

Mon-Fri 10.00-16.00. Closed Bank Hol Mon
Admission Free

discount offer: 10% off ANY product displayed

Historical

Albany
Albany Court Yard Piccadilly London W1
[Tube: Green Park / Piccadilly Circus]

These desirable and discreet bachelor apartments, half hidden through an entrance off Piccadilly, were built in 1803 by Henry Holland. Notable residents have included the poet Lord Byron, novelist Graham Greene, two Prime Ministers and the actor Terence Stamp. Married men were admitted in 1878 but could not bring their wives to live with them until 1919. Women are not allowed to live here in their own right.

To view from the outside only, any reasonable time
Admission Free

Alexandra Palace Trading Limited
Alexandra Palace Way Wood Green London N22 7AY
[M25 signposted. Tube: Wood Green. Bus: W3. Plenty of parking on site]
Tel: 020 8365 2121 Fax: 020 8883 3999
www.alexandrapalace.com

Opened in 1873, this majestic building is one of London's most famous landmarks, renowned as the birthplace of television. Set in 200 acres of parkland, it offers spectacular views of London's skyline. Attractions include a boating lake, pitch and putt golf course, Children's Playground, animal enclosure, conservation area, ice-skating and ice hockey, a café and the Phoenix Bar.

visitor comments: Great fun! The ice-skating is particularly enjoyable, and the stewards are a great help for first-timers.

Palm Court: All year daily 10.00-23.00.
Alexandra Park: All year daily 10.00-23.00
Admission Free

discount offer: Two For The Price Of One For

Ice Rink

↓ *special events*

▶ **Sailboat and Windsurf Show 2000**
4/3/00-5/3/00
Call the organiser, the Royal Yachting Association, on 01703 627425 for details

▶ **Alexander Palace Antique and Collectors Fair**
12/3/00-12/3/00
For more information please call the organisers, Pig and Whistle Promotions on 020 8883 7061

▶ **Antique and Collectors Fair**
12/3/00-19/11/00
Held on Mar 12, May 14, Sept 24 and Nov 19 only. London's largest Antiques Fair with over 700 stands plus furniture selling wide range of quality items

▶ **The London Classic Motor Show**
18/3/00-19/3/00
Commences 10.00-18.00. A£7.50 C(5-16)£3.00 OAPs£6.50

▶ **Spring Craft Fair**
22/4/00-24/4/00
Please call Marathon Event Management on 01273 833884 for more details

▶ **Afro Hair & Beauty 2000**
28/5/00-29/5/00
The latest hair and beauty ideas for black women, including fashion shows.

▶ **Children's Summer Fun Fair**
10/6/00-10/9/00
Family fun held on the boating lake car park, with a selection of rides and stalls themed for children and parents. Open weekends only up to July 16, 12.00-19.00 and then daily 12.00-20.00

▶ **The Evening Standard Hot Tickets Theme World Experience Show '99**
16/6/00-18/6/00
A show for all the family featuring theme parks, visitor attractions and fun days out!

▶ **Cyprus Wine Festival**
1/7/00-2/7/00
Promoting Cypriot products, especially the wine, and bringing the Cypriot Community together

▶ **4th Mind Sports Olympiad**
19/8/00-28/8/00
Call MSO Worldwide Ltd on 01707 659080 for further details

▶ **Iftex 2000**
2/9/00-3/9/00
Please call the organisers, Nexus Media Ltd/Nexus Horticulture on 01322 660070 for details

▶ **The National Self Build Homes Show**
14/9/00-17/9/00

▶ **The Knitting and Stitching Show**
12/10/00-15/10/00
For further details, please call Creative Exhibitions Ltd on 020 8690 8888

▶ **Dolls House Fair and Teddy Bear Fair 'The Event of 2000'**
25/11/00-26/11/00

Open 10.00-17.00 daily. Sat: Collector's day tickets £8.00-£10.00 in advance by calling 01903 244900... One of the largest fairs of its type anywhere in the world, with hundreds and hundreds of stands to see, with stalls for everyone from the fascinated newcomer to the avid collector

▶ **Christmas Craft Fair and Festive Table**
1/12/00-3/12/00
Please call Marathon Event Management on 01273 833884 for more information

Blewcoat School Gift Shop

23 Caxton Street Westminster London SW1H 0PY
[near the junction with Buckingham Gate, Tube: St James's Park. BR: Victoria]
Tel: 020 7222 2877
A National Trust Property. Built in 1709 at the expense of William Green, a local brewer, to provide an education for poor children. The building was in use as a school until 1926, bought by the Trust in 1954 and restored in 1975. It is now the NT London Information Centre and Shop.
All year Mon-Fri 10.00-17.30 Thur 10.00-19.00. Open Sat 28 Nov, 5, 12 & 19 Dec 11.00-16.30. Closed Bank Hol Mon, Good Fri & 25 Dec-1 Jan inclusive
Admission Free

Boston Manor House

1-19 Boston Manor Road Brentford Middlesex TW8 9JX
[in Boston Manor Road, Tube: Boston Manor]
Tel: 020 8560 5441 Fax: 020 8862 4595
Boston Manor House is a fine Jacobean Manor built in 1623, extended in 1670 when the Clitherow family bought the house. It was their family home until 1924. Boston Manor is renowned for its fine English Renaissance plaster ceilings and contains a selection from the local collection of paintings.
Weekends & Bank Hol Mon from first Sat in Apr-end Oct 14.30-17.00
Admission Free

Brunel's Engine House

Railway Avenue Rotherhithe London SE16 4LP
[Tube: Rotherhithe, situated behind the tube station. Brunel Road the B205. Situated at the heart of the St Mary's Rotherhithe conservation area]
Tel: 0207 231 3840 Fax: 020 8806 4325
The Tunnel was the first major underwater thoroughfare in the world. It construction, between 1825 and 1843, was a triumph of

ingenuity and perseverance in the face of floods, financial losses and human disaster. The Tunnel was opened as a pedestrian route but was sold to a railway company in 1865. It now carries London Underground East London Line trains between Rotherhite. An 80ft diameter shaft, dating from 1825, stands next to the engine house. The shaft was used for building the tunnel and was later adapted for the pedestrian staircase in use between 1843 and 1869. It is now disused but a similar shaft on the north bank of the Thames now forms part of the East London Line's Wapping station. The Engine House, now designated an ancient monument and listed building grade II, contains the sole surviving example of a compound horizontal V steam pumping engine, built by J & G Rennie of Southwark in 1885, and a fascinating exhibition 'Brunel's Tunnel and where it led.'

Apr-Oct Sat & Sun 13.00-17.00, Nov-Mar 1st Sun of every month 13.00-17.00. Other times by arrangement
Last Admission: 15.30
A£2.00 C£1.00 Family Ticket £5.00
Concessions£1.00

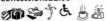

Burgh House
New End Square London NW3 1LT
[end of M1 then A502 via Golders Green / Hampstead Village or from Central London via Swiss Cottage or Camden Town. Tube: Hampstead]
Tel: 020 7431 0144
A Grade I listed building of 1703 in the heart of old Hampstead with original panelled rooms, 'barley sugar' staircase balusters and a Music Room. Home of the Hampstead Museum, permanent and changing exhibition. Prize-winning terraced garden and licensed basement Buttery. Regular programme of Concerts, Art Exhibitions, and Meetings. Receptions, Seminars and Conferences. Licensed for Weddings. Rooms for hire.
All year Wed-Sun 12.00-17.00, Good Fri & Bank Hol Mon 14.00-17.00
Admission Free
↓ *special events*
▶ **From a Wild Heath in Wales**
1/3/00-5/3/00
▶ **Heath and Hampstead Society Walk**
5/3/00-5/3/00
▶ **Face to Face Discussion Series**
9/3/00-9/3/00
Two leading contemporary architects debate the uses and misuses of architecture. Call for details, £8.00, wine included
▶ **Music Concert**
12/3/00-12/3/00
A variety of music at 14.30. Tickets A£8.00, Concessions£6.00 in advance only. Call 020 8341

6073 or 020 8455 4009
▶ **Pupil's Concert**
12/3/00-12/3/00
Musical soirèe of all ages and stages at 18.00. A£4.00, £1.00 non-performing children
▶ **Hampstead Music Club**
14/3/00-14/3/00
Master Class given by Norma Fisher for piano, solo, duet or with instrument
▶ **"The Haydn Interview"**
19/3/00-19/3/00
Dramatised biography of Haydn, in period costume including sonatas for piano. Tickets A£6.00 and Concessions £4.00. Call 020 8904 6100
▶ **Musical Concert**
26/3/00-26/3/00
Including work by J S Bach. Tickets A£10.00 and Concessions £5.00. Call 020 8341 9897
▶ **Print and Drawing Exhibition**
29/3/00-16/4/00
Two printmakers working mostly in wood, lino and silkscreen. Strong and colourful landscapes and abstracts

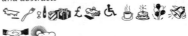

Carew Manor And Dovecote
Church Road Wallington Surrey SM6 7NH
[Church Road Beddington off A232 1m E of junction with A237 BR: Waddon then bus 407 or 408]
Tel: 020 8770 4781 Fax: 020 8770 4666
Grade I listed late-medieval Great Hall, with its arch-braced hammer-beam roof, together with the restored early 18th century Dovecote.
June-July & Aug. Guided tours for Groups in School Holidays and weekends
A£2.00 C&Students£1.00

Carlyle's House
24 Cheyne Row Chelsea London SW3 5HL
[off Cheyne Walk between Battersea & Albert Bridges on Chelsea embankment or off Oakley Street. Tube: Sloane Sq, BR: Victoria]
Tel: 020 7352 7087
A National Trust Property. This Queen Anne town house was the home of the Victorian writer and historian Thomas Carlyle, and his wife Jane from 1834 until their deaths. The life and times of the Carlyles can be seen through the original furniture and decoration of the house, together with the many books, portraits and personal relics acquired by the Carlyles.
1 Apr-1 Nov Wed-Sun & Bank Hol Mon 11.00-17.00. Closed Good Fri
Last Admission: 16.30
A£3.40 C(5-16)£1.70. NT Members Free

London

Carshalton House

St Philomena's School Pound Street Carshalton Surrey SM5 3PN
[at junction with Carshalton Road BR: Carshalton]
Tel: 020 8770 4781 Fax: 020 8770 4666
A mansion built around 1707 with grounds laid out originally by Charles Bridgeman. The principal rooms contain 18th century decoration and garden buildings include a Hermitage and unique Water Tower, with Delft-tiled plunge bath. Guided tours and refreshments available. Free parking.
Open on limited occasions during Spring & Summer. Please call for details. Water Tower open Easter-end Sept Sun 14.30-17.00
Last Admission: 16.15
A£3.00 C£1.50

Chenies Manor House

Chenies Rickmansworth Hertfordshire WD3 6ER
[J18 M25, off A404 between Amersham & Rickmansworth BR: Chorleywood]
Tel: 01494 762888 Fax: 01494 762888
15/16th century Manor House with fortified tower. Housing contemporary tapestries and furniture, hiding places, collection of antique dolls, medieval undercroft and well. Surrounded by beautiful gardens, a Tudor sunken garden, a white garden, herbaceous borders, a fountain court, a physic garden containing a large selection of medical and culinary herbs and much more. Member of the Historic Houses Association.
First week in Apr-end Oct Wed & Thur 14.00-17.00, Bank Hol Mon 14.00-17.00
Last Admission: 16.15
House and Gardens: A£4.20 C(0-14)£2.00. Party bookings by arrangement. Gardens only: A£2.10

Chiswick House

Burlington Lane Chiswick London W4 2RD
[signposted off A4. Tube: Turnham Green. BR: Chiswick, 0.25m]

Tel: 020 8995 0508 Fax: 020 8742 3104
Lord Burlington's masterpiece built circa 1728 is one of England's first and finest Palladian villas. The ornately decorated interior includes the dazzling Blue Velvet Room. Beautifully laid out classical gardens with statues, urns and obelisks surround the House, as well as the newly restored water cascade. It has been said that a ghost of one of the past cooks prepares a full English Breakfast in the last afternoon. Such visitations are few and far between, and, when you consider that smell eminates from kitchens which have not existed for over 100 years it is rather spooky!
1Apr-30 Sept daily 10.00-18.00. 1 Oct-31 Oct daily 10.00-17.00. 1 Nov-31 Mar Wed-Sun 10.00-16.00. Closed 24-26 Dec
A£3.00 C(0-5)£Free C(5-16)£1.50 Concessions£2.30. EH Members £Free Price alterations from 1 Apr A£3.30 Concessions£2.50

↓*special events*

▶ **May Day, 1740**
30/4/00-1/5/00
From Noon. Celebrate May Day in period style! Make garlands and see the crowning of the May Queen

▶ **The Soprano In Pink**
10/6/00-11/6/00
From 13.00. Delightful Georgian song and spinet music, with gossip and talks about period fashion

▶ **Jurassic Giants!**
17/6/00-18/6/00
From Noon. Meet two 17th century comic archaeologists and help them reconstruct dinosaur skeletons

▶ **Tea and Scandal!**
27/8/00-28/8/00
From Noon. Enjoy the latest scandalous London gossip with Lady Devonshire!

▶ **Georgian Christmas Fun**
9/12/00-10/12/00
From Noon. Meet Lady Burlington and make an 18th century mask. Fun for all the family!

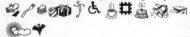

Coalhouse Fort

Princess Margaret Road East Tilbury Village Tilbury Essex RM18 8PB
[A13, signposted from junction of A13 and A128]
Tel: 01375 844203
The best example of a Victorian case mate fortress in the South East. Living history displays and museums. All set in an attractive riverside park. Thought to be the largest scheduled monument in voluntary care.
Last Sun Mar-Oct, 2nd Sun Apr-Sept, 4 days of Easter, all Bank Hol Mon 11.00-17.00

Last Admission: 16.00 or 60mins before closing
Queuing Times: Tours may be by timed ticket
A£2.00 Accompanied C(5-16)£1.00

College of Arms

Queen Victoria Street London EC4V 4BT
[N side of Queen Victoria Street, S of St Paul's
Cathedral. Tube: Blackfriars / St Paul's]
Tel: 020 7248 2762 Fax: 020 7248 6448
1670's mansion housing English Officers of
Arms and their records. Earl Marshal's Court
open to public. Record Room open for tours
(groups up to 20) by prior arrangement with
Officer in Waiting. Advice on Arms and geneal-
ogy available on request.
All year Mon-Fri 10.00-16.00. Closed Public Hol,
State and Special Occasions
Last Admission: 16.00
Admission Free Parties by arrangement

Dennis Severs House

18 Folgate Street London E1 6BX
[Tube/BR: Liverpool Street]
Tel: 020 7247 4013
The house is a time capsule - sometimes
opened. It's owner, Dennis Severs, is an artist
who uses his visitor's imagination as his canvas, and who lives in the house in much the
same way today as its original occupants
might have done in the early 18th century. The
Experience, conducted in silence, titled by Mr
Severs as 'Still-life Drama' enables the visitor
to become lost in another time as they appear
to be on their own.
All year, 1st Sun of each Month 14.00-17.00 no
booking necessary. 1st Mon of each Month,
evenings, booking essential
Sunday tour: A£7.00. Monday tour: A£10.00

Down House - Home of Charles Darwin
Luxted Road Downe Orpington Kent BR6 7JT
[off A233 signposted]
Tel: 01689 859119 Fax: 01689 862755
www.english-heritage.org.uk
See the home of one of the world's greatest
scientists, Charles Darwin. It was from his

study in Down House that Darwin worked on
his most famous and controversial life and work, 'On
the Origins of Species.' The ground floor has
been recreated to its appearance in Darwin's
time. The first floor contains an interactive
exhibition detailing Darwin's life and work.
Down House operates a timed ticket system
(12 July-10 Sept if travelling by car).
1-31 Mar Wed-Sun 10.00-16.00. 1 Apr-31 Oct
Wed-Sun 10.00-18.00, 17.00 in Oct. 1 Nov-31
Dec Wed-Sun 10.00-16.00. Closed 24-26 Dec &
Jan 2001.
Last Admission: 30mins before closing
A£5.50 C(0-5)£Free C(5-16)£2.80
Concessions£4.10. EH Members £Free

Eastbury Manor House

Barking Essex IG11 9SN
[in Eastbury Square 10mins walk S from Upney
station. BR: Barking then one stop on Tube:
District Line to Upney]
Tel: 020 8507 0119
An important example of a medium-sized
Elizabethan manor house. Eastbury Manor
House is let to the London Borough Council of
Barking and Dagenham for use as an Arts and
Cultural Centre. Limited street parking. Dogs
in garden only.
By appointment with Administrator. Also open
first Sat in each month except Aug 10.00-16.00,
call for details
£1.60. Group visits by prior arrangement, rates
on application. 1999 price due for review April
1999

Fenton House

Windmill Hill Hampstead London NW3 6RT
[Visitors' entrance on W side of Hampstead
Grove. Tube: Hampstead. BR: Hampstead
Heath]
Tel: 020 7435 3471 Fax: 020 7435 3471
A National Trust Property. A delightful late
17th century merchant's house, set on the
winding streets of Old Hampstead. The charming interior contains an outstanding collection
of porcelain, needlework and furniture. The
Benton Fletcher Collection of Early Keyboard
Instruments is also at Fenton; sometimes visitors will find a music scholar playing one of
the instruments. Fenton is set in walled gardens, with formal lawn and walks, an orchard
and vegetable garden, and fine wrought iron
gates. Disabled access to ground floor only.
6 Mar-4 Apr Weekends only 14.00-17.00. 7 Apr-
31 Oct Wed-Fri 14.00-17.00 Sat-Sun & Bank Hol
Mon 11.00-17.00. Groups at other times by
appointment
Last Admission: 30mins before closing

A£4.10 C£2.05 Family Ticket £10.250. No reduction for Groups

⌖ ❀

Freud Museum

20 Maresfield Gardens Hampstead London NW3 5SX

[Tube: Finchley Road]

Tel: 020 7435 2002/435 5167 Fax: 020 7431 5452

Sigmund Freud left his home in Vienna (1938) as a refugee from Nazi occupation and chose exile in England, transferring his entire domestic and working environment to this house. He resumed work until his death a year later. Bequeathed by his daughter Anna Freud whose pioneering development of her father's work is also represented. Freud's collections include: Egyptian, Greek, Roman, and Oriental antiquities, plus fine Oriental rugs. The household contains Biedermeier furniture. Guided Tours for pre-booked groups.

All year Wed-Sun 12.00-17.00. Closed Bank Hol, 24-26 Dec

A£3.00 C(0-12)£Free C(12-18)&Concessions£1.50

Geffrye Museum

Kingsland Road London E2 8EA

[Buses: 149 / 242 / 243 or 67. Tube: Liverpool Street then bus 149 or 242 / Old Street (exit 2), then bus 243, situated on A10 Kingsland Road. Meter parking in surrounding streets]

Tel: 020 7739 9893 Fax: 020 7729 5647

www.geffrye-museum.org.uk

One of London's most friendly and enjoyable museums, the Geffrye specialises in the domestic interiors of the urban middle class. Its displays span from 1600 to 2000, forming a sequence of period rooms which capture the quintessential nature of English interior style. The museum is set in elegant, 18th century buildings, just north of the City. It is surrounded by beautiful gardens including an award-winning walled herb garden and a series of historical garden rooms which highlight the key changes in urban middle-class gardens from the 17th to the 20th centuries (open April to October). The museum and gardens are regularly brought to life through an innovative programme of special exhibitions, seminars, workshops, drama and music. New for this year is the 70 seater restaurant.

visitor comments: Interesting period gardens. The herb garden is particularly fascinating, as it shows the uses for each herb. One of London's best kept secrets! A great place to take visitors.

All year Tue-Sat 10.00-17.00, Sun & Bank Hol Mon 12.00-17.00. Closed Mon, Good Fri, 24-26, 31 Dec & 1 Jan

Admission Free

↓ special events

► **Matthew Hilton - Furniture for our time**

15/2/00-9/7/00

Exhibition will feature some of the most successful designs of Matthew Hilton, one of the UK's leading furniture designers

► **Contemporary Furniture 1 & 2**

23/2/00-2/7/00

Show #1, 23 Feb -30 Apr 2000. Show #2, 3 May-2 July. Two consecutive shows highlight the fine quality and innovative work of selected furniture designers from East London

► **Contemporary Furniture 1 and 2**

23/2/00-2/7/00

Show 1 Feb 23-Apr 30 and Show 2 May 3-July 2. Shows featuring recent work by five East London furniture designers

► **Eco Furniture: Workshop for Adults**

4/3/00-4/3/00

► **Heavy Metal: Workshop for Adults**

25/3/00-1/4/00

Two-day workshop in which participants have the opportunity to explore casting with metal. Tickets £36.00 (inc materials but not lunch) 11.00-16.00

► **Fantastic Plastics**

8/4/00-8/4/00

For teenagers aged 13-15. Participants make their own light or clock using fun coloured plastic. £5.00 per ticket, 11.00-16.00

► **Easter Workshop: Material World**

25/4/00-28/4/00

For ages 6-15, 10.30-12.45 and 14.00-16.00. Design with plastics, metals and wood. Children under 8 must be accompanied. First served basis 30 mins in advance

► **Easter Workshops: Making a Mirror Frame**

29/4/00-29/4/00

For children aged 3-5. 14.00 and 15.15. Children must be accompanied. First served basis 30 mins in advance

George Inn

77 Borough High Street Southwark London SE1

[on E side of Borough High Street near London Bridge Station. Tube BR: London Bridge]

Tel: 020 7407 2056

A National Trust Property. The only remaining galleried inn in London, famous as a coaching inn in the 17th century, and mentioned by Dickens in Little Dorrit. The George Inn is leased to and run by Whitbread plc as a public house. Children admitted subject to normal licensing regulations.

During licensing hours

Admission Free

Guildhall

Gresham Street London EC2P 2EJ
[Tube: Bank / St Paul's]
Tel: 020 7606 3030 Fax: 020 7332 1987
The Court of Common Council administers the
City of London and meets in the Guildhall.
Dating from 1411 the building was badly
damaged in the Great Fire and the Blitz.
Beneath it lies a 15th century crypt. The Clock
Museum charts 500 years of time-keeping. The
Guildhall Library has an unrivalled collection
of manuscripts, books and illustrations. Pre-
booked Guildhall Guided Tours by calling The
Keepers Office 0171 332 1460. To view the
Clock Museum contact the Guildhall Library.
All year. Winter: Mon-Sat 10.00-17.00.
Summer: Mon-Sun 10.00-17.00. Closed during
functions
Admission Free

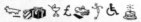

Hall Place

Bourne Road Bexley Kent DA5 1PQ
[BR: Bexley. Nr J of A2 and A233 signposted]
Tel: 01322 526574 Fax: 01322 522921
Hall Place is an attractive mansion of che-
quered flint and brick, but it is most interest-
ing for its garden. Topiary in the form of the
'Queen Beasts'; rose, rock, peat and water gar-
dens; and a herb garden with a fascinating
range of plants for medicine and cooking.
Photography allowed by permit.
All year House: Summer Mon-Sat 10.00-17.00,
Sun & Bank Hol 14.00-18.00. Winter Mon-Sat
10.00-16.15. Gardens: Mon-Fri 07.30-dusk, Sat
& Sun 09.00-dusk
Admission Free

↓*special events*
▶ **Chronical of the Century Exhibition**
12/1/00-2/4/00
A collection of photographs covering events in
Bexley during the last century
▶ **Tilting at Windmills Exhibition**
25/2/00-26/3/00
Around Bexley in the 1820s with Paul Linington
▶ **Book Fairs**
4/3/00-4/11/00
Held on Mar 4, Apr 22, Aug 5, Sept 23 and Nov 4

only
▶ **Rush on Paper Exhibition**
1/4/00-1/5/00
Life size papier mache by sculptor Peter Rush
▶ **Pans and Polish Exhibition**
15/4/00-18/6/00
The life of a maid in Victorian Times
▶ **International Marquetry Exhibition**
6/5/00-29/5/00
Woodcraft at its finest
▶ **World Wildlife Photographer of the Year**
Exhibition 1999
3/6/00-9/7/00
▶ **Bexley 2000 Exhibition**
4/7/00-4/11/00
From settlement to suburb
▶ **Paladins of Chivalry Weekend**
15/7/00-16/7/00
A Middle Ages encampment with jousting etc.
▶ **Bexley Local Studies History Trail**
1/8/00-2/8/00
An outdoor event for children
▶ **Bexley Garden Festival Weekend**
2/9/00-3/9/00
▶ **Bexley Local Studies History Fair**
16/9/00-16/9/00
▶ **Open Art Exhibition**
4/11/00-2/12/00
Bexley Arts Council

Ham House

Ham Street Richmond Surrey TW10 7RS
[on S bank of Thames W of A307 at Petersham.
Tube/BR: Richmond, then Bus: 371]
Tel: 020 8940 1950 Fax: 020 8332 6903
A National Trust Property. Outstanding Stuart
house built on the banks of the River Thames
in 1610 and enlarged in the 1670's. Contains
rare survivals of the 17th century, including
exquisite closets, fine furniture, textiles and
pictures. Garden returned to its 17th century
framework with continuing work to reinstate
it to its former glory. South Terrace borders
replanted in formal late 17th-century style;
kitchen restored to early 18th-century original
appearance.
House: 1 Apr-29 Oct Sat-Wed 13.00-17.00.
Garden: Sat-Wed 10.30-18.00 or dusk if sooner.
Orangery tea-room, tea garden & shop: Mar,
Nov & Dec Sat & Sun 11.00-16.30. Apr-Oct Sat-
Wed 11.00-17.30. Closed 25-26 Dec & 1 Jan
Last Admission: 30mins before closing
House: A£5.00 Family Ticket £12.50. Garden:
£1.50 Pre-booked Groups 15+ A£4.00 C£2.00.
Parking: £Free not NT
↓*special events*
▶ **Spring Plant Fair**
14/5/00-14/5/00
Buy plants and enjoy a walk around Ham

House. Telephone 020 8940 1950 for information, 11.00-15.00, usual admission

▶ **Last Night of the Summer Proms**

25/6/00-25/6/00

British Concert Orchestra. Bring a picnic and seating. Send a SAE and cheque to Princess Alice Hospice, West End Lane, Esher, KT10 8NA or phone 01372 461855, A£16.00 C£8.00, 18.00 for 19.00

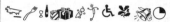

Hogarth's House

Hogarth Lane Great West Road Chiswick London W4 2QN

[50yds W of Hogarth roundabout on Great West Road. Tube: Turnham Green]

Tel: 020 8994 6757

Small Georgian house once the home of William Hogarth, now a print gallery and has on view many of his famous engravings. It has a secluded garden and Hogarth's Mulberry Tree. Has recently been refurbished with money from the National Lottery Heritage fund. New exhibition celebrating the tri-centenary of his birth, including detailed information on the pictures, Hogarth and what it was like to live in London during his lifetime.

Nov-Mar Tue-Fri 13.00-16.00, Weekends 13.00-17.00. Apr-Oct Tue-Fri 13.00-17.00, Weekends 13.00-18.00. Closed 25 & 26 Dec, Jan & Good Fri

Admission Free

Horse Guards

Whitehall London SW1

[Tube: Westminster]

Tel: 0891 505452

Once Henry VIII's tiltyard (tournament ground), the Changing of the Guard still takes place here every day. The elegant buildings, completed in 1755, were designed by William Kent. On the left, as you pass on to the parade ground, is the Old Treasury, also by Kent.

Changing of the Guard & Dismounting Ceremonies: All year daily, please see special events for details

Admission Free

↓*special events*

▶ **Changing The Guard Ceremonies**

1/1/00-31/12/00

Mon-Sat 11.00, Sun 10.00 at Tilt Yard, forecourt of Horse Guards building.

Iveagh Bequest, Kenwood House

Hampstead Lane London NW3 7JR

[Bus: 210 from; Tube: Golders Green / Archway or Hampstead (then 20 min walk)]

Tel: 020 8348 1286 Fax: 020 7973 3891

www.english-heritage.org.uk

Visit the idyllic country retreat of Kenwood, remodelled by Robert Adam in the 1760s including the magnificent library. The house is home to the world famous Iveagh Bequest collection of paintings, which includes masterpieces by Rembrandt, Vermeer, Turner and Gainsborough. Outside, enjoy over a hundred acres of landscaped parkland with ornamental lakes and amazing views over London. Wheelchair access to ground floor only. Enjoy a season of summer concerts at the Kenwood Lakeside.

1 Apr-30 Sept daily 10.00-18.00. 1-31 Oct daily 10.00-17.00. 1 Nov-31 Mar daily 10.00-16.00. Closed 24-25 Dec

House & Grounds: Admission Free. Some Special Events are charged

↓*special events*

▶ **East, Drink and be Merry!**

27/6/00-24/9/00

A fascinating exhibition of food which explores the history and habits of the British at table, 1600-2000.

▶ **Victorian Vittles!**

9/7/00-9/7/00

Visit the 1900 kitchen, learn about Mrs Beeton, household management and recipes to try at home

▶ **Georgian Grub!**

16/7/00-16/7/00

The fad for French food in 1800 Britain, with salads, jellies and crystallised fruit. Plus the history of tea

▶ **Tudor Tucker!**

23/7/00-23/7/00

From comfits of cloves to sweetmeats and handraised pies - Tudor cookery of 1600

▶ **Victorian Vittles!**

10/9/00-10/9/00

See entry for 9 July

▶ **Georgian Grub!**

17/9/00-17/9/00

See entry for 16 July
► **Tudor Tucker!**
24/9/00-24/9/00
See entry for 23 July

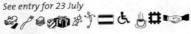

Jewel Tower
Abingdon Street Westminster London SW1 3JY
[Tube: Westminster, opposite South end of Houses of Parliament. No parking except public car parks]
Tel: 020 7222 2219
www.english-heritage.org.uk
The Jewel Tower is one of two surviving buildings of the original Palace of Westminster. It was built circa 1365 to house the personal treasure of Edward III. The Jewel Tower is currently home to the 'Parliament Past and Present' exhibition and a new touch screen computer gives a virtual reality tour of both Houses of Parliament.
1Apr-30 Sept daily 10.00-18.00. 1-31 Oct daily 10.00-17.00. 1 Nov-31 Mar 2001 daily 10.00-16.00. Closed 24-26 Dec
A£1.50 C(0-5)£Free C(5-16)£0.80 Concessions£1.10. EH Members £Free

Keats House
Keats Grove Hampstead London NW3 2RR
[Tube: Hampstead]
Tel: 020 7435 2062 Fax: 020 7431 9293
The two Regency houses were occupied by John Keats and his fiancée Fanny Brawne. They have now been converted into one building and form a museum devoted to the life of this famous poet. Manuscripts, letters and personal mementoes are displayed.

CLOSED UNTIL FURTHER NOTICE FOR URGENT REPAIR WORK. PLEASE CALL: FOR CURRENT INFORMATION. All year Apr-Oct Mon-Fri 10.00-13.00 & 14.00-18.00, Sat 10.00-13.00 & 14.00-17.00, Sun & Bank Hol 14.00-17.00, Nov-Mar Mon-Fri 13.00-17.00, Sat 10.00-13.00 & 14.00-17.00, Sun 14.00-17.00. Closed Good Fri, Easter eve, May Day, 24-26 Dec, 1 Jan
Admission Free

Lincoln's Inn
London WC2A 3TL
[Tube: Chancery Lane / Holborn / Aldwych]
Tel: 020 7405 1393 Fax: 020 7831 1839
www.lincolnsinn.org.uk
In the heart of Central London lies Lincoln's Inn, the oldest of the Inn's of Court a haven from the roar of traffic and crowded pavements. The buildings complex includes The Great Hall, one of London's finest Tudor Revival buildings, The Old Hall, erected in 1490 and the Chapel whose bell is said to have been brought back from Spain in 1596 as part of the spoils of Cadiz. The grounds can be explored freely during opening times.
All year Mon-Thur 09.00-17.30, Fri 9.00-17.00

Lindsey House
99-100 Cheyne Walk London SW10 0DQ
[on Cheyne Walk W of Battersea Bridge near junction with Milman's Street on Chelsea Embankment, Tube: South Kensington BR: Victoria]
Tel: 01494 528051 Fax: 01494 463310
A National Trust Property. Part of Lindsey House was built in 1674 on the site of Sir Thomas More's garden, overlooking the River Thames. It has one of the finest 17th century exteriors in London. Nearest parking Battersea Park. Inaccessible to wheelchairs.
Ground floor entrance hall & garden room, main staircase to first floor and the front and rear gardens by written appointment only on the following dates: 16 Apr, 21 May, 20 June, 9 July, 19 Sept & 15 Oct 14.00-16.00. Please write to R Bourne, 100 Cheyne Walk, London SW10. Admission Free

Linley Sambourne House
18 Stafford Terrace Kensington London W8 7BH
[Tube: High Street Kensington]
Tel: 020 7937 0663 Fax: 020 7371 2467
The home of Linley Sambourne (1844-1910), chief political cartoonist at Punch, has had its magnificent artistic interior preserved, almost unchanged since the late 19th century. Step back in time into the best surviving middle-

class victorian Town House in Britain.
*Mar-Oct Wed 10.00-16.00, Sun guided tours
only: 14.15, 15.15 & 16.15 (tours 45min). For
Groups of 12+ by appointment only
Last Admission: 30mins before closing
A£3.50 C£2.00 OAPs£2.50 Family Ticket(2A&2C)
£ 10.00. Group rates on application*

London Wall
Tower Hill London EC3
*[Tube: Tower Hill. BR: Fenchurch Street 0.5m.
Bus: frequent from surrounding areas]*
Tel: 020 7222 1234
The best preserved piece of the Roman Wall,
heightened in the Middle Ages, which formed
part of the eastern defences of the City of
London.
*Any reasonable time
Admission Free*

Marble Hill House and Park
Richmond Road Twickenham London TW1 2NL
[Tube: Richmond. BR: St Margaret's]
**Tel: 020 8892 5115 Fax: 020 8607 9976
www.english-heritage.org.uk**
This perfect English Palladian villa, set beside
the River Thames, was built in 1724 for
Henrietta Howard, Countess of Suffolk and
mistress of King George II. The house contains
important early Georgian paintings and furniture and the lavishly gilded Great Room. There
are a range of sports facilities to be enjoyed in
the park and concerts through the summer.
Limited disabled access.
*1 Apr-30 Sept daily 10.00-18.00. 1-21 Oct daily
10.00-17.00. 22 Oct-31 Mar Wed-Sun 10.00-
16.00. Closed 24-26 Dec & 1-16 Jan
A£3.30 C(0-5)£Free C(5-16)£1.70
Concessions£2.50. EH Members £Free*

↓*special events*
► **Easter Fun**
23/4/00-24/4/00
*From 12.00 with Beaux Stratagems. Enjoy an
Easter Egg Hunt and make your own Easter hat*
► **A Regency Tea-Break**
13/5/00-14/5/00

*From 12.00 with Hogarth's Heroes Comic
Georgian decorators bravely recreating the
Battle of Waterloo using everyday objects!*
► **The Soprano in Pink**
28/5/00-29/5/00
*With Rhiannon Gayle, from 13.00. Delightful
Georgian song and spinet music, with gossip
and talks about period fashion*
► **Ghostly Goings On**
28/10/00-29/10/00
*From 12.00 with Beaux Stratagems. Wear your
scariest Halloween costume, join the footman
for a ghostly tour of the house and listen to
chilling tales*
► **Georgian Christmas Fun**
16/12/00-17/12/00
*Fun for all the family at 12.00 with Beaux
Stratagems. Meet Lady Suffolk and make an
18th century mask*

Middle Temple Hall
The Temple London EC4Y 9AT
*[Tube: Temple / Blackfriars, no parking in the
near vacinity]*
Tel: 020 7427 4800 Fax: 020 7427 4801
Middle Temple Hall is a fine example of Tudor
architecture and was built during the reign of
Elizabeth I completed around 1570. Pre-
booked guided tours available upon request,
groups only, small charge may be applicable.
*All year Mon-Fri 10.00-12.00 & 15.00-16.00, if
available. Closed Bank Hol
Admission Free*

Museum of Fulham Palace
Bishops Avenue London SW6 6EA
[Tube: Putney Bridge]
Tel: 020 7736 3233 Fax: 020 7736 3233
The former residence of the Bishop of London
(Tudor with Georgian additions and a
Victorian chapel). Three rooms available for
functions including receptions. The museum
(in part of the Palace) tells the story of this
ancient site. The displays include paintings,
archaeology, garden history and architecture.
Tours visit the gardens and Palace.
*Grounds, Botanic Garden and herb collection:
daily during daylight hours. Museum: Mar-Oct
Wed-Sun 14.00-17.00 and Bank Hol Mon Nov-
Feb Thur-Sun 13.00-16.00. Guided Tours every
2ns Sun of the month at 14.00. Closed Good Fri
& 25 Dec
A£0.50 (accompanied)C£Free Concessions£0.25.
During Exhibitions A£1.00 accompanied C£Free
Concessions£0.50. Guided Tours: A£2.00*

Number Two Willow Road

2 Willow Road Hampstead London NW3 1TH

[Car Parking: limited street parking, East Heath Road municipal car park (100mtrs). Tube: Hampstead / Belsize Park, BR: Hampstead Heath]

Tel: 020 7435 6166 Fax: 020 7435 6166

A National Trust Property. Erno Goldfinger's house designed and built by him in 1939. The central part of a block of three, it was his family's home until his death in 1987, and that of his widow Ursula until 1991. Filled with furniture designed by Goldfinger and works of art he collected. Cinema showing introductory film. 1998 London Small Attraction of the Year.

1 Apr-30 Oct Thur-Sat 12.00-17.00. Closed Good Fri. Entry by Guided Tour only every 45mins from 12.15-16.00 60mins duration max. 12 persons

Last Admission: 16.00

A£4.10. Pre-booked Groups max 12

Old Speech Room Gallery

Harrow School High Street Harrow Middlesex HA1 3HP

[off the High Street]

Tel: 020 8869 1205/422 2196

Situated in the Old Schools at Harrow School, Old Speech Room Gallery was designed by Alan Irvine in 1976. It houses the School's collections: Egyptian and Greek antiquities, watercolours, some Modern British pictures, printed books, natural history. Tour parties can be arranged, call 0181 422 2303

Term time daily Mon-Sun 14.30-17.00. Closed Wed

Admission Free

Pitshanger Manor and Gallery

Mattock Lane Ealing London W5 5EQ

[on the A3001 Ealing Green, 5mins from BR/Tube: Ealing Broadway. Buses: 207, 65 & 83]

Tel: 020 8567 1227 Fax: 020 8567 0595

Set in an attractive park, Pitshanger Manor was built 1800-04 by the architect Sir John Soane 1753-1837 as his family country villa. The house incorporates a wing of the late 1760's by George Dance. The Art Gallery houses a changing programme of exhibitions. Short Courses, Lectures and Gallery Events details are available quarterly - call for details. Picnic area in the adjacent park. Guided tours for pre-booked parties.

All year Tue-Sat 10.00-17.00. Closed Easter, Christmas & New Year

Admission Free. Groups by arrangement

↓ *special events*

▶ **Underground**

7/4/00-13/5/00

Stunning photographic study of the world's Underground systems, shown for the first time in the UK.

▶ **Private Myths**

26/5/00-8/7/00

Watercolours by Shanti Panchal of an autobigoraphical nature

▶ **An Overview of Social and Political Art**

20/10/00-16/12/00

Produced in Northern Ireland 1969-1994. A major retrospective and positive appreciation of art produced during the troubles

Prince Henry's Rooms and Samuel Pepys Exhibition

17 Fleet Street London EC4Y 1AA

[Tube: Temple]

Tel: 020 7936 4004

One of the few buildings to survive the Great Fire of London in 1666. Original 16th century wood panelling. Collection of items on loan from the Pepys Society contained within one room.

All year Mon-Sat 11.00-14.00. Closed Sun & Bank Hol

Admission Free

Queen Ann's Gate

Queen Ann's Gate London SW1

[Tube: St James Park]

The spacious terraced houses at the west end of this well-preserved enclave date from 1704 and are notable for the ornate canopies over their front doors. At the other end are houses built some 70 years later, sporting blue plaques that record former residents, such as Lord Palmerston, the Victorian Prime Minister.

To view from the outside only, any reasonable time

Admission Free

Queen Charlotte's Cottage

Royal Botanic Gardens Kew Richmond Surrey TW9 3AB

[Tube: Kew Gardens. BR: Kew Bridge]

Tel: 020 8781 9500 Fax: 020 8781 9669

www.hrp.org.uk

This rustic cottage was the summer retreat of George III, Queen Charlotte and their growing family. Set amidst the splendour of Kew Gardens and a landscape designed by Capability Brown, it's thatched roof and timber framing present a charming picture. From the rooms used by the royal household, to the domestic chambers of the servants, visitors may explore this setting of late 18th century royal life. Features include the Picnic Room, decorated to resemble a bower of flowers, and probably designed by Princess Elizabeth, daughter of George III, and the Print Room lined with the works of William Hogarth.
Cottage: Apr-Sept Sat Sun & Bank Hol 10.30-16.00
Admission Free with ticket to the Botanic Gardens. Please see the entry for Kew Gardens for facilities...

Queen Elizabeth's Hunting Lodge
Ranger's Road Chingford London E4 7QH
[A1069, Tube: Walthamstow Central. BR: Chingford. Limited on site parking]
Tel: 020 8529 6681
The royal hunting grandstand was built for Henry VIII in 1543. It is one of the finest examples of timber framed architecture in the UK. It houses displays about timber-framed architecture and Royal hunting in Epping Forest.
All year Wed-Sun 14.00-17.00 or dusk if sooner
Last Admission: 16.45
A£0.50 C(accompanied)£Free
discount offer: Two Adults For The Price Of One

Queen's House
Greenwich Park Greenwich London SE10 9NF
Tel: 020 8858 4422 Fax: 020 8312 6632
www.nmm.ac.uk
The first Palladian-style villa in England, designed by Inigo Jones for Anne of Denmark and completed for Queen Henrietta Maria, wife of Charles I. Includes a Loggia overlooking Greenwich Park. Until Sept 24 2000, contains The Story of Time, a superb exhibition of important artefacts from around the world covering stories from creation to the after-life.
Open until Sept 25 2000 10.00-17.00, after this time please call for details
Last Admission: 16.00
A£7.50 C£3.75 Concessions£6.00

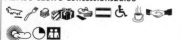

Rainham Hall
The Broadway Rainham Essex RM13 9YN
[S of the church 5m E of Barking BR: Rainham]

Tel: 01494 528051 Fax: 01494 463310
A National Trust Property. An attractive red-brick house with stone dressing, built in 1729 on a symmetrical plan. There are fine contemporary wrought-iron gates in front of the house and original panelling inside. Guide dogs by arrangement with tenant. Parking limited. No toilet facilities.
Apr-end Oct Wed & Bank Hol Mon 14.00-18.00 also Sat by written application to tenant
A£2.10. No reduction for groups

Ranger's House
Chesterfield Walk Blackheath London SE10 8QX
[just off A2 on Blackheath 0.5m from Greenwich, signposted in Greenwich. BR: Blackheath / Greenwich]
Tel: 020 8853 0035 Fax: 020 8853 0090
www.english-heritage.org.uk
This charming and intimate early Georgian house stands on the edge of Greenwich Park. It houses the superb Suffolk collection of paintings including stunning full length Jacobean portraits in the gallery, which overlooks the beautiful rose garden. The Coach House contains a unique collection of architectural features from 18th and 19th century London buildings.
1 Apr-30 Sept daily 10.00-18.00. 1-31 Oct 10.00-17.00. 1 Nov-31 Mar Wed-Sun 10.00-16.00. Closed 24-26 Dec. May close due to refurbishment, please call
A£2.80 C(0-5)£Free C(5-16)£1.40 Concessions£2.10. EH Members £Free

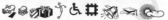

Ritz Hotel
Piccadilly London W1
[Tube: Green Park]
Tel: 020 7493 8181
Cesar Ritz, the Swiss hotelier who inspired the word "ritzy", had virtually retired by 1906, when this hotel was built and named after

London

him. The colonaded front of the dominant chateau-style building was meant to suggest Paris. It is a popular stop, among those who are suitably dressed, for afternoon tea.

All year daily to take Tea, or view from the outside,

Admission Free, Tea is charged

&

Rose Theatre Exhibition

56 Park Street London SE1 9AR
[BR: Waterloo/London Bridge. Tube: Mansion House, Cannon Street or London Bridge. Buses: 45, 63, 172 to Blackfriars Bridge; 15, 17 to Cannon Street; 11, 15, 23, 26, 76 to Mansion House; 149, 344, P11 to Southwark Street]
Tel: 020 7593 0026 Fax: 020 7633 0367
www.rdg.ac.uk/Rose

The first purpose-built theatre on Bankside, the Rose is the only Elizabethan theatre site with remains completely available for modern exploration. Its covered remains are tucked into the basement of an office block, submerged beneath a protective pool of water. This atmospheric site not only provides an insight into Shakespeare and Marlowe's London, it offers the opportunity to 'tread the boards' in their footsteps. The exhibition, which unfolds the fascinating story behind this unique fragment of history, centres around a multi-media presentation narrated by Sir Ian McKellen, and designed by award winning theatre designer William Dudley.

All year daily 10.00-17.00
Last Admission: 16.30
A£3.00 C(under 5)£Free C(5-16)£2.00 Family Ticket (A2+C3)£8.00 Concessions£2.50
Registered Disabled £2.50 + escort £Free
discount offer: Two For The Price Of One

Royal Mews at Buckingham Palace

Buckingham Palace Road London SW1W 0QH
[Tube: Victoria]
Tel: 020 7839 1377 Fax: 020 7839 8168
www.royal.gov.uk

As one of the finest working stables in existence, the Royal Mews at Buckingham Palace provides a unique opportunity for visitors to see a working department of the Royal Household. The Monarch's magnificent gilded State Carriages and Coaches, including the unique Gold State Coach are housed here, together with their horses and State liveries.

1 Oct 99-1 Aug 2000 Tue-Thur 12.00-16.00
Last Admission: 30 mins before closing
A£4.20 C(0-17)£2.00 OAPs£3.20. Groups 15+ entitled to 10% discount. Advance bookings can be made

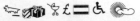

Royal Naval College

King William Walk Greenwich London SE10 9NN
[M25 A2 or A13 or from London take A206, BR: Greenwich / Cannon Street]
Tel: 020 8858 2154

The Royal Naval College occupies one of the masterpieces of English architecture; the grand sequence of buildings originally planned by Sir Christopher Wren towards the end of the 17th century as a hospital and refuge for disabled or veteran seamen of the Royal Navy. Was formerly used as a naval hospital.

All year daily 14.30-16.45
Last Admission: 16.30
Admission Free

Royal Opera Arcade

Royal Opera Arcade London SW1
[Tube: Piccadilly Circus]

London's first shopping arcade, it was designed by John Nash and completed in 1818, behind the Haymarket Opera House (now called Her Majesty's Theatre.) It beat the Burlington Arcade by a year or so. Farlows sell shooting equipment, fishing tackle, including the famous Hunter's green wellington boots, and a broad range of other essentials for traditional country living.

Dependant on individual shop opening hours
Admission Free

Shakespeare's Globe

21 New Globe Walk Bankside London SE1 9DT
[Tube: London Bridge / Mansion House]
Tel: 020 7902 1500 Fax: 020 7902 1515
www.shakespeares-globe.org

The biggest exhibition of its kind devoted to the world of Shakespeare, from Elizabethan times to the present day - situated beneath the Globe Theatre itself. Explore Bankside, the Soho of Elizabethan London, follow Sam Wanamaker's struggle to recreate an authentic Globe for the twentieth century and beyond, and take a fascinating guided tour of today's working theatre. Globe Education provide workshops, lectures and courses for students of all ages and nationalities. For further information please call (020) 7902 1433. GlobeLink is the Globe's association for schools and colleges and provides a range of services including a designated website, examination hotline, regular newsletters and priority booking. Globe Performances 12 May - 24 September 2000. Box Office (020) 7401 9919. The Globe Café offers light refreshments and main dishes from £6.00. The Globe Restaurant offers main dishes starting at £9.00. Two courses with coffee from £15.00.

visitor comments: Tour guides are "performing actors" adding new and fascinating dimensions to the visit.

Shakespeare's Globe Exhibition: May-Sept daily 09.00-12.00. Oct-Apr daily 10.00-17.00. Performance season: May-Sept. Globe Café: daily 10.00-23.00. Globe Restaurant: daily 12.00-23.00 (reservations 020 7928 9444) A£7.50 Concessions£6.00 C£5.00 Family Ticket £23.00. Admission includes a guided tour of the Theatre. Group rates 10+ available

↓*special events*

► Child's Play
1/5/00-30/9/00
An active introduction for 8-11 year olds exploring Shakespeare's work.

Somerset House
Strand London WC2R 1LA
[Tube: Covent Garden/Temple/Embankment]
Tel: 020 7845 4600
www.somerset-house.org.uk
Somerset House, Sir William Chambers' 18th century architectural masterpiece, will open to the public from May 2000. Situated in the heart of London and already home to the Courtauld Institute Gallery of world famous paintings, this great building will also house the new museum for the Gilbert Collection of decorative arts, gold and silver. Open-air events will be staged in the magnificent Courtyard. The River Terrace will open as a public promenade for the first time in over a

hundred years, together with an open-air cafe, restaurant and shop. A new pedestrian link from Waterloo Bridge onto the Terrace and through the restored Seamen's Hall will link the South Bank to Covent Garden, via Somerset House.

All year Mon-Sat 10.00-18.00, Sun & Bank Hol Mon 12.00-18.00
Last Admission: 17.30
Admission to Somerset House: £Free (For Gilbert Collection and Courtauld Gallery, see separate entries)

Southside House
3-4 Woodhayes Road Wimbledon Common London SW19 4RJ
[on S side of Wimbledon Common B281 beside Kings College School, opposite The Crooked Billet and the Hand in Hand Public Houses. Tube: Wimbledon / Putney Bridge. Buses: No 93 to Wimbledon War Memorial, 6min walk]
Tel: 020 8946 7643
Built by Robert Pennington, the friend of the future King Charles II, as a safe retreat for his family after his little son died in the London Plague in 1665. An old family home from William and Mary's time, built around a Tudor farmhouse with Dutch Baroque influence. Interesting connections with and visits by members of the Royal family, the Hamiltons, and Nelson among others. In this century it has been one of the homes of the Swedish Doctor and philanthropist Axel Munth who wrote one of his best selling works 'The Story of San Michele' which was later saved from sale by his widow Hilda Pennington-Mellor-Munth by creating an Educational Trust which allows the family to continue to live here and let visitors enjoy its uniqueness - 310 years of occupancy by the same family. Still lived in by the Pennington/Mellor/Munth descendants to this day surrounded by family portraits, and an atmosphere of living history.

1 Jan-21 June, Guided Tours: Tue, Thur, Sat & Bank Hol 14.00, 15.00 & 16.00. Group Visits 15+ by written appointment Mornings Mon-Sat 10.30, not Sun afternoons also Mon, Wed & Fri 14.00
A£5.00 C(accompanied by adult)£3.00

Spencer House
27 St. James's Place London SW1A 1NR
[Tube: Green Park]
Tel: 020 7499 8620
Spencer House built 1756-66 for the first Earl Spencer, an ancestor of Diana, Princess of Wales (1961-97), is London's finest surviving 18th Century townhouse. This magnificent pri-

London

vate palace, overlooking Green Park, has regained the full splendour of its 18th Century appearance after a ten year restoration.

Feb-July & Sept-Dec Sun only 10.30-16.45

Queuing Times: Tours every 20mins

A£6.00 C(10-15)&Concessions£5.00 No Children under 10 admitted.

Strawberry Hill, Horace Walpole's Gothick Villa

Waldegrave Road Twickenham Middlesex TW1 4SX

[BR: Strawberry Hill. Bus No: 33]

Tel: 020 8240 4224 Fax: 020 8255 6174

Horace Walpole bought Strawberry Hill in 1749 and converted the modest house into his own vision of a 'gothick' fantasy. It is widely regarded as the first substantial building of the gothick revival and as such internationally known and admired.

Easter Sun-10 Oct Sun 14.00-15.30 and week-days for pre-booked groups

A£4.75 Concessions£4.25

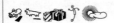

Sutton House

2 & 4 Homerton High Street Hackney London E9 6JQ

[at the corner of Isabella Road & Homerton High Street. BR: Hackney Central / Hackney Downs]

Tel: 020 8986 2264

A National Trust Property. A rare example of a Tudor red-brick house, built in 1535 by Sir Rafe Sadleir, Principal Secretary of State for Henry VIII, with 18th century alterations and later additions. The recent restoration has revealed many 16th century details which are displayed. Ground floor only accessible for wheelchairs.

3 Feb-24 Nov & 2 Feb 2000 onwards Wed, Sun & Bank Hol 11.30-17.30, Sat 14.00-17.30. Closed Good Fri. Group visits by prior arrangement on Thur & Fri

Last Admission: 17.00

A£2.00 C£0.50 Family Ticket £4.50

Syon House and Gardens

Syon Park London Road Brentford Middlesex TW8 8JF

[approach via A310 Twickenham Road into Park Road]

Tel: 020 8560 0883 Fax: 020 8568 0936

Syon House is the London home of the Duke of Northumberland. It is built on the site of a medieval abbey dissolved by Henry VIII. The present house is Tudor in origin but famed for its splendid Robert Adam interiors. Member of the Historic Houses Association.

15 Mar-29 Oct Wed, Thur, Sun & Bank Hol 11.00-17.00

Last Admission: 16.45

Gardens: A£3.00 Concessions£2.50. Combined ticket for House & Gardens: A£6.00 Concessions£4.50 Family Ticket £15.00

discount offer: Two For The Price Of One Full Paying Adult For Combined Ticket Only

↓*special events*

► **Spit and Polish**
22/4/00-24/4/00
Come and see a Victorian dishwasher in action! Experience live demonstrations of 19th century gadgets, housework techniques and recipes

► **Absolutely Georgian**
30/4/00-1/5/00
Rhiannon Gayle gives a lively performance with music, song and gossip on the most controversial women of the 18th century

► **Countryside Live**
19/5/00-21/5/00
A new event with demonstrations and displays about our rural heritage

► **The 1900 House Guests**
28/5/00-29/5/00
Hoi Polloi demonstrate what it was like to be a Syon House Guest at the turn of the century. For the first time, the nursery wing will be on view

► **Start of the London to Brighton Classic Car Run**
4/6/00-4/6/00

► **Craft Fair**
27/7/00-30/7/00

► **Death by Chocolate**
27/8/00-28/8/00
Baroque 'n' Roll present music and dance reflecting the gossip and intrigues of Chocolate, the drink introduced to Europe in the 17th and 18th centuries

The Old Palace
Old Palace Road Croydon Surrey CR0 1AX
[in Croydon Old Town Adjacent to Parish Church. BR: East Croydon / West Croydon]
Tel: 020 8688 2027
Seat of Archbishops of Canterbury since 871. 15th century Banqueting Hall and Guardroom, Tudor Chapel, Norman undercroft. Queen Elizabeth's bedroom and one of the country's oldest Long Gallerys. Run by the Whitgift foundation
Daily on the following dates only: 10-15 Apr, 29 May-3 June, 10-15 July, 17-22 July. Conducted tours last 2 hours and commence 14.00-14.30 Last Admission: 14.30
A£4.00 C&OAPs£3.00 Family Ticket £10.00 including afternoon tea served in the undercroft

Tilbury Fort
No 2 Office Block The Fort Tilbury Essex RM18 7NR
[0.5m E of Tilbury off A126]
Tel: 01375 858489
The best and largest example of 17th century military engineering in England, the fort dates from the reign of Henry VIII, but is most famous for Queen Elizabeth I's review of the fleet and her stunning speech to her troops on the eve of the Spanish Armada. Visitors can visit the militaria museum and enjoy extensive views of the River Thames.
27 Mar-31 Oct daily 10.00-18.00 or dusk if sooner (17.00 in Oct). 1 Nov-31 Mar Wed-Sun 10.00-16.00. Closed 24-26 Dec
A£2.50 C£1.30 OAPs&Students&UB40£1.90
↓*special events*

► **The Military Vehicle Rally**
2/4/00-3/12/00
08.00-13.00. Tilbury Fort welcomes militaria enthusiasts with its popular collectors' fair. On 2 Apr, 7 May, 4 June, 2 July, 6 Aug, 3 Sept, 1 Oct, 5 Nov & 3 Dec

► **1940's Children's Easter**
23/4/00-24/4/00

► **WWII Artillery Firing Days**
14/5/00-22/10/00
Living history and firing of a 25-pounder field gun on 15 May, 25 June, 16 July, 24 Sept & 22 Oct

► **Tilbury Tales**
21/5/00-9/7/00
At 11.00 & 14.30.   Find out about the Fort's colourful past, including the secrets of the "Dead House" on 21 May, 19 June & 9 July

► **Essex Classic Military Vehicle Rally**
26/8/00-28/8/00
Stalls, driving displays, and a dozens of vehicles from World War II to the present

Tower of London
Tower Hill London EC3N 4AB
[Tube: Tower Hill]
**Tel: 020 7709 0765 Fax: 020 7480 5350
www.hrp.org.uk**
Perhaps the most famous tower in the world, it was used as the State Prison where King Henry VIII had two wives executed, Sir Walter Raleigh was imprisoned for 13 years and during both World Wars German spies were incarcerated here. It is home to the Crown Jewels and famous ravens. Includes the Royal Fusiliers Museum. The Jewel House was refurbished in 1994 and is now accessible for Wheelchairs. Wheelchairs available Free. Free Beefeater Tours and talks throughout the year. During school holidays free Family Trails. The armoury display in the White Tower opened in 1998. The Tower of London is the worst haunted places in Britain with the ghost of Thomas a Becket who appeared in the mid 13th century during the building of the inner curtain wall. He apparently reduced the work to rubble by striking it with his cross. The ghosts of the Little Princes (12 year old King Edward V and his 9 year old brother Richard, Duke of York) have occasionally been seen in the Bloody Tower dressed in white nightgowns. The grisliest haunting of the Tower if that of the 70 year old Countess of Salisbury - 'The last of the Plantagenets' - executed by Henry VIII (to awful to describe ask at the Tower!) The most persistent ghost if that of Queen Anne Boleyn drifting from Queen's House to the Chapel of St Peter ad Vincula where she floats down the aisle to the site of her final resting place under the chapels's alter. And finally, the most haunted part of the Tower is the Salt Tower, not only do dogs refuse to enter but Yeoman Warders are unwilling to visit after nightfall. The following events are free to Tower ticket holders.

visitor comments: Long queues during Summer, get there early. Beefeater tour has some wonderful stories to tell and really involves the children. Expensive, but there's lots to see.

All year Mar-Oct Mon-Sat 09.00-17.00, Sun 10.00-17.00. Nov-Feb Tue-Sat 09.00-16.00, Mon & Sun 10.00-16.00. Closed 24-25 Dec & 1 Jan Last Admission: Closes 30 mins after last admission

A£10.50 C(under 5)£Free C(5-16)£6.90 Family Ticket (A2+C3/A1+C4) £31.00 OAPs&Students&Disabled£7.90. Wheelchair pushers £Free

↓ *special events*

▶ **The Tower Menagerie**
27/10/99-31/3/00
The fascinating development of the Tower's collection of exotic animals prior to their removal to form London Zoo.

▶ **Opening of Thomas More's Cell**
10/1/00-10/12/00
St Thomas More was imprisoned in the Bell Tower in 1534 for refusing to acknowledge Henry VIII as head of the English Church. Entrance by guided tour only.

▶ **Gun Salutes 2000**
7/2/00-4/8/00
Actual Dates: Feb 7, Apr 21, June 2, 10, Aug 4. Gun salutes have been fired on important state and royal events since Tudor times

▶ **The Rise and Fall of Anne Boleyn**
19/2/00-27/2/00

▶ **The Ceremony of the Constable's Dues**
24/3/00-14/10/00
To be held on Mar 24, May 12, June 24, Sept 9 and Oct 14 only. Celebrates the ancient custom of paying dues if moored in the Pool of London.

▶ **The Royal Armouries' Millennium Exhibition**
15/4/00-31/12/00
Celebration of 2000 years of Tower history. Exhibits to include a volume of the Domesday Book

▶ **King Richard III: Man and Myth**
22/4/00-30/4/00
Was Richard III responsible for the deaths of the Princes in the Tower or was it malicious gossip?

▶ **State Parades**
23/4/00-17/12/00
Apr 23, May 28 and Dec 17 only. Yeoman Warders in State Dress escort Resident Governor from Queen's House to Chapel Royal St Peter ad Vincula.

▶ **Shakespeare at the Tower**
27/5/00-4/6/00
Scenes from Shakespeare will be performed alongside presentations of the historical events portrayed

▶ **The Great Crown Jewels Robbery**
21/10/00-29/10/00
Follow Captain Blood through the unsuccessful 1671 attempt to steal the Crown Jewels

▶ **The King's Medieval Christmas**
27/12/00-31/12/00
Period musicians, music and merriment fill the Medieval Palace for a Christmas celebration

Travellers Club
106 Pall Mall London SW1Y 5EP
[Tube: Piccadilly Circus]
Tel: 020 7930 8688 Fax: 020 7930 2019
Built in 1829-33 by Sir Charles Barry
By prior arrangement Mon-Fri only from 09.30-12.00
A£8.00

Whitehall
1 Malden Road Cheam Sutton Surrey SM3 8QD
[on A2043 just N of junction with A232. BR: Cheam]
Tel: 020 8643 1236 Fax: 020 8770 4777
www.sutton.gov.uk

A unique timber-framed house built 1500. Displays include medieval Cheam pottery; Nonsuch Palace; timber-framed buildings and Cheam School.

Apr-Sept Tue-Fri Sun 14.00-17.30, Sat 10.00-17.30. Oct-Mar Wed, Thur, Sun 14.00-17.30, Sat 10.00-17.30, also Bank Hol Mon. Closed 24 Dec-2 Jan
A£1.20 C£0.50

discount offer: Two For The Price Of One

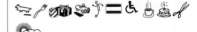

Landmarks

Albert Memorial
Princes Gate Kensington Gore Kensington London SW7 2AN
[Buses frequent from surrounding areas BR: Victoria 1.5m, Tube: South Kensington 0.5m]
Tel: 020 7298 2117

An elaborate national memorial by George Gilbert Scott to commemorate the Prince Consort. The monument has undergone extensive conservation - details are displayed in an exhibition and video in the visitor centre.

All year, at any reasonable time
Admission Free

British Airways London Eye

Jubilee Gardens The Southbank London SE1 7SW

[Tube: Embankment, Waterloo, Charing Cross & Westminster. Access will be via the river utilising the new Waterloo Millennium Pier to be built adjacent to the London Eye.]

Tel: 020 77074159 Fax: 020 7465 0923
www.ba-londoneye.com

Sweeping one of the world's most famous skylines at 135m (450ft) high, British Airways London Eye is London's fourth tallest structure. Its gradual 30 minute 360 degree rotation will give passengers totally new perspectives of some of the Capital's most famous landmarks and provide a birds-eye view usually accessible only by helicopter or aircraft. Unrivalled views from 32 fully enclosed, high tech capsules, each accommodating up to 25 people, will be enhanced by commentary designed to enable visitors to get the most out of the experience.

All year daily, 1 Nov-31 Mar 10.00-18.00, 1 Apr-31 Oct 09.00-late evening. Call 0870 5000 600 Advance ticket hotline. Group bookings 0870 400 3005
A£7.45 C£4.95 Concessions£5.95. Tickets can be booked in advance on 0870 5000 600

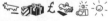

Cenotaph

Whitehall London SW1
[Tube: Westminster]

This suitably bleak and pale monument, completed in 1920 by Sir Edwin Lutyens to commemorate the dead of World War I, stands in the middle of Whitehall. On Remembrance Day every year - the Sunday nearest 11 November - the monarch and other dignitaries place wreaths of red poppies on the Cenotaph.
All year any reasonable time

Hyde Park

London W2
[Tube: Hyde Park Corner / Marble Arch]

Situated to the west of Park Lane, between Knightsbridge and Bayswater and formerly a Royal hunting park, Hyde Park now consists of 340 acres of grass and trees. The Serpentine is at it's centre. It was the venue for the Great Exhibition in 1851. Hour-long horse riding

lessons are available at the Hyde Park Riding Stables (Tel 0171 723 2813). The lessons are mainly aimed at beginners but more advanced riders are welcome and can be catered for.
Riding Lessons: Tue-Fri 07.00-Sunset, Sat-Sun 09.00-16.00
Admission Free. Horse Riding Lessons: £25.00 for one hour session

↓*special events*
▶ **London to Brighton Veteran Car Run**
5/11/00-5/11/00
▶ **Peter Pan Swimming Race**
25/12/00-25/12/00

London Balloon

Spring Gardens Vauxhall London SE11 5HF
[Tube: Vauxhall - 100m from here, opposite The Tate Gallery. Parking is available 100m away on Tyres Street, just off Kennington Lane.]

Tel: 020 7587 1111 Fax: 020 7587 1113
www.londonballoon.co.uk

The London Balloon is established as a leading tourist attraction offering panoramic views from hundreds of feet above the city. Not only can you experience a flight in the world's largest balloon but at the same time enjoy spectacular views of London's major buildings - Big Ben is only 500 meters away. The London Balloon is an exciting leisure attraction for people of all ages, including disabled and wheelchair access. We recommend that you call and check our flying status before travelling to fly The London Balloon. The name of our balloon is 'BIG BOB' and is the world's largest tethered passenger balloon ride and the first of it's kind in the UK. Big Bob has enough helium inside to fill half a million children's balloons and is strong enough to lift a London Double Decker Bus! Ascending to a height of 400 feet (120m) the views are absolutely breathtaking. The Gondola can take up to 30 passengers at a time enabling you to walk all round taking in 360 degree views. Bring your camera/binoculars because this is one view you won't want to miss!
All year daily 10.00-dusk every 15 mins. Fri, Sat & Sun till midnight for night flights (subject to weather)
A£12.00 C£7.50 Family Ticket £35.00. Group rates upon request. Bookings are not required (except for night flights).

Pall Mall

Pall Mall London SW1
[Tube: Charing Cross]

This dignified street is named from the game of palle-maille, a cross between croquet and golf, which was played here in the early 17th century. For more than 150 years Pall Mall has

London

London

been at the heart of London's clubland. Here exclusive gentlemen's clubs were formed to provide members with a refuge from their womenfolk.

To view from the outside, any reasonable time
Admission Free

Parliament Square

London SW1
[Tube: Westminster]
Laid out in the 1840's to provide a more open aspect for the new Houses of Parliament, the square became Britain's first official roundabout in 1926. Today it is hemmed in by heavy traffic. Statues of statesmen and soldiers are dominated by Winston Churchill in his greatcoat, glowering at the Houses of Commons.
Any reasonable time
Admission Free

Piccadilly Circus

London W1
[Tube: Piccadilly Circus]
Sited in the heart of London's West End, Piccadilly Circus is overlooked by buildings covered with famous neon slogans from Coca Cola to Kodak. The focal point is a fountain and the statue of Eros, the Angel of Christian Charity, which is surrounded by steps. It is a regular meeting spot for tourists.
All Year

Statue of Eros

Piccadilly Circus London W1
[Tube: Piccadilly Circus]
For years people have congregated beneath the symbolic figure of Eros, originally intended as an angel of mercy but renamed after the Great god of love. Poised delicately with his bow, Eros has become almost a trade mark for the capital. Piccadilly Circus has been considerably altered in recent years and consists chiefly of shopping malls.
All year, any reasonable time
Admission Free

Thames Barrier Visitors Centre

1 Unity Way Woolwich London SE18 5NJ
[BR: Charlton, in Charlton signposted from
Greenwich]
Tel: 020 8305 4188 Fax: 020 8855 2146
Built to prevent the possibility of flooding, the Thames Barrier is the world's largest moveable flood barrier. The Visitor Centre explains the flood threat and the construction of this £480 million project, now valued at £1 billion. All 10 gates are tested each month for two hours with full day closure in the autumn. See special events for some closure times, they may vary as a result of testing or weather conditions, please call on the day to check.
visitor comments: Interesting and reasonably entertaining.
All year Mon-Fri 10.00-17.00, Sat & Sun 10.30-17.30. Evening opening by special arrangements for groups, call for details
Last Admission: 1hr before closing
A£3.40 C&OAPs£2.00 Family Ticket £7.50. Car park £1.00. Coach park £Free

The Mall

London SW1
[Tube: Charing Cross / Green Park / Piccadilly Circus]
This broad triumphal approach to Buckingham Palace was created by Aston Webb when he redesigned the front of the palace and the Victoria Monument in 1911. It follows the course of the old path at the edge of St James's Park, laid out in the reign of Charles II when it became London's most fashionable promenade.
Any reasonable time
Admission Free

The Monument

Monument Street London EC3R 8AH
[Tube: Monument]
Tel: 020 7403 3761
Designed by Wren and erected in 1671-7, the Monument commemorates the Great Fire of 1666. 311 stairs with viewing platform at the top, all round view of the City of London. Access for disabled is almost impossible because of the steps.
All year daily 10.00-18.00, Weekends 14.00-17.40
Last Admission: 17.40
A£1.50 C£0.50

Tower Bridge Experience

Tower Bridge London SE1 2UP
[in centre of London signposted. Bus: 15 / 25 / 40 / 42 / 27 / 78 / 100 / D1 / P11. Tube: Tower Hill / London Bridge. Car Parking in: Tooley Street & Lower Thames Street]
Tel: 020 7378 1928 Fax: 020 7357 7935

www.towerbridge.org.uk

One of London's most unusual and exciting exhibitions is situated inside Tower Bridge. Animatronic characters from the bridge's past guide you through a series of audio-visual presentations, telling the story of this world famous landmark. From the high-level walkways above the Thames, you'll also enjoy one of the memorable panoramic views of London. The Tower Bridge Experience has won the 'England for Excellence' award for London: All areas of The Tower Bridge Experience are accessible to disabled visitors, including those in wheelchairs. Ramps and wheelchair accessible toilets are provided, and if any of the party are unable to climb stairs, a guide will be happy to arrange for use of the lift.

All year Apr-Oct daily 10.00-18.30. Nov-Mar daily 09.30-18.00. Closed Good Fri, 24-25 Dec, 19 Jan
Last Admission: 75mins before closing
Queuing Times: 10mins max
A£6.15 C(5-15) & OAPs&Students £4.15 Family Ticket (A1+C2)£13.95 (A2+C2)£15.50 (A2+C3)£17.50 (A2+C4)£19.50. Group rates: A£5.55 C(5-15) & OAPs&Students £3.75. Prices expire 31 Mar 2000

↓*special events*

▶ **Tower Bridge Lifts**
1/1/00-31/12/00
Lifts 500 times a year , 10 times a day during the summer months. A 24 hour dedicated phone line 020 7378 7700 will give details.

▶ **Super Sleuth Quiz**
19/2/00-27/2/00
Put yourself to the test as you race around the Bridge trying to solve the mystery word.

▶ **Kite-Making Workshops**
27/5/00-2/6/00
The workshops allow kids (and Mums and Dads) to make a specially designed Tower Bridge Kite which they can then try out for size outside the Bridge's Engine Rooms.

Trafalgar Square
London W2
[Tube: Charing Cross / Embankment]
In this famous meeting area stands Nelson's Column, built to commemorate Admiral Nelson, who was killed during his victorious battle against Napoleon's navy off Trafalgar in Spain in 1805. At the top of the 56 metre high column is a statue of Nelson with one arm and one eye which he lost in battle. On October 21st each year a service is held to commemorate Nelson. At Christmas time Norway always sends a huge Christmas tree that stands in the square, as a token of gratitude for Britain's help during the Second World war. Trafalgar Square is also the centre of London's New Year's celebrations when thousands of party goers herald in the New Year.
All Year
♿

Wellington Arch
London SW1
[Tube: Hyde Park Corner]
A vast archway, designed by Decimus Burton and called Wellington Arch, was erected in 1828. The sculpture, by Adrian Jones, was added later, in 1912. It is sometimes referred to as Constitution Arch.
All year daily 05.00-24.00
Admission Free

Literature & Libraries

British Library
96 Euston Road London NW1 2DB
[BR: St Pancras. Tube: King's Cross / St Pancras / Euston. Bus: 10 / 30 / 73 / 91 / SL1 & SL2]
Tel: 020 7412 7332 Fax: 020 7412 7340
www.bl.uk

The British Library is the national library of the UK and one of the great libraries of the world. The new St Pancras building in London is it's headquarters. The spectacular new building designed by Colin St John Wilson, will open fully to the public on 21st April 98. The reading rooms will open over a two year period as follows: Humanities now open, Rare Books and Music 23/3/98 Oriental and India Office Aug 98, Maps Aug 98, Manuscripts Jan 99 and Science March-May 99. The large Piazza is a new public space for London, with a bronze statue of Isaac Newton and the Amphitheatre will be used for poetry reading, outdoor performances and other public events. From April 98 a full programme of talks, seminars, films and musical and dramatic performances will commence. The main venue will be the purpose-built Conference Centre which has a raked (seating arranged so that everyone has an optimum view as in a cinema) 255 seat auditorium.

All year daily, Mon, Wed, Thur & Fri 09.30-18.00, Tue 09.30-20.00, Sat 09.30-17.00, Sun 11.00-17.00. Closed 3-4 Apr
Last Admission: Mon-Fri 18.00, Sat 16.30
Admission Free, reader passes can only be issued in person. Admission to events are by ticket from the Box Office. Doors open 15mins before the advertised start time

↓*special events*

▶ **Chapter and Verse: One Thousand Years Of Literature**
10/3/00-15/10/00
Ten themes, including Love, Loss and Laughter, which have inspired writers over the last 1,000 years.

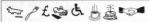

Dickens House Museum
48 Doughty Street London WC1N 2LF
[Tube: Russell Square]
Tel: 020 7405 2127 Fax: 020 7831 5175
www.dickensmuseum.com
Charles Dickens lived in Doughty Street in his twenties and it was here that he worked on his first full-length novel, The Pickwick Papers, Oliver Twist and Nicholas Nickelby. Pages of the original manuscript are on view. Dickens' drawing room has been reconstructed.
All year Mon-Sat 10.00-17.00 incl 24-26 Dec 10.30-18.00
Last Admission: 16.30
A£4.00 C(5-15)£2.00 Family Ticket £9.00
OAPs&Students£3.00
discount offer: Two For The Price Of One

Dr Johnson's House
17 Gough Square London EC4A 3DE
[Tube: Temple / Blackfriars / Chancery]
Tel: 020 7353 3745 Fax: 020 7353 3745
The celebrated literary, Dr Samual Johnson, lived between 1748 and 1759 and wrote his first English Dictionary, a first edition is on display. The house is a handsome example of 18th century architecture and exhibits include fine prints, letters and other memorabilia. Guided tours by arrangement for pre-booked parties.
All year May-Sept Mon-Sat 11.00-17.30. Oct-Apr Mon-Sat 11.00-17.00. Closed Bank Hol & Christmas
A£3.00 C(0-10)£1.00 Concessions&Groups£2.00

Royal Geographical Society (with the Institute of British Geographers)
1 Kensington Gore London SW7 2AR
[Tube: South Kensington]
Tel: 020 7591 3000 Fax: 0171 591 3001
World famous map library with over 1 million maps, covering the world, from 1480 to modern topographic mapping available for reference. For full information about joining the society call the above number.
All year Mon-Fri 11.00-17.00 closed June
Admission Free

Living History Museums

Age Exchange Reminiscence Centre
11 Blackheath Village Blackheath London SE3 9LA
[junction of Lee Road / Belmont Road in Lewisham]
Tel: 020 8318 9105 Fax: 020 8318 0060
A 'Hands-On' museum of everyday objects from the 1920's-40's. Includes regular changing exhibitions on themes.
All year Mon-Sat 10.00-17.30. Closed Bank Hol
Last Admission: 17.30
Admission Free. Parties £1.50

Sir Winston Churchill's Britain at War Experience
64-66 Tooley Street London Bridge London SE1 2TF
[close to London Bridge]
Tel: 020 7403 3171 Fax: 020 7403 5104
www.britain-at-war.co.uk
Take an unforgettable journey back in time to the dark days of the Second World War and experience the fury and danger of war torn Britain and life on the Home Front. Special effects recreate the gihts and sounds of the London Blitz. Special children's activities during school holidays.
All year Mar-Oct daily 10.00-17.30, Oct-Mar daily 10.00-16.30. Closed 24-26 Dec & Jan 1
Last Admission: Summer 17.30, Winter 16.30

A£5.95 C£2.95 Family Ticket £14.00
Concessions£3.95
discount offer: One Child Free When
Accompanied By A Full Paying Adult

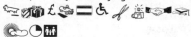

Maritime

Cutty Sark Clipper Ship
Greenwich Pier King William Walk Greenwich
London SE10 9HT
[A2 / A102(M), off A206 signposted to
Greenwich. Tube: Island Gardens BR: Greenwich]
Tel: 020 8858 3445 Fax: 020 8853 3589
www.cuttysark.org.uk
The fastest tea clipper to be built once sailed
363 miles in a single day. She has been pre-
served in dry dock since 1957 and her graceful
lines dominate the riverside at Greenwich.
Exhibitions and video presentation on board
tell the story of the ship and there is a magnif-
icent collections of ships' figureheads.
All year daily 10.00-17.00. Closed 24-26 Dec
Last Admission: 30mins before closing
A£3.50 Family Ticket £8.50 Concessions£2.50.
Passport Ticket (including National Maritime
Museum & Royal Observatory) A£12.00
Concessions£9.60
discount offer: Two For The Price Of One

Golden Hinde
St Mary Overie Dock Cathedral Street London
SE1 9DE
[between London Bridge and Shakespeare's
Globe on the south side of the Thames]
Tel: 020 7403 0123 Fax: 020 7407 5908
www.goldenhinde.co.uk
The reconstruction of Sir Francis Drake's ship
Golden Hinde has a permanent berth on the
Thames in the heart of London. The ship is a
'Living History' museum with a variety of pro-
grammes suited to schools and families. These
include guided tours, workshops and the
opportunity to spend a night aboard the ship
on an imaginary voyage. Dressed in period
clothes, Drake's new recruits learn 16th century sailors skills, eat Tudor food and experience
life 400 years ago. Booking Number: 08700
118700
All year daily 10.00-18.00 unless a special event
is taking place, check before visiting.
Last Admission: 17.30
A£2.50 C£1.75 Family Ticket £6.50
Concessions£2.10 Pre-booked guided tours
A£2.80 School parties £2.00 each

National Maritime Museum
Romney Road Greenwich London SE10 9NF
[J2 M25 then A2 and A206, follow signposts
into central Greenwich. BR: Maze Hill DLR:
Cutty Sark]
**Tel: 020 8858 4422/312 6565 Fax: 020 8312
6521**
www.nmm.ac.uk
See how the sea affects our daily lives in this
impressive modern museum. Themes include
exploration and discovery, Nelson, 20th century seapower, trade and empire, passenger
shipping and luxury liners, maritime London,
costume, art and the sea, the future of the sea
and the global garden. Exhibition will take
place in the Queen's House in the year 2000.

London

This definitive exhibition will tell the 'Story of Time' with over 300 exhibits from around the world, with a unique mix of the arts and sciences, the works of mankind, and the natural world.

visitor comments: The newly refurbished museum is fantastic and employs the latest technology. Definitely worth a visit.

All year daily 10.00-17.00. Closed 24-26 Dec
Last Admission: 16.30
A£7.50 C(Under16)£Free Concessions£6.00
Group rates available. Story of Time extra charge

discount offer: One Free Ticket When An Adult Ticket Is Purchased. Ref: DOG

↓*special events*

▶ **Story of Time**

1/12/99-26/9/00

Exhibition of Man's Study of Time with world famous exhibits.

Markets

Berwick Street Market

Berwick Street London W1

[Tube: Piccadilly Circus]

Surrounded by the sex shops and chi-chi coffee houses of Soho, Berwick Street is one of London's finest fruit, veg and fish markets. The stalls are works of art in themselves. Plus Points: A rare groove from one of the record shops that line the street (Selectadisc and Daddy Kool), fresh tune steaks from the fishmongers and feather boas and leopard-print fabrics from the dressmakers' stores. Minus Points: Prices can be high for the home-grown British produce.

All year Mon-Sat 08.00-17.30
Admission Free

Billingsgate Fish Market

West India Docks London E14

[DLR: West Inda Quay]

Established by the Romans and referred to by Shakespeare, London's premier fish market is legendary, as is the salty language used by its traders. It moved from the city in 1982 to the Docklands, and it's still doing a roaring trade. Plus Points: Fish, fish and more fish in the freshest of states at the lowest of prices. Minus Points: The smell!! and the early closing.

All year Tue-Sat 05.00-08.30
Admission Free

Brick Lane

Bethnal Green Road and Cheshire Street and

Brick Lane London E1 / E2

[Tube/BR: Liverpool Street / Aldgate East]

A vast car-boot sale, Brick Lane is bustling, brazen and brilliant for all your cut-price bric-à-brac, clothes, fruit and veg. Don't be tempted to leave your car on a yellow line - parking is restricted until after 14.00. Plus Points: City boys' discarded office furniture from Charlie Burns' stall (haggle for those swivel chairs), sari silks, Britain's best bagels from the 24-hour Beigel Bake and kitchenware from Irvin Keyes. Minus Points: Lycra leggings that'll only cling for a day, the so-hot-they're-burning bicycles, ancient spanner and socket sets, old plugs and half-empty bottles of shampoo!

All year Sun 06.00-13.00
Admission Free

Brixton Market

East of Brixton Road and Electric Avenue and Granville Arcade London SW9

[Tube/BR: Brixton]

Fruit and veg, clothes and records in this six days a week genuinely popular market. Plus Points: Since the arrival of the West Indian population in the 1950s and 1960s, Brixton Market has been the place for Afro-Caribbean foodstuffs especially along Electric Avenue, while the African and Asian fabrics are also worth a look. Check out the biggest Ghana Yams in London - they're the size of a small child. Minus Points: The usual suspect market goods - nylon undies, fluorescent pink candy and cut-price electrical goods.

All year Mon, Tue, Thur & Sat 09.00-17.30, Wed 09.00-13.00
Admission Free

Camden - The Stables

Chalk Farm Road London NW1

[Tube: Camden Town]

This weekend special, adjacent to the Lock, is probably the best market experience in the area. Follow your nose to the burning joss sticks and veggie curry stalls, through to the indoor stalls straining under the weight of so much collectable vintage clothes and cutting-edge club-wear. Plus Points: Usually it's the beaded dress buried either at the bottom of an enormous impenetrable vintage clothes or hung up on the highest hook. Names to spot include Cyberdog for clubby fluorescent T-shirts, Clip's vintage jackets, Gary Holder's bleached velvet jackets and trousers; Mothball's second-hand gear, Retropolis, Threads, and the Hat Shop for old-fashioned bowler hats. Minus Points: Too many nutty sticky buns from the patisserie stall. Those Seventies hipsters demand flat stomachs.

All year Sat & Sun 09.00-18.00

Admission Free

Camden Lock
Chalk Farm Road London NW1
[Tube: Camden Town]
The markets of Camden are London's fourth biggest tourist attraction and the alleys and stalls apparently have the highest retail turnover in Europe. The five million visitors a year can make Camden a high-stress, high-price, no-go area but there are still bargains and good times to be had. The Lock section is best for ethnic goods, gifts and home furnishings. During the week, there are less stalls, but equally, less punters. Plus Points: The weekend food stalls opposite Middle Yard selling cheap cooked breakfasts alongside Thai and Japanese fast food, the vegetable-dyed cotton drapes at only £15 a double, and the canal cruises to Little Venice. Minus Points: Being there on Sundays between 10.00-16.00!
All year daily 10.00-18.00
Admission Free

Camden Market
Camden High Street London NW1
[Tube: Camden Town]
This is a bit for leather (or 'levva' in Camden parlance), second-hand flares and up-and-coming young designers. Plus Points: Hard to say with the hoards of Eurostar bargain-hunters pushing prices up but with luck and haggling, the second-hand leather jackets can be wardrobe classics. Minus Points: The new leather (not the best in town), Lycra boob-tubes and anything with a Union Jack on it.
All year Thur-Sun 09.00-17.00
Admission Free

Chapel Market
off Liverpool Road London N1
[Tube: Angel]
Everything and then some, all at below-average prices. The shops along the street tend to be of the tackier end of the high street staples (Superdrug, Iceland etc.), but the stalls are full of bargains. Plus Points: The 'Under a Fiver' stall for cheap presents, hair and make-up for ethnic groups not usually catered for in Boots, and Arsenal memorabilia. Minus Points: Buying cheap for cheapness' sake.
All year Tue-Thur 09.00-16.00, Fri & Sat 09.00-18.00, Sun 09.00-14.00
Admission Free

Columbia Road
Columbia Road London E2
[Tube/BR: Liverpool Street]

Flowers and plants sold direct to the public. London's complete horticultural needs are met by stalls selling the cheapest bedding plants, hanging baskets, cut flowers, ferns and shrubs. It's also a lot more fun than a garden centre. Plus Points: Almost anything green along with Terracotta urns, scented candles and oils from The Flower Room and 'squid for a quid' from Just Fish. Minus Points: Things green and living lurking on your Lobelia.
All year Sun 07.00-14.00
Admission Free

Covent Garden
Covent Garden London WC2
[Tube: Covent Garden / Holborn]
Tel: 020 7375 0441
An excellent place to hang out with children. Covent Garden is one of London's few pedestrianised areas. Street entertainers, covered stalls and shops keep you all amused for hours. Covent Garden is home to the London Transport Museum, Cabaret, Mechanical Theatre and the Theatre Museum.
All year daily 10.00-19.00
Admission Free

East Street Market
East Street London SE17
[Tube: Elephant & Castle / Kennington]
General, fruit and veg at lower-than-supermarket prices.
All year Tue-Sun from 09.00
Admission Free

Gabriel's Wharf
59 Upper Ground London SE1
[Tube: Waterloo / Temple / Blackfriars]
As part of a massive movement to reclaim the once ghostly Southbank, Gabriel's Wharf was transformed into a thriving market for the very best in new designers and jewellers. A perfect day in London would be to pop into the units here, have lunch in the Oxo Tower and the stroll down to Shakespeare's Globe Theatre. Plus Points: Made-to-meausre clothes from Callan White and Mantie Maker, recycled wear from Lauren Stanley and geometric jewellery from David Ashton. Minus Points: It's far too classy to let in any rotten elements.
Hours depend on individual units and some are by appointment only
Admission Free

Greenwich Markets
Greenwich High Road and Greenwich Church Street and Stockwell Street and College Approach and Thames Street London SE10

[BR: Greenwich]

Lazy Sundays are perfectly spent at the markets spread across Greenwich: Antiques Market, Bosun's Yard, Central Market, Craft Market and Flea Market. Plus Points: The Thai food stall at The Central Market, cute children's clothes at the Craft Market and any old iron from the Flea Market. Minus Points: Watch out for the brand-new 'antiques' and the crafts that take the adjective 'crafty' to previously unknown depths of whimsy.

All year Sat & Sun 09.00-17.00
Admission Free

Kensington Market

49-53 Kensington High Street London W8
[Tube: Kensington High Street]
The most claustrophobic indoor market in London has been popular since the early days of punk in 1976. Myriad grungy units selling T-shirts, caps and black leather set amid tattoo parlours and tarot-reading stalls. Plus Points: Original clubwear from Children of Vision, Ad Hoc and Strip. Minus Points: Shockingly expensive second-hand denim jackets, nickel gothic crucifixes and getting a tattoo inscribed with the name of your present lover.

All year Mon-Sat 10.00-18.00
Admission Free

Leather Lane

Leather Lane London EC1
[Tube: Chancery Lane / Farringdon]
Now that Clerkenwell is newly trendy it's good to be reminded that there are people that have lived in the environs for a lot longer than the recent refugees from Notting Hill. Jewellers from parallel Hatton Garden, office workers, Italians from nearby Little Italy and stall-holders mingle for cheap fruit and clothes. Not a lot of leather, despite its name! Plus Points: Lycra leggings for under a fiver, rip-off perfumes, bootleg cassettes, cheap lingerie and second-hand magazines. Minus Points: All of the above!

All year Mon-Fri 09.00-14.00
Admission Free

Oxo Tower

Bargehouse Street Southbank London SE1
[Tube/BR: Waterloo. Tube: Blackfriars]
Following a three-year, £20-million refurbishment plan, Oxo Tower opened its doors to the public as a centre for contemporary textile designers, jewellers and enamellists. Don't expect to snack on a bag of greasy chips at this market - food and fine views are to be found at the pricey Harvey Nichols' Roof-top Restaurant Bar and Brassiere.

All year Tue-Sun 11.00-18.00
Admission Free

Petticoat Lane

Middlesex and Wentworth Streets London E1
[Tube/BR: Liverpool Street / Aldgate East / Aldgate]
Over a thousand stalls selling clothes, shoes, trainers and electrical goods. Plus Points: High-street seconds, batteries and, if you look hard enough, bags of whelks. Minus Points: Dodgy electrical goods and tacky lingerie.

All year Mon-Fri (Wentworth Street only) 10.30-14.30, Sun (all streets) 09.00-14.00
Admission Free

Portobello Green Arcade

281 Portobello Road London W10
[Tube: Ladbroke Grove / Notting Hill]
Hidden away from the hoards that visit Portobello Market, this is a tiny shopping arcade full of individual designers each with their own unit. It was built in 1981, yet it remains a secret from all but the most determined shoppers, and consequently has a rather forlorn feel in contrast to the bustle outside. Plus Points: Lucy Barlow's Holly Golightly hats, Anna Scholz's 'non-sizest' designs (sizes 10-28) in the Morgana shop and exhibitionist evening wear at Preen. Minus Points: If you don't go clubbing now, you never will. Don't kid yourself - you will never wear those spangly disco hotpants and skin-tight midriff tops.

Hours depend on individual units - some are by appointment. Most Mon-Sat 10.00-18.00
Admission Free

Portobello Road Market

Portobello Road London W11
[Tube: Ladbroke Grove / Notting Hill]
It's an institution and a tourist attraction that during the week really is the place to go for all your everyday needs. The antiques stalls and shops are at Notting Hill end of Portobello Road, while the vintage clothing is piled high under the Westway at the northern end. According to the Evening Standard's style doyenne, Mimi Spencer, Britain's top stylists and fashion editors can be spotted seeking inspiration early on Friday mornings. Plus Points: The vintage shoe stall under the Westway for Fifties dancing shoes, the second-hand cashmere stalls for skinny-fit sweaters and cheap batteries from the chirpy stall-holder on the corner of Elgin Crescent. Minus Points: Moth-eaten suede jackets.

All year daily 09.00-17.00
Admission Free

Roman Road Market

Roman Road London E3

[DLR: Beckton]

One of the largest and oldest of the East End markets, marred only by inaccessibility by public transport. Plus Points: High-street stock at knock-down prices, market copies of catwalk styles and anything from the bargain-bucket shops lining Roman Road. Minus Points: Some woefully mass-produced sad-rags.

All year Tue Thur & Sat 08.30-15.00
Admission Free

Shepherd Market

London W1

[Tube: Green Park]

This Bijou pedestrianised enclave of small shops, restaurants, and outdoor cafes, between Piccadilly and Curzon Street, was named after Edward Shepherd, who built it in the mid-18th century. During the 17th century the annual 15 day May Fair was held on this site, and today Shepherd Market is still very much the centre of Mayfair.

Dependant on individual shops
Admission Free

Shepherd's Bush Market

Between the Goldhawk and Uxbridge Roads London W12

[Tube: Goldhawk / Shepherd's Bush]

Fantastically eclectic market selling the usual tacky clothes but with food stores and stalls laden with exotic fodder. It divides into two parallel streets: the original market and 'New Shepherd's Bush.' The former is more of a treasure trove. Plus Points: Luggage is a speciality with bargain brand names like Samsonite. Exotic food - try five different types of mango, both ripe and green plantains, Halal meat and obscure delights like roti, tinda, long dudhi, karela, blogo and eddoes. On top of that there's a specialist linoleum shop, religious kitsch, hair pieces and fabrics at £1 a metre. Minus Points: Clothes that look like rejects from a Spice Girl's wardrobe.

All year Mon-Sat 08.00-17.00
Admission Free

Smithfields Meat Market

Farringdon Street and Charterhouse Street London EC1

[Tube/BR: Farringdon / Barbican / City Thameslink]

Not for the faint-hearted or vegetarian, Smithfields is a temple to carnivorous habits.

Every conceivable part of every conceivable animal is jointed, carved and minced in these portals. The covered market is currently being modernised but is due for completion in 1998. Plus Points: Simply Sausages (341 Central Markets) is London's premier sausage shop with over 40 different types of meaty (and vegetarian) tubes including Wild Boar and Juniper, Duck and Apricot, and Steak and Guiness Stout. If you're out late from the nigh before, Smithfields is the place to head for an early morning point - special licensing laws mean that pubs like the Cock Tavern in the Poultry Market can serve pints from 06.00, while the surrounding cafés do sterling cooked breakfasts. Minus Points: The smell can be overwhelming and the stalls, with names like M&L Offals, encourage latent vegetarianism.

All year Mon-Fri 04.00-10.00
Admission Free

St James's Antiques Market

197 Piccadilly London W1V 0LL

[BR: Victoria / Caring Cross. Tube: Piccadilly Circus / Green Park. Bus: 3 / 6 / 9 / 12 / 14 / 15 / 19 / 22 / 38]

Tel: 020 7734 4511 Fax: 020 7734 7449

A specialist Antiques and Collectors' Market on Tuesdays and Crafts / Tourist Market Wednesday to Saturday. Enjoy a little piece of Heaven in Piccadilly.

Antiques: all year Tue 08.00-18.00. Craft / Tourist Market: all year Wed-Sat 08.00-18.00. Closed Easter
Admission Free

Whitechapel Market

Whitechapel Road London E1

[Tube: Whitechapel / Aldgate East]

A glorious combination of colours aromas and cultures, Whitechapel Market has been around for centuries. Plus Points: Fruit, flowers and unusual groceries. Minus Points: The clothes are nothing special. With suits going for as little as £12.99 you don't expect last-a-lifetime quality.

All year Mon-Sat 08.30-17.30, Thur 08.30-13.00
Admission Free

Medical Museums

Alexander Fleming Laboratory Museum

St Mary's Hospital Praed Street London W2 1NY

[BR/Tube: Paddington]

Tel: 020 7725 6528 Fax: 020 7725 6739

Opened in 1993 The Alexander Fleming Laboratory Museum leads you in the footsteps

of Fleming in the days when antibiotics were not being used to fight often lethal bacteria. See the small laboratory in which he discovered penicillin, now restored to it's cramped condition in 1928 when a petri dish of bacteria became contaminated with a mysterious mould, and experience the thrill of the story of the discovery of penicillin. Then retrace through the displays and a video the remarkable story of Fleming, the man and scientist. The museum also offers illustrated lectures to schools and other groups, on their own premises, on the history of hospitals, nursing and antibiotics.
All year Mon-Thur 10.00-13.00 and at other times by appointment Mon-Fri. Closed Bank Hols
A£2.00 Concessions£1.00

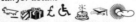

Florence Nightingale Museum
Gassiot House 2 Lambeth Palace Road London SE1 7EW
[on site of St Thomas' Hospital. Tube: Westminster / Waterloo]
Tel: 020 7620 0374 Fax: 020 7928 1760
This museum shows that Florence Nightingale was more than 'The Lady with the Lamp.' Beautifully designed, the museum creates the personal setting in which Florence's prized possessions, a lamp from the Crimean War and nursing artifacts are shown. Resource Centre by appointment for research.
All year Tue-Sun & Bank Hol Mon 10.00-17.00 Last Admission: 16.00
A£3.50 Family Ticket (A2+C2)£7.00 Concessions£2.50. Groups of 11+ discounted call for details

Museum of The Order of St John
St John's Gate St John's Lane London EC1M 4DA
[Tube: Farringdon]
Tel: 020 7253 6644 Fax: 020 7336 0587
Knights Hospitallers Priory with Tudor Gatehouse, Church and Norman Crypt. Armour; manuscripts; medals; silver and religious art are among the treasures on display. An interactive gallery uses oral histories, film, uniforms and photographs to tell the story of St John Ambulance, founded by the British Order of St John.
All year Mon-Fri 10.00-17.00, Sat 10.00-16.00. Tours of Gate Church & Crypt Tue, Fri & Sat 11.00 & 14.30
Museum: admission Free; Tours: donation requested

Peter Pan Gallery, The Museum of the history of Geat Ormond Street Hospital
1st Floor 55 Great Ormond Street London WC1 3JH
[Tube: Holborn / Russell Square On the 1st floor of an eighteenth century house opposite the main hospital building]
Tel: 020 7405 9200 X 5920
Artefacts and memorabilia of the hospital covering the time since its opening as the first hospital for children in Great Britain in 1852. Connections with Charles Dickens and Sir James Barrie. It also includes the Felix Besser Collection of Books on the history of Medicine, the Charles West Collection and the Peter Pan Collection of the story in many languages.
By special appointment only Mon-Fri 10.30-16.00
Admission free

Royal College of Surgeons
35-43 Lincoln's Inn Fields London WC2A 3PN
[Tube: Holborn / Temple]
Tel: 020 7312 6694/973 2190 Fax: 020 7405 4438
The four museums of the Royal College of Surgeons are the Hunterian, the Odontological and the Wellcome museums of Pathology and Anatomy. The Hunterian museum contains about 3,500 surviving specimens from John Hunter's 18th century collection of anatomical and pathological preparations both human and animal. Three paintings from George Stubbs are also on display. The Odontological museum is a museum about teeth, it has displays on dental anatomy, instruments and dentures. The Wellcome museums of Pathology and Anatomy contain over 2,300 specimens dating from the 19th century to the present day. There is also an Historical Instrument Collection of surgical instruments.
Hunterian & Odontological Museums Mon-Fri 10.00-17.00. Wellcome Museums by appointment only. Tel before visiting
Admission free, donations are encouraged

Royal Hospital Museum
Royal Hospital Road Chelsea London SW3 4SR
[adjacent to the London Gate Royal Hospital. Tube: Sloane Square]
Tel: 020 7730 0161 x203
Hospital run by retired Military Officers for the benefit of the occupants who are former soldiers. Small museum reflecting the history of the Royal Hospital with a range of pictures, plans and maps. The large medal collection, bequeathed by former pensioners, date from 1793 to present day. The collection of uniforms show examples that have been worn during the last 100 years. Parking only for coach parties pre-booked.
Museum: Mon-Sat 10.00-12.00 & 14.00-16.00, Apr-Sept Sun 14.00-16.00

Admission Free

The Old Operating Theatre, Museum and Herb Garret

9a St Thomas Street Southwark London SE1 9RY

[Tube: London Bridge]

Tel: 020 7955 4791 Fax: 020 7378 8383

Climb up a steep spiral staircase and into the roof of a church, which houses the oldest surviving operating theatre in Britain dating back to 1821 before the advent of antiseptic surgery or anaesthetic. Complete with wooden operating table, blood box and tiered stands from which spectators witnessed the ordeal of surgery. Pill making equipment, surgical paraphernalia and specimens, lurk amidst a cornucopia of medicinal herbs in the 300 year old apothecary's garret of Old St. Thomas Hospital.

All year Tue-Sun 10.00-17.00. Open most Mon - call to check. Closed 25 Dec
A£2.90 C£1.50 Family Ticket £7.25 Concessions£2.00

discount offer: Two For The Price Of One

Military & Defence Museums

Cabinet War Rooms

Clive Steps King Charles Street London SW1A 2AQ

[Tube: Westminster or St. James's Park. Buses: 3, 11, 12, 24, 53, 77A, 88, 109, 159, 184, 211]

Tel: 020 7930 6961 Fax: 020 7839 5897

www.iwm.org.uk

T he underground emergency accommodation used to protect the Prime Minister, Winston Churchill, his War Cabinet and the Chiefs of Staff during the Second World War provide a fascinating insight into those tense days and nights. There are 21 rooms in all, all carefully preserved. New acoustiguide audio tours for adults and children in six languages.

All year Apr-Sept daily 09.30-18.00. Oct-Mar 10.00-18.00. Closed 24-26 Dec
Last Admission: 17.15
A£4.80 C£Free OAPs&Students£3.50 Unemployed£2.20 Disabled visitors and carers A£2.30 OAPs&Students£1.80. Group rates 10+ A£3.40 OAPs&Students£2.70. Booked School parties £Free. Unbooked school parties C£1.80 C(ages 16+)£2.70 A£3.30

Guards Museum

Wellington Barracks Birdcage Walk London SW1E 6HQ

[Tube: St. James's Park]

Tel: 020 7414 3428/414 3271 Fax: 020 7414 3411

The story of the Foot Guards, a superb collection of uniforms, weapons and memorabilia illustrating their martial history and service to The Sovereign and The City of London for over three centuries. Magnificent venue for all types of functions. Details on request. Guide Tours for pre-booked groups.

All year daily 10.00-16.00 & Bank Hol. Closed Christmas
A£2.00 Family Ticket £4.00, Concessions & Group rates 25+ £1.00. Guided Tours charged, please call for details

HMS Belfast (Imperial War Museum)

Morgan's Lane Tooley Street London SE1 2JH

[BR/Tube: London Bridge. Tube: Tower Hill / London Bridge. DLR: Tower Gateway]

Tel: 020 7940 6328 Fax: 020 7403 0719

www.iwm.org.uk

HMS Belfast - the last of the Royal Navy's big-gun armoured warships from the Second World War. With nine huge decks, you can see for yourself where 850 men lived, worked and fought. Visitors can explore from the captain's bridge all the way down to the massive six inch gun turrets, boiler rooms, hammock-slung messdecks, galley, sick bay, punishment cells and more. Leave at least two hours for whole visit. Free Birthday Party facilities on board for pre-booked groups.

Mar-Oct daily 10.00-18.00. Nov-Feb daily 10.00-17.00. Closed 24-26 Dec. 1 June-8 July 1999 HMS Belfast will be in dry dock and therefore closed
Last Admission: Mar-Oct 17.15, Nov-Feb 16.15
Queuing Times: Minimal
A£4.70 C(0-16)£Free Concessions£3.60. Group bookings £3.40 £2.60 & £1.70. Group bookings call for details. Pre-booked schools: One Teacher Admitted Free Per Ten Pupils

Honourable Artillery Company

Armoury House City Road London EC1Y 2BQ

[Tube: Old Street]

Tel: 020 7382 1537 Fax: 020 7382 1538

Display of uniforms, old arms, awards, campaign medals, regimental colours, pictures, trophies and souvenirs.

By appointment 12.00-18.00. Weekdays tours of Armoury House also available 15.00-18.00
A£2.00

Inns of Court and City Yeomanry Museum

10 Stone Buildings Lincolns Inn London WC2A 3TG

[Tube: Chancery Lane]

London

Tel: 020 7405 8112/831 1693 Fax: 020 7414 3496

Small but interesting display of uniforms, medals and equipment of the Inns of Court Regiment and the City of London Yeomanry (the Rough Riders) which together comprise the Inns of Court and City Yeomanry covering period 1798 to date. Occasional exhibitions and events.

By appointment only with Curator please call to arrange
Admission Free, donations appreciated

£ 🍴

Museum of Artillery in the Rotunda

Royal Artillery Institution Old Royal Military Academy Woolwich London SE18 4DN
[BR: Arsnal. Tube: Woolwich]
Tel: 020 8316 5402 Fax: 020 8781 5929
The guns, muskets, rifles and edged weapons that form the collections in this museum are contained in the rotunda designed by John Nash that once stood in St James's Park. The collection tells the story of the gun from its beginning in the 13th century to the present day, in an unrivalled display of ordnance, including ammunition.
All year Mon-Fri 13.00-16.00. Closed all Bank Hol
Admission Free

National Army Museum

Royal Hospital Road Chelsea London SW3 4HT
[BR: Victoria, Tube: Sloane Square, Bus: 11 / 19 / 22 & 211 along King's Road; 137 to Pimlico Road; 239 (Mon-Sat) stops immediately outside the Museum]
Tel: 020 7730 0717 Fax: 020 7823 6573
www.national-army-museum.ac.uk
Discover some of Britain's finest military treasures. Displays include weapons, paintings, equipment, uniforms, models, medals, reconstructions. Exhibits include nine Victoria Crosses, a model of the Battle of Waterloo, Florence Nightingale's jewellery, and the skeleton of Napoleon's horse. A new permanent exhibition, The Modern Army, is now open.
All year daily 10.00-17.30. Closed Good Fri, May Day, 24-26 Dec & 1 Jan
Admission Free

↓ *special events*

▶ **String of Pearls Activities**
5/2/00-3/12/00
A series of events and activities in Chelsea on the first weekend of every month throughout 2000. Call for date confirmation and details
▶ **2000 Soldiers' Lives and Soldiers' Wives**
4/3/00-5/3/00

Royal Air Force Museum

Grahame Park Way Hendon London NW9 5LL
[signposted from A1 / A5 M1 N Circular. BR: Mill Hill. Tube: Colindale. Bus: 303]
Tel: 020 8205 2266 Fax: 020 8205 8044
www.rafmuseum.org.uk
There's something to entertain everyone with over 70 legendary planes, fascinating exhibits and an art gallery telling the story of aviation from the Wright Brothers to the RAF Eurofighter of the 21st century. Free return visit within six months of issue of individual tickets, ask for details. Please check info line for possible changes. Major new interactive gallery opens in the Spring - 'fun 'n' flight.'
All year daily 10.00-18.00. Closed 24-26 Dec & 1 Jan. Info line: 0891 600 5633 24hr
Last Admission: 17.30
A£6.50 C(0-5)£Free C(5-16)£3.25 Family Ticket (A2+C2)£16.60 Additional C£1.65 OAPs£4.90 Students&UB40s£2.25. Groups of 10+ 20% discount. School discounts: £1.50 1 Adult leader Free per 5 Children.
discount offer: Two For The Price Of One (based on highest priced ticket)

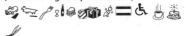

✂

Royal Armouries

HM Tower of London London EC3N 4AB
[BR: Fenchurch Street. Tube: Tower Hill. Bus: 15,

X15, 25, 47, 78, 100, D1, D9, D11]
Tel: 020 7480 6358 Fax: 020 7481 2922
Britain's oldest museum, the Royal Armouries
at the Tower is re-displaying its collections in
the White Tower, to tell the stories of the
building and of the Armouries which has occupied it for 400 years, storing and displaying
royal armours and military weapons.
*All year Mar-Oct Mon-Sat 09.00-18.00, Sun
10.00-18.00. Nov-Feb Mon-Sat 09.00-17.00, Sun
10.00-17.00*
*Last Admission: Tower: 1 hour, Armouries: 1
hour 30mins*
*Royal Armouries: Admission Free. Tower: A£8.50
C£5.60 Family Ticket £25.40*

Royal British Legion Poppy Factory
20 Petersham Road Richmond Surrey TW10
6UR
[Tube: BR: Richmond. Bus: 65]
Tel: 020 8940 3305 Fax: 020 8332 1205
By appointment only. Makers of poppies,
wreaths and remembrance crosses.
Wheelchairs and pushchairs on ground floor
only.
*All year for guided tours only. Mon-Thur 10.00
& 13.30, Fri 10.00. Tours last about 2 hours
Admission Free*

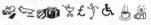

Mills - Water & Wind

Wimbledon Windmill Museum
Windmill Road Wimbledon Common
Wimbledon London SW19 5NR
[Windmill Road off Parkside (A219)]
Tel: 020 8947 2825
www.wpcc.org.uk
The history of windmills and windmilling told
in pictures, models and the machinery and
tools of the trade. The Museum is housed in
the historic Wimbledon Windmill which was
built in 1817 and ended its working life in
1864. Set within the 1100 acres of Wimbledon
Common.
*Easter-Oct Sat Sun and Public Hol 14.00-17.00
A£1.00 C£0.50 Concessions£0.50. Group visits
by arrangement*

Multicultural Museums

Commonwealth Experience
Commonwealth Institute Kensington High
Street London W8 6NQ
*[Tube: High Street Kensington then 5mins walk
towards Holland Park. Bus: 9 / 9a / 10 / 27 / 28
/ 31 / 49 / C1 Hoppa]*
Tel: 020 7603 4535 Fax: 020 7602 7374

www.commonwealth.org.uk

Embark on a fun-packed adventure around
the globe. Start with Helride, a thrilling simu-
lator helicopter ride over Malaysia, continue
with Interactive World, a 'hands-on' activity
centre that illuminates the fascinating world
of natural phenomena. Before finally exploring two floors of intriguing displays featuring
the diverse landscapes, history and cultures of
over 40 Commonwealth countries.

*This venue is now CLOSED UNTIL JUNE 2000
(2.12.99)*

Last Admission: 16.30

Closed until further notice.

Grange Museum of Community History

Neasden Lane Neasden London NW10 1QB

[on Neasden Roundabout. Tube: Neasden]

**Tel: 020 8452 8311/937 3600 Fax: 020 8208
4233**

Housed in a building that was originally an
18th century stable block, the Grange Museum
tells the story of the Peoples of Brent. The
Brent People Gallery is a multicultural and historical journey through the peoples of Brent
from the 1920s to the present day, and features audio listening posts and CD's.
Wheelchair access is limited to the ground
floor, guided tours are available for pre-
booked groups. The Ground floor consists of
Victorian and Edwardian room sets and the
current community project. Conservatory and
Garden with picnic areas and shop.

*All year Sept-May Mon-Fri 11.00-17.00, Sat
10.00-17.00. June-Aug Tue-Fri 11.00-17.00, Sat
10.00-17.00, Sun 14.00-17.00. Closed Public Hol*

Admission Free, donations welcome

London

Horniman Museum and Gardens

100 London Road Forest Hill London SE23 3PQ

*[situated on the South Circular. BR: Forest Hill,
Bus: 176 / 185 / 312 / 63 / 122 / P4 / P13 / 352]*

Tel: 020 8699 1872 Fax: 020 8291 5506

www.horniman.ac.uk

Set in 16 acres of beautiful gardens, this fascinating, free Museum houses a number of
unique exhibitions to delight adults and children alike. The African Worlds gallery is dedicated to African art and culture and includes
the largest African mask, the Natural History
gallery echoes the Victorian age with many
original specimens, while the Living Waters
Aquarium explores marine ecology with tropical fish and seahorses. (The Music collection is
currently off display due to a £13m lottery
project to build a new extension). The
Horniman has an extensive events and activities programme ranging from art workshops
to live music performances.

*All year Mon-Sat 10.30-17.30, Sun 14.00-17.30.
Closed 25 & 26 Dec. Gardens close at sunset*

Last Admission: 17.20

Admission Free

Jewish Museum

Raymond Burton House 129-131 Albert Street
Camden London NW1 7NB
*[off Camden High Street / Parkway. Tube:
Camden Town]*
Tel: 020 7284 1997 Fax: 020 7267 9008
www.jewmusm.ort.org

Opens a window on to the history and religious life of the Jewish community in Britain
and beyond. Its attractive galleries tell the
story of the Jewish community from the
Norman Conquest until recent times, and
illustrate Jewish religious life with outstanding examples of Jewish ceremonial art. The
Museum has been awarded Designated Status
in recognition of the national importance of
its collections. Guided walks of Jewish London
can be arranged. Education programmes and
group visits by prior arrangement.

*All year Sun-Thur 10.00-16.00. Closed Jewish
Festivals & Bank Hol*
Last Admission: 30mins before closing
A£3.00 Family Ticket £7.50 Concessions£1.50

↓ *special events*

► **"The Jewish Dickens" Israel Zangwill and
the Wanderers of Kilburn**
3/11/99-14/3/00
*The life and works of Zangwill, prolific novelist,
playwright and campaigner for political causes*
► **The Crystal Den - a new play by Marion
Baraitser**
14/3/00-14/3/00
*at 19.30. Premiere of performed extracts of a
new play set in 1880s London about the life of
Eleanor Marx Aveling, call 020 7794 0022*
► **Victorian Jews through British Eyes**
14/3/00-14/3/00
*Illustrated talk by Anne Cowen, 19.00. £6.50
(£5.00 Museum Friends, full-time students)
Includes gallery admission and refreshments*
► **Judaica 2000 - Contemporary British Jewish
Ceremonial Art**
5/4/00-3/9/00
*Outstanding examples of contemporary Jewish
ceremonial art by British craftsmen and
women. Work ranges from textiles, metalwork
and glass to ceramics, wood and calligraphy.*

Jewish Museum - Finchley, London's Museum of Jewish Life

80 East End Road London N3 2SY
[on A504. Tube: Finchley Central. 12mins walk via Station Road / Manor View]
Tel: 020 8349 1143 Fax: 020 8343 2162
www.jewmusm.ort.org
Social history displays tracing Jewish immigration and settlement in London including reconstructions of East End tailoring and cabinet-making workshops. Mezzanine gallery has special exhibition on Leon Greenman, British citizen and Holocaust survivor. Education programmes and group visits by prior arrangement. Guided walks of Jewish London also available.
All year Mon-Thur 10.30-17.00, Sun 10.30-16.30. Closed Jewish Festivals, Public & Bank Hol, 24 Dec-4 Jan. Also closed Sun in Aug and Bank Holiday Weekends
Last Admission: 30mins before closing
A£2.00 C£Free Concessions£1.00
discount offer: Two For The Price Of One Full Paying Adult
↓*special events*
▶ **Taxi!**
10/2/00-29/10/00
An exhibition about Jewish taxi drivers and the London cab trade. Call 020 8349 1143 for further details.

Kent House (Czech Memorial Scrolls Trust)

Rutland Gardens London SW7 1BX
[Tube: Knightsbridge opposite Knightsbridge Barracks]
Tel: 020 7584 3741
The permanent exhibition tells the unique story of the rescue from Prague in 1964 of 1,564 Torah scrolls and of their restoration and distribution to communities throughout the world. The exhibits include some of the scrolls, a remarkable display of Torah binders, some dating from the 18th century and other moving reminders of the vanished communities of Bohemia and Moravia. The expert restoration with traditional materials and calligraphy is also featured.

All year Tue & Thur 10.00-16.00 other times by appointment

Music & Theatre Museums

British Library National Sound Archive

29 Exhibition Road London SW7

[Tube: South Kensington]

Tel: 020 7412 7440

Library and listening facilities by appointment only. Holds one million discs of all kinds and more than 80,000 hours of recorded tape. Collection of music, wildlife sounds, drama, spoken literature and sound effects.

Admission Free

Cabaret Mechanical Theatre

33-34 The Market Covent Garden London WC2E 8RE

[Tube: Covent Garden]

Tel: 020 7379 7961 Fax: 020 7497 5445

www.cabaret.co.uk/

The museum offers entertainment for the whole family with an impressive collection of Automata. Buy a ticket in the foyer area, get it stamped by the mechanical stamping man and enter the magical world of Cabaret, where at the touch of a button or the insertion of a coin, machines are set in motion.

All year Mon-Sat 10.00-18.30, Sun 11.00-18.30. School holidays daily 10.00-19.00. Closed 25-26 Dec & 1 Jan

Last Admission: 18.15

A£1.95 Family Ticket £4.95 C&Concessions£1.20

discount offer: £1.00 Off Family Ticket

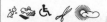

London

Musical Museum

368 High Street Brentford Middlesex TW8 0BD

Tel: 020 8560 8108

This museum will take you back to a bygone age to hear and see a marvellous working collection of automatic musical instruments from small music boxes to a mighty Wurlitzer theatre organ. Working demonstrations. Tour lasts 90mins. Registered Charity No. 802011.

Apr-Oct Sat & Sun 14.00-17.0. July-Aug Wed 14.00-16.00, Sat & Sun 14.00-17.00

A£3.20 C&OAPs£2.50 Family Ticket £10.00

discount offer: Two For The Price Of One. Not Valid For Special Events. Valid Until 31 Oct 2000

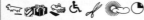

Rock Circus

The London Pavilion 1 Piccadilly Circus London W1V 9LA

[Tube: Piccadilly Circus]

Tel: 020 7734 7203 Fax: 020 7734 8023

www.madame-tussauds.com

London's Rock Circus is where the spirit of rock speaks to you, sings to you, plays for you, moves and touches you. Audio-animatronic moving and static wax figures, lasers, authentic memorabilia, videos, archive film and personal stereo sound surround you and astound you. There's a change of pace at every pace, a new rock turn at every turn. Rock Circus' award winning exhibition and show is the ultimate rock experience and will take you 90mins to see.

All year Sun-Thur 11.00-21.00, Tue 12.00-21.00, Fri & Sat 11.00-22.00. Rocking for Easter 1999, after transformations

A£8.25 C(0-16)£6.25 Concessions£6.95. Groups Rates of 10+: A£6.95 C(0-16)£5.10 Concessions£5.90

Royal College of Music Department of Portraits and Performance History

Prince Consort Road South Kensington London SW7 2BS

Tel: 020 7591 4340 Fax: 020 7589 7740

An extensive collection of portraits of musicians, comprising some 320 original portraits and many thousands of prints and photographs. Also houses the College's important collection of concert programmes.

Term time Mon-Fri by appointment, parties by arrangement

Admission Free

Royal College of Music Museum of Instruments

Prince Consort Road South Kensington London SW7 2BS

[Tube: South Kensington]

Tel: 020 7591 4346/589 3643 Fax: 020 7589 7740

Internationally renowned collection of musical instruments. Over 600 keyboard, stringed and wind instruments from circa 1480 to the present day, including the Donaldson, Tagore, Hipkins, Ridley and Hartley collections. Guided tours available for pre-booked parties.

Closed Wed during term-time 14.00-16.30. Closed Jan; groups and special visits by appointment

A£1.20 Concessions£1.00

Theatre Museum

(Public Entrance) Russell Street Covent Garden London WC2E 7PA

[Tube: Covent Garden]

Tel: 020 7836 7891 Fax: 020 7836 5148

http://theatremuseum.vam.ac.uk

Discover the magic of the stage past and present - exhibitions on the British stage and its stars from Shakespeare's time to the present. Daily Costume workshops and demonstrations on the art of stage make-up available for all ages. Postal address: 1e Tavistock Street, London, WC2E 7PA.

All year Tue-Sun 10.00-18.00

Last Admission: 30mins before closing

A£4.50 Concessions£2.50. Booked groups 10+ A£3.00, Concessions£2.50

London

Natural History Museums

Natural History Museum
Cromwell Road London SW7 5BD
[Tube: South Kensington]
Tel: 020 7942 5000 Fax: 020 7942 5536
www.nhm.ac.uk
A day out for all the family. Highlights include 'Dinosaurs,' 'Creepy Crawlies,' 'Human biology' and 'The power within' where you can experience an earthquake and investigate the causes and devastating effects of volcanoes. Opening in July 2000 'Rhythms of life' will take a quirky look at the roles of rhythm and time in nature. Ideal for all age groups - closes Spring 2001. October 2000 - February 2001 BG Wildlife Photographer of the Year 2000, internationally famous exhibition of stunning wildlife photography.
visitor comments: Terrific value. Very interesting displays and lots of touch screens. Wide variety of refreshments with quick service and pleasant surroundings. The Earth Gallery is fabulous!
All year Mon-Sat 10.00-17.50, Sun 11.00-17.50. Closed 23-26 Dec
Last Admission: 17.30
A£6.50 C£Free Concessions£3.50. Groups call for details.

↓ *special events*
► **Voyages of Discovery**
4/7/99-1/3/00
► **BG Wildlife Photographer of the Year Exhibition**
23/10/99-29/2/00

Nature & Conservation Parks

Beckton Creek Trail
Beckton Sewage Works Jenkins Lane Beckton London IG11 0AD
[Tube: Barking on the District and Metropolitan lines]
Tel: 020 8507 4721
Situated next door the Europe's largest sewage treatment works and the ancient Barking Creek, this special spot for wildlife and visitors alike. It is one of the most important ecological communities in London, and has developed undisturbed for over 20 years. At the end of the trail is a birdhide which is suitable for disabled visitors and provides magnificent views over the river Thames. The Creek Trail is not really suitable for wheelchair users but the birdhide is.
All year daily by appointment - tides may limit access
Admission Free

East Ham Nature Reserve
Visitor Centre Norman Road East Ham London E6 4HN
[Tube: East Ham]
Tel: 020 8470 4525
This 10 acre nature reserve with grasslands and woodland, has two nature trails with printed guides. One trail is suitable for all disabled visitors. There is a visitor centre with displays relating to local and natural history and the history of the churchyard nature reserve.
Visitor Centre: All year Weekends 14.00-17.00. Nature Reserve: Summer months Tue-Fri 09.00-17.00, Weekends 14.00-17.00, Winter months Tue-Fri 09.00-16.00, Weekends 13.00-16.00
Admission Free

King George V Reservoir
Lee Valley Road Chingford London RM
[BR: Ponders End J25/26 M25, A110 or A112]
Tel: 020 8808 1527
This is the largest body of water in Greater London and forms part of the Lee Valley reservoir complex. The site is a site of special scientific interest and holds internationally important numbers of overwintering wildfowl, as well as being important for summer migrants and moulting species. Permit holders have access to both reservoirs from which there is excellent visability
Access throughout the year
Season Ticket holders only

London

London Wildlife Trust
Harling House 47-51 Great Suffolk Street
London SE1 OBS
Tel: 020 7278 6612
www.wildlifetrust.org.uk/london/
London Wildlife Trust Key Project. The London
Wildlife Trust manages nearly 60 nature
reserves in the Greater London area and runs a
free annual programme of events and activities for Londoners to discover more about
nature in the capital. It is the only organisation in the Capital involved in all aspects of
nature conservation and campaigns to protect
wildlife whenever it is under threat, as well as
providing a popular information service to
Londoners offering a series of wildlife information leaflets and packs. The Trust also has a
junior environmental club called Wildlife
Watch and educational work is targeted at all
ages working with schools, universities and
community groups.
Phone enquiries: All year Mon-Fri 10.00-17.00
Membership: A£15.00 per year, Wildlife Watch
C£6.50 per year; 01732 520040

Ramblers' Association
1-5 Wandsworth Road London SW8 2XX
[Various venues around the country]
Tel: 020 7339 8500 Fax: 020 7339 8557
The Ramblers' Association is a voluntary
organisation founded in 1935. It promotes
walking and works to protect right of way, to
campaign for access to open country and to
defend the beauty of the country side. It has
over 197,000 supporters consisting of 122,000
individual members and 77,000 members of
its affiliated clubs and socities.
See events
Free walks

Tree Council
51 Catherine Place London SW1E 6DY
**Tel: 020 7828 9928 (Hotline) Fax: 020 7828
9060**
The British Isles are less well wooded than anywhere else in Europe, although we do have
more than our fair share of really ancient veteran trees. We also have a splendid Victorian
heritage of city parks and street trees, though
in the past few years they have suffered badly
from neglect, air and ground pollution and
damaging cable and service trenching.
Landmark Trees are any trees that are special
or important to us. It could be our own personal tree, planted to mark a birth or special
event, or one of the veteran trees mentioned
before.
Admission Free

On the Water

Batchworth Lock Centre
99 Church Street Rickmansworth Hertfordshire
WD3 1JD
*[A404 Rickmansworth / Northwood. BR:
Marylebone / Aylesbury. 10mins walk from
Rickmansworth station]*
Tel: 01923 778382 Fax: 01923 710903
Batchworth Lock is an historic setting on the
Grand Union Canal. The Canal Centre is
housed in former stables where horses rested
overnight whilst the boatmen refreshed themselves in the adjacent Boat Inn. Maps showing
the network of waterways around Batchworth
are available in the Centre, which also stocks a
wide range of other books, guides, leaflets,
videos, souvenirs, hand painted canalware etc,
plus an exciting range of ice-creams. The Trust
welcomes educational visits on weekdays by
arrangement. Enquiries should be made to the
Canal Centre. Enjoy a half hour trip on the
canal to Stockers Lock and back. Operates on
Sundays from 11.00-17.00.
*Easter weekend-end Oct Mon, Tue, Thur, Fri
10.00-15.00, Sat & Sun 11.00-17.00*
*Admission Free. Whilst there is no charge for
admission to any of the events listed, donations
are always welcomed towards the costs of
maintaining the Centre and promoting the
activities.*

Bateaux London
Embankment Pier Victoria Embankment
London WC2N 6NU
[Tube: Embankment]
Tel: 020 7925 2215 Fax: 020 7839 1034
Imagine dining on the finest international
gourmet cuisine in luxurious surroundings
while some of London's most famous sights -
The Houses of Parliament, St. Paul's Cathedral,
Tower Bridge, The Tower of London and more -
float majestically past your window. You've
just imagined a lunchtime or evening aboard
the Restaurant Symphony. Available for pri-
vate hire and includes a private suite for
groups of up to 82 people.
Please call for departure times
*Four Course Evening Meal with Cabaret: £55.00.
Sunday Lunch: £27.00. Mon-Sat Lunch: £21.00.
Booking by telephone only.*

Canal Cruises - Jenny Wren
250 Camden High Street London NW1 8QS
[Tube: Camden Town]
**Tel: 020 7485 4433/6210 Fax: 020 7485
9098**
Cruise along the picturesque Regent's Canal
aboard the Jenny Wren, a traditionally

London

designed and decorated canal boat. 90mins going through a lock, past London Zoo, Regent's Park to Little Venice and return with an interesting commentary on the canal's history. Evening buffet cruises for groups of 20/40. Call for details.

Mar-Oct daily all day
A£5.40 C&OAPs£3.25. School Groups each £2.00. Groups rates call for details

Canal Cruises - My Fair Lady

250 Camden High Street London NW1 8QS
[Tube: Camden Town]
Tel: 020 7485 4433/6210 Fax: 020 7485 9098

Enjoy a leisurely cruise along the Regent's Canal aboard the My Fair Lady, a luxury cruising restaurant. Whilst cruising an excellent three-course meal is served freshly cooked in the galley. My Fair Lady is also available for hire throughout the year for luncheon or dinner for a maximum of 80 guests.

All year, public cruise for lunch of Sunday, public cruise for dinner Tue & Sun
A£16.95-£29.85

Catamaran Cruisers

Charing Cross Pier Victoria Embankment London WC2N 6NU
[Tube: Embankment]
Tel: 020 7987 1185 Fax: 020 7839 1034
See the heart of London from the Thames. Daily sightseeing journey including commentary, from Charing Cross Pier to Tower Pier to Greenwich.

All year daily 09.30-16.30. Please telephone for departure times.
Last Admission: 16.30
A£7.00 C£3.80. Group Rates and School Parties available

Circular Cruise

HMS President (1918) Victoria Embankment London EC4Y 0HJ
[Tube: Embankment / London Bridge / Waterloo / Westminster]
Tel: 020 7839 2111 Ticket Box Fax: 020 7936 3383

A visit to London should always include a trip on the Thames. A trip on London's river provides a whole new perspective to many of London's world famous tourist sights. Historic riverside attractions include the Houses of Parliament, Big Ben, Lambeth Palace, the Tower of London, Tower Bridge. Shakespeare's Globe Theatre, Cleopatra's Needle and HMS Belfast. They merge with new waterside developments such as Butler's Wharf and the Design Museum, London Bridge City with the shopping and restaurant complex of Hays Galleria and the South Bank Arts Centre including The Festival Hall and National Theatre. All times subject to tide conditions, total cruise time approximately 1 hour.

All year. From: Westminster Pier Mid-Winter Season (Dec, Jan and Feb) weekends only at 11.00, 12.20, 13.40 and 15.00. Winter Season (Mar 6-Apr 2 and Oct 30-Nov 26) daily at 11.00, 12.20, 13.40 and 15.00. Summer Season (Apr 3-May 28 and Sept 4-Oct 29) daily, every 40 mins from 11.00-17.00. Peak Summer Season (May 29-Sept 3) daily, every 30 mins from 11.00-18.30.
Queuing Times: minimal
Circular Cruise: A£5.80 C(2-15)£2.90 Family Ticket (A2+C2)£15.50 OAPs/Students£4.80. Singles to London Bridge City: A£4.20 C(2-15)£2.10 Family Ticket (A2+C2)£10.60 OAPs&Students£3.20. Singles to St Katharine's: A£4.60 C(2-15)£2.30 Family Ticket (A2+C2)£11.60 OAPs&Students£3.60. Groups 10+ discounts available.

City Cruises

Cherry Garden Pier Cherry Garden Street London SE16 4TU
[Tube: Tower Hill]
Tel: 020 7237 5134/7488 0344 Fax: 020 7237 3498/7480 6289

The London Showboat: Imagine your favourite songs from the world's famous musicals as the perfect accompaniment to the sights of London. Add a river trip, a superb five course dinner, cocktails with the captain, dancing and you have the perfect combination for an unforgettable evening. City Cruises have unveiled their first package for the millennium - with an all-in price of £30 including Millennium dome offering a direct link from Central London each day in year 2000. The first aerial view of the Dome since construction work was completed in August. City Cruises will operate from a new pier just a few yards from the entrance. To link the Greenwich site with Central London in 2000 City Cruises will build a fleet of luxury craft based on the successful design of Millennium of London, which entered service in 1996. The new boats will provide the backbone of an extended sightseeing network on the river, which will build on the company's existing successful year round operations. The Red Fleet Sightseeing Cruises: Explore the River Thames from Westminster Pier or Tower Pier and back again. From the deck of one of our Red Fleet there are superb views of all that London has to offer. London's mixture of historic and modern buildings is well illustrated on our tours. In whichever direction you travel, you will normally enjoy a full commentary, so you will not miss anything at all. Lunch Cruises: daily from St Katharines Pier by the Tower Hotel 12.30-13.45, hot two course meal with coffee, Afternoon Tea Cruises: daily from St Katharines Pier 15.00-16.30 sandwiches, scones, cakes, tea and coffee.

The London Showboat: May-Oct Wed-Sun & Nov-Apr boarding from Westminster Pier at 19.00 returning 22.30. Red Fleet: Mar-Nov Westminster to Tower Pier daily from 10.30 then every 30mins til 16.30. Tower Pier to Westminster daily from 11.00 then every 30mins til 16.30. June-Aug evening trips daily Westminster to Tower Pier from 17.30 then every 20mins til 21.30. Tower Pier to Westminster from 18.00 then every 20mins til 21.30

The London Showboat: £45.00 inclusive of welcome drink and half bottle of wine. Red Fleet: Single A£4.80 C£2.50 Return A£6.00 C£3.10. The Millennium Dome: £30.00

John Lyon Narrow Boat Project

Brent Children's Play Service 1st Floor Middlesex House Northwick Road Alperton Middlesex HA0 1LG
[A40 / A406 (North Circular) to Hanger Lane Gyratory, then 0.5m N along A4005 - enter Sainsbury car-park. BR: Alperton]
Tel: 020 8810 9126 Fax: 020 8810 5356
The Brent Children's Play Service Narrowboat trips provide an ideal social and educational experience of the canalscape. The boat is available for school groups, playgroups, youth groups, people with special needs and other community organisations and families. Users may have a try at steering or just enjoy the journey.
Apr-end Nov daily 10.00-dusk
Boat Hire Charge (inc Steerer) £20.00 per hour for first hour, £5.00 for each subsequent hour, max. 12 passengers

London Waterbus Company

58 Camden Lock Place London NW1 8AF
[nearest coach park for all waterbus departure points is at London Zoo. Both areas have restricted parking. At Little Venice some parking is available at weekends. Camden Lock access: Bus: 24 / 27 / 29 / 31 / 68 (Sun) / 74 / 134 / 135 / 168 / 214 / 253 / C2. Tube: Camden Town / Chalk Farm. Little Venice access: Bus: 6 / 8 / 16 / 16a / 18 / 46. Tube: Warwick Avenue]
Tel: 020 7482 2660/2550
The London Waterbus Company operates four converted traditional working narrowboats, Milton, Perseus and Gardenia (68 seats), Water Ouzel (50 seats) and a purpose-built wideboat, Water Buffalo (75 seats). The waterbuses

have full protection against unpredictable weather and large opening windows to make the most of fine days. Boat trips along the historic Regents Canal. Through Regents Park, the Maida Hill Tunnel and stopping at London Zoo for admission. From Camden Lock or Little Venice. We regret that we cannot take pets or bicycles on board the boats. Wheelchair can only be carried if folded. Since the landing stage for London Zoo is within Zoo grounds, passengers intending to disembark at the Zoo must buy a combined ticket including Zoo admission. Private charter information is available on request.

All year Apr-Oct daily on the hour from 10.00-17.00. Nov-Mar Sat & Sun 10.30-15.00. It is possible to catch a later boat for return trips
Last Admission: Apr-Oct 17.00, Nov-Mar 15.00
One Way Trips: Little Venice-Camden Lock/Camden Lock-Little Venice A£3.900 C&OAPs£2.50. London Zoo-Little Venice A£2.70 C&OAPs£1.80, London Zoo-Camden Locl A£1.50 C&OAPs£1.10. Return Trips: Little Venice-Camden Lock-Little Venice A£5.40 C&OAPs£3.20, Camden Lock-Little Venice-Camden Lock A£5.40 C&OAPs£3.20, Zoo-Little Venice-Zoo A£3.70 C£2.50, Zoo-Camden Lock-Zoo A£2.40 C&OAPs£1.80. Combined Ticket one way trip and zoo entrance: Little Venice-Zoo £9.90 C£7.00, Camden Lock-Zoo A£9.00 C£7.00. C(0-3)£Free. C(0-4)£pay for boat trip but not entrance to Zoo. Group rates 20+ available

Puppet Theatre Barge

Little Venice Blomfield Road London W9 2PF
[Tube: WarwickAvenue. All buses on the Edgware Rd]
Tel: 020 7249 6876 Box Office Fax: 020 7683 0741
The Hare and the Tortoise and other tales from Aesop are brought to life with drama and humour. Staged with beautiful lighting and carved marionettes, enchantment is guaranteed. Brer Rabbit visits Africa - This specially written play tells of Brer Rabbit arriving in Africa, in his new waistcoat, feeling rather proud of himself. He is staying with his old grandmother when he finds himself in trouble. All the animals including the elephant, the lion and the tortoise gather together to help. Brer Rabbit returns home much the wiser. A Shipful of Verse matinees for the family, inspired by R L Stevensons A Childs' Garden of Verses and Macbeth, evenings for adults, a new production. Full details from the box office.
All year weekends and School Hols.
Last Admission: Latecomers admitted in performance break
Matinees: A£6.00 C&Concessions£5.5 Evenings: A£7.50 C&Concessions£6.00. Apply to Box

Office for Group Rates and School Parties. Seats can be booked in advance.
discount offer: One Ticket Free With Every Four Seats Booked

Queen Mary Reservoir
Ashford Road Sunbury Middlesex
Tel: 0118 939 9254
At 283 hectares this is the largest single body of water in southern Britain. Permit holders have access to the whole of the 4 mile walk on the top of the reservoir giving coastal-like views. The reservoir is used by resident migrating duck and is a prime winter location for Great Crested Grebe, with Shoveler, Tufted Duck and Gadwall also appearing in large numbers.
Season Ticket only Wed-Sun

Richmond Bridge Rowing Boat Hire
1-3 Bridge Boathouses Richmond Surrey TW9 1TH
[free parking at The Old Deer Car Park on the A316 on Sundays and parking under the boathouse is available. Tube: Richmond]
Tel: 020 8948 8270
What is a skiff ; a wood rowing boat about 24 feet long built for ease of handling and efficient travelling. At night a canvas cover converts the entire craft into a snug tent with room for 3 people to sleep aboard, the cover can also provide weather protection throughout the day. You can expect to travel about 12-25 miles in a day and by the 3rd day even a complete beginner will find that boat handling and the work involved is not as daunting as it first appeared. A map is available of the reach of this section of the river that will detail good stopping off points for picnics etc. A new rowing club is being formed call for details. Featured on the BBC Holiday Programme in July 1997.
All year daily 09.00-19.00, Winter hours may vary
A£3.00 per hour daily A£12.00 per day C(0-14)£half price. Weekend rowing from £80.00 2 nights inclusive, Week rowing hire from £120.00 7 nights inclusive

Westminster-Greenwich Thames Boat Passenger Boat Services
Westminster Pier Victoria Embankment London SW1A 2JH
[Tube: Westminster]
Tel: 020 7930 4097 Fax: 020 7930 1616
The Royal River Thames Cruise. Cruises commence at either Westminster Pier or Greenwich Pier. Boats are covered in winter and have both open and closed decks in summer. A trip down the Thames from Westminster to Greenwich offers a superb introduction to many of London's sights and attractions. Most of the city's greatest buildings were designed to be seen from the river and they are still being built that way today. A lively english commentary is provided as well as a written guide with French, German, Italian, Spanish & Russian translations.
Nov-March 10.40-15.20 every 40mins April-Oct 10.30-17.00 every 30mins there are extra departures during June and Aug. Closed Christmas Day, Boxing Day & New Years Day
From Westminster to Greenwich return A£7.00 C£3.60 Concessions £5.80 Family Ticket £18.60

Palaces

Banqueting House
Whitehall London SW1A2ER
[Tube: Westminster / Embankment / Charing Cross]
Tel: 020 7930 4179 Fax: 020 7930 8268
www.hrp.org.uk
This fascinating building offers a haven of tranquility amidst the bustle of Westminster. Designed by Inigo Jones in 1619, the Banqueting House is all that survives of the Palace of Whitehall, that was destroyed by fire in 1698. It has been the scene of many historic events including the execution of Charles I and restoration of Charles II. Features include magnificent ceilings painted by Rubens in 1635 and the Undercroft, where James I used to retreat from the commotion of court life.
All year Mon-Sat 10.00-17.00. Closed Good Fri, 24 Dec-2 Jan, Bank Hol & Government Functions
Last Admission: 16.30
A£3.80 C£2.30 Concessions£3.00
↓*special events*
► **The Faerie Queen (Purcell)**
6/3/00-6/3/00
► **Performed by Alibas**
3/4/00-3/4/00
► **Mistresse Musicke**
8/5/00-8/5/00

London

London

▶ **Court Dance**
5/6/00-5/6/00
▶ **Restoration London**
3/7/00-3/7/00
▶ **The Merrie Monarch**
7/8/00-7/8/00
▶ **Performance to be confirmed**
11/9/00-11/9/00
▶ **Mistresse Musicke**
9/10/00-9/10/00
▶ **The Merrie Monarch**
13/11/00-13/11/00

Buckingham Palace
Buckingham Palace Road London SW1 1AA
[Tube: Victoria / Green Park]
Tel: 020 7839 1377 Fax: 020 7930 9625
www.royal.gov.uk
Here among some of the finest pictures and works of art in the world, visitors can see where The Queen and Members of the Royal Family receive and entertain their guests on State, ceremonial and Official occasions. From the pomp and ceremony of a State Visit, when the Guard of Honour is mounted in the Quadrangle and The Queen entertains the visiting Head of State at a ceremonial banquet, to ministerial and diplomatic audiences, receptions and other events, the State Rooms provide a majestic backdrop to the on going work of the Monarchy. Masterpieces by Vermeer, van Dyck, Rubens, de Hooch, Zuccarelli and Rembrandt are among the forty or so paintings which hang in the Picture Gallery. Fine sculpture, including two groups by Antonio Canova, line the Marble Hall and, in the splendour of the White Drawing Room visitors can see the secret door used by The Queen and the Royal Family. To help visitors enjoy their visit fully, a comprehensive Official Guide is available for purchase in English, German, Italian, French, Spanish and Japanese languages. Wheelchair users are required to pre-book for the Summer Opening of the State Rooms. Regrettably, due to architectural limitations, The Queen's Gallery is inaccessible to wheelchair users. The Royal Mews, however is fully accessible.
6 Aug-3 Oct daily 09.30-16.30. Ticket Office: 31 July-3 Oct daily 09.00-16.00. The Changing of the Guard takes place at 11.30 daily from 1 Apr-early July and on alternate days thereafter. 24 hour information line: 0171 799 2331
Last Admission: 16.00
Queuing Times: 15-20mins
A£10.00 C£5.00. Over 60's £7.50. Advance Purchase via Credit Card (0171 321 2233) or from the Ticket Office in Green Park. Groups discounts to Summer Opening (min 15): 15-250 people £9.50 per person; 251-1000 £9.25 per person; 1001-2000 £9.00 per person; 2001-3500

£8.50 per person; 3501+ to be negotiated, please telephone

↓ *special events*

▶ **Changing of the Guard Ceremonies**
2/1/00-31/12/00

Eltham Palace
Court Yard Eltham London SE9 5QE
[1m N of A20 off Court Yard. BR: Eltham or Mottingham 0.50m. Plenty of on site parking available]

Tel: 020 8294 2548

www.english-heritage.org.uk

Recently opened. Discover this unique site - home to a spectacular 1930s Art Deco country house and a magnificent medieval Great Hall. Scene of many society parties, the home of millionaire Stephen Courtauld evokes the style and glamour of the 1930s era. Then step back in time and marvel at the 15th century Great Hall which stood at the heart of the medieval palace, the boyhood home of Henry VIII.

All year. 1 Apr-30 Sept Wed-Fri & Sun 10.00-18.00. 1-31 Oct Wed-Fri & Sun 10.00-17.00. 1 Nov-31 Mar Wed-Fri & Sun 10.00-16.00. Also open Bank Hol Mon. Closed 24-26 Dec

House & Grounds: A£5.90 C£3.00 Concessions£4.40. Grounds only: A£3.50 C£1.80 Concessions£2.60. Group rates 11+ 15%

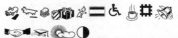

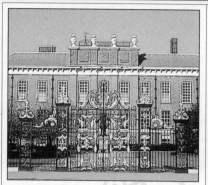

Kensington Palace State Apartments

Kensington Gardens Palace Green London W8 4PX

[Tube: High Street Kensington]

Tel: 020 7376 2858 Fax: 020 7376 0198

www.hrp.org.uk

Designed by Sir Christopher Wren for William III and Mary II, this peaceful royal retreat was the childhood home of Queen Victoria. Features include the magnificent State Apartments and 'Dressing for Royalty', a stunning presentation of Royal Court and Ceremonial Dress dating from the 18th century. Multi language sound guides are available to lead visitors around the magnificent State Apartments. Highlights include the splendid Cupola Room, the most lavishly decorated State Room in the palace where Queen Victoria was baptised, and the beautifully restored King's Gallery. 'Dressing for Royalty' allows visitors to participate in the excitement of dressing for court - from invitation to presentation. There is also a selection of 16 dresses owned and worn by HM Queen Elizabeth II.

Mid Mar-mid Oct daily 10.00-18.00, mid Oct-mid Mar daily 10.00-17.00

Last Admission: 60mins before closing

A£8.50 C£6.10 Family Ticket £26.10 Concessions£6.70 (Entrance prices increase by £1.00 between 1 Oct 1999 - 31 March 2000)

↓*special events*

▶ **Diana, Princess of Wales - a Collection of her Dresses**

1/10/99-31/3/00

14 dresses that belonged to Diana, Princess of Wales and show her approach to dressing for royal occasions, are on display

Kew Palace

Royal Botanic Gardens Kew Richmond Surrey TW9 3AB

[BR: Kew Bridge. Tube: Kew Gardens]

Tel: 020 8781 9540 Fax: 020 8332 5197

www.rbgkew.org.uk

Kew was the site of several royal houses although only three remain. A modest red-brick building, in Dutch style with gables, Kew Palace was built in 1631 and used for nearly a century until 1818 when Queen Charlotte died. Opened to the public in 1899 and remains much as it was in George III's time. Closed for refurbishment.

Closed for refurbishment Autumn 1996-Spring 2000

Closed for refurbishment Autumn 1996-Spring 2000

Palace of Westminster including Westminster Hall

Westminster London SW1A 0AA

[Tube: Westminster]

Tel: 020 7219 4272 Fax: 020 7219 5839 info fax

Palace of Westminster is a working Parliament and Westminster Hall, where Charles I was tried (1649), has survived virtually intact since it was remodelled at the end of the 14th century. It escaped the fire in 1834 which destroyed much of the medieval Palace of Westminster. It can only be viewed by those on a tour of the Houses of Parliament.

Must be arranged with an MP or Peer, if you are a resident in this country. Overseas Visitors need to apply in writing to the Deputy Education Officer, House of Commons as above Admission Free though guides require a payment if employed which is £25.00 approx per group of 16

Winchester Palace

Corner of Clink Street / Storey Street Southwark London SE1

[behind Southwark Cathedral Buses are frequent from surrounding areas. BR/Tube: London Bridge 0.25m]

Tel: 020 7222 1234

The west gable end, with its unusual rose window, is the prominent feature of the remains of the Great Hall of this 13th century town house of the Bishops of Winchester, damaged by fire in 1814.

All year any reasonable time

Admission Free

Performing Arts

Adelphi Theatre

18-20 Maiden Lane London WC2E 7NA

[Tube: Charing Cross / Embankment]

Tel: 020 7344 0055

www.ticketmaster.co.uk

Built in 1930 by Ernest Schaufelberg on a site

occupied by three earlier theatres since 1806, The Adelphi boasts a Proscenium arch stage. The raked auditorium has a capacity of 1,500 while backstage, there are 15 dressing rooms which can accommodate up to 90 performers at one time. It has be reported that the theatre is often visited by the ghost of William Terriss.
Mon-Sat 20.00 mats Wed & Sat 14.30
£16-£36 (inc booking fee) booking to Jan 30 1999

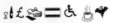

Aldwych Theatre
49 Aldwych London WC2B 4DF
[on the corner of Alwych & Drury Lane. Tube: Covent Garden / Holborn. NCP Car Park in Drury Lane]
Tel: 020 7416 6000 Box Office
Based on the much loved film, Whistle Down The Wind is set in America's deep South in the late fifties. A young girl, Swallow, struggling to come to terms with the death of her mother, discovers a mysterious stranger who she believes is Jesus. In a town where a miracle is long overdue, the children fight to protect the stranger from an adult world determined to catch the fugitive hiding in their midst. Andrew Lloyd Webber's powerful music combines with lyrics by acclaimed rock'n'roll songwriter Jim Steinman. They fuse epic storytelling with intimate emotion as the innocence of children collides with the cynical adult world.
Mon-Sat 19.45. Thur & Sat Matinees 15.00
Seat Prices: Stalls £32.50, £30.00, £25.00; Dress Circle £32.50, £30.00, £27.50; Upper Circle £27.50, £22.50, £17.50, £15.00, £10.00. Box Office & Credit Cards subject to £1.00 Booking Fee 0171 416 6000. Credit Card Bookings subject to £1.50 Booking Fee Ticketmaster 0171 957 4001, and with booking fee from Ticketmaster Ticket Centres including selected HMV, Tower and Waitrose stores nationwide. Group bookings 0171 416 6075/0171 413 3321, £5.00 off £32.50, £30.00 & £27.50 seats for groups of 12+ excluding Sat eve performances and subject to availability

Almeida at the Albery Theatre
St Martin's Lane London WC2N
[Tube: Leicester Square. Buses: 24 / 29 / 176. NCP Car Parks in Bedfordbury and Upper St Martin's Lane]
Tel: 020 7369 1740 (24hrs)
A season opens... Racine's two great tragedies in repertoire launch a new season from 3rd September. 24 hours booking line, no booking fee.
Seasonal opening
Ticket Prices: Mon-Thur & Sat matinèes £27.50,

£25.00, £22.00, £18.00, £16.00, £13.50, £10.00 & £5.00. Fri & Sat evenings: £29.50, £27.50, £25.00, £19.50, £17.50, £15.00, £11.50 & £5.00. Previews: Fri & Sat evenings: £27.50, £25.00, £22.00, £18.00, £16.00, £13.50, £10.00 & £5.00

Almeida Theatre
Almeida Street off Upper Street London N1 1TA
[Tube: Angel / Highbury & Islington. Buses: 4 / 19 / 30 / 43 (St Mary's Church). 38 / 73 / 171 (Islington Green). 271 / 277 (Highbury Corner). Some on street parking restrictions around the theatre end after 18.30 Mon-Fri and after 13.30 on Sat. Upper Street is a Red Route Zone: restrictions apply Mon-Fri 08.00-19.00. There is also an off street car park on Islington Green]
Tel: 020 7359 4404
www.almeida.co.uk
The Almeida is accessible to the disabled: there is a lift giving wheelchair access to the stalls and there are disabled toilet facilities in the foyer. Please inform the Box Office of any special requirements when booking your tickets. The Almeida has a full range of sign-interpreted performances during its season. The signer is Mary Connell. Please contact the Box Office for further details. Snacks and refreshments are available outside the Café-Bar opening times.
Seasonal opening. Café-Bar Mon-Sat 11.00-14.30 and from 17.30-19.30.
Ticket Prices vary according to the programme. There are concessions and supporters' discounts available

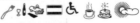

Apollo Victoria
17 Wilton Road London SW1V 1LG
[BR/Tube: Victoria - opposite theatre]
Tel: 020 7416 6070
Speed straight into the next millennium with Starlight Express, the fastest show on earth. Board the white knuckle ride of your life as electrifying songs and music combine in an awesome light show of fantastic characters. Andrew Lloyd Webber's high velocity musical is a dazzling theatrical experience light years ahead of the rest. Re-energised for a new generation of families, with great new songs and even more thrills, Starlight Express is a guaranteed trip of a lifetime.
Mon-Sat 19.45, Tue & Sat Matinees 15.00
Mon-Thur eve & both mats: Stalls £27.00, £24.00, £21.00, £16.50, £12.50(restricted view); Dress Circle £24.00, £21.00, £16.50, £12.50. Fri & Sat eve: Stalls £30.00, £27.00, £23.00, £17.50, £12.50(restricted view); Dress Circle: £27.00, £23.00, £17.50, £12.50. Group discounts available, please call for details 0171 420 0200.
Tickets from: First Call 0171 420 0000 or with booking fee from First Call Ticket Shops includ-

ing Selfridges, Debenhams Oxford St, Virgin Megastore Oxford St, Bentalls of Kingston & Metro Central (Holborn)

Arts Theatre
Great Newport Street London WC2H 7JA
[Tube: Leicester Square]
Tel: 020 7836 3334

BAC
Lavender Hill Battersea London SW11 5TF
[BR: Clapham Junction + 5min walk. Buses: 35 / 37 / 345 / 77 / 77a / 115 / 319 / 337 / C3 / G1.]
Tel: 020 7223 2223 Box Office
Box Office: Mon 10.30-18.00, Tue-Sat 10.30-21.00, Sun 16.00-19.00
Tickets by post: send your cheque made payable to BAC to the above address. Unpaid reservations should be collected one hour before the performance.

Barbican Concourse Gallery
Ground Floor Level 0 Barbican Centre Silk Street London EC2Y 8DS
[the Barbican Centre is well signposted & has 4 car parks, 2 off Beech Street & 2 off Silk Street. Call Box Office for Disabled Parking Permit. Rail savings available through the Theatre and Concert Travel Club call 01727 841115. Tube: Barbican / Moorgate / St. Paul's / Liverpool Street / Bank / Mansion House. BR: Liverpool Street / Farringdon / Blackfriars / City Thameslink / Barbican / Moorgate]
Tel: 020 7638 8891
www.barbican.org.uk
The Barbican Centre is a showcase for British culture. The Corporation of London's considerable investment in the arts keeps London at Europe's cultural forefront, enhancing the name of the City, London and Britain on the world stage.
All year Mon-Sat 10.00-19.30, Sun & Bank Hol 12.00-19.30
Admission Free

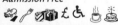

Barbican Craftspace
Ground Floor Level 0 Barbican Centre Silk Street London EC2Y 8DS
[see Barbican Concourse Gallery details]
Tel: 020 7638 8891 Box Office
www.barbican.org.uk
The Barbican Centre is a showcase for British culture. The Corporation of London's considerable investment in the arts keeps London at Europe's cultural forefront, enhancing the name of the City, London and Britain on the world stage.
All year Mon-Sat 10.00-19.30, Sun & Bank Hol 12.00-19.30

Admission Free

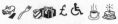

Barbican Craftspace
Ground Floor Level 0 Barbican Centre Silk Street London EC2Y 8DS
[see Barbican Concourse Gallery details]
Tel: 020 7638 8891 Box Office
www.barbican.org.uk
The Barbican Centre is a showcase for British culture. The Corporation of London's considerable investment in the arts keeps London at Europe's cultural forefront, enhancing the name of the City, London and Britain on the world stage.
All year Mon-Sat 10.00-19.30, Sun & Bank Hol 12.00-19.30
Admission Free

Barbican Foyer Gallery
Level 0 Barbican Centre Silk Street London EC2Y 8DS
[see Barbican Concourse Gallery details]
Tel: 020 7638 8891 Box Office
www.barbican.org.uk
The Barbican Centre is a showcase for British culture. The Corporation of London's considerable investment in the arts keeps London at Europe's cultural forefront, enhancing the name of the City, London and Britain on the world stage.
All year Mon-Sat 10.00-19.30, Sun & Bank Hol 12.00-19.30
Admission Free

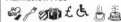

Barbican Hall
Barbican Centre Silk Street London EC2Y 8DS
[see Barbican Concourse Gallery details]
Tel: 020 7638 8891 Box Office Fax: 020 7588 9023
www.barbican.org.uk
A simply marvellous venue for all types of music and dance. A full programme of updated events each month can be seen on our internet pages or by calling the box office for a monthly programme. All of the FreeStage events are Free and take place on Ground Floor level 0.
Opening details are dependant on dates and times of performances, see special events or call the box office for full programme
Prices are dependant on performances and seats chosen, call the box office for full programme, with the exception of the FreeStage events which are Free.

Barbican Library
Library Floor Level 2 Barbican Centre Silk Street

London EC2Y 8DS
[see Barbican Concourse Gallery details]
Tel: 020 7638 0569
www.barbican.org.uk
The Barbican Library is the City's leading lending library with books, tapes, compact discs, videos and CD ROMs. Membership is open to those who live, work or study in the City of London, and regular visitors to the Barbican Centre. Music Library 0171 638 0672, Children's Library 0171 628 9447.
All year Mon, Wed-Fri 09.30-17.30, Tue 09.30-19.30, Sat 09.30-12.30
Admission Free

Barbican: The Pit

Silk Street Barbican London EC2Y 8DS
[Tube: Barbican / Moorgate]
Tel: 020 7638 8891

Baron's Court Theatre, The Curtain's Up

28a Comeragh Road London W14 9RH
[Tube: Baron's Court / West Kensington]
Tel: 020 8932 4747 Fax: 020 7603 8935
The theatre is sited underneath the Curtain's Up wine bar and restaurant in which excellent pre-performance meals can be obtained. The menu offers a large and inexpensive selection. Book tables on 0171 385 4064. It is advisable to start your meal no later than 19.00.
Box Office: All year daily. Performances: All year Tue-Sun, times varying according to programme see individual items
from £7.00 Concessions from £4.00

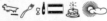

Bloomsbury Theatre

15 Gordon Street London WC1H 0AH
[BR/Tube: Euston / Euston Square, 2mins walk. Bus: 10 / 18 / 24 / 29 / 73. 24hr Car Park under Euston Station and free on-street parking after 18.30]
Tel: 020 7388 8822 Box Office Fax: 020 7383 4080
www.ucl.ac.uk/BloomsburyTheatre/
The Bloomsbury Theatre is a 550 seat venue situated in the Bloomsbury area. We offer a diverse and international artistic programme in comedy, opera, music, dance and drama. With comfortable seats, affordable ticket prices, a welcoming bar and friendly staff, a visit to this leading off West-End venue is a great way to spend an evening! So easily accessible by public transport too!
Box Office: Mon-Sat 10.00-18.00
Dependent on Show. Concessions are discounted tickets for students, OAPs, Friends of UCL, disabled persons and holders of UB40, NCA, Equity or UCL Alumni Association cards. If a disabled

person requires assistance we can offer a free ticket for a helper or friend.

Bridewell Theatre

Bride Lane Off Fleet Street London EC4Y 8EQ
[Car: Parking space can be located on New Bridge Street and around Fleet Street after 18.30. BR: City Thameslink (2 mins). Tube: Blackfriars (3 mins) / St Paul's (7 mins). Bus: Fleet Street 4 / 11 / 15 / 23 / 26 / 76; New Bridge Street 45 / 63 / 172]
Tel: 020 7936 3456/353 0259 Fax: 020 7583 5289
The Bridewell Theatre lies off Fleet Street in a former Victorian bath house in Bride Lane. The pool had been dry for 22 years when, in 1994, the cobweb filled vault was dusted off and renovated to become one of London's most popular theatres. Since then, the audiences have been charmed by the venue and the quality of work presented there. Wrought iron balconies, pillars, staircases and the sunken pool area have become adaptable and much loved playing spaces for actors, directors, designers and musicians. As well as becoming one of London's most popular venues for visiting companies, the Bridewell also produces its own work. The Bridewell Theatre Company presents 3 or 4 productions each year with a particular interest in music theatre, epic classical drama and some new work. The Bridewell Youth Theatre (BYT) is committed to fostering the creativity of young people through their involvement in theatre. BYT offers weekly workshops, productions and special projects for young people aged 6-26. Wheelchairs: spaces available by prior arrangement on 0171 936 3456 (2-inch step at entrance, wheelchair lifts inside, wheelchair toilet).
Please see separate performances
Please see separate performances. By Phone: Credit Card Booking (no booking fee) 10.30-19.00 Tue-Fri, 10.30-18.00 Mon. Plus 24 hour answering machine. Please leave a message. We will get back to you as soon as possible. In Person: Cash, Credit Cards & Cheques 10.30-19.30 Tue-Fri, 10.30-18.00 Mon, 14.30-15.30 Sun. By Post: Please make cheques payable to 'Bridewell Theatre' (enclose SAE). Concessions: Registered Disabled, Unemployed, Senior Citizens. ID cards for all concessions to be presented when collecting tickets

Bush Theatre

Goldhawk Road Shepherd's Bush Green London W12 8QD
[Tube: Shepherd's Bush / Goldhawk Road. Free parking in local streets after 18.30. Situated above the Fringe and Ferkin public house on the corner of Shepherds Bush Green and Goldhawk

Road]
Tel: 020 8743 3388 Fax: 020 7602 7614
For over 25 years the Bush has been at the forefront of the sharpest new drama. This intimate space provides an unrivalled setting for trailblazing new plays, world-class performances and non-stop dramatic invention. Drinks may be taken into the show. The Bush Theatre is fully air-conditioned, and receives support from London Weekend Television.
Box Office: Mon-Fri from 18.30, Sat from 19.00. Performances at 19.00.
£10.00. Concessions £7.00. Group rates: free ticket ration 1:10. Mastercard/Visa (no booking fee)

Cambridge Theatre
Earlham Street London WC2H 9HU
[Tube: Covent Garden / Leicester Square. Bus: 14 / 19 / 24 / 29 / 38 / 176]
Tel: 020 7494 5080 Box Offic
Now showing, Grease in it's 6th year!
Mon-Sat 19.30; Wed & Sat Matinees 15.00
Mon-Thur evenings & Sat Matinees: Stalls £27.50, £22.50, £17.50, £15.00. Royal Circle £27.50. Upper Circle £20.00, £15.00, £10.00. Fri & Sat Evenings: Stalls £30.00, £25.00, £20.00, £17.50. Royal Circle £30.00. Upper Circle £22.50, £17.50, £12.50. Wed Matinees: Stalls £20.00, £15.00, £10.00. Royal Circle: £20.00. Upper Circle £15.00, £10.00. Box Office and Credit Card Bookings Open 24 hours / 7 days a week, £1.00 Booking Fee. Reduced prices for groups of 10+ excluding Sat eve performances. Standby: OAP, Student & UB40 £12.50 from half an hour before the performance. Subject to availability and on production of valid identification. Subject to availability. For further information call Stoll Moss Group Sales on 0171 494 5454

Courtyard Theatre Club
10 York Way Kings Cross London N1 9AA
[BR/Tube: King's Cross (out of side exit on Platform 1 & opposite side of Street). Bus: 73 / 30 / 214 / 10 / 17 / 18 / 45 / 46 / 63 / 91 / 221 / 259 / C12. Free parking in the area after 19.00]
Tel: 020 7833 0870 Fax: 020 7833 0870
Pay What You Can operates on Sunday nights for all shows except Music Hall. Book 3 shows for the price of 2. Discounts on all groups bookings. No performance on Mondays

Croydon Clocktower
Katharine Street Croydon Surrey CR9 1ET
[BR: East & West Croydon Stations]
Tel: 020 8253 1030 Fax: 020 8253 1032
www.croydon.gov.uk
The Croydon Clocktower is a multi-disciplinary arts and cultural centre. It opened in 1995 and is a striking fusion of Victorian and modern architecture at the heart of Croydon's cultural quarter. It houses a state-of-the art public library, a cinema, three exhibition galleries and a performance space. The Exhibition Gallery holds exhibitions from Picasso to Cyber Art, Lifetimes. The Interactive Museum tells the story of Croydon through the personal experiences of it's people. The Riesco Gallery, a national treasure, houses a stunning collection of Chinese ceramics and pottery dating from 2500BC. A full range of exhibitions and events are held throughout the year.
visitor comments: Excellent use of interactive media, with lots of films on interesting local personalities.
All year Exhibitions Mon-Sat 11.00-17.00 Sun 12.00-17.00
Lifetimes: Admission £Free. The Riesco Gallery: Admission £Free. Exhibitions entrance prices are dependent on exhibition.

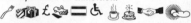

Dominion Theatre
Tottenham Court Road London W1A
[Tube: Tottenham Court Road]
Tel: 020 7656 1888
Disney's Beauty and the Beast is this year's smash hit musical. The world's favourite love story comes to life before your very eyes through the magic of live theatre. Winner of London's coveted Olivier Award for Best New Musical, this spectacular show should be on every visitor's list of must-see attractions. For performance times and prices please tel: 0171 656 1888.
Please telephone
Please telephone

Donmar Warehouse
41 Earlham Street London WC2H 9LD
[Tube: Covent Garden / Leicester Square / Charing Cross / Holborn. Bus: Destination Leicester Sq 14 / 19 / 24 / 29 / 38 / 176. NCP parking at Drury Lane]
Tel: 020 7369 1732
Depending on Show
Depending on Show. Box Office and Credit Cards No Booking Fee 0171 369 1732. Telephone bookings 7 days a week. Personal callers Monday-Saturday. Ticketmaster 0171 344 4444, Credit Card 24 hours, Booking Fee and with booking fee from all Ticketmaster Ticket Centres including HMV and Tower stores in London and the South East. Standby: £5.00 off top two prices 30 minutes before performance (Students/OAPs/UB40s/West Res Card/CGCA/Under 18s/Equity) (subject to avail-

London

ability)

£

Finborough Theatre
118 Finborough Road London SW10 9ED
[Tube: Earl's Court. Buses: C3 & 31]
Tel: 020 7373 3842 Box Office Fax: 020 7835 1853

The Steam Industry has completely transformed the Finborough Theatre into an evocative and atmospheric setting for four major productions, directed by core members of the company. Using to the full their proven ability with both reviving classic plays and developing the best new playwrights, The Steam Industry turn their attention to the law and those who break it. In a year already mounting up with criminal scandals and with more miscarriages of justice being exposed every month, The Steam Industry presents some of the theatre's most extraordinary pieces addressing these issues. Alongside, the company brings forward new voices to explore related themes.

Dependent on show
Dependent on show
↓ *special events*
▶ **A Child of the Forest directed by Neil McPherson**
7/3/00-1/4/00
Eastern Europe. 1947. But the war is not over... A World Premiere of a new play by the award winning playwright Anthony Melnikoff.

Gate Theatre
11 Pembridge Road Notting Hill London W11 3HQ
[Tube: Notting Hill Gate. Buses: 12 / 27 / 28 / 31 / 52 / 94 / 302 - all to the door. Theatre located above the Prince Albert Public House.]
Tel: 020 7229 0706 Box Office Fax: 020 7221 6055

1999 is a special year for the Gate Theatre and to mark our 20th Birthday celebrations we are introducing Gate 2000 scheme. Since 1979, London's Home of International Drama, has launched the careers of actors, directors and playwrights and made some theatre history on the way. This year we are inviting our audiences and supporters to ensure the Gate's life journey. With the Gate 2000 scheme we are asking 2000 friends to donate a minimum of £20.00, to launch the Gate into the new millennium and to enable us to continue to produce the best International Drama in London.

Greenwich Theatre
Crooms Hill London SE10 8ES
[parking available off Burney Street opposite the theatre]
Tel: 020 8858 7755

As the Theatre Royal Stratford East is currently closed for refurbishment until it's re-opening in Autumn 2000, it will be in residence at Greenwich Theatre.
Box Office: Mon-Sat 10.00-20.00
Prices vary according to chosen performance
↓ *special events*
▶ **Marie**
1/3/00-11/3/00
Life story of singer and emtertainer Marie Lloyd singer of 'My Old Man said Follow the Van.'

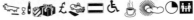

Grinlings Restaurant
62 Carter Lane London London (East) [Tube: Blackfriars / St Pauls]
Tel: 020 7248 2255

Her Majesty's Theatre
Haymarket London SW1Y 4QL
[Tube: Piccadilly Circus. Bus: 6 / 12 / 15 / 22B / 38 / 53 / 88 / 159]
Tel: 020 7494 5400 Box Office
www.stoll-moss.com

Margaret Rutherford star of the film 'Blithe Spirit' and the plays of Agatha Christie's novels, witnessed the apparition of a former theatre manager, John Buckstone, who died over 120 years ago. An actor opened the door of a dressing room, saw the familiar shape of a man wearing a frock coat seated in a chair. He closed and locked the door. When witnesses arrived they found nothing. The ghost seems only appear when productions are successful!
Performance times: Evenings 19.45, Wed & Sat Matinees 15.00. The performance runs 2.5 hours
Ticket prices: Stalls £32.50, £27.50, £18.50*; Dress Circle £32.50, £27.50, £22.50, £18.50*; Upper Circle £27.50, £22.50, £16.50, £14.00*, £10.00*; Balcony £10.00; *restricted view

IMAX Cinema (BFI London)
Museum of the Moving Image South Bank Waterloo London SE1 8XT
[situated outside BR/Tube: Waterloo on the South Bank. Bus: stops nearby on Waterloo Bridge and South Bank. 10mins walk from Covent Garden / Leicester Square via Waterloo Bridge or Hungerford Bridge. Coach parking on Belvedere Rd]
Tel: 020 7815 1330/1331 Fax: 020 7815 1419
www.bfi.org.uk

The BFI London IMAX Cinema offers the biggest cinema screen in Europe - ten stories high - housed inside a spectacular £20m glass building. Showing breathtaking 2D and IMAX 3D films. IMAX is the world's biggest screen experience, recognised worldwide for providing high quality family entertainment. For 3D films the audience wear special glasses which trick the eye into seeing images in three dimensions.

visitor comments: Everything seems to jump out at you!

Films showing each hour every hour, 12.00-22.00 daily

A£6.50 C(5-16)£4.50 Concessions£5.50. Advance bookings (with no booking fee) are available on 0171 902 1234. Discounts for groups of 10+. For advanced group bookings, whether for family and friends, corporate events or education groups, please call 0171 902 1220.

Jerwood Gallery

Jerwood Space 171 Union Street London SE1 OLN

[Tube: Borough / London Bridge]

Tel: 020 7654 0171 Fax: 020 77654 0172

www.jerwoodspace.co.uk

The Jerwood space is a new and innovative facility in London for the creation and development of new work by young drama and dance groups and young artists. Located in Southwark Bankside, and created out of a former Victorian school building it is five minutes walk from the projected new Tate Gallery. The gallery has a year round programme of work by emerging artists as well as the established and prestigious Jerwood Painting Prize. There is also a Sculpture Space and Café. A film and fashion prize are two of a series of new large-scale sponsorships created by the Jerwood foundation that are being launched this year.

All year Mon-Sat 10.00-18.00, Sun & Bank Hol 12.00-18.00

Admission free

↓*special events*

▶ Martin Boyce

15/1/00-27/2/00

Labatt's Apollo Hammersmith

Queen Caroline Street Hammersmith London W6

[Tube: Hammersmith. Buses: 9 / 9a / 10 / 27 / 34 / R69 / 72 / H91 / 19- / 211 / 220 / 267 / 283 / 295 / 366 / 391 / 415]

Tel: 020 7416 6075

Dr Dolittle. The combining of the unique talents of Phillip Schofield with the technical wizadry of Jim Henson's world-famous Creature Shop is going to take this production beyond the depth and breadth of conventional theatre. This eagerley awaited stage musical has its world premiere at the Labatt's Apollo Hammersmith.

All year, Mon-Sat evenings 19.30, Wed & Sat matinees 14.30, until further notice

Mon-Sat evenings and Sat matinees Stalls & Circle: £32.50 & £27.50. Circle: also £22.50, £17.50 & £12.50. Wed matinees Stalls & Circle: £27.50 & £22.50. Circle: also £17.50 & £12.50. C(under 16) Mon-Fri evenings £5 Off all prices subject to availability. Groups of 12+ save 10% on all prices (excluding all Sat performances)

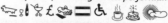

Lion & Unicorn Pub Theatre

42-44 Gaisford Street London NW5 2ED

[Tube: Kentish Town]

Tel: 020 7482 0850 24 hr

Please call for details

By phone: 24 hour booking line. Reservations: all tickets can be reserved in advance and must be paid for 15 minutes prior to the performance

London Palladium

Argyll Street London W1

[Argull St which runs between Oxford St / Great Marlborough St. Tube: Oxford Circus.. TNCP Car Park is in Cavendish Square]

Tel: 020 7494 5020 Box Office

www.stoll-moss.com

The haunted old Crimson Staircase by a beautiful lady in a marvellous crinoline dress. The phantom is supposed to be the ghost of Helen Campbell, a former resident of Argyll House, which once stood on this site. Others say she is the phantom of a former actress, for the Crimson Staircase was built as part of the theatre, not in the home of the Duke of Argylll. Alternatively, she could be one of the distinguished guests or a member of the Royal Family.

Performance Times: Monday-Saturday Evenings 19.30, Wednesday and Saturday Matinees 14.30. The performance runs approximately 2.5 hours including an interval. Christmas Performances: Christmas Eve 14.30 only, No performance on Christmas Day. All other performances as normally scheduled

Booking information, Box Office and 24 hour Credit Card Hotline 0171 494 5030. Ticketselect 0171 494 5386. Reservations, Telephone and Credit Card Bookings. With £1.00 Service Charge. Seat Prices: Stalls £32.50, £30.00, £25.00, £20.00; Royal Circle £32.50; Upper Circle £17.50, £10.00. School Groups call 0171 494 5456 for details on special group and school rates. Group Sales call Stoll Moss Groups 0171 494 5454 Monday-Friday 09.00-18.00, Saturday 11.00-18.00.

Lyric Theatre Hammersmith Ltd

2 King Street London W6 0QA

[Tube: Hammersmith / Piccadilly. Bus: 9 / 209 / 10 / 27 / 33 / 72 / 91 / 211 / 220 / 266 / 267 / 283 / 290 / 702 / 740 / 700 / 390 / 190 / 391 / 609. Car parks close to the theatre at Kings Mall and Centre West]

Tel: 020 8741 2311 Box Office Fax: 020 8741 7694

www.lyric.co.uk

During July and August our Main House Theatre underwent a dramatic change; the gilt and velvet Victorian auditorium was transformed into an intimate new 175 seat Studio space specially created to house the British premieres of new plays from two exciting contemporary writers. Visitors with disabilities welcome. Facilities in both our Main House and Studio theatres include dedicated spaces for wheelchair users, lifts to all levels, wheelchair accessible toilets, a loop, Infra-red Sennheiser system and minicom (0181 741 3119). If you are using the loop or Sennheiser please tell the box office so that they can advise on the best seats for reception. If you have any queries contact Howard Meaden, Theatre Manager on 0181 741 0824 or fax 0181 741 7694. The Café Brera famous for its special blend of coffee - also serve pastries, desserts, pannini, hot and cold antipasti and a variety of authentic Italian pastas and drinks.

Depending on show. Children's Shows: Every Sat shows at 11.00 and 13.00 (from 19 Sept). Café Brera: from 09.30

Depending on show. Call the Box Office for your free copy of our children's shows leaflet.

Millfield Theatre

Silver Street London N18 1PJ

[located just off the Cambridge roundabout at the J of the North Circular and the A10. BR: Silver Street]

Tel: 020 8807 6680 Box Office Fax: 020 8803 2801

There is level access to the auditorium, box office, bar, toilets and car park. We can accommodate a limited number of wheelchair users in the auditorium. There is an induction loop in the auditorium for the hard of hearing, hearing aids should be turned to T. An Infra-Red Audio System is now installed in the theatre. Headsets are essential. A limited number are available from the Box Office when you arrive. Please advise us when you book if you require a headset.

Box Office: Mon-Sat 11.00-17.00. Also open for an hour before an event outside these hours, for that event only. Closed Bank Hol unless performances on that day.

By Phone: during opening hours and quote

your Credit Card / Debit Card number and your tickets will be sent to you (£0.50 handling fee per transaction)

Mountview Theatre School

104 Crouch Hill London N8 9EA

Tel: 020 8347 3601 Fax: 020 8348 1727

The ghost of a young girl about 12 years old, dressed in a smock dress has been seen several times. On one occasion a younger member of the theatre who found her presence difficult to believe, felt someone take his hand and lead him across the darkened stage one night. The girl is understood to be either the victim or even the perpetrator of a murder which was responsible for the closure of the school in the 1890s.

Box Office: Mon-Fri 14.00-17.00, booking for the Autumn Season 1999 will open 9th Sept 99. A£7.50 Concessions£5.00.

Open Air Theatre

Chester Road Regent's Park London NW1 4NP

[Tube: Baker Street. Bus: 13 / 18 / 27 / 30 / 74 / 82 / 113 / 159 / 189. Parking is free on the Inner and Outer Circles after 18.30 Mon-Fri, after 13.30 on Sat, and all day Sun. Pay & Display at all other times; maximum stay 4 hours. Coaches may set down on the Inner Circle and park in the Outer Circle Coach Park (near London Zoo). Designated parking for the disabled on the Inner Circle near the theatre entrance, and level access via the Main or Stage Door entrances.]

Tel: 020 7486 2431/1933 Box Fax: 020 7487 4562

www.open-air-theatre.org.uk

A trip to see a production at the Open Air Theatre along with a cool drink and a picnic has often been described as the total alfresco experience. So, once again, we are delighted to offer London and her visitors an exciting season in one of the most beautiful theatre settings to be found anywhere in this country. As ever, we combine a little of the old with the new. No summer is complete without at least one trip to the Open Air Theatre, so please join us, take in the enchanting atmosphere and witness magic. Adapted male and Female toilets for disabled. Performances are never cancelled before the advertised starting time, and only then in the event of very bad weather. If cancellation is avoidable, ticket holders will be entitled to seats for any other performance, subject to availability. Refunds are not given, except to school groups, subject to certain conditions (details from the Box Office).

See separate performances. Box Office: Mon-Sat 10.00-20.00, Sun 12.00 to start of performance only

London

Tickets telephone 0120 7379 6722 for details. Wheelchair spaces available (bookable in advance) £6.00 each

Orange Tree Theatre
1 Clarence Street Richmond Surrey TW9 2SA
[BR/Tube: Richmond. Buses: 65 / 190 / 290 / 371 / 391 / 415 / 490 / 938 / 963 / 967 / H22 / H37 / R61 / R68 / R70 / N9 or a short walk from 33 / 337 / 415 and R69. NCP Car Parking at Richmond station and at the car and coach park opposite the Old Deer Park off the A316.]
Tel: 020 8940 3633

The Orange Tree Theatre welcomes disabled people. Simply notify the box office when booking if you would like to use any of the following facilities: spaces for wheelchair users, ramp and rail lift, lift, induction loop, infra-red facility, sign-language interpreted performances and audio described performances. A touch guide to the set and props can be arranged. Guide dogs welcome. Disabled parking by prior arrangement. Please contact the Front of House Manager on 0181 940 0141.
Seasonal programme. Box Office open Mon-Sat 10.00-19.00. New Box Office situated in Kew Road will full disabled access (day time only) Main House Tickets: Mon evenings & Thur matinèes £5.00. Tue evenings & Previews£9.00 Concessions£7.00. Wed-Fri evenings & Sat matinées £11.50 Concessions£9.00. Sat evenings £14.50. Concessions are available to students, under 16's, OAPs, all recipients of state benefit (including Child Allowance) and Stagepass members. Special tickets for under 25s - £2.50 for the first Wed of each main house production, bookable in advence

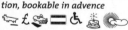

Oval House
52-54 Kennington Oval London SE11 5SW
[BR: Vauxhall (8 mins walk). Tube: The Oval. Bus: 36 / 185 / 133 / 109 / 3 / 155. Car Park for disabled visitors]
Tel: 020 7582 7680 Box Office
www.ovalhous.dircon.co.uk
Oval House Theatre: for theatre, music and dance. No wheelchair access to Upstairs theatre. Full ground floor wheelchair access to cafe area, downstairs theatre and adapted toilets. Induction Loop.
Dependent on event. Open theatre nights from 18.30 for selection of beers, wines & homemade bar snacks

Palace Theatre
93-107 Shaftesbury Avenue London W1V 8AY
[Tube: Piccadilly Circus / Tottenham Court Road. BR: Charing Cross. Serviced by buses: 38 / 19 / 24 / 22 & 176 all of which stop very near the Theatre. NCP Parking in Cambridge Circus, which is reached by taking the 1st L in Shaftsbury Avenue and Cambridge Circus, travelling towards Piccadilly Circus]
Tel: 020 7434 0909 Box Office Fax: 020 7734 6157

Les Misérables has indisputably become the world's most popular musical, having been seen worldwide by over 40 million people. The Palace was first opened as the Royal English Opera House on 31st January 1891 by Richard D'Oyly Carte and the first production was Ivanhoe by Arthur Sullivan the composing half of Britain's most famous musical team Gilbert and Sullivan. On December 10th 1892 the theatre reopened as the Palace Theatre of Variety and saw the London debute in 1910 of the ballerina Pavlova. Thus the theatre made variety 'respectable' and it was at the Palace that the first Royal Command took place in 1912. This performance prompted Sir Oswald Stoll to remark 'The Cinderella of the Arts at last went to the Ball'. Subsequently the Palace became better known for its musicals. Rome wasn't built in a day, and the Palace is a working theatre with working productions and working people who have in some cases given an extraordinary amount of time to the building. It is therefore not possible to close the theatre and expensively refurbish it without preventing continual existence of what the theatre's very life blood; the shows and the loyalty of the staff, although we know this will eventually have to take place. - Andrew Lloyd Webber (1985)

Box Office: Mon-Sat 10.00-20.00 for personal callers and telephone bookings. Between 19.30-10.00 the telephone line is switched over to Ticketmaster who will charge a booking fee for out of hours service. Performance Times: All year evenings at 19.30. Matinees: Sat & Thur at 14.30. Christmas performances: 22-27 Dec daily 14.30 & 19.30. No performances: 24 & 25 Dec Les Misérables: Stalls & Dress Circle £32.50, £27.50, £23.50. Upper Circle: £23.50, £20.00. Balcony: £8.50, £7.00. Apply daily for returns. Ticketmaster: 0171 344 4444 (24hrs) First Call: 00171 420 0000 (24hrs). Group Bookings: 0171 494 1671 & 0171 436 5588. Ticketmaster: 0171 413 3321

Place Theatre
17 Dukes Road London WC1H 9AB
[Tube/Rail: Euston and King's Cross stations (5min walk). Buses: 10, 30, 91, 73]
Tel: 020 7387 0031 Box Office
www.theplace.org.uk
The Place is the centre for dance in the heart of London. For thirty years it has been at the forefront of the development of contemporary dance in the UK. Many of the world's leading

London

dance companies have made their British debut at The Place Theatre including Wim Vandekeybus, Mark Morris, S.O.A.P Dance Theatre Frankfurt, Saburo Teshigawara, Adventures In Motion Pictures, DV8, The Cholmondeleys and The Featherstonehaughs, V-Tol and Random Dance Company. A major refurbishment and renovation of The Place began in June. The £7 million project is funded by the National Lottery through the Arts Council of England, King's Cross Partnership, and through privately raised partnership funding. It is scheduled for completion in Summer 2001. Contemporary Dance Trust has been based at The Place since 1969. The site has been developed piecemeal fashion from three separate buildings and is now in need of urgent repair and refurbishment. The Place is intensively used seven days a week and the facilities have become shabby and well below the standard required by the dance profession. *Box Office: Mon-Fri 10.30-20.00, Sat 12.00-20.00 (18.00 on days of no performance) A£10.00 Concessions£7.00*

Pleasance Theatre
Carpenters Mews off North Road London N7 9EF
[Tube: Caledonian Road, left out of station and first left into North Road. Bus: 10 / C12 / 259 / 274 / 17 / 91 & N92. Plentiful parking in the evening]
Tel: 020 7609 1800
Dependent on Show
Dependent on Show. All telephone bookings attract a £0.50 booking fee.

Polka Theatre for Children
240 The Broadway Wimbledon London SW19 1SB
[BR/Tube: South Wimbledon. Bus: 57 / 93 / 155 stop outside; 131 / 156 / 163 and 200 stop nearby. Parking: there are Pay and Display bays near the theatre in Latimer Road and Bridges Road and a number of car parks in Wimbledon Town Centre, including: Wimbledon Broadway (next to Wimbledon Theatre) 70 spaces; Queens Road 700 spaces; Hartfield Road 70 spaces; St George's Road 190 spaces & Hartfield Crescent 250 spaces]
Tel: 020 8543 4888 Box Office Fax: 020 8542 7723
www.polkatheatre.com
Britain's only theatre producing works for children. We create our own productions, designing the sets and costumes and provide an opportunity to see the best work from around the world. Workshops, show-related exhibitions, café, playground and small shop. School parties and the public on Saturdays during the

holidays. Equipped for wheelchair users and hearing-aid users (induction-loop). Advance scripts available. Recommended age-ranges - please abide by these. Please respect and explain to children other people's wish to see an uninterrupted performance. Events listed are for the first quarter of the year only, please contact the venue directly or visit their web site for upcoming performances.
Dependent on event. Two performances per day, Tue-Fri term-time. Times can be flexible to suit circumstances. Specially requested evening performances available
Dependent on event. Payment by tel: Mon 09.30-16.30; Tue-Fri 09.00-18.00; Sat 10.00-17.00. In Person: Tue-Fri 09.30-16.30; Sat 11.00-17.30. Advance booking recommended, (pay within two weeks). Group bookings, reductions and family tickets available (specified performances). Call for further details
discount offer: Two For The price Of One At Saturday Second Main House Performance

↓ *special events*

▶ **Saturday Adventures**
8/1/00-27/5/00
A wonderful array of magical theatrical productions to keep the Saturdays in your family life exciting. Prices: Public £2.00, Schools and concessions £4.00. Durations are variable, please call for fuller details

▶ **Drama for 3 to 5s**
1/2/00-11/4/00
(10 weeks). Drama, improvisation and theatre crafts. With Marleen Vermeulen. 16.00-17.00. £45.00.

▶ **Music for 3 to 5s**
3/2/00-13/4/00
(10 weeks). Music, rhythm and percussion. 16.00-17.00. £45.00

▶ **Youth Theatre for 13 to 16s**
3/2/00-13/4/00
(10 weeks). Weekly drama sessions exploring all aspects of acting, including improvisation, script-work and voice. With Juliet Peters. 18.45-20.15. £55.00.

▶ **Drama for 9 to 12s**
3/2/00-13/4/00
(10 weeks). Weekly drama sessions exploring all aspects of acting, including improvisation, script-work and voice. With Juliet Peters. 17.00-18.30. £55.00.

▶ **Drama for 6 to 8s**
4/2/00-14/4/00
(10 weeks). Drama, storytelling, music and movement. With Marleen Vermeulen. 16.00-17.30. £55.00

▶ **No Worries by David Holman**
10/2/00-25/3/00
Told through narration, song and exhilarating action, this is a moving and joyful play for younger children. Recommended for children aged 6-10 and their families!

► **Bike**
22/2/00-26/2/00

► **The Mamas and the Papas**
29/2/00-4/3/00

A game of hide and seek slips into a magical parallel universe down the plughole where Harry and his mum both learn a lot about play and responsibility!

► **The Lottie Project by Jacqueline Wilson**
13/4/00-29/4/00

Back by popular demand. share Charlie's extraordinary adventures both in real life and in her imaginary Victorian diary. Suitable for children 8 and over and their families. Please call for performance times and dates. Ticket Prices: Public Performances £8.00 Concessions £5.50 Schools's Performances £3.50 Previews £3.50 Family Ticket (Sat 17.30 and Tue & Thur 11.00) £28.00

► **Dogworthy's Summer Magic**
18/4/00-22/4/00

Summer is on its way! Dogworthy is off to the seaside with his speical Imagination Shell. You are invited to join him explore the beach and meet some wonderful creatures

► **Easter Drama Schools and Special Days**
25/4/00-28/4/00

Richmond Theatre

The Green Richmond London TW9 1JQ
[approach by A316. There is free parking on Richmond Green and the Old Deer Park after 18.30. BR: Waterloo (10mins). Tube: Richmond / Hammersmith (12mins). Silverlink from N London]

Tel: 020 8940 0088 Box Office Fax: 020 8948 3601

At Richmond Theatre you can be among the first to enjoy the latest shows, including world premieres, before they go to the West End, in the comfort of our beautifully restored Victorian building. With the latest technology, including air-conditioning and state-of-the-art sound and lighting you'll have a top quality experience to remember.

Times are dependent on Show. Box Office: Mon-Sat 10.00-20.00 on performance days and 10.00-18.00 when there is no evening performance. Closed until 11.00 on the first Thur of the month for staff training. Theatre tours: first Sat of every month at 12.00
Dependent on Show

Royal Albert Hall

Kensington Gore London SW7 2AP
[parking nearby can be booked in advance at a cost of £6.00. Tube: Knightsbridge / South Kensington / High Street Kensington]
Tel: 020 7589 8212 Fax: 020 7584 1406

World famous concert and event venue. Opened in 1871 and named after Queen Victoria's consort Albert. Apart from the distinctive domed exterior an interesting feature is The Great Organ, with over 10,000 pipes, one of the largest and finest in the world.

Box office open 09.00-21.00. Doors normally open 45 mins before the start of each show

Admission varies according to event

↓ *special events*

► **BBC Henry Wood Promenade Concerts**

14/9/00-9/10/00

Call 020 7765 5575 for information.

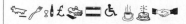

Royal Court Theatre

St. Martin's Lane London WC2N 4BG

[Theatre Upstairs: St Martin's Lane Covent Garden WC2. Theatre Downstairs: West Street WC2. Both of the Theatres are within 5mins walking distance from each other. Tube: Leicester Square 5mins walking / Charing Cross. Buses: many buses run to and from Trafalgar Square which is within easy walking distance of both theatres]

Tel: 020 7565 5000 Fax: 020 7565 5001

The Royal Court Theatre has been awarded a National Lottery Award, through the Arts Council of England, to re-build our Sloane Square home. The Lottery Fund will pay up to 3/4 of the total cost of the £25million project, but we must raise £7million ourselves. We are aiming to raise £500,000 from our Stage Hands appeal to loyal audience members. We have already secured over £300,000 in pledges and donations, but need more supporters to help finish the re-building.

All year

Ticket Prices: Downstairs - Best Seats (Evenings) £19.50 (Matinees) £15.00, Good Seats - (Evenings) £15.00 (Matinees) £12.00, Economy Seats - (Evenings) £10.00 (Matinees) £8.00, Restricted View - (Evenings) £5.00 (Matinees) £5.00, Benches* - (Evenings) £0.10 (Matinees) £0.10. Upstairs - Best Seats (Evenings) £10.00 (Matinees) £5.00, Restricted View - (Evenings) £5.00 (Matinees) £5.00, Benches* - £0.10 (Standing). * In person only, one hour before performance, two tickets per person.

London

Royal Festival Hall and Hayward Gallery
Belvedere Road London SE1 8XX
[South Bank. Tube: Waterloo]
Tel: 020 7960 4242 Fax: 020 7921 0821
www.sbc.org.uk
London's South Bank plays host to the finest
artists from the worlds of music, drama,
dance, literature, film and visual arts. The
sheer scale of events is very impressive, with
the best in classical, contemporary and the
cutting edge, all represented. There are also
free exhibitions and concerts in the foyers,
which are open throughout the day. All this
plus a wide range of food and drinks, and
shops with books, records and gifts mean
there is never a shortage of things to do at the
world's largest centre for the arts.
All year daily 10.00-22.00. Closed 25 Dec
Admission Free
↓ *special events*
► Classic International
22/9/99-2/6/00

Royal National Theatre and Tours
South Bank London SE1 9PX
*[Rail: Waterloo. Tube: Waterloo or cross the river
from Charing Cross, Embankment or Temple.
Car Park: Spaces in the car park below the
National, managed by Central Parking System,
are £5.50 after 17.00. If you attend a daytime
ticketed event, the rate is also £5.50, but validation must be obtained from the Information
Desk. There is Free parking for Orange Badge
holders - validation required when booking*

*tickets or on the day from the Information
Desk. Phone 020 7452 3400 for details.]*
Tel: 020 7452 3000 Box Office
www.nt-online.org
The National is one the South Bank of the
Thames, just minutes from Covent Garden and
the West End. It is one of the worlds most successful theatres, renowned for its first-class
productions and with awards to its credit. On
its three stages the National offers a wealth of
drama to suit every age and interest ranging
from great classics to award-winning new
plays; from comedies to shows for young people and spectacular musicals. There are also
backstage tours offering the chance for visitors
to see one of the most technically advanced
theatres in the world, including a well-
informed guided journey through all three
auditoriums, front-of-house, scenic workshops
and backstage areas. In addition, the National
offers places to eat and drink, bookshops, early
evening events, free foyer exhibitions and live
music. Information and Backstage Tours: 020
7452 3400; Mezzanine Restaurant: 020 7452
3600; Terrace Café: 020 7452 3555.
*All year Foyers Mon-Sat 10.00-23.00. Open from
16.00 on Mon 31 Aug. Mon-Sat Backstage
Tours: Mon-Sat. Main Foyer Bookshop: Mon-Sat
10.00-22.45. Olivier & Cottesloe Bookshops
open from 1 hour before performances.
Costume Hire Dept: by appointment Mon-Fri
10.00-13.00 & 14.00-18.00 (020 7735 4774 /
020 7587 0404. Mezzanine: 12.00-23.00.
Terrace Café: opens 17.30 and from 12.00 on
Lyttleton matinee days, to 19.30. Circle Café:
open from 17.30-19.30 on Olivier performance
days and from 12.00 on Olivier matinee days.
Espresso Bar: Mon-Sat 09.00-20.00 (summer),
Mon-Fri 09.00-16.00, Sat 09.00-20.00 (winter).
Lyttleton Buffet: 12.00-23.00.
Prices vary according to performance and seating areas, see events. To book by post: Write
enclosing payment, including a £0.50 handing
charge for return of tickets. Mailing list members are given priority by phone, 020 7452
3030. No further written confirmation is need-
ed. Minicom for deaf people: 020 452 3009
Mon-Sat 10.00-17.00. By Cheque: made payable
to Royal National Theatre. By Card: Access /
American Express / Artscard / Diners Club /
Mastercard / Switch or Visa. Overseas payment
by credit card (as above), Eurocheque, international money order or bankers draft in £ sterling drawn on a London bank. Ticket Exchange:
Tickets may be exchanged for later performances or credit vouchers, provided 5 days'
notice is given. The handing charge is £1.00 per
ticket. Tickets cannot be refunded. Standing
tickets are only sold after all seats have been
sold. Backstage Tours: £4.00 per person. Groups
12+, Students, OAPs, unemployed, Equity, SOLT
& BECTU £3.50.*

London

↓special events

▶ **The Merchant of Venice by William Shakespeare (1594/95)**
11/6/99-23/3/00
At the Olivier. Generally considered a comedy but also one of Shakespeare's most grippingly dramatic plays

▶ **Summerfolk - venue: Olivier Theatre**
27/8/99-18/3/00
Gorky's mighty naturalistic masterpiece shows us a diverse group of Russians meeting and responding to the prospect of great upheaval

▶ **The Oresteia - venue: Cottesloe Theatre**
24/9/99-1/4/00
An adaptation by Ted Hughes of, 1 The Home Guard, 2 The Daughters of Darkness by Aeschylus (458BC). A contemporary version that rises to the tragic vision of the original

▶ **Battle Royal**
9/12/99-8/4/00
Nick Stafford's witty play about the tempestuous marriage of George IV and Caroline of Brunswick charts a fascinating chapter in British monarchy

▶ **Honk! The Ugly Duckling - NT Ensemble**
11/12/99-25/3/00
Hans Christian Andersen's inspirational tale has been turned into an exhilarating musical for the whole family

▶ **Talk Shows in the Lyttelton**
22/2/00-20/3/00
Hear from the writers, actors, directors and other members of the creative teams about the National's current productions

▶ **Tear from a Glass Eye**
24/2/00-17/3/00
By Matt Cameron and directed by Erica Whyman

▶ **Baby Doll - in the Lyttelton**
3/3/00-4/4/00
Tennessee Williams' passionate tale of the Deep South is both a searing examination of racial bigotry and corruption, and a tender portrait of love and loneliness.

▶ **Judi Dench in the Lyttelton**
10/3/00-10/3/00
At 18.00, the recent Oscar-winner and National Theatre favourite will talk about her work, with biographer John Miller

▶ **Theatre of the Seasons**
13/3/00-22/4/00
Photography by Carlos Guarita. Lyttelton Exhibition Foyer, 10.00-23.00, not on Sundays, admission free.

▶ **The Villains' Opera**
4/4/00-15/4/00
A dynamic new piece of music theatre, John Gay's conception of The Beggar's Opera has been updated to a contemporary London

▶ **Simon Callow in the Lyttelton**
7/4/00-7/4/00
Callow reads and talks about romance and the

Bard at 18.00.

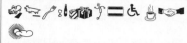

Royal Opera House
Covent Garden London WC2E 9DD
[Disabled Access: a lay-by allows vehicles to pull off Bow Street immediately outside the Floral Hall to drop off disabled passengers. Disabled parking bays are on the opposite side of Bow Street in Floral Street (which caters for the whole area and NOT just the Royal Opera House). Ample wheelchair spaces are available within the Stalls, Grand Tier, Balcony, Upper Amphitheatre and the Studio Theatre. A lift service to all levels. The Box Office will be pleased to advise customers with mobility dificulties of the most easily accessible seats. Guide Dogs are welcome in the auditoria or can be looked after at the foyer cloakroom by front-of-house staff.]
Tel: 020 7304 4000 (27/9/99) Fax: 020 7212 9460 (27/9/99)
www.royaloperahouse.org
The Royal Opera House will be open to the general public in December 1999. From 6th December visitors will be able to see the beautifully refurbished foyer areas and view permanent displays and temporary exhibitions sited around the building. Some areas may be temporarily unavailable if events are taking place during the day. When the Royal Opera House is open to the public the Link will connect Bow Street to Covent Garden Piazza from 10.00 to the end of the evening performance, Monday to Saturday. The Link holds: the Box Office (from October) and the Royal Opera House Shop, the Coffee Shop, the Information Point. Backstage tours: From Jan 2000, specific tours, which have been designed with wheelchair users in mind, will guide visitors through the new building, unravelling the history and the hidden areas of the theatre. Departs the Information Desk three times daily at 10.30, 12.30 and 14.30. Booking for these tours opens on Monday 11 October (though 8 places for the first public tour will be reserved for people to buy on that day). Ballet Classes: From Monday 11 October, it will be possible to book tickets to watch members of The Royal Ballet taking their daily ballet class in the new Studio Upstairs.
Box Office: a temporary Box Office located in Floral Street will open from 27 Sept for personal callers. On that day only the Box Office will open 08.00-22.00. Normal opening hours from 28 Sept are 10.00 until the end of the first interval or 20.00 on non-performance days. You can also book using the web address above. Coffee Shop: Mon-Sat 10.00-20.00. Information Point: Mon-Sat 10.00-curtain up. Amphitheatre Restaurant & Bar: from Mon 6 Dec Mon-Sat

10.00-15.00 (except when there is a performance of special event during the day). For ticket holders the Restaurant will open one and a half hours before curtain-up for performances starting at 19.00 or later. For matinees or early performances, restaurants and bars will open one hour before curtain-up.

Admission to the Royal Opera House is Free, ticket prices to special events are dependant on event being booked. Backstage tours: £6.00. Ballet Classes: £10.00, concessions available.

↓ *special events*

► Coppélia
8/2/00-14/5/00
► Roméo et Juliette
18/2/00-9/3/00
► La bohème
24/2/00-13/3/00
► Ashton Revisited
29/2/00-22/3/00
► Der Rosenkavalier
14/3/00-10/4/00
► Der fliegende Holländer
21/3/00-11/4/00
► Manon
28/3/00-19/4/00
► The New World
12/4/00-4/5/00
► The Greek Passion
25/4/00-8/5/00
► The Diaghilev Legacy
9/5/00-20/5/00
► Die Meistersinger von Nürnberg
16/5/00-31/5/00
► Norma in Concert
24/5/00-26/5/00
► Birmingham Royal Ballet
29/5/00-10/6/00
► Kirov Opera and Ballet
12/6/00-15/7/00
► The Royal Ballet
17/7/00-29/7/00

Sadler's Wells

Rosebery Avenue Islington London EC1R 4TN
[situated at the top of Rosebery Avenue the theatre is in the heart of London's popular Islington area. Free Bus Travel Sadler's Wells and Arriva buses will be launching a promotion for free travel to SW on the 38, 19, 341 and 73 routes (further details will be sent with tickets). Tube: Angel Northern Line (City Branch) is a 6min walk from Sadler's Wells. Trains run every few minutes northbound to Kings Cross and Euston, and southbound to Bank and London Bridge.]
Tel: 020 7863 8000 Box Office
www.sadlers-wells.com
Sadler's Wells Theatre presents a programme of national and international dance, lyric the-

atre and opera, the variety and excellence of which can be seen at no other British venue. The auditorium seats 1500 which can be extended to 1800 or reduced to 900 for more intimate performances. The new Autumn Season, starting in September, presents an array of dance, opera and music theatre. The season opens with a captivating new star of Flamenco - Sara Baras and ends with a brand new musical version of Dick Whittington.
Box Office: Mon-Sat 10.00-20.00. There is a minicom for hearing impairments 0171 863 8015. Alternatively there is 24 hour booking through First Call on 0171 420 1166.
Group Bookings: Adult groups of 10+, 10% discount on Stalls prices. Adult groups of 30+, 15% discount on Stalls prices. For Dick Whittington adult groups of 12+ receive 20% off any seats in the auditorium except First Circle Superseats (discounts apply to off-peak performances only). School Groups: One teacher free for every ten pupils for specific performances. For details and special school offers please call the Education Department on 0171 863 8092. Standbys (from 1hr before the performance). For students, unwaged, children under 16, over 60s, from £7.50 (subject to availability and proof of status). A transaction charge of £1.90 will be added to all ticket bookings and reservations.

↓ *special events*

► Tango por Dos Una Noche de Tango
23/2/00-1/4/00

Shaftesbury Theatre

210 Shaftesbury Avenue London WC2H 8DP
[Tube: Holborn / Tottenham Court Road]
Tel: 07000 211221 Fax: 020 7836 0466
www.lifecafe.com
New York Office: 31 West 56th Street, New York NY10019, Tel: (212) 245 4680.
Performance times: Mon-Sat 19.30, Sat & Wed matinee 15.00
Ticket prices: Stalls £32.50, £30.00, £26.00; Royal Circle £32.50, £30.00, £20.00; Grand Circle £26.00, £20.00, £12.50. First two rows of the stalls go on sale two hours before curtain-up. Two seats per person cash only £10.00 at the Box Office. Groups: £5.00 off top two prices of 12 or more, excluding Sat evenings

The Prince Theatre, Prince Of Orange

Greenwich BR Station Forecourt Greenwich High Road London SE10 8JA
[BR: Greenwich]
Tel: 020 8858 9256
The Prince Theatre was set up in 1996 and in the last two years, has housed 38 full scale productions, provided work for over 400 the-

atre practitioners and entertained approximately 22,000 people. The Price Theatre is now entering a crucial stage of its future development with plans to convert it into a 100 seater all day opening Arts Centre, which will ensure its future as one of London's leading theatre spaces. The Galleon Theatre Company was founded in 1988 and his since produced theatre throughout England, Scotland and Europe. In the last two years, in residency at The Prince Theatre, the company has presented twenty-two theatre productions

Performance dates and times are given in the events section or by calling the Box Office Tickets are dependant on the current production, details given in the events section or by calling the Box Office

The Questors Theatre Studio
12 Mattock Lane London W5 5BQ
[Tube: Ealing Broadway]
Tel: 020 8567 5184 Box Office
www.questors.org.uk
Questors Theatre is the largest non-professional theatre in the UK, and was founded in 1929. It has a reputation for the highest standards not only in acting, but also in direction and design. The theatre has over 3000 members including 300 actors and a further 350 involved in production and managing all aspects of the theatre. The main playhouse, which was completed in the mid sixties, was the first flexible theatre in the country. A studio theatre was established in the early seventies. There is usually one production in the playhouse and one in the studio every three weeks during the season. The playhouse, studio and supporting facilities are superbly equipped to professional standards.
Dependent on performance
You need to be a member to enjoy this facility call 0181 567 8736 for details

The Space
269 Westferry Road Isle of Dogs London E14 3RS
[DLR: Mudchute - bearing right, walk the length of Spindrift Avenue. Turn right at West Ferry Road (T-Junc) and the Space is 400 yards up on the right (10 min walk) or Tube: Mile End then Bus: D7 to the Space]
Tel: 020 7515 7799 Box Office
Landy's bar and bistro. Fully licensed bar, homemade natural food, breakfasts, special £5.00 two course lunch, parking for patrons, private function room for day or evening events. Cafe reservations 0171 515 5577.
Box Office: Mon-Fri 10.00-17.00 & evenings / weekends with events. Landy's Bar & Bistro: 11.00-23.00 daily

Tonybee Studios
28 Commerical Street London E1 6LS
[Tube: Aldgate East. Buses: 15 / 25 / 40 / 67 & 253]
Tel: 020 7928 6363 Box Office
Please call for details
Please call the Young Vic Studio on the number above

Tower Theatre
Canonbury Place Islington London N1 2NQ
[BR: Silverlink Metro or Great Northern) to Tube: Highbury & Islington. Bus: 271 to Canonbury Sq 4 / 19 / 30 / 277 to St Pauls Rd (Highbury Corner); 4 / 19 / 30 / 43 to Islington Town Hall; 38 / 56 / 73 / 171a to Essex Rd Station. Car: The theatre is in Canonbury Place, which leads out of the NE corner of Canonbury Sq, quite nr Highbury Corner roundabout at the S end of the Holloway Road (A1). Local street parking is available]
Tel: 020 7226 3633 Box Office
www.tower-theatre.org.uk
The Tower Theatre, the oldest established little theatre in Islington, has been providing first-class entertainment for over 40 years. Presenting a new show every two weeks, our repertoire aims to cover a wide theatrical spectrum, from the classics to traditional panto and new plays. There's bound to be something to interest you! The Theatre has an audio induction loop for the hard of hearing. We regret the theatre has space for only one wheelchair; fire regulations state that any other wheelchairs must be removed to the foyer after the occupants have been seated.
Dependent on Show
Seats: A£7.00 Concessions£5.00. Sat eve: £8.00 Concessions£6.00. Sun Matinees all seats £5.00. Tue two seats for £7.00. Credit/Debit Cards accepted for advance bookings (for Switch, please quote issue no). A £0.50p service charge will be added for all transactions (except Switch) up to £30.00 (£1.00 above £30.00). Provisional bookings are held only for four working days or until 19.00 on the performance night, whichever is the sooner, after which they will be sold. Tickets accepted for resale on the understanding that the theatre's own unsold tickets take priority. Box Office hours 14.00-20.00 Mon-Sat, 14.00-16.00 performance Sun. Closed Public hol and non-performance Sun

Tricycle Theatre
269 Kilburn High Road London NW6 7JR
[Tube: Kilburn. Buses: 16, 28, 31, 32, 98, 206, 316. Also 139/139N to Messina Ave (5 mins walk)]

Tel: 020 7328 1000

The Tricyle incorporates a Theatre, Cinema and Gallery. All areas of the Tricycle are fully accessible to wheelchair users. Please inform the Box Office of any special requirements when booking your tickets. Hot and cold meals are served daily in the cafe and bar. Children's workshops are held during the school holidays. Please contact the Box Office for detailed listing.

Box office: All year daily 10.00-21.00. Cafe & Bar: Mon-Sat 12.00-20.45, Sun 13.00-20.45

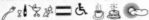

Tristan Bates Theatre, The Actors Centre
1a Tower Street London WC2H 9NP

[Tube: Covent Garden / Leicester Square. Buses: 24 / 29 / 176. NCP car parks: Upper St Martins Lane / Drury Lane]

Tel: 020 7240 3940

The Tristan Bates Theatre was created through the generosity of Alan Bates and his family, and is dedicated to the memory of Mr Bates' own son Tristan, who died tragically at the age of twenty as he embarked on his acting career.

Box Office: daily from 10.00
Ticket Prices vary according to the programme, please see the individual details

Unicorn Theatre For Children
at Pleasance Theatre Carpenters Mews North Road London N7 9EF

[Tube: Caledonian Road]

Tel: 020 7609 1800 Fax: 020 7700 7366

Unicorn Theatre for Children present top quality performances for children, their families and teachers.

During Performances: Mon-Sat 10.00-18.00, Sun 12.30-16.00
Tickets prices range from: £4.50-£11.00

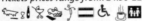

Upstairs at The Gatehouse
The Gatehouse Highgate Village London N6 4BD

[situated at the corner of Hampstead Lane and North Road. Tube: Highgate. Bus: 143 / 210 / 214 / 271. Parking in Hampstead Lane]

Tel: 020 8340 3488

Like most London Fringe Theatres, The Gate House relies on private funding to keep the Theatre open. We are always looking for those who would like to become patrons and lend their support.

During Season Tue-Sun
Unless stated otherwise Ticket prices for all shows: Tue £7.00 Concessions£5.00; Wed-Fri £8.00 Concessions£6.00; Sat £10.00 Concessions£8.00; Sun Matinees £7.00 Concessions£5.00

Warehouse Theatre
Dingwall Road Croydon CR0 2NF

[follow signs to Fairfield Halls, then East Croydon Railway Station. Tube: East Croydon (adjacent). Bus: 54 / 64 / 130 / 166 / 197 / 353 / 367 / 726. Multi-storey car pars are located on Dingwall Rd and Hazledean Rd]

Tel: 020 8680 4060 Box Office Fax: 020 8688 6699

www.uk-live.co.uk/warehouse_theatre

South London's only producing theatre dedicated entirely to new writing.

Dependent on Show. Box Office: Mon 10.00-17.00, Tue 10.00-20.30, Wed-Sat 10.00-22.00, Sun 15.00-19.00
Dependent on Show. Group bookings: One EXTRA ticket FREE for every 10 booked on Tue, Wed, Fri & Sun. Special discounts can also be arranged for larger groups - please call the Box Office Manager for further information. School groups will also receive one free ticket for a teacher in the group. Reservations: Tickets can be reserved, but must be paid for within 3 days of booking or 45 mins before the performance, whichever is the sooner. Tickets cannot be exchanged or money refunded.

Whitehall Theatre
14 Whitehall London SW1A 2DY

[Tube: Charing Cross]

Tel: 020 7925 2107 Fax: 020 7839 3462

Built in 1930, the plain white front seems to emulate the Cenotaph at the other end of the street, but, inside, the theatre boasts some excellent Art Deco detailing. From the 1950's to the 1970's it was noted for staging a wide range of farces.

All year for performances or private hire
Prices vary according to performance call for details

Wyndham's Theatre
Charing Cross Road London WC2H 0DA

[Tube: Leicester Square]

Tel: 020 7369 1736

Performance times: Evenings Tue-Sat 20.00, Matinees Wed 15.00, Sat & Sun 17.00
Box Office 0171 369 1756 No Booking Fee.
Ticket prices: £9.50-£27.50

Young Vic and Young Vic Studio
66 The Cut London SE1 8LZ

[Tube/BR: Waterloo. Bus: 1 / N1 / P11 / 26 / 45 / 63 / 68 / X68 / 76 / N81 / 149 / 168 / 171 / 171a / N171 / 176 / N176 / 188 / 501 / 505 / 521.]

London

Tel: 020 7928 6363 Box Office
Mon-Sat: 10.00 - curtain up
All tickets can be reserved in advance. By post: please send a SAE for the return of your tickets.

Places of Worship incl Cathedrals

Highgate Cemetary
Swains Lane London N6 6PJ
[Tube: Archway]
Tel: 020 8340 1834
The most impressive series of large, formally arranged and landscaped cemeteries which were established around the decades of Queen Victoria's reign. A wealth of fine sculptures and architecture amongst the tombstones, monuments and mausoleums as well as the graves of such notables as the Rossetti family, George Elliot, Michael Faraday and Karl Marx.
Eastern: A£1.00. Guided Tours of Western: A£3.00 C£1.00

Kensal Green (All Souls) Cemetary
Green Dragon Lane Brentford Middlesex W10 4RA
[Tube: Gunnersbury. BR: Kew Bridge]
Tel: 020 8960 1030
Interesting variety of Victorian memorials and mausoleums. Chapel and catacombs can be viewed by appointment. Anthony Trollope is here along with William Makepeace Thackeray and Wilkie Collins.
Tours every Sun 14.00 from Anglian Chapel (15mins walk from gate)
A£4.00 Concessions £3.00

Shri Swaminarayan Mandir
105-119 Brentfield Road Neasden London NW10 8JP
[Tube: Neasden / Wembley Park. Bus: PR2 from Wembley Park]
Tel: 020 8965 2651 Fax: 020 8961 2444
Inspired by His Holiness Pramukh Maharaj the Shri Swaminarayan Mandir is the first traditional Hindu Mandir in Europe, carved and constructed entirely according to the ancient Shilpashastras (the treatise on Temple architecture). No steel has been used. Over 2820 tonnes of Bulgarian limestone and 2000 tonnes of marble were shipped to India. More than 1500 craftsmen worked at over 12 sites in India. Over 26300 carved pieces including amazingly intricate ceilings were shipped to London. Within 3 years they were finally assembled like a giant jigsaw by volunteers. On the ground floor is an exhibition of the study of the Hindu religion. This amazing building has been described by The Sunday

Telegraph as 'the most remarkable London monument of the late 20th century.' Allow 90 minutes to enjoy your visit and do not forget to visit the café for mouth-watering vegetarian delicacies. As this is a place of worship mini skirts, shorts, sleeveless tops and revealing clothes should not be worn.
All year daily from 09.00-18.00
There is no charge to visit the Mandir.
Exhibition & video show: A£2.00 C(6-16)£1.50

Southwark Cathedral
Montague Close London SE1 9DA
[Tube: London Bridge]
Tel: 020 7407 3708 Fax: 020 7357 7389
For over 1,000 years Southwark Cathedral has been a centre for Christian worship. The oldest part of the present building dates from 1215 with additions in the 1500's and 1800's. Monuments include one of Shakespeare and Sam Wanamaker, founder of the International Globe Centre, Bankside. Guided tours may be booked in advance. Lunch time instrumental concerts and organ recitals take place regularly.
All year daily 08.00-18.00
Admission free, donation of £2.00

St Bride's Church
Fleet Street London EC4Y 8AU
[Tube: Blackfriars]
Tel: 020 7353 1301/583 0239 Fax: 020 7583 4867
St Bride's is often termed 'the Cathedral of Fleet Street' since 1500 it has had an intimate relationship with people engaged in printing. In 1500 Wynkyn de Woede set up Caxton's alongside the church yard. It's spire is the highest Christopher Wren ever built and was the inspiration for the first tiered wedding cake. The site was first built on by the Romans 1800 years ago and it has been a monument and an illustration of England's history ever since. Lunch time recitals are held every Tuesday, Wednesday and Friday.
All year daily

St Clement Danes Church
Strand London WC2R 1DH
[Tube: Temple]
Tel: 020 7242 8282 Fax: 020 7404 2129
Built in it's present form in 1682 by Sir Christopher Wren, the steeple was added to the tower by James Gibbs in 1719. St Clement Danes was destroyed by enemy action in May 1941, with only the walls and steeple left standing. After the war the Royal Air Force launched an appeal fund to restore the church

London

and in Oct 1958 the completely restored church was reconsecrated as the Central Church of The Royal Air Force. The church contains many Royal Airforce memorials and over 800 badge inscriptions.
All year daily 09.00-17.00
Admission free, donations accepted

St James's Church
197 Piccadilly London W1V 0LL
[BR: Victoria / Charing Cross. Tube: Piccadilly Circus / Green Park. Bus: 3 / 6 / 9 / 12 / 14 / 15 / 19 / 22 / 38]
Tel: 020 7734 4511 Fax: 020 7734 7449
Among the many churches Wren designed this is said to be one of his favourites. It has been altered over the years and was half-wrecked by a bomb in 1940, but it maintains its essential features from 1684 - the tall arched windows, thin spire (a 1966 fibre glass replica of the original) and a light, dignified interior. A specialist Antiques and Collectors' Market is held on Tuesdays, please see the main listing under Markets.
All year daily 08.30-19.00. Craft Market: Wed-Sat 09.30-18.00. Closed Easter
Admission Free

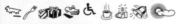

St Margaret's Church
Parliament Square London SW1
[Tube: St. James's Park / Westminster]
Tel: 020 7222 5152 Fax: 020 7233 2072
Overshadowed by the Abbey, this early 15th century church has long been a favoured venue for political and society weddings, such as Winston and Clementine Churchill's. Although much restored, the church retains some Tudor features, notably a stained-glass window that celebrates the engagement of Catherine of Aragon to Arthur, Henry VIII's eldest brother.
All year Mon-Sat 09.30-17.00, Sun 13.00-17.30
Admission Free

St Martin-in-the-Fields
Duncannon Street Trafalgar Square London WC2N 4JJ
[Tube: Charing Cross / Embankment]
Tel: 020 7930 0089/1862 Fax: 020 7839 5163
The current building is the fourth to stand on the site, completed in 1726 to a design by James Gibbs. The magnificent facade was a new style, with Corinthian columns supporting a pediment, with a graceful steeple, topped with a gilt crown. Visit the Gallery with frequently changing exhibits, or create a medieval knight in the Brass Rubbing Centre.

The Cafe-In-The-Crypt serves hot drinks and pastries or a full menu in the excellent restaurant. St Martin-In-The-Fields hosts concerts held in the evenings and lunchtimes (bookings on 0171 839 8362).
visitor comments: A variety of things to do - visit the church, gallery, brass rubbing, cafe and the fascinating gift shop.
All year daily 09.00-18.00
Admission free

↓ *special events*
► **Le Concert Spirituel**
9/3/00-9/3/00
► **String Favourites**
8/6/00-8/6/00

St Paul's Cathedral
St Paul's Churchyard London EC4M 8AD
[Tube: St Paul's]
Tel: 020 7236 4128 Fax: 020 7248 3104
Sir Christopher Wren's architectural masterpiece. Climb to the Whispering Gallery where your whisper can be heard on the other side and visa-versa.
All year Mon-Sat 08.30-16.00, Sun services only Cathedral, crypt & galleryA£7.50 C£3.50 Family Ticket £16.50 Concessions£6.50 Guided tours and group booking available

Wesley's Chapel, Museum and House
49 City Road London EC1Y 1AU
[Tube: Old Street / Moorgate]
Tel: 020 7253 2262 Fax: 020 7608 3825
Mother Church of World Methodism since 1778. Crypt houses a museum tracing the development of Methodism from the 18th century to the present. Visit Wesley's house built by him in 1779 and discover the day to day running of a small Georgian townhouse.
visitor comments: Very interesting, very unusual.
All year Mon-Sat 10.00-16.00, Sun 12.00-14.00. Closed Bank Hol, Christmas and New Year A£4.00 C&OAPs&Students£2.00. Parties of 20+ 10% discount

Westminster Cathedral
Clergy House Victoria Street London SW1P 1QW
[300 yards from BR: Victoria Station, Tube: Victoria]
Tel: 020 7798 9055 Fax: 020 7798 9090
www.westminstercathedral.org.uk
A fascinating example of Victorian architecture. It was designed in the Early Christian Byzantine style by John Francis Bentley and its strongly oriental appearance makes it very distinctive. The foundation stone was laid in 1895

London

but the interior is still not complete though its fine marble work and mosaics are awesome.
Cathedral: All year Mon-Fri 07.00-19.00, Sat 08.00-19.00, Sun closes 20.00. Tower: Apr-Nov daily 09.00-17.00. Dec-Mar Thur-Sun 09.00-17.00
Admission Free, Tower lift charged

Police, Prisons & Dungeons

Central Criminal Court (Old Bailey)
London EC4M 7EH
[Tube: St. Pauls]
Tel: 020 7248 3277 Fax: 020 7248 5735
The site of Old Newgate Prison, the public galleries are open for viewing. No admission for children under the age of 14 years.
Gallery: All year daily 09.30-13.00 & 14.00-16.30
Admission Free

Clink Prison Museum
1 Clink Street Bankside London SE1 9DG
[Tube: London Bridge]
Tel: 020 74036515 Fax: 020 7378 1558
Enter The Clink Prison Museum, on the original site of the prison that gave it's name to all others, and you enter a world of cut-purses, gibbets, and torture chairs. A dark and mysterious world, whose long and gory history is charted in this fascinating, not to be missed exhibition.
All year daily Apr-Sept Mon-Sun 10.00-18.00. Oct-Mar 10.00-18.00
Last Admission: 18.00 or 20.00
Queuing Times: 5mins
A£4.00 Family Ticket £9.00 Concessions£3.00. Group rate £2.00. Guided Tours are extra and arranged with our resident guide

House of Detention
Clerkenwell Close Clerkenwell Green London EC1R 0AS
[signposted from Tube: Farringdon]
Tel: 020 7253 9494 Fax: 020 7251 1897
London's underground prison built upon one of London's earliest prison sites originally dating back to 1616. Educational Pack available.
All year daily 10.00-18.00
Last Admission: 17.15
A£4.00 C£2.50 Family Ticket £10.00 OAPs£3.00 Concessions£3.00. School Parties £2.50. Group Rates £3.00

London Dungeon
28-34 Tooley Street London SE1 2SZ
[Tube: London Bridge]
Tel: 020 0891 6000 666 Fax: 020 7378 1529
www.dungeons.com
Deep in the heart of London, buried beneath the paving stone lies the world's most chillingly famous museum of horror. The London Dungeon brings more than 2,000 years of gruesomely authentic history vividly back to life - and death. Visit the carnage and stench of a recently ransacked medieval village or wander through into the horrors committed under the name of God and the King before coming face to face with your own 'Judgement Day.' This recent £3.5million addition will take you on the ride of your death through the sewers of London. Finally find out more than you would really care to know about Jack the Ripper. A warning - in the Dungeons dark catacombs it always pays to keep your wits about you ... some of the exhibits have an unnerving habit of coming back to life! New for Easter 2000: Firestorm - new £1m feature.
visitor comments: Fantastical horror museum - but it may frighten younger children.
All year daily Apr-Sept 10.00-17.30 Oct-Mar 10.30-17.00
Last Admission: Mar-Oct 17.30, Nov-Feb 16.30
Queuing Times: 1-2 hours in Summer
A£9.50 C&OAPs£6.50 Students£8.50 Group rates available

North Woolwich Old Station Museum
Pier Road North Woolwich London E16 2JJ
[Pier Road next to both Woolwich Ferry and Silverlink Line at North Woolwich. DLR: Gallions Reach]
Tel: 020 7474 7244 Fax: 020 7473 6065
Railway engines, carriages, photographs, models and memorabilia; The story of Newham's Railway Industry and those who worked on it in a dignified Edwardian station. Education Service, holiday activities, special events every Wednesday during holidays. Engines in steam first Sunday, miniature railway 3rd Sunday of summer months.

London

Jan-Dec Sat & Sun 13.00-17.00. Closed Dec. Open Newham school half terms, Easter and summer Hol. Mon, Tue & Wed 13.00-17.00 Admission Free

Southall Railway Centre

Glade Lane Southall Middlesex UB2 4PL
[BR: Southall. S of the main line entrance via footbridge linking Merrick Road / Park Avenue. Car parking in Arches Business Centre in Merrick Road]
Tel: 020 8574 8100 Fax: 01753 831169
www.daysout.co.uk/colourapore/IA106.ht ml
Based in the former steam and diesel engine shed near Southall Station, the Centre is home to the G.W.R. Preservation Group's 10 pre-served locomotives and collection of rolling stock. Regular steam events are held as well as special events including Santa Specials and vintage vehicle rallies.
Every weekend for stationary display 10.00-18.00, 17.00 in Winter. Monthly steam days and special events. Closed Christmas & New Year Last Admission: 60mins before closing A£4.25 C&OAPs£2.25 Family Ticket (A2+C3)£12.00. Stationary weekends: A£2.00 C&OAPs£1.00 Family Ticket £5.00. Different prices may apply for special events

Roman Era

Crofton Roman Villa

Crofton Road Orpington Kent BR6 8AD
[J4 M25, A232 adjacent Orpington BR station, signs on cover building, BR: Orpington]
Tel: 01689 873826
The only Roman Villa in Greater London which is open to the public. Ten rooms of a villa-house with tiled floors and underfloor heating systems, protected inside a public viewing building. Graphic displays, children's activity corner, schools service. Alternative phone number 020 8462 4737.
2 Apr-29 Oct Wed & Fri 10.00-13.00 & 14.00-17.00, Sun 14.00-17.00, Bank Hol Mon 10.00-13.00 & 14.00-17.00
Last Admission: 16.30
A£0.80 C£0.50 (Alternative phone number: 020 8462 4737)

Roman Bath (National Trust)

5 Strand Lane London WC2R 2NA
[W of Aldwych station approach via Surrey Street. Tube: Temple / Embankment, BR: Blackfriars / Charing Cross]
Tel: 020 7641 5264
A National Trust Property. The remains of a bath, restored in the 17th century, believed by some to be Roman. No toilet facilities. Bath visible through window from pathway all year.
May-end Sept Wed 13.00-17.00 by appointment only.
£0.50 C&Concessions£0.25

Science - Earth & Planetary

Faraday's Laboratory and Museum

The Royal Institution of Great Britain 21 Albemarle Street London W1X 4BS
[Tube: Green Park]
Tel: 020 7409 2992 Fax: 020 7629 3569
Michael Faraday's Laboratory, where many of his most important discoveries were made, has been restored to the form it was known to have in 1845. An adjacent museum houses a unique collection of original apparatus arranged to illustrate the more significant aspects of Faraday's contribution to the advancement of science.
All year Mon-Fri 09.00-17.00. Groups at other times, by arrangement
A£1.00

Grant Museum of Zoology and Comparative Anatomy

University College London Gower Street London WC1E 6BT
[Tube: Euston Square]
Tel: 020 7504 2647 Fax: 020 7380 7096
Specialised teaching collection of Zoological material, covering the whole animal kingdom. Includes rare and extinct specimens and many whole articulated skeletons.
By arrangement only
Admission Free

London Planetarium

Marylebone Road London NW1 5LR
[Tube: Baker Street]
Tel: 020 7935 6861 Fax: 020 7465 0862
www.madame-tussauds.com
Star shows are performed throughout the day and visitors can experience a 3 dimensional journey through space. Interactive "Space Zone" exhibition areas provide up-to-date information about the stars and planets through touch-sensitive screens. Not recom-mended for the under 5's.
visitor comments: Queued for ages in boring surroundings. But the boys loved it once we got in.
All year daily, shows every 40 minutes from 12.20. Closed 25 Dec

Last Admission: 16.30
Queuing Times: 15mins
A£6.00 C£4.00 OAPs£4.60. Combined ticket
with Madame Tussaud's A£12.25 C£8.00
OAPs£9.30

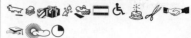

Museum of the Royal Pharmaceutical Society

1 Lambeth High Street London SE1 7JN
[opposite Lambeth Palace. Tube/BR: Waterloo / Vauxhall. Tube: Lambeth North]
Tel: 020 7735 9141 x354 Fax: 020 7735 7629

The rich, specialist collections of the Museum offer visitors and researchers a treasure trove of unexpected objects, images and insights into more then 5 centuries' history of medicinal drugs and their use in Britain. In a series of exhibition spaces set in the Society's impressive Headquarter building in Lambeth, the museum traces the long and complex history of our medicines, the scientists and traders who have invented, developed, compounded and sold them and the patients who have swallowed the pills and fed the leeches!
All year by appointment only Mon-Fri 09.00-13.00 & 14.00-17.00
Admission Free

Royal Observatory Greenwich

Greenwich Park Greenwich London SE10 9NF
[off the A2. BR: Maze Hill DLR: Cutty Sark]
Tel: 020 8312 6565 Fax: 020 8312 6521
www.rog.nmm.ac.uk
Stand on the longitude zero, the Greenwich Meridian, the home of time. Explore the history of time and astronomy in this charming Wren building. see the Astronomer Royal's apartments. Watch the time-ball fall at 1 o'clock. Admire Harrison's amazing time-keepers and other historic clocks. Climb to the giant refracting telescope.
visitor comments: Very popular. Many visitors. Interesting and pleasing experience.

All year daily 10.00-17.00. Closed 24-26 Dec
Last Admission: 16.30
A£6.00 C£Free OAPs&Students£4.80. Combined Admission with National Maritime Museum also available
discount offer: One Free Ticket When An Adult Ticket Is Purchased. Ref: DOG

Science Museum

Exhibition Road South Kensington London SW7 2DD
[Buses: 9 / 10 / 14 / 345 / 49 / 52 / 74 / C1. Tube: South Kensington]
Tel: 020 7942 4354
www.nmsi.ac.uk
When the Wellcome Wing at the Science Museum opens in the summer of 2000, it will be the world's leading centre for the presentation of contemporary science and technology open to the public. The wing will be a breathtaking theatre of science. The exhibition spaces in the Wellcome Wing will feature interactive exhibitions devoted to some of the most important areas of modern science and technology - notably genetics, brain science, artificial intelligence and digital technology. The latest ideas and issues in science and technology will be presented using the most innovative, fast changing displays ever undertaken in the Science Museum. The Wellcome Wing marks a new era, enabling the Museum to do justice not only to the past work of the scientists and technologists but also the work they are doing today. The Wellcome Wing will house the state-of-the-art IMAX (large screen) 3D film theatre and catering and retail facilities.
visitor comments: Children loved the interactive parts. The 'Basement' really graps your attention! Excellent water play.
All year daily 10.00-18.00. Closed 24-26 Dec
A£6.50 C£Free Concessions£3.50, all visitors to the Museum after 16.30 £Free

↓ *special events*
▶ **It's About Time**
1/3/99-1/3/00
▶ **The Art of Invention**
15/10/99-24/4/00
Exhibition bringing to life the incredible engineering projects which revolutionised design and architecture in Renaissance Italy. Open daily, 10.00-18.00. Closed 24-26, 31 Dec, 1 Jan. Admission A£3.00, C£2.00 and concessions £2.00. Also entry to museum: A£6.50; concessions, £3.50.

The Dome

Greenwich Peninsular London SE10 OBB
[Tube: North Greenwich, by river: shuttle boats between historic Greenwich and the Dome; by foot and by bike, new walkways and cycle routes; by rail, new Millennium Transit link to the rail network; by tube, the largest underground station in Europe has been built at the heart of the Dome to serve the new Jubilee line extension, 12 mins from Central London]

Tel: 0870 606 2000 ticket line
www.dome2000.co.uk

Opened on time by the Queen on 31st Dec 1999 The Sixteen Zones are: 1 Central Show - Tells the story of a tragic larger-then-life family, played by a cast of 70 aerial acrobats. 2a Work- Discover the skills you need in the workplace of the future, 2b Learn - Test yourself in the orchard of learning and access the Tesco SchoolNet 2000 project. 3 Money - The walls are lined with £1million of legal tender! experience spending this much money and see what impact it has. 4 Our Town Stage - More than 200 performances by local communities and international visitors in the World Stage Season. 5 Rest - There is nothing at all here, just a soothing light and sound show. 6 Mind - An exploration of the power of thought. 7 Faith, 7 Talk - Everything communication is here, create a web site send an email or leave a message for the future. 9 Self Portrait - A national portrait of how we see Britain. 10 Home Planet - Take a British Spaceways flight to future spacetravel. 11 Living Island - Virtual seaside resort made from recycled household waste. 12 Journey - Explores the history and future of motion from horses to sci-fi machines. 13 Shared Ground - The world's largest recycled cardboard structure created with items collected by Blue Peter Viewers. 14 Play - Video arcade for the future. 15 Body - Take a trip through the human body.

visitor comments: A simply superb day out, the Body Zone - it's not as good as the other zones... which are highly entertaining. So much to see, well worth the money, the building is amazing with much more than just the Dome. NO picnic areas! But you can eat picnics at food outlets. Lost Children: make sure you tell your child to ASK for help, then YOU ASK too, you will be reunited, NO tannoy system.

Make sure you see the SHOW and the Black Adder Film... they're great. In all the Dome does not deserve the bad press it has had, I whole-heartedly recommend a visit - Editor (I paid for my tickets)

All year daily from 1st Jan 2000 for 366 days till 31 Dec 2000. Daily 10.00-18.00 with late opening till 23.00 planned from Apr

Last Admission: Timed Tickets

Tickets must normally be purchased in advance, however, if available they can be be purchased at the Dome. A£20.00 C(0-5)£Free C(5-15) & Students£16.50 OAPs£18.00 ES40£12.00 Family Ticket (either A2+C3 or A1+C4)£57.00; Group rates 15+ A£17.50 OAPs£12.00 Students£14.50 Schools£8.00

↓ *special events*

▶ **Daily Shows**
1/1/00-31/12/00

Sealife Centres & Aquariums

London Aquarium

County Hall Riverside Building Westminster Bridge Road London SE1 7PB
[Tube: Westminster, across Westminster Bridge from the Houses of Parliament]

Tel: 020 7967 8000 Fax: 020 7967 8029
www.londonaquarium.co.uk

The London Aquarium, housed within County Hall on the Thames, is three levels of exciting and educational exhibits, featuring hundreds of varieties of fish and marine life, many of which have not been seen before on these shores. The main attraction will give visitors the chance to enjoy an uninterrupted view of marine life via a huge twin tank display. Also included are some hands-on and interactive displays, where you can touch the starfish, crabs, mussels and rays. Additional tanks display aspects of sea and marine life from different regions and habitats around the world. There is a new interactive Coral display and our new exhibits include The Bizarre Nautilus.

visitor comments: Feel really close to fish and sharks. Good opportunity to touch some fish. The kids loved the day.

All year daily 10.00-18.00

Last Admission: 17.00

Queuing Times: Up to 3 hours

A£8.50 C(3-14)£5.00 Family Ticket (A2+C2)£24.00 Concessions£6.50

discount offer: £2.00 Off Published Admission Price

London

Social History Museums

Gunnersbury Park Museum
Popes Lane Acton London W3 8LQ
[J of A4, M4, North Circular. Bus: E3 Tube: Acton Town]
Tel: 020 8992 1612 Fax: 020 8752 0686
Set in 186 acres of parkland the Mansion was built circa1802 by architect owner Alexander Copland. Later enlarged by Sidney Smirke for N M Rothschild. Now a museum with constantly changing exhibitions, our collections represent social and local history, fashion and childhood. Special group tours can be arranged of Gunnersbury Mansion, phone for details.
Museum: Apr-Oct Mon-Fri 13.00-17.00, Sat, Sun & Bank Hol 13.00-18.00. Nov-Mar Mon-Fri 13.00-16.00. Closed 25-26 Dec & 1 Jan. House: Group tours by arrangement
Last Admission: 15min before closure
Admission Free
discount offer: Any Three Postcards Free

Imperial War Museum
Lambeth Road London SE1 6HZ
[Tube: Lambeth North, Waterloo, Elephant & Castle, well signposted]
Tel: 020 7416 5320 Fax: 020 7416 5374
www.iwm.org.uk
Features all aspects, of all wars involving Britain and the Commonwealth since 1914. Modern exhibitions using the latest technology. Includes special exhibitions and an extensive programme of events, as well as an art gallery. As part of the Millennium Commission for development, a new Holocaust and Total War gallery is due to open in June 2000. A major new exhibition runs to 30 May 2000, "From the Bomb to the Beatles: 1945 - 1965." Sir Terence Conran designed this special exhibition, which will chronicle the changing face of Britain in the post war years. Special features include a 1940's prefab. home, a 1950s coffee bar with a jukebox.
visitor comments: Very interesting - we all learnt a lot, and there's no charge for kids.
All year daily 10.00-18.00. Closed 24-26 Dec
A£5.20 C£Free Concessions£4.20. Group rates 10+ on application. Admission Free from 16.30 daily

↓*special events*
► **Sporting Heroes**
27/2/00-27/2/00
► **'From the Bomb to the Beatles'**
24/4/99-29/5/00
► **Enigma and the Code-breakers**
1/1/00-2/7/00
This special interactive display, designed with the needs of the younger visitor in mind, explores the intriguing world of code-breaking in wartime
► **February Film Shows**
1/2/00-29/2/00
► **Spitfire Summer Films**
6/2/00-27/2/00
► **Spitfire Summer**
18/2/00-26/11/00
An exhibition marking the 60th anniversary of the events of 1940 - a key year for Britain in the Second World War
► **Do Touch the Exhibits**
19/2/00-27/2/00
► **Signs of the Times**
24/2/00-7/5/00
An exhibition of over 100 superb examples of graphic design from Eastern Europe
► **Go To It!**
1/3/00-1/12/00
Actual dates to be announced (call for details) A display to mark the contribution made by the many people who worked on the Home Front during WWII, often in dangerous and difficult conditions.
► **Recent Acquisitions**
1/3/00-1/1/01
A chance to see some of the latest acquisitions made by the museum, including objects, film, photographs and works of art
► **Korea**
14/4/00-1/12/00
Fifty years ago British and Commonwealth troops went off to fight in Korea. This exhibition looks at the experiences of those who were involved. End date not confirmed - please call for details
► **Spitfire Summer Films**
16/4/00-31/5/00
Angles One Five (1952) (98mins) 16 Apr only at 14.00. This Week: from Gaumont British News (1939-1940). (30mins) 3-28 Apr, 1-26 & 30-31 May weekdays at 16.00
► **Spitfire Scramble Easter Egg Hunt**
20/4/00-30/4/00
Free mini chocolate eggs for all those taking part
► **The Holocaust**
1/6/00-1/6/00
A major permanent exhibition about one of the most chilling events of the 20th century. Opens mid 2000 this date is to be confirmed

Museum of London
150 London Wall London EC2Y 5HN
[Tube: St Paul's / Barbican]
Tel: 020 7600 3699 Fax: 020 7600 1058
www.museum-london.org.uk
Officially opened in December 1976, the collec-

tions of the former London and Guildhall museums were brought together in one specially designed building. Detailing all aspects of London life from pre-history to contemporary times. The London Now Gallery looks at the city today, at why London and Londoners are special and different, and explores some of the big issues facing the capital as it approaches the Millennium.

All year Mon-Sat 10.00-17.50, Sun 12.00-17.50.
Closed 22, 24-26 & 29 Dec & 1 Jan
Last Admission: 17.30
A£4.00 C(0-4)£Free C(2+)£2.00 Family Ticket £9.50 Concessions£2.00

↓ *special events*
► **London Eats Out With Simply Food Co UK**
22/10/99-27/2/00

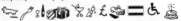

Spectator Sports

Arsenal Football Stadium Tour
Avenell Road Highbury London N5 1BU
[Tube: Arsenal]
Tel: 020 7704 4000 Fax: 020 7704 4101
www.arsenal.co.uk
Stadium tour of Marbel Hall, dressing rooms, trophy cabinet, manager's dugout and museum. Tours by arrangement, call for details.
By appointment only. Please telephone for details
A£4.00 C&OAPs£2.00

Chelsea Football Club
Stamford Bridge Fulham Road London SW6 1HS
[Tube: Fulham Broadway. Plenty of parking on site]
Tel: 0870 603 0005 Booking
www.chelseafc.co.uk
Sit on the seat of your favourite player, in the Manager's seat in the dugout. Walk up the players tunnel and hear the crowd roar. Find out how Chelsea Football Club are preparing for the 21st Century, how security and technology provide safety for the supporters, discover the secrets of the hallowed turf. Tour duration is 1.5hrs. For disabled visitors the tour will be specially arranged.
All year daily except Match and Event days, tour times 11.00, 13.00 & 15.00. Booking Hotline No: 0870 603 0005
Last Admission: 15.00
A£8.00 C&OAPs£5.00 Family Ticket (A2+C3)£26.00 - 3rd C goes FREE. Group rates 15+ 10% discount. Birthday Parties (ages 6-12) 15+ £15.00-£17.00 per head. To book call 020 7915 1924
discount offer: 4th Child Free When Family

Ticket Purchased

Kempton Park Racecourse
Kempton Sunbury-on-Thames Middlesex TW16 5AQ
[J1 M3. BR: Kempton Park Racecourse. Helicopter landing by permission]
Tel: 01932 782292 Fax: 01932 782044
www.demon.co.uk/racenews/rht
Major races run: Jubilee Handicap; Coral Rosebery H'cap Stakes; Pertemps King George VI Chase; Pertemps Christmas Hurdle; Lanzarote Hurdle; Charisma Gold Cup Chase; Easter Stakes; Masaka Stakes; Sirenia Stakes; Adonis Hurdle; Crawley Warren Heron Stakes; Gala Stakes; Racing Post Chase; Rendlesham Hurdle; Queens Prize; Quail Stakes; Feltham Novices' Chase.
Please see Special Events
Feature Days: £10.00-£14.00, Premier Days: £12.00-£16.00. Parking £5.00

Wembley Stadium Tours
Empire Way Wembley Middlesex HA9 0WS
[M1, M4, M40, A406, well signposted from all major approach roads. Tube: Wembley Park / Wembley Stadium]
Tel: 020 8795 5733 Fax: 020 8900 1045
www.wembleynationalstadium.com
World famous stadium and unique in the history of sport and entertainment. Many millions of people have experienced the magic of Wembley Stadium. On your tour you will visit behind the scenes areas not generally seen, and explore Wembley's unique history. The Stadium is scheduled to close for redevelopment in August 2000.
visitor comments: A surprisingly good time
All year daily: Summer 10.00-16.00, Winter 10.00-15.00. Closed for major special events & 25-26 Dec. Due to redevelopment scheduled August 2000 please call to check availability

ЕЕЕ ЕЕ

before making a special journey
Last Admission: Summer 16.00 Winter 15.00
Available on request

↓ special events

▶ **England v Hungary**
25/3/00-25/3/00
Schools International Football

▶ **The F.A. Cup Semi Finals**
8/4/00-9/4/00
Sponsored by AXA

▶ **The Auto Windscreens Shield Final**
16/4/00-16/4/00

▶ **The F.A. Carlsberg Vase Final**
6/5/00-6/5/00

▶ **The F.A. Umbro Trophy Final**
13/5/00-13/5/00

▶ **The F.A. Cup Final**
20/5/00-20/5/00
Sponsored by AXA

▶ **The Nationwide Football League Playoffs**
27/5/00-29/5/00
May 27 Division 3, May 28 Division 2 and May 29 Division 1

▶ **Tina Turner in Concert**
15/7/00-15/7/00

▶ **Oasis in Concert**
22/7/00-22/7/00

▶ **The One-2-One F.A. Charity Shield**
30/7/00-30/7/00

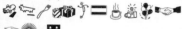

West Ham United Football Club
Boleyn Ground Green Street Upton Park
London E13 9AZ
[Tube: Upton Park]
Tel: 020 8548 2777 Fax: 020 8548 2758
www.westhamunited.co.uk
A stadium with 100 years of history, memories and non-league football to the premiership featuring players from 1895 to the present day including 7 Cup Finals.
All year daily from 10.30
A£3.50 C&OAPs£2.00

Sport & Recreation

Beckenham Place Park
Beckenham Place Park London SE6
[BR: Ravensbourne / Beckenham Hill]
Within meadowland and woods, there are paths to walk and explore, butterflies, mushrooms, birds to see and a great kite flying slope. Other attractions include a public golf course, putting green and tennis courts.
All year daily dawn till dusk
Admission Free

Bushy Park
Teddington London *[BR: Hampton Wick / Teddington, close to Hampton Court]*
Situated close to Hampton Court, this is one of London's ten Royal Parks, formerly hunting preserves, which were opened to the public by Charles I and Charles II. Bushy Park has a famous .75 mile Chestnut Avenue which runs from Hampton Court to the Teddington Gate. This superb double row of enormous tress, laid out by Wren, is best seen in springtime.
Any reasonable time
Admission Free

Castle Climbing Centre
Green Lanes Stoke Newington London N4 2HA
[Tube: Manor House]
Tel: 020 8211 7000 Fax: 020 8211 7720
www.castle-climbing.co.uk
The premier climbing wall in London and South East England is located at the Castle between Manor House and Stoke Newington, North London. It is set in an atmospheric grade 2 listed Victorian Folly based on Stirling castle (a former water pumping station) and is often filmed and used in adverts. There are climbing courses for adults and children. 12 metre tall top roping and lead climbing walls. The best Bouldering wall in the South East (Used for the past two years as the Head to Head Final wall for the Southern Bouldering League). A coffee bar, climbing shop, outdoor courses, Facilities for Film Shoots, Parties & function rooms, Corporate Training, Art Exhibitions and lots more.
All year Mon to Fri 14.00 to 22.00 Sat & Sun 10.00 to 19.00
A£6:00 per day (One Off £4 Membership registration) C£3:50 per day (One Off £2 Membership registration)

Crystal Palace Park
Thicket Road Penge London SE20 8UT
[BR: Crystal Palace, turn right out of station]
Tel: 020 8778 9496 Eventsline Fax: 020 8659 8397
A great park for all the family. Highlights include the T-maze built in 1854, a mini fair for young kids, the Palace Farmyard featuring sheep, goats, cows, pigs and shire horses which can be ridden. There is also a fishing lake with special fishing days during the summer and peddloes for hire. There is a 1'o'clock club held on weekdays, children attending must be accompanied by an adult. The mini fair has rides with wheelchair access and children in wheelchairs go free of charge on the Land-Train that runs around the park. Within the Park is the Crystal Palace Sports Centre (Tel

0181 778 0131) with many activities for kids including a ski slope, climbing wall and fun station. The Sports Centre also runs children's camps and courses.

All year daily 07.30-Sunset
Palace Farmyard: A£1.10 C£0.55 Family Ticket £2.75, Land-Train: A£1.00 C£0.60, Fishing Days: A£2.60 C£1.30 (bring own equipment), Mini fair: £0.30 per ride, Shirehorse rides: £0.50

↓*special events*

► **11th London to Brighton Classic Car Run**
4/6/00-4/6/00
Route Two: Starts here. Check point 1. Groombridge Gardens, Kent, Check Point 2. Michelham Priory, Sussex. Finishing at Maderia Drive, Brighton. No charge to visitors at the Start and Finish points

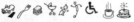

Discovery Zone
1st Floor The Junction Shopping Centre St Johns Hill Clapham Junction London SW11 1SA
[on the A3036 just off the A3, between Wandworth & Clapham, inside Clapham Junction's mainline BR: Clapham Junction]
Tel: 020 7223 1717 Fax: 020 7223 0409
A huge indoor adventure play centre, designed by fitness experts for children up to 12 years old. Parent and Toddler groups 10.00-13.00 and 13.00-15.00 - term time only for £1.99 and the 4 O'Clock Club every day after school where kids can play and get fed for £1.99 Mon-Wed, and Thur & Fri term time only for £2.49. Action packed Birthday parties can also be arranged.
All year Mon-Fri 10.00-18.00, Sat Sun & all School Hol 10.00-19.00
Mon-Fri C£3.99, Sat & Sun C£4.99 for unlimited play. Groups rates C£2.99. Birthday Parties £3.99-£9.99 call for details

Fun House
Edmonton Leisure Centre Plevna Road Edmonton North London N9 0BU
Tel: 020 8807 0712
Let your imagination run wild! Be Superman or Superwoman on the Giant Serpent Spiral. Travel the Overhead Aerial Runway. Be mangled in the Horizontal Rollers or succumb to blood curdling screams of "The Bones". And for the under 5's a totally separate soft play environment where tots can explore the secrets of the Magic Garden free from the constraints of hard surfaces and sharp edges. Parents can relax in the cafeteria whilst the children enjoy the thrill of The Fun House supervised by fully trained staff.
All year daily 10.00-19.00
A£Free C£2.45 (10.00-16.00 Mon-Fri), C£2.85 (Evenings, weekends and Holidays). Off Peak

Mon 16.00-19.00: Free Hot Dog, Crisps & Squash included in entrance fee per paying customer. Group rates £2.00. School parties £2.00, Tue 12.30-16.00 & Wed 10.00-12.30: C£1.50

Green Park
London SW1
[Tube: Green Park]
The smallest of the central London parks, Green Park has the Tyburn stream running just below its surface, maintaining it's lush verdancy. Situated in a triangle formed by Piccadily, The Mall and Constitution Hill.
Admission Free

Greenwich Park and Kesslers Café
Charlton Way Greenwich London SE10 8QY
[Bus: 1 / 53 / 177 / 180 / 188 / 286. Riverboat: to Greenwich Pier. Tube: Blackheath / Greenwich / Maze Hill. BR: Island Gardens. DLR then Greenwich foot tunnel]
Tel: 0181 293 0703 café Fax: 020 7935 5894
200 acres of parkland including a duck pond, putting green, a large playground with safety surfaces and with an attendant supervising at all times and the oldest enclosed deer herd in the UK. Numerous events take place at the playground during the Summer including clowns, magicians, storytelling and circus workshops. Don't miss the Accurist Millenium Countdown Clock which is counting down the days to the new Millenium.
All year daily: Pedestrians 05.00-dusk. Cars: 07.00-dusk
Admission Free

Lee Valley Watersports Centre
Banbury Reservoir Harbet Road Chingford London E4 8QB
[BR: Angel Road, off North Circular road]
Tel: 020 8531 1129 Fax: 020 8527 0969
The Centre has been in existence for 25 years and specialises in teaching sailing, waterskiing, windsurfing and canoeing to all ages and at many levels. The extensive experience of fully qualified staff are available to provide courses to suit your every need. Lessons and courses are available from three hours to five days. We are recognised by all the relevant National Governing Bodies and hold the Adventure Activities License.
All year 10.00-sunset
Members only, new members welcome. Membership from £80 per annum

Monkey Business
220 Green Lanes Green Lane Palmers Green London N13 5UD
[Entrance via Lodge Drive Public Car Park]

Tel: 020 8886 7520

Children's adventure playground for children up to 12 years of age. Height restriction of 4ft 11 inches. Includes slides, swings, net climbs, ball pools, biff 'n' bash bags etc.

All year daily 10.00-19.00. Closed Wed during Term Time

Last Admission: 18.00

A£Free C£2.75. Special toddler rate of £2.00 per child on Tue & Thur a.m. in Term Time.

Children's Parties also catered for

Outfall Sailing Club

Jenkins Lane Barking Essex IG11 0AD

[access from A406 or A123]

Tel: 020 8507 4711/989 0986

This Thames Water club has 1/3 of its membership available to the public. The club is based on the River Thames and has 20 moorings. It is the only one with its shore base at a sewage works. The club has the challenging tidal Thames to provide an exciting sailing environment.

All year to members. New members welcome

Membership £25 per year

Primrose Hill

London NW3

Once part of the same hunting forest as Regent's Park, Primrose Hill retains in its name the rural character and charm that it undoubtedly had in the past. The view from the summit is panoramic and encompasses virtually the whole of central London. In 1842 its 62 acres gained gaslights, a gymnasium and respectability as a Royal Park.

Any reasonable time

Admission Free

Queen's Ice Bowl

17 Queensway London W2 4QP

[Tube: Bayswater / Queensway]

Tel: 020 7229 0172 Fax: 020 7229 5207

Situated in the heart of London we offer an enjoyable day out for the whole family. Kids can skate and bowl while mum and dad can relax in our new licensed bar, or enjoy a Wimpey meal from our new restaurant.

All year daily 10.00-24.00. Sessions: 10.00-12.00, 12.00-14.00, 14.00-17.00, 17.00-19.00, 20.00-22.00 Sun-Thur; 20.00-23.00 Fri & Sat

Last Admission: 23.15

£6.00 per person per session including ice skates

Regent's Park

London NW1

[N of Marylebone Road. Tube: Baker Street]

John Nash laid out this elegant park along with the imposing surrounding terraces as part of a plan for a new palace which was never built. It contains London Zoo, a boating lake, open air theatre, Regent's Canal and Queen Mary's Rose Garden. The Royal Botanic Gardens were once situated here. The New Shakespeare Company holds an Open Air Theatre here during the summer months (see events) there will also be a number of Sunday concerts and late night shows during the season including the Traditional Free Midsummer Night Concert on 20th June.

Any reasonable time

Admission Free

Richmond Park

London TW10 5HS

[BR/Tube: Richmond]

Tel: 0181 9483209

With its herds of deer, abundant wildlife and centuries-old oaks, Richmond is a favourite haunt for visitors and naturalists. There is a formal garden at Pembroke Lodge, and the various plantations show a wealth of exotic shrubs and wild flowers. Model sail boats are allowed on Adam's Pond, where the deer drink, and the 18 acre Pen Ponds have been specially made for angling (permits required).

Mar-Sept daily 07.00-30mins before dusk

Admission Free

St James's Park

Horse Guards Parade London SW1

[between Buckingham Palace / Whitehall Tube: St James's Park / Piccadilly Circus]

Tel: 020 7930 1793

This is the oldest of the Royal Parks in London. Drained and converted into a deer park by Henry VIII in 1532, Charles II had the park redesigned in the style of Versailles, but the park as it exists today was created by Nash for George IV.

All year daily dawn-midnight

Admission Free

The Playhouse

The Old Gymnasium Highbury Grove School London N5

Tel: 020 7704 9424

A medium-sized play room for children aged from six months to 12 years. It has a three-level playframe, 40-foot slide, ball ponds, crawl tunnels and rope bridges, plus a soft play area for under-fives.

London

The Ridgeway
Thamesmead London E
Tel: 0118 939 9254
This 4km footpath on top of the biggest sewer pipe in south London. It runs from Plumstead to Abbey Wood and links with several local footpaths in the area. This raised walk has good views over the surrounding area and although the path is surfaced it is not suitable for wheelchairs.
Any reasonable time
Admission Free

UK Bungee Club
194 New Kings Road London SW6 4NF
[Central London, call for details]
Tel: 07000 286 433/07000BUNGEE Fax: 020 7731 3734
www.adren-a-line.com
The UK Bungee Club is the largest club in the UK, offering nationwide events. Once based at Chelsea Bridge the club has successfully jumped over 100 000 people. If you are 14+ you can take part in the ultimate andrenalin experience in London! Bungee supporters welcome.
All year Sat & Sun 11.00-16.00. Plus Bungee Roadshows around the country. Phone for details
Last Admission: 17.30
Bungee Jump: £35 Tandem Jump: £70 Cage Spectators: £5.00. Ground Spectators: £Free
Groups: 10% for booking of 5+
discount offer: Two For One. One Person Jumps Free - The Other Pays Full Price. (NB: All Jumpers MUST Pay The £15 Membership and Insurance)

Victoria Park
Old Ford Road London E3
[Bus: 2 / 8 / 55 / 253 / 277. Tube: Mile End. BR: Cambridge Heath]
Tel: 020 8985 6186
This East End Park has two lakes, a deer herd, playgrounds and sports facilities. The oldest model boat club in the world (The Victoria Model Boat Club) meets here most Sunday mornings. Also features: animal enclosure, athletics track, football and cricket pitches, bowls green, café, playgrounds.
All year daily 08.00-dusk
Admission Free

Walthamstow Reservoirs
Ferry Lane Tottenham London N17 9NH
[Tube: Tottenham Hale / Black Horse Lane]
Tel: 020 8808 1527
Venue for Fishing and Bird Watching only. Site comprises 10 water bodies, including the Coppermills stream, some of which are classed as sites of special scientific interest. Some of the waters have dense vegetation by the bankside and islands in the centre, others provide an open water habitat. The site is famous for its large heronry. Children under 8 years are not permitted, and from 8 years to 16 years must be accompanied by an adult.
All year daily 07.30-dusk. Closed 25 Dec
Season tickets available for course fishing and birdwatching. Day tickets available for all activities please call for details.

Sporting History Museums

FA Hall of Fame
County Hall Riverside Building Westminster Bridge Road London SE1 7PB
[Tube: Westminster]
Tel: 0870 8488484/0171 9283636 Fax: 020 7928 3939
www.hall-of-fame.co.uk
The F.A. Premier League Hall of Fame is a multi-themed new visitor centre. It is an entertaining celebration of English football from the past to the present day. The main entrance is located on Westminster Bridge, adjacent to the magnificent Member's Carriageway gate. There are five themed areas. The Hall of Legends featuring a spectacular stroll through the history of English football. The F.A. Premier League Hall of Fame, a living history of the Premier League. The Hall of Fans, a unique tribute to the heritage and culture of football fanaticism. Hope and Glory, a special film depicting the dreams of a young boy inspired by the stars of today's Premier League. Virtual Stadium, offers visitors the chance to test their skills on interactive football games.
visitor comments: Well-presented new attraction. Very clean, very new - my son loved it.
Opens 12th June 1999. All year10.00-18.00 closed Christmas day.
Last Admission: 17.00
Queuing Times: 10 min
£9.95 C(4-15)£6.50 Student rate £7.50 Group 15+ Group & Corporate booking 0171 928 1800

Finsbury Park
Seven Sisters Road London
A huge park with lots to do and many activities throughout the summer. It features a boating lake, playground, athletics track and an orienteering course. (This is a 2-hour trail going throughout the Park). Maps can be pur-

chased for £1.00 at the Athletics Track and children must be accompanied by adults.
All year daily dawn to dusk
Admission Free

M.C.C. Museum and Tour of Lord's
Lord's Ground St John's Wood London NW8 8QN
[Tube: St John's Wood]
Tel: 020 7432 1033 Fax: 020 7266 3825
www.lords.org
Lord's was established in 1787 and is the home of the MCC and cricket. When you tour this famous arena you follow in the footsteps of the 'great's' of the game, from W G Grace to Ian Botham. Daily guided tours take you behind the scenes at this venue. You will visit the Members' Pavilion including the hallowed Long Room and the Players' Dressing Room, the MCC Museum where the Ashes Urn is on display and many other places of interest including the newly constructed Grand Stand and futuristic Natwest Media Centre.
All year Tours normally 12.00 & 14.00, vary on cricket days, call to book
A£6.00 C&OAPs&Students£4.40 Family Ticket £18.00
discount offer: Two For The Price Of One

Museum of Rugby and Twickenham Stadium Tours
Rugby Football Union Rugby Road Twickenham Middlesex TW1 1DZ
[follow A316 from Central London and Richmond then turn R at the Currie Motors roundabout onto Whitton road, at mini roundabout turn R into Rugby Road. Keep stadium to your L, turn L at the Tesco Roundabout into Whitton Dene Road. Entrance to the North Car Park is on the L, approximately 25 metres. BR: Twickenham 10mins walk from the ground]
Tel: 020 8892 2000 Fax: 020 8892 2817
www.rfu.com
A fascinating behind the scenes Guided Tour. Includes breathtaking views from the top of the North Stand, and a visit to the players tunnel and the famous changing rooms with their 60 year old baths. The new multi-media Museum of Rugby appeals to enthusiasts of all

ages and charts the history and world-wide growth of rugby, using touchscreens, video clips and film.
All year, Non-Match Days: Tue-Sat & Bank Hol 10.00-17.00, Sun 14.00-17.00. Closed Mon, Good Fri & 24-26 Dec. Match Days: 11.00-1 hour prior to kick-off. Match ticket holders only. Open for 1 hour after Match.
Last Admission: 16.30
Museum/Tour: A£3.00 C&Concessions£2.00. Museum & Tour: A£5.00 C&Concessions£3.00 Family Ticket (A2&C3)£15.00. Groups of 15+ 10% discount, for Group Catering Requirements, please pre-book on 0181 891 4565. School Parties Welcome, call for details. Identification is required for Students & Senior Citizens for concession price
discount offer: One Child Free When Accompanied By A Full Paying Adult
↓*special events*
► Tetleys Bitter Cup Final
13/5/00-13/5/00

Wimbledon Lawn Tennis Museum
All England Lawn Tennis & Croquet Club Church Road Wimbledon London SW19 5AE
[Tube: Wimbledon Park / Southfields. Car: from central London take the A3 Portsmouth Road to Tibbet's Corner, at the underpass turn L towards Wimbledoon, down Parkside. Entrance is in Church Road, ample free parking from Aug-May - drive in the Museum gates]
Tel: 020 8946 6131 Fax: 020 8944 6497
Wimbledon is synonymous with lawn tennis and the museum in the grounds of the All England Lawn Tennis Club is the only one of its kind in the world. Trophies, pictures, equipment, displays and memorabilia trace the development of the game over the last century. See the famous Centre Court and the enjoyable interactive quizzes and data banks for all ages. New for this year is the Costume Gallery where 100 years of changing Ladies' Fashions at Wimbledon are depicted. The Library containing the finest collection in the world of books and periodicals relating to Lawn Tennis is open by appointment.
All year daily 10.30-17.00. Tea Room: As Museum but 10.00-17.00. Open to tournament visitors only during Championship. Closed Fri, Sat and Sun before Championships, middle Sun and Mon after Championships.
A£5.00 C&OAPs&Students£4.00. Group rates 20+ on application
discount offer: £1.00 Off Adult Admission
↓*special events*
► Wimbledon Lawn Tennis Championships
26/6/00-9/7/00

Note their is no play on Sun 2nd July. Call 020 8946 2244 for information.

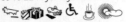

Theme & Adventure Parks

Fantasy Island Playcentre

Vale Farm Watford Road Wembley Middlesex HA0 3HG

[next to Vale Farm Sports Centre. Buses: 18, 92, 182, 245, H17. Tube: North Wembley or Sudbury Town]

Tel: 020 8904 9044 Fax: 020 8904 9046

The South's most thrilling indoor children's entertainment centre towering to a breathtaking 33 feet. Heart stopping slides, monster ball pools and rope climbs. Talking logs and much, much more. Separate area for under 5's. Kids go-karting, supervised birthday parties, safe and secure.

visitor comments: Overall a fun attraction for both children and adults.

All year daily 10.00-18.00
Last Admission: 16.30, subject to change
A£Free C(0-5)£3.50 C(5+)£4.50. Group and school rates on application

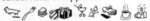

Namco Station

County Hall Riverside Building Westminster Bridge Road London SE1 7PB

[opposite Big Ben & Houses of Parliament on South Bank of Thames. Tube: Waterloo / Westminster, 5 mins. Bus]

Tel: 020 7967 1066 Fax: 020 7967 1060

It's a dazzling, brilliant, interactive experience on a massive scale. 35,000 square feet of pulsating fun, developed and operated by the global Japanese entertainment corporation, Namco. The kind of environment that provides the setting for a Party that will live in history. See it, feel it, hear it, do it. Experience the ultimate in mind-blowing interactive entertainment. From Techno Bowling to Bumper Cars and Shooting to Pool, plus all the latest and greatest video games and simulators including Downhill Skiing, Skateboarding, Cyber-Cycles, Grand Prix Racing, Martial Arts, Jet-Skiing, Soccer, Horse Racing and much more in one vast circular arena.

All year daily 10.00-24.00
Admission Free but charges on individual games. Price ranges from £0.50-£2.00. For bookings of between 100-750 people please contact Justin Thomas 0171 967 1067

Segaworld

1 Coventry Street London W1V 8DH

[Tube: Piccadilly Circus]

Tel: 020 7734 2777 Fax: 020 7734 7654

Indoor theme park featuring virtual reality and motion simulation rides, lots of arcade type games. Ideal for children 8yrs and upwards.

All year 10.00-24.00. Closed 25 Dec
Admission £Free. Multi-ride ticket (4 rides): £8.00 each, coin operated games: £0.20-£2.00 each

discount offer: Two Multi-Ride Tickets For The Price Of One

Trocadero

1 Piccadilly Circus London W1V 7DD

[Tube: Piccadilly Circus]

Tel: 020 7434 0030 Fax: 020 7434 1413

The Trocadero in Piccadilly Circus is Europe's largest one-stop entertainment destination. The massive multi-level complex houses over 400,000 square feet of white knuckle rides, state of the art video games, hi tech exhibitions and screen entertainment attractions - all under one roof in the heart of London's West End. The complex also boasts the capital's most exciting theme restaurants and offers the chance to play, dine and shop - without getting wet! The Trocadero has been called the Theme Park of the Future as it combines all the fun of a traditional fairground with the latest virtual reality techniques to give everyone a glimpse of the future of entertainment. The Trocadero also houses, actually within its vast 9 storey atrium, the world's first and only indoor free fall drop ride - The Pepsi MAX Drop - 130 feet of vertical madness - roof to basement in one terrifying second. Visitors can choose from Planet Hollywood, Rainforest Café, McDonalds, marco's Pizzeria or Ed's Easy Diner if they want to eat, drink or just hang out watching the world go by!

All year daily, Sun Thur 10.00-24.00, Fri & Sat 10.00-01.00
Admission Free. Individual rides and games are on a pay as you play basis. Power Passes packaging four rides together £7.90. Pepsi MAX Drop £3.00 per ride.

↓*special events*
► Fantasia 2000
1/1/00-30/4/00
In the Pepsi Imax theatre. Box office 020 7494 4153

Tourist & Visitor Information Centres

Bexley Tourist Information Centre

Hall Place Visitor Centre Bourne Road Bexley

London

Kent DA5 1PQ
Tel: 01322 526574 Fax: 01322 522921
Tourist Information Centre supplies:
Accommodation Booking Service; Museum
Displays; Art Displays.
Easter-Oct Mon-Sat 10.00-17.00 Sun 14.00-18.00
Admission Free

Bexleyheath Tourist Information Centre
Central Library Townley Road Bexleyheath Kent
DA6 7HJ
Tel: 020 8303 9052 Fax: 020 8303 7872
*All year Mon-Wed & Fri 09.30-17.30, Thur
09.30-20.00, Sat 09.30-17.00, Sun 10.00-14.00*

Britain Visitor Centre
1 Regent Street London SW1Y4XT
[Tube: Piccadilly Circus]
www.visitbritain.com
Friendly staff offer free advice and assistance
to visitors to London, Britain, Northern Ireland
and Ireland. The centre is run by the British
Tourist Authority and the National Tourist
Boards of England, Scotland, Wales, Northern
Ireland and Ireland. There are a number of
booking services also available: Globaltickets
central booking 020 7734 4555 for theatre,
sightseeing and events tickets; Thomas Cook
Hotel and Travel Reservations Ltd 020 7808
3861 offer a hotel booking service and travel
agency; FEXCO 020 7808 3880 are a bureau de
change, also selling phone cards and making
money transfers. The Stanford's book shop
sells travel books and maps
*Mon 09.30-18.30 Tue-Fri 09.00-18.30 winter Sat
& Sun 10.00-16.00, summer Sat 09.00-17.00
Sun 10.00-16.00*

↓ *special events*
► **Oxford & Cambridge Boat Race**
25/3/00-25/3/00
*Putney to Mortlake, River Thames. Starts 16.10,
for more information call Robert Mitchell 020
7379 3234.*
► **Lord Mayor's Show**
11/11/00-11/11/00
*Through the streets of the City of London. Call
020 7606 3030 for information.*

Croydon Tourist Information Centre
Katharine Street Croydon Surrey CR9 1ET
Tel: 020 8253 1009 Fax: 020 8253 1008
*All year Mon-Wed 09.00-18.00, Thur 09.30-18.00, Fri 09.00-18.00, Sat 09.00-17.00 & Sun
12.00-17.00*

Gravesend Tourist Information Centre
18A St Georges Square Gravesend Kent DA11
0TB

Tel: 01474 337600 Fax: 01474 337601
2 Jan-24 Dec Mon-Sat 09.00-17.00

Greenwich Tourist Information Centre
46 Greenwich Church Street Greenwich
London SE10 9BL
Tel: 020 8858 6376 Fax: 020 8853 4607
*Apr-Sept daily 10.15-16.45. Winter: daily with
reduced hours*

↓ *special events*
► The Thames Festival
27/5/00-30/5/00

Harrow Tourist Information Centre
Civic Centre Station Road Harrow Middlesex
HA1 2XF
Tel: 020 8424 1103 Fax: 020 8424 1134
www.harrowlb.demon.co.uk
All Year Mon-Fri 09.00-17.00
Last Admission: 16.45

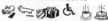

**Heathrow Airport Tourist Information
Centre**
Terminal 1,2 & 3 Underground Station
Concourse London Heathrow Airport
Hounslow TW6 2JA
Tel: 020 8897 3781
Tourist Information Centre supplies:
Accommodation Booking, National Express
and Euroline Bus Tickets, Theatre Ticket Agent,
Stamps, Phone Cards, Great Britain Heritage
Pass and Literature on all of Britain.
All year daily 08.00-18.00

**Heathrow Airport Tourist Information
Centre**
Heathrow Terminal 3 Arrivals Concourse
Hounslow Middlesex TW6 2JA
Tel: 020 7759 8983
All year daily 06.00-23.00

Hillingdon Tourist Information Centre
14-15 High Street Central Library Uxbridge
Middlesex UB8 1HD
Tel: 01895 250706 Fax: 01895 239794
www.hillingdon.gov.uk
*All year Mon, Tue & Thur 09.30-20.00, Wed
09.30-17.30, Fri 10.00-17.30, Sat 09.30-16.00*

Hounslow Tourist Information Centre
The Treaty Centre High Street Hounslow
Middlesex TW3 1ES
Tel: 020 8583 2929 Fax: 020 8583 4714
*All year Mon, Wed, Fri & Sat 09.30-17.30, Tue &
Thur 09.30-20.00*

Islington Visitor Information Centre
44 Duncan Street Islington London N1 8BW
Tel: 020 7287 8787 Fax: 020 7833 2193
1 Apr-28 Oct Mon 12.00-17.00, Tue-Sat 10.00-17.00. Closed Sat 13.30-14.30. Reduced Winter opening hours

Kingston-upon-Thames Tourist Information Centre
The Market House Market Place Kingston Upon Thames KT1 1JS
Tel: 020 8547 5592 Fax: 020 8547 5594
All year Mon-Fri 10.00-17.00, Sat 09.00-16.00

Lewisham Tourist Information Centre
199-201 Lewisham High Street Lewisham Library Lewisham London SE13 6LG
Tel: 020 8297 8317 Fax: 020 8292 9241
All year Mon 10.00-17.00, Tue-Fri 09.00-17.00 closed Sat Sun & Bank Hol

Liverpool Street Tourist Information Centre
Travel and Tourist Centre Liverpool Street Underground Station Liverpool Street London EC2M 7PN
[by main entrance to Liverpool Street tube]
Tel: 020 7932 2020 Booking
Tourist Information Centre supplies: Accommodation Bookings in London and Britain; Free London and Britain Information; National Express and Eurolines Coach Tickets; London Maps, Guides and Merchandise; Beat the Queue Tickets for Tower of London and Madame Tussauds.
All year Mon-Fri 08.00-18.00, Sat & Sun 08.45-17.30
Admission Free

Richmond Tourist Information Centre
Old Town Hall Whittaker Avenue Richmond Surrey TW9 1TP
[J2 M4 over Kew Bridge to Richmond, M3 to A316 to Richmond, M25 to J12 M3]
Tel: 020 8940 9125 Fax: 020 8940 6899
www.richmond.gov.uk
Tourist Information Centre supplies: Accommodation Booking Service; Guided Walks June-October.
All year Mon-Fri 10.00-17.00, Sat 10.00-17.00, May-Sept Sun 10.15-16.15
Admission Free

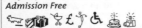

Southwark Tourist Information Centre
Unit 4 Lower Level Cottons Centre Middle Yard London SE1 2QJ

[BR/Tube: London Bridge, opposite London Dungeon]
Tel: 020 7403 8299
Tourist Information Centre supplies: Bureau De Change; Accommodation Booking; Theatre Booking; National Express Booking; Sightseeing Tours of London and UK.
All year Apr-Oct Mon-Fri 10.00-17.00, Sat & Sun 10.30-17.00, Nov-Mar Mon-Fri 10.00-16.00, Sat & Sun 11.00-16.00
Admission Free

Swanley Tourist Information Centre
London Road Swanley Kent BR8 7AE
Tel: 01322 614660 Fax: 01322 666154
All year Mon-Thur 09.30-17.30, Fri 09.30-18.00, Sun closed

Tower Hamlets Tourist Information Centre
107a Commercial Street London E1 6BG
Tel: 020 7375 2549 Fax: 020 7375 2539
All year Mon-Fri 09.00-16.30

Twickenham Tourist Information Centre
The Atrium Civic Centre York Street Twickenham Middlesex TW1 3BZ
Tel: 020 8891 7272
All year Mon-Thur 09.00-17.15, Fri 09.00-17.00

Victoria Tourist Information Centre
Victoria Railway Station London SW1V 1JU
[Tube: Victoria]
Tourist Information Centre supplying: Accommodation Booking Book-A-Bed-Ahead Scheme; Sales of Travelcards; Sightseeing Bus Tours; Theatre Tickets via Ticketmaster; Information On London and Britain.
Easter-2 Nov daily 08.00-19.00. 3 Nov-Easter Mon-Sat 08.00-18.00, Sun 08.30-16.00
Admission Free

Waterloo International Tourist Information Centre
London Visitor Centre Arrivals Hall London SE1 7LT
All year daily 08.30-22.30

Toy & Childhood Museums

Bethnal Green Museum of Childhood
Cambridge Heath Road London E2 9PA
[Tube: Bethnal Green (500yds). Buses 106/253/309/D6 (Cambridge Heath Road) 8 (Roman Road) 26/48/55 (Hackney Road). Meter parking 500 yards from the tube station. Free on Sat, Sun & Bank Hol at other times £3.00 for 2

hours]

Tel: 020 8983 5200Switchboard Fax: 020 8983 5225

The National Museum of Childhood at Bethnal Green is a fascinating blend of toys and other nursery objects that belong to the experience of childhood. The ground floor is packed full of playthings, ranging from dolls' houses, dolls and games to teddy bears, toy soldiers and trains, dating from the 17th century to the present day. The upper gallery explores the process of growing up from birth through to the teenage years, including baby equipment, nursery furniture and children's dress, from working smock to party dresses. Education: The child-friendly atmosphere of the Museum also makes it an excellent resource for schools, while the familiar world of toys and childhood allows children to access the collections easily and quickly. Ring for a copy of the Education leaflet, offering: free direct teaching sessions related to the National Curriculum, free group visits, free use of picnic room and Resource Pack for Teachers. Guided Tours: For adult groups, the Museum has a rare nostalgic appeal; book a guided tour, focusing on some of the showstoppers in the collections, and reminisce over your old favourite toys. Access: The Museum has steps throughout. Help is available but must be arranged in advance. There is a wheelchair accessible toilet, two steps down from the Museum's main floor and three steps up from the entrance. There is parking available for wheelchair users, please call in advance, 020 8983 5205. Shop: The Museum Shop sells souvenirs, books, postcards and toys. Café: The licensed Café serves salads, sandwiches, cakes, children's lunch boxes and hot and cold drinks, also offers children's birthday parties.

visitor comments: Wonderful, big airy building, helpful staff, much to see. Exhibitions & events are brilliant!

All year Mon-Thur & Sat-Sun 10.00-17.50. Closed Fri, 24-26 Dec & 1 Jan. Recorded information line: 020 8980 2415

Admission Free. Education & Group booking and access help: 020 8983 5205.

London Toy and Model Museum

21-23 Craven Hill London W2 3EN

[Tube: Bayswater / Paddington / Lancaster Gate]

Tel: 020 7706 8000 Fax: 020 7706 8823

Reopened in 1995 after being extensively redeveloped, the museum has 21 themed galleries all with sounds and smells to create the atmosphere. A fascinating display of over 7000 exhibits including detailed working models,

villages, railways and funfairs. There are vintage roundabout and train rides for children.

visitor comments: Not very "hands-on" for younger visitors.

All year daily 09.00-17.30
Last Admission: 16.30
A£5.50 C(0-4)£Free C£3.50 Family Ticket £15.00 Concessions£4.50. Group 10+: A£4.00 C£2.50. Schools: A£5.50 C£3.20 (1 Free adult for every 10 children). Wheelchair users and visually impaired visitors £Free

Pollock's Toy Museum

1 Scala Street London W1P 1LT

[Tube: Goodge Street]

Tel: 020 7636 3452

Displays include teddy bears, wax and china dolls, dolls' houses, board games, toy theatres, tin toys, mechanical and optical toys, folk toys and nursery furniture. Items from all over the world and all periods are here in two small interconnecting houses. Toy theatre performances available for school visits and during school holidays. Pushchairs need to be left downstairs.

All year Mon-Sat 10.00-17.00. Closed Public Hol
Last Admission: 16.30
A£2.50 C£1.00

Transport Museums

London Canal Museum

12-13 New Wharf Road London N1 9RT

[Buses: 10 / 17 / 30 / 45 / 46 / 63 / 73 / 91 / 214 / 259 / A2 / C12. Tube: Kings Cross 5 mins walks]

Tel: 020 7713 0836 Fax: 020 7713 0836
www.charitynet.org/~LCanalMus

The museum tells the story of the development of London's Canals. Visitors can learn about the people who strove to make a meagre livelihood by living and working on them, the horses which pulled their boats, and the cargoes they carried. Housed in a former ice warehouse built in the 1860s for Carlo Gatti, the famous ice cream maker, this Museum also features the history of the almost forgotten trade in natural ice. Visitors can peer down into a huge ice well, where the ice was once stored. Temporary exhibitions, book and gift shop.

All year Tue-Sun & Bank Hol Mon 10.00-16.30. Closed 24-26 & 31 Dec 1 Jan
Last Admission: 15.45
A£2.50 C&Concessions£1.25

↓ *special events*

► **The Croydon Canal**
29/12/99-26/3/00
A tape-slide presentation about the canal will

be the centrepiece of the exhibition

▶ **Lecture Working and Living on the Cut**
2/3/00-2/3/00
Experiences of hotel boating in the 1999s

▶ **Science Engineering and Technology Week**
21/3/00-24/3/00
A series of workshops for schools

▶ **Posters of the Canals**
28/3/00-26/6/00

▶ **Lecture**
6/4/00-6/4/00
Home is Where My Boat Is

▶ **Lecture**
4/5/00-4/5/00
The Regent's Canal - Yesterday and Today

▶ **Lecture**
1/6/00-1/6/00
The World's Oldest Private Canal Company

▶ **Lecture**
6/7/00-6/7/00
The Wild Waterside

▶ **Lecture**
7/9/00-7/9/00
The Royal Military Canal

▶ **London Open House weekend**
23/9/00-24/9/00
Free admission. Refreshments available. Guide service.

▶ **Lecture**
5/10/00-5/10/00
The Great Grand Union

▶ **Lecture**
2/11/00-2/11/00
Background to Battlebridge - King's Cross and St. Pancras

▶ **Lecture**
7/12/00-7/12/00
Enchanted Waters of the Basingstoke Canal

▶ **Lecture**
4/1/01-4/1/01
The Lime Juice Run

London Transport Museum

Covent Garden Piazza Covent Garden London WC2E 7BB
[Tube: Covent Garden / Leicester Square / Holborn. Bus: to Strand or Aldwych 1, 4, 6, 9, 11, 13, 15, 23, 26, 68, 77A, 188, 501, 171 and 171A]
Tel: 020 7836 8557/565 7299 Fax: 020 7836 4118
www.ltmuseum.co.uk
Travel through time at the London Transport Museum. It's London history. It's London people. It's trams, trains, buses, and more. It's a hands-on moving experience right in the heart of Covent Garden. As well as the stunning collection, actors, working models and videos plus special Fun Bus for the Under 5's. There are special exhibitions, talks and family activities, all bringing the Museum's story to life. For

details of school visits and educational material contact the Education Service 0171 379 6344. A lift and ramps give access throughout the Museum. Disabled toilets. From December 1997 the Museum launches "Kid Zones" - fifteen hands-on zones marking an easy-to-follow route around the Museum. Each zone will feature a fun activity to help kids and families learn a different part of the Museum's story.

visitor comments: Excellent. Friendly staff and helpers. Attractively and interestingly presented. Plenty of activities for older children. Definitely worth another visit.

All year Sat-Thur 10.00-18.00, Fri 11.00-18.00. Closed 24-26 Dec
Last Admission: 17.15
A£5.50 C&Concessions£2.95 C(0-5)£Free Family Ticket(A2+C2)£13.95
discount offer: £1.00 Off Adult, 50p Off Child Admissions & £2.00 Off Family Ticket(A2+C2)

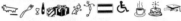

Victorian Era

Leighton House Museum and Art Gallery

12 Holland Park Road London W14 8LZ
[Tube: High Street Kensington. Buses: 9 / 9a / 10 / 27 / 28 / 31 / 33 / 49 to Odeon Cinema / Commonwealth Institute, the museum is N of Kensington High Street, off Melbury Road]
Tel: 020 7602 3316 Fax: 020 7371 2467
A uniquely opulent and exotic example of high Victorian taste, Leighton House was built for Frederic Lord Leighton (President of the Royal Academy). Leighton was one of the great Victorian artists and much of his work is displayed here. The Arab Hall is the centrepiece of Leighton House, evoking the world of the Arabian Nights. The dazzling gilt mosaic frieze, depicting birds and scenes of mythology, the calming murmur of the fountain in the centre of the Arab Hall, and the intricate designs of the Isnik tiles, all contribute to an extraordinary vision of the Orient. The opulent fantasy extends throughout the other rooms of the House culminating in Leighton's Studio, the heart and purpose of the House, with its great north windows and gilded dome and apse. Leighton House may be booked for concerts, lectures, receptions and private functions, for further information contact the Curator's office.
Jan-Mar Mon-Sat 11.00-17.30. Closed Sun. 1 Apr-Dec Wed-Mon 11.00-17.30. Closed Tue. Guided tours take place every Wed & Thur at 12.00 also tour groups can be made by appointment.
Last Admission: 17.00
Admission Free. A charged is levied for tours.

Wax Works

Madame Tussaud's
Marylebone Road London NW1 5LR
[Tube: Baker Street]
Tel: 020 7935 6861 Fax: 020 7465 0862
www.madame-tussauds.com
Madame Tussaud's world-famous waxwork collection was founded in Paris in 1170. It was moved to England in 1802 and to London's Marylebone Road in 1884. A star studded cast of sportsmen, world leaders and movie actors will make a visit to London's premier attraction a real winner. Mingle with the stars and meet the likes of Kate Winslet and Robert Carlyle; part of the brand new 'Superstars and Legends'. Our new infamous Chamber of Horrors is sure to give you a fright. Dare you enter? As a finale to Madame Tussaud's you will take a spectacular moving journey through London's extraordinary past. Visit the Planetarium, where you will enter the magnificent space age dome to be taken on Planetary Quest, a breathtaking cosmic journey through the splendours of our Universe!
visitor comments: Quite amazing - lovely watching the kids faces light up.
All year daily 10.00-17.30 (earlier opening throughout the summer). Groups can book a guaranteed timed admission between 09.30-16.30 daily, please telephone for details.
Last Admission: 17.30
A£10.00 C(under 16)£6.50 OAPs£4.60. Combined ticket with Planetarium A£12.25 C£8.00 OAPs£9.30

Zoos

Battersea Park Children's Zoo
Battersea London SW11
[Tube: Sloane Square BR: Battersea Park then Bus: 137]
Tel: 020 8871 7540 Fax: 020 7350 0477
Small zoo housing domestic farm and non domestic animals including monkeys, otters, birds, wallabies, pot bellied pigs, cows, reptile house. Animal contact area where children can touch, feel and feed the animals, pony rides and carousel rides.
visitor comments: Excellent value for money. Interesting with lots to see and do. Educational features a must for older children.
Mar-Sept Mon-Sun 10.00-17.00. Oct-Feb weekends only 11.00-15.00. Closed 25 Dec, 1 Jan
Last Admission: 16.30
A£1.20 C£0.60 OAPs£0.60. School groups £0.40 per pupil

London Zoo
Regents Park London NW1 4RY
[Tube: Camden Town / Great Portland Street / Regents Park]
Tel: 020 7722 3333 Fax: 202 7586 5743
www.weboflife.co.uk
Home to over 12,000 animals, insects, reptiles and fish. Opened in 1827 and claims the world's finest aquarium, insect and reptile house. Rare and exotic animals, many participating in captive breeding programmes. Daily events give visitors an insight to animal behaviour. Children's Zoo and whole range of educational programmes for schools. The new Web of Life biodiversity exhibition, a Millennium Commission project, opened in April 99. It uses a unique combination of 61 live animal exhibits, interactive displays and on-show breeding habitats to astonish the visitor with the complexity of nature and its myriad habitats.
visitor comments: Plenty to see. Opportunity to see animals being fed. Possibly more suitable for older children. The guide leaflet is very helpful.
All year daily Summer: 10.00-17.30 Winter: 10.00-16.00. Closed 25 Dec
Queuing Times: 10mins
A£9.00 C(3-14)£7.00 OAPs&Students£8.00 Saver Ticket £28.00 (2A+2C or 1A+3C) Group rates 15+
discount offer: One Child Free With A Full Paying Adult

↓ special events

▶ **Daily Events**
1/1/00-31/12/00
11.30-12.30 - Dliscovering Reptiles in the Reptile House. 12.30 - Feeding the Pigs
in the Children's Zoo. 13.00 - Feeding the Pelicans near the Fountain Court. 13.30 - Animals in Action in the Lifewatch Centre not suitable for very young children. 14.00 - Wonders of the Web in the Web of Life. 14.30 - Feeding the Fish in the Aquarium.
NB: Please note that different fish are fed on different days. Check the noticeboard at the Aquarium entrance for details. 15.00 - Elephant Time (Weekends and school holidays only) in the Elephant House. NB: All events are subject to the availability of animals and suitable weather conditions.

Plashet Park Zoo
Plashet Park Rutland Road (off Shrewsbury Road) Forest Gate London E7

[A406 to Ilford, turn off, L onto Romford Road (towards Stratford) L down Shrewsbury Road, Rutland Road and Park entrance of the L]

Tel: 020 8503 5994

An opportunity to see wide ranges of cage and aviary birds as well as a variety of pheasant and waterfowl species. There are also breeding llamas, wallabies & pygmy goats. A tropical Butterfly House. Falconry displays during high season.

All year Tue-Sun, Summer 10.00-17.00, Winter 10.00-16.00

Last Admission: 10mins before closing

Admission Free

Surrey

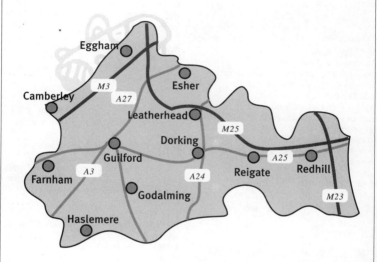

Eggham

Esher

Camberley
M3
A27

Leatherhead

Dorking
M25

Guilford
A3
A24
Reigate
A25
Redhill

Farnham

Godalming

M23

Haslemere

Abbeys

Waverley Abbey
Farnham Surrey GU
[J10 M25, 2m SE of Farnham off B3001, BR: Farnham 2m]
First Cistercian house in England, founded in 1128. The remaining ruins date from the 13th century.
All year any reasonable time
Admission Free

Agriculture / Working Farms

Coxbridge Farm
West Street Farnham Surrey GU9 7AS
[A31 and A325 at Coxbridge roundabout, on the corner. Plenty of parking on site]
Tel: 01252 715 539
Beautiful, historic family farm of 100 acres. Attractions include indoor and outdoor play areas and picnic facilities, with areas to feed the animals. Tractor-trailer rides and horse-wagon rides (occasional). Enjoy snacks and homemade cakes in the tearoom.
All year
Last Admission: 15.30
A£4.50 C£3.50

Rural Life Centre
The Reeds Tilford Farnham Surrey GU10 2DL
[off A287 halfway between Frensham / Tilford follow brown signposts]
Tel: 01252 792300/795571 Fax: 01252 795571
www.surreyweb.org.uk/rural-life/
The Old Kiln houses a collection of farm implements and machinery, and examples of the craft and trades allied to farming may be seen. The larger exhibits are displayed in the pleasant garden and woodland surrounds which cover some ten acres. In the old farm buildings

are a smithy and a wheelwright's shop, hand tools and other artifacts. Plenty to interest all age groups.
1 Apr-30 Sept Wed-Sun & Bank Hol Mon 11.00-18.00
Last Admission: 17.00
A£4.00 C£2.00 OAPs£3.00
discount offer: Two For The Price Of One

↓ *special events*
► **Easter Eggstravaganza**
23/4/00-23/4/00
Come and join the fun!
► **Miller's Ark Animals**
23/4/00-28/8/00
Apr 23-24, Apr 30-May 1, May 28-29 and Aug 27-28 only. Includes rides on the Old Kiln Light Railway
► **Global Party**
21/5/00-21/5/00
World celebration of music, culture, costume, food and games from around the world
► **Think Water**
18/6/00-18/6/00
An environment family day with pond dipping, "toys for free" with water, games and demonstrations
► **A Day of Cricket with a Difference**
2/7/00-2/7/00
The re-erected Godalming Cricket Pavilion (1883) opens at 14.30. A junior cricket team in Victorian dress will entertain
► **Rustic Sunday**
30/7/00-30/7/00
Traditional country event with crafts, music and demonstrations
► **Hops, Hogs and Harleys**
20/8/00-20/8/00
The history of hops, brewing, pubs and beer! See and hear Harley Davidson Motorcycles and raise funds for MENCAP and the Rural Life Centre
► **Keep it in the Family**
17/9/00-17/9/00
Family heirlooms and how to research your family history
► **The Broomsquire**
17/9/00-17/9/00
Dramatisation of Sabine Baring-Gould's 1896 book described by David Bellamy as "my firm favourite"
► **Harvest Home**
1/10/00-1/10/00
Traditional ceremony with corn dollies, countryside produce and a harvest festival in the chapel
► **Santa Specials**
9/12/00-17/12/00
Dec 9-10 and 16-17 only. Ride on the light railway to the magic wood and Santa's grotto

Animal Attractions

Godstone Farm

Tilburstow Hill Road Godstone Surrey RH9 8LX
[J6 M25, follow signs to Godstone Village]
Tel: 01883 742546 Fax: 01883 740380
The most popular children's farm in the south east. The animals are very friendly and children are encouraged to stroke and cuddle the smaller ones. The play areas are enormous and great fun. There is also a large indoor play barn, making it worthwhile for a winter visit. The views are superb and the tea cakes legendary!
visitor comments: A large number of animals, hands-on experience. Well worth paying 50p for the large indoor play area with tea shop and picnic area close by. Educational and good value.
Daily Summer 10.00-18.00, Winter 10.00-17.00
Last Admission: 1 hour before closing
£3.80 per person aged 2+. One adult free with each paying child. OAPs£2.80

Horton Park Children's Farm

Horton Lane Epsom Surrey KT19 8PT
[J9 M25 between Epsom and Chessington]
Tel: 01372 743984 Fax: 01372 749069
Friendly and informal, ideal for 2-8 year olds. Staff encourage children to pet and enjoy the animals. The adventure playgrounds are expanding each year with specially designed mazes. Food is simple, but good and excellent value for money.
Summer daily 10.00-18.00, Winter 10.00-17.00
A£3.65 C£3.65 OAPs£2.65 One Adult Free With Each Paying Child

Arts, Crafts & Textiles

Watts Gallery

Down Lane Compton Guildford Surrey GU3 1DQ
[3m from south from Guildford]
Tel: 01483 810235
Paintings by G F Watts O.M.R.A.
All year Fri-Wed 14.00-18.00, Oct-Mar Mon-Tue 14.00-16.00, Wed & Sat 11.00-13.00
Admission Free

Birds, Butterflies & Bees

Birdworld and Underwater World

Holt Pound Farnham Road Holt Pound Farnham Surrey GU10 4LD
[3m S on A325]
Tel: 01420 22140 Fax: 01420 23715
28 acres of garden and parkland are home to a wide variety of birds including many rare and unusual species. Rare baby birds can be seen at the Incubation Research Station during breeding times. Shop and café, special penguin feeding times and animal handling sessions.
visitor comments: Excellent value. Brilliant entertainment for under 5's. Very easy access for prams. Extremely friendly staff.
5 Jan-11 Feb weekends only, 12 Feb-ealy Nov daily, early Nov-early Dec weekends only, early Dec-24 Dec daily. Summer 09.30-18.00, Winter 09.30-16.40
Last Admission: Summer 17.00 Winter 15.30
A£7.95 C(3-14)£4.75 Family Ticket (A2+C2)£22.95 Extra C£4.25 Concessions£6.50

↓ *special events*

► **Craft Fair**
20/5/00-21/5/00

► **Old Macdonald's Farm Fun Day**
1/6/00-1/6/00
Rustic fun and games for the whole family

► **Birdwolds' Bird Extravaganza Day**
25/6/00-25/6/00
A must for all bird enthusiasts. Bird shows, stands and fun things to do.

► **Teddy Bears Picnic**
3/8/00-3/8/00
If you go down to Birdworld on this day, you're sure of a big surprise!

► **Treasure Island Fun Day**
17/8/00-17/8/00
Yo-ho-ho and a big bottle of fun on this great day out with a swashbuckling pirate theme!

► **Mad Hatters Party**
31/8/00-31/8/00
Alice and her friends will all be there to greet you at this mad fun day out

► **Santa Specials**
30/11/00-24/12/00
A magical train ride for children to Santa's Grotto to meet Santa

Country Parks & Estates

Box Hill - The Old Fort

Box Hill Road Box Hill Tadworth Surrey KT20 7LB
[1m N of Dorking, 2.5m S of Leatherhead on A24. Bus: London & Country 516. BR: Boxhill & Westhumble 0.5m]
Tel: 01306 885502 Fax: 01306 875030
On the edge of the North Downs rising some

Surrey

130 metres above the River Mole this Country Park consists of acres of woods and chalk downland, with magnificent views to the South Downs. Dogs under strict control.
All year any reasonable time
Admission Free

↓*special events*

► **Pre-Spring Walk**
19/3/00-19/3/00
Meet in the main car park (TQ179514) for this 2-mile walk, £1.00, 10.30-12.00

► **Easter Egg Trail**
23/4/00-24/4/00
Follow a trail, answer clues and win a prize, £1.50, 11.00-15.00

► **Woodland Folklore**
6/5/00-6/5/00
Meet in the main car park (TQ179514) for this 2-mile walk, £1.00, 14.00-16.00

► **Woodland Discovery Day**
31/5/00-31/5/00
Take part in art and environmental activities, suitable for all over 5 years old! Booking essential - tickets from North Downs office. Telephone 01306 742809 for information, A£2.00 C£4.00, 10.00-16.00

► **Summer Buterflies**
30/7/00-30/7/00
Meet in the main car park (TQ179514) for this 2-mile walk, £1.00, 10.30-12.00

► **Children's Activity Afternoon**
8/8/00-22/8/00
Environmental games and activities with the Wardens on Box Hill. Tickets in advance from the North Downs Office. Telephone 01306 742809 for information, C£2.50 incl refreshments, 14.00-16.00 on 8, 15 and 22 Aug

► **Plants: Poison or Medicines?**
16/9/00-16/9/00
Meet in the main car park (TQ179514) for this 2-mile walk, £1.00, 14.00-16.00

► **Woodland Discovery Day**
25/10/00-25/10/00
Create and explore in a superb natural setting. Suitable for all over 5 years old! Tickets in advance from North Downs office. Telephone 01306 742809 for information, A£2.00 C£4.00, 10.00-16.00

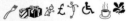

Leith Hill
nr Coldharbour Dorking Surrey RH5 6LX
[on summit of Leith Hill, 1m SW of Coldharbour on A29 / B2126. Bus: Surrey Hills Leisure Bus 433 / Tillingbourne 21.
BR: Holmwood 2.5m / Dorking 5.5m]
Tel: 01306 711777 Fax: 01306 712153
The highest point in south-east England, crowned by an 18th-century Gothic tower, from which there are magnificent views. The surrounding woodland contains ancient stands of hazel and oak, and there is a splen-

did display of rhododendrons in May-June. (There is limited disabled access to the rhododendron wood).
Tower: 1 Apr-end Sept Wed 12.00-17.00, Sat-Sun Bank Hols 11.00-17.00, Oct-end Mar Sat-Sun 11.00-15.30
Last Admission: Apr-Sept 16.30. Oct-Mar 15.00
Tower £0.80 Rhododendron Wood £1.50 per car. No reduction for groups. No coaches. Circular trail guide available from dispenser £1.00

↓*special events*

► **A Walk Through the Rhododendrons Woods**
10/5/00-24/5/00
Meet at the Rhododendron Woods car park (TQ131427) for this less-than-1-mile walk. Sorry, no dogs, £1.00, 14.00-15.30

► **Discover Leith Hill**
14/5/00-14/5/00
Meet your guide at Coldharbour Cricket Pitch (TQ147438) for this 2/3-mile walk, £1.00, 10.00-12.30

► **All the Way to the Top**
14/6/00-14/6/00
Catch a lift in a National Trust minibus to Leith Hill Tower. Ideal for those who have difficulty in walking. Meet at Starveall car park (TQ131434) for this 1.5-mile walk, £1.00, 10.30-13.00

► **Evening Stroll to Leith Hill Tower**
18/6/00-18/6/00
Meet at the Plough Pub, Coldharbour (TQ149438) for this 3-mile walk, £1.00 (non-member), NT members free, 19.00-20.30

► **Children's Activity Days**
3/8/00-17/8/00
Play some exciting environmental games. Meet at Windy Gap car park (TQ139430, TQ139429). Suitable for 6-9 year olds, C£2.00, 14.00-16.00 on 3 and 17 Aug

Runnymede
Coopers Hill Lane Egham Surrey TW20 0AU
[J13 M25. On the Thames 2m W of Runnymede Bridge on S side of A308. 6m E of Windsor. BR: Station Egham 2m]
Tel: 01784 432891 Fax: 01784 479007
A National Trust Property. Riverside wildflower meadows where King John sealed the Magna Carta in 1215. there is an American Bar Associations Memorial to Magna Carta, the John F Kennedy memorial and the Fairhaven Lodge's and Kiosks designed by Edwin Lutyens. Fishing available. Seasonal boat trips.
All year. Riverside grass car park open Apr-end Sept daily when ground conditions allow 10.00-19.00.Tea-room car park (hard standing) all year Apr-Sept 09.00-19.00, Oct-Mar 10.00-17.00
Admission Free. Fishing charge. Parking charge

↓*special events*

► **Mad as a March Hare**
12/3/00-12/3/00

Meet at the Magna Carta tea-room car park, Windsor Road (A308), Egham (TW995733) for this 2-mile walk, A£1.00 C&OAP£0.50p (non-member), NT members free, 11.00-13.00

► **Woodland Spring Awakening**
16/4/00-16/4/00
See entry for 12 March

► **Birds Before Breakfast - A Dawn Chorus**
7/5/00-7/5/00
See entry for 12 March except meet at 05.00-07.30

► **A King's Ransom - The Magna Carta Walk**
11/6/00-11/6/00
See entry for 12 March except meet at 11.00-12.30

► **Country Craft Fayre**
4/8/00-6/8/00
Craft and entertainment with a Viking and Saxon theme, 10.00-18.00. A£3.50 C£1.50 OAPs£3.00 (member and non-member)

► **A Royal River Ramble**
13/8/00-13/8/00
See entry for 12 March except mee at 11.00-13.00

► **The Good, The Bad and The Ugly**
1/10/00-1/10/00
See entry for 12 March except meet at 11.00-13.30

Exhibition & Visitor Centres

Sandown Exhibition Centre
Sandown Park Esher Surrey KT10 9AJ
[BR: Esher]
Tel: 01372 467540 Fax: 01372 465205
Exhibition, Conference and Banqueting Centre, see special events for details.
Times vary dependent on event
Prices dependent on event

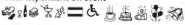

Festivals & Shows

Autocavan VW-Audi Swapfest
Festival Office: Lower Weybourne Lane Badshot Lea Farnham Surrey GU9 9LG
[held at T S Swiftsure, Lower Weybourne Lane, Badshot Lea - adjacent to Autocavan Head Office - please call or fax for a map]
Tel: 01252 346810 Fax: 01252 346811
www.autocavan.com
A great day out for all motor enthusiasts! Sunday 26th September sees the return of the hugely successful Autocavan Swapfest. Last year VW enthusiasts flocked from around the country to enjoy the inaugural event and this

year's show promises to be even better. Attractions include thousands of new and used parts for sale, Show 'n' Shine, race and custom car display, competitions, a prize draw and on-site refreshments.
Sept 2000, dates to be confirmed please call
A£2.00 C£Free Parking £1.50

Old Fair of Abinger 2000
Abinger Common Abinger Surrey *[Turn off A25 in Abinger Hammer and follow yellow fair signs.]*
Tel: 01306 731083 Fax: 01306 731083
The Old fair of Abinger celebrates the old pilgrimage to Canterbury and Compostella in Spain. The fair is held on Abinger Common with food and produce stalls, refreshments and bar. The programme will include Maypole dancing, Jousting Knights, Morris dancing, Punch and Judy, Tug of war and plenty of traditional sports. There will also be music and madrigals in the Church adjacent to the Common.
June 10 2000 14.00
Free Entry unless using Car Park where £2.00 per car.

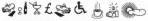

Tilford Bach Festival
All Saint's Parish Church Tilford Farnham Surrey GU9
[Tilford can be reached from the M3 via Farnham, or from the A3 exit at Godalming or Hindhead]
Tel: 01252 721605
A festival largely based around and celebrating the works of JS Bach and his contemporaries.
May 18-20 2000 All concerts begin at 20.00
A£12.00 with Concessions for students. Tickets available from the Secretary on 01252 782167

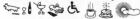

Working Beer Festival
Woking Leisure Centre Woking Park Kingfield Road Woking Surrey GU22 9BA
[just ouside main town centre]
Tel: 01483 771122
www.camrabranches.org.uk/surrey/
Sixth Woking Beer Festival. Over 70 real ales, plus ciders and imported beers, live bands, Wurlitzer organ, food and juice bar. Bring the whole family Saturday lunchtime. Children's entertainment in separate areas; family room, face painting, Punch & Judy, Magic Shows and use of the Pick 'N' Mix Playstore. Evening sessions over 18's only.
Nov 2000, dates to be confirmed, call for details
£4.00 in advance

Surrey

Folk & Local History Museums

Bourne Hall Museum
Spring Street Ewell Epsom Surrey KT17 1UF
[Nearest BR Ewell West]
Tel: 020 8394 1734
A museum of Epsom & Ewell with relics of
Henry VIII's Nonsuch Palace, the Epsom Spa
visited by Samuel Pepys and Surrey's largest
Roman town.
All year Mon-Sat 09.00-17.00, Sun 09.00-12.00.
Closed 25 Dec & Bank Hol
Admission Free

Chertsey Museum
The Cedars 33 Windsor Street Chertsey Surrey
KT16 8AL
[J11 M25 or A320]
Tel: 01932 565764 Fax: 01932 571118
www.runnymede.gov.uk/cmintro.htm
Housed in a Regency Town house, collections
include items illustrating life in the
Runnymede borough from pre-history to the
present day. Costumes, accessories, furniture,
clocks, ceramics and archaeology. Lively exhibi-
tions and events programme complements
permanent displays, see Special Events.
Wheelchair access limited to ground floor only.
All year Tue-Fri 12.30-16.30, Sat 11.00-16.00
Admission Free

Egham Museum
The Literary Inst High Street Egham Surrey
TW20 9EW
[J13 M25, follow A30 to Egham]
Tel: 01344 843047
Local history and archaeology exhibits from
Egham, Englefield Green, Thorpe and Virginia
Water.
All year Tue-Thur 10.00-12.30 & 14.00-16.30,
Sat 10.00-12.30 & 14.00-16.30
Admission Free

Elmbridge Museum
Church Street Weybridge Surrey KT13 8DE
[J11 M25 A317 Weybridge road or leave A3 at
Painshill Park roundabout take A245 then B374
to Weybridge BR: Weybridge]
Tel: 01932 843573 Fax: 01932 846552
Elmbridge Museum situated above the Public
library in Church Street, Weybridge, tells the
story of the towns and villages of the Borough
of Elmbridge. Refurbished in 1995/96 and has
new and exciting displays.
All year Mon-Wed & Fri 11.00-17.00, Sat 10.00-
13.00 & 14.00-17.00
Last Admission: 16.45
Admission Free

Godalming Museum
109A High Street Godalming Surrey GU7 1AQ
[signposted within the town centre. Near South
street car-[ark]
Tel: 01483 426510 Fax: 01483 869495
The museum is housed in a 15th-century town
house. Displays relate to the local history of
Godalming. There is a room dedicated to the
architect and gardener team Edwin Lutyens
and Gertrude Jekyll; a display about Jack
Phillips, wireless operator on the Titanic and
also James Oglethorpe who founded the
colony of Georgia in America. The museum is
currently undergoing major refurbishment
work and is CLOSED UNTIL JULY 1998 when
there will be access downstairs only. Please
ring for details.
All year Tue-Sat 10.00-17.00 From end Oct-Mar
10.00-16.00 closed 25-26 Dec Research Library
Tue & Sat 10.00-16.00
Admission Free

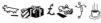

Guildford Museum
Castle Arch Guildford Surrey GU1 3SX
[200yds down Quarry St. from High Street.]
Tel: 01483 444750 Fax: 01483 532391
www.surreyweb.org.uk/guildfordmuseum
A local museum with history, archaeology and
needlework displays. Collections relating to
Lewis Carroll and the garden designer
Gertrude Jekyll.
All year Mon-Sat 11.00-17.00. Closed 24-26 Dec
& Good Fri
Admission Free

Kingston Museum
Wheatfield Way Kingston-Upon-Thames
Surrey KT1 2PS
[Kingston town centre next door to the library]
Tel: 020 8546 5386 Fax: 020 8547 6747
www.kingston.gov.uk
Local history displays telling the story of
Kingston from pre-history to today in 'Ancient
Origins' & newly-opened 'Town & Kings' gal-
leries; Martinware pottery, Eadweard
Muybridge Gallery; temporary exhibitions in
the art gallery. Local History room now located
at the North Kingston Centre, Richmond Road,
Kingston upon Thames KT2 5PE Tel 0181 547
6738.
All year Mon, Tue, Thur-Sat 10.00-17.00. Local
History Room: Mon-Fri 10.00-17.00 Tue until
19.00
Admission Free

Surrey

Museum of Farnham
38 West Street Farnham Surrey GU9 7DX
Tel: 01252 715094 Fax: 01252 715094
Exciting displays tell the story of Farnham and its people, in this newly refurbished Grade 1 listed Georgian townhouse. William Cobbett memorabilia is also shown , and there is a walled garden.
All year Tue-Sat 10.00-17.00. Closed Christmas-New Year
Admission Free

Reigate Priory Museum
Bell Street Reigate Surrey RH2 7RL
[in Reigate centre]
Tel: 01737 222550
The museum is housed in Reigate Priory which was originally founded before 1200, this Grade I listed building was converted to a mansion in Tudor times. Notable features include the magnificent Holbein fireplace, 17th century oak staircase and murals. The small museum has changing exhibitions on a wide range of subjects.
Wed & Sat 14.00-16.30 in term time
Admission Free

Surrey Heath Museum
Surrey Heath House Knoll Road Camberley Surrey GU15 3HD
[in town centre within main council offices. BR: Camberley]
Tel: 01276 707284 Fax: 01276 707177
An attractive museum combining permanent displays on local history and environment with a lively programme of temporary displays of local and regional interest.
All year Tue-Sat 11.00-17.00
Admission Free

Forests & Woods

Alice Holt Woodland Park
Forestry Commission Bucks Horn Oak Farnham Surrey GU10 4LS
[near A325 between Farnham & Bordon well signposted from both directions]
Tel: 01420 23666 Fax: 01420 22082
Whether you come to walk, cycle, picnic or see wildlife, there is something at Alice Holt for everyone who loves the countryside. The Easy-Access trail, Family Cycle Trail and children's play areas means everyone can relax in this beautiful woodland. Learn about the forest, purchase rustic gifts at the Visitor Centre - Enjoy!
Forest open all the time Visitor Centre June-Sept daily 09.30-17.00 Oct-May Wed-Sun 09.30-

16.30
Admission Free

Gardens & Horticulture

Bromages Bonsai Centre
St. Marys Gardens Worplesdon Guildford Surrey GU3 3RS
[A322 Bagshot road out of Guildford]
Tel: 01483 232893
Finest range of Japanese and English Bonsais in the country. Range of all sizes from Baby bonsais up to magnuficent specimens. Bonsai bowls and sundries also stocked. 10% discount for Bonsai club members
All year daily10.00-16.00 closed Wed &   25-26 Dec & 1 Jan

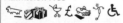

Claremont Landscape Garden
Portsmouth Road Esher Surrey KT10 9JG
[S edge of Esher, E side of A307. BR: Esher 2m, Hersham 2m, Claygate 2m]
Tel: 01372 467806 Fax: 01372 464394
One of the earliest surviving English landscape gardens, restored to its former glory. Features include a lake, island with pavilion, grotto and turf amphitheatre. Dogs on leads Nov to Mar and not admitted Apr to Oct. Coach parties by arrangement only.
All year, Jan-end Mar Tue-Sun 10.00-17.00 or sunset if sooner. Apr-end Oct Mon-Fri 10.00-18.00, Sat Sun & Bank Hol Mon 10.00-19.00. Nov-end Mar Tue-Sun 10.00-17.00 or sunset if sooner. Closed 25 Dec
Last Admission: 30mins before closing
A£3.20 C£1.60 Family Ticket £8.00. £0.50 discount if arriving on public transport please present valid ticket. Guided Tours 15+ £1.00 extra. All coach parties must book

↓*special events*

► **Walk Through the History and Beauty of Claremont**
1/4/00-30/4/00
Guided tours on the 1, 12, 15 & 30 April, looking at the history and beauty of Claremont. Meet at entrance kiosk. Sorry, no dogs, A£1.00 C£0.50p plus usual admission, 14.00-15.30

► **Easter Egg Trail**
22/4/00-22/4/00
Fun for the family, C£1.50 plus usual admission, 11.00-16.00

► **Walk Through the History and Beauty of Claremont**
6/5/00-28/5/00
See entry for 1 April except tours are on the 6, 10, 20, 27 & 28 May

► **Spring Plant Fair**
14/5/00-14/5/00
Volunteer-grown plants, garden bric-a-brac, etc.,

Surrey

all for sale, 11.00-16.00

▶ **Walk Through the History and Beauty of Claremont**
3/6/00-30/7/00
See entry for 1 April except tours on 3, 14, 17, 24 & 25 June, 1, 19, 22, 29 & 30 July

▶ **Claremont Carnival & Millennium Fete**
13/7/00-16/7/00
A spectacular open air, fancy dress extravaganza, offering non-stop entertainment culminating in a fantastic fireworks finale over the lake. Prizes for the best themed fancy dress. Thur A£17.00 C£10.00, Fri A£20.00 C£14.00, Sat A£22.00, Sun A£18.00 (No child prices Sat & Sun). 10% discount for groups 15+ on Thur & Fri, 19.00-23.00

▶ **Treasure Hunts**
31/7/00-4/8/00
Call 01372 467806 for full details

▶ **Walk Through the History and Beauty of Claremont**
5/8/00-29/10/00
See entry for 1 April except tours on the 5, 9, 19, 26 & 27 Aug, 2, 13, 16, 23 & 24 Sept, 7, 11, 21 & 29 Oct

Coverwood Lakes, Gardens and Farm

Coverwood Cottage Peaslake Road Ewhurst Cranleigh Surrey GU6 7NT

[from A25 through Gomshall S to Peaslake then 0.5m S, there are many posters to show the way]

Tel: 01306 731103 Fax: 01306 731103

Landscaped water and cottage gardens of 14 acres, including 9 year old 3.5 acre Arboretum; rhododendrons, azaleas, candelabra primulas, Lysecitums, taxodiums and many other bog garden plants. Marked trail through the farm to see pedigree Poll Hereford cattle, sheep and many horses. Home-made teas during April and May, hot soup and sandwiches in October.
Open for the National Gardens Scheme: Apr: Sun 18 & 25 14.00-18.00. May: Sun 2, 9, 16, 23, 30 & Wed 12 14.00-18.00. Oct: Sun 17 11.00-16.30
A£2.50 C£1.00

Millais Rhododendrons

Crosswater Farm Crosswater Lane Churt Farnham Surrey GU10 2JN

[Farnham/Haslemere 6m From A287 turn East into Jumps Road 0.5m N of Churt village centre. After 0.25m turn left into Crosswater Lane]

Tel: 01252 792698 Fax: 01252 792526

6-acre woodland garden surrounded by acres of National Trust property. Plantsman's collection of Rhododendrons and Azaleas including many rare species collected in the Himalayas, and hybrids raised by the owners. Pond, stream and companion plantings. Plants for

sale from specialist nursery which is open throughout the year.

May-early June daily 10.00-17.00

Last Admission: 16.30

A£1.50 C£Free

Painshill Landscape Garden

Portsmouth Road Cobham Surrey KT11 1JE

[J10 M25 and A3 exit at A245. 200 metres east of A245/A307 roundabout in Between Streets. Plenty of on site parking.]

Tel: 01932 868113/864674 Fax: 01932 868001

Painshill, contemporary with Stourhead and Stowe, is one of Europe's finest 18th century landscape gardens. Created by the Hon. Charles Hamilton between 1738 and 1773 - a garden of different moods and variety to surprise and mystify visitors leaving them spellbound at every turn. Visitors can take a circuit walk through a series of delightful scenes - a Gothic temple, a Chinese bridge, a ruined abbey, a crystal grotto, a Turkish tent, a spectacular waterwheel, 14 acre lake and much, much more.

Apr-Oct Tue-Sun & Bank Hol 10.30-18.00, Nov-Mar Tue-Thur, Sat, Sun & Bank Hol 11.00-16.00 or dusk if sooner. Closed 25-26 Dec. Guided Tours Sat & Sun 14.00

Last Admission: Apr-Oct 16.30 Nov-Mar 15.00

A£3.80 C(under 5)£Free C(5-16)£1.50 Concessions£3.30. Group rates 10+ £3.00. Special arrangements for school parties contact Education Department 01932 866743

RHS Garden Wisley

RHS Garden Wisley Woking Surrey GU23 6QB
*[J10 M25 on A3, London 22m, Guildford 7m.
Plenty of on site parking available.]*
Tel: 01483 224234 Fax: 01483 211750
www.rhs.org.uk
Voted Visitor Attractions of the Year 1999 in
the English Tourism Council's England for
Excellence Awards, Wisely demonstrates
British gardening at it's best in all aspects.
Covering over 240 acres, highlights include the
Alpine Meadow carpeted with daffodils in
Spring, Battleston Hill, brilliant with rhodo-
dendrons in early Summer, the heathers and
Autumnal tints. New for this year is the Daily
Telegraph 'Reflective Garden,' winner of Best
Garden Award and Gold Medal at the 1999
Chelsea Flower Show. For the following walks
and demonstrations, tickets are £5.00 for
Members and £10.00 for non-members. Send a
cheque made payable to RHS, enclosing a SAE
and daytime telephone number to the
Administration Dept., RHS Garden, Wisley,
Woking, GU23 6QB.
*Garden: Mon-Fri 10.00-18.00 or sunset if soon-
er, Sat-Sun 09.00-18.00 or sunset if sooner. RHS
Members only on Sun*
*A£5.00 C(0-6)£Free C(6-16)£2.00. Groups 10+
£4.00 if booked 21 days in advance*
discount offer: Two For The Price Of One.
Valid Oct 2000-Mar 2001, Mon-Sat only

↓*special events*

▶ **Rose Pruning**
1/3/00-5/3/00
*Demonstrations on Mar 1 at 14.00 and Mar 5 at
10.30*
▶ **Getting Started in the Greenhouse**
3/3/00-3/3/00
10.00-16.00. Please call for further details

▶ **Garden Crafts**
3/3/00-14/3/00
Live demonstrations by practising craftsmen
▶ **Winter-flowering Heathers**
5/3/00-5/3/00
A walk at 10.30
▶ **Container Gardening**
16/3/00-16/3/00
From 10.00-16.00, please call for more details
▶ **Spring Flowers at Wisley**
19/3/00-19/4/00
A walk at 10.30 on Apr 9 and 12 only
▶ **Practical Gardening Skills**
22/3/00-26/3/00
*Demonstrations at 14.00 on Mar 22 and 10.30
on Mar 26*
▶ **Flower Arranging Workshops**
22/3/00-23/11/00
*Themed workshops from 10.00-15.30 on Mar
22, Sept 6 and Nov 23 only. Please call for
details*
▶ **Garden Design Weekends**
23/3/00-12/11/00
*Weekends run on Mar 23-26 and Nov 9-12.
Please call for further details*
▶ **Two-day Botanical Art Courses with Niki
Simpson**
29/3/00-21/11/00
*Workshops at beginners/intermediate level held
on Mar 29-30 and Nov 20-21 at 10.00-16.30.
Call for details*
▶ **Alpine Specialist Day**
5/4/00-5/4/00
*From 10.00-16.00. Please call for further infor-
mation*
▶ **Photographic Workshop Weekends**
8/4/00-26/11/00
*Workshops for beginners on Apr 8-9, Nov 25-26
and for intermediates on Sept 16-17. Please call
for details*
▶ **The Rock Garden, Alpine Meadow and
Alpine House**
9/4/00-12/4/00
A walk at 10.30 on Apr 9 and 12 only
▶ **Plantsman's Days**
10/4/00-23/10/00
*Held on Apr 10, May 5, June 30, Sept 4, 29 and
Oct 23. Please call for more details*
▶ **Silk Painting Workshops**
15/4/00-26/11/00
*Held on Apr 15-16, May 15-16 and Nov 25-26
from 10.00-16.30. Please call for more information*
▶ **Water Gardens Specialist Signs**
18/4/00-20/4/00
*Apr 18 is for beginners and Apr 20 for those
with more experience. Courses run from 10.30-
16.30. Call for more details*
▶ **Flower Arranging Demonstrations**
19/4/00-22/11/00
*Demonstrations with differing themes on Apr
19, May 10, June 14, July 19, Aug 9, Oct 18 and*

Nov 22 only. Please call for details

▶ **Trees, Shrubs and Herbaceous Perennials**
26/4/00-26/4/00
A walk at 10.30

▶ **The Mixed Border**
26/4/00-13/9/00
Demonstrations at 14.00 on Apr 26 and Sept 13 only

▶ **Botanical Art Weekends**
27/4/00-29/10/00
Beginners courses Apr 27-30, advanced June 15-18 and intermediate Sept 21-24 and 26-29. Call for further details. Necessary to have art if not botanical art experience

▶ **Wisley's Birds**
30/4/00-14/5/00
A walk at 10.30 on Apr 30 and May 14 only

▶ **Science Open Day**
11/5/00-11/5/00
From 10.00-16.00. Please call for more information

▶ **Potager Day**
31/5/00-31/5/00
Runs from 10.30-16.30. Call for more information

▶ **A Summer Stroll in the Garden**
4/6/00-7/6/00
Walks to be held at 10.30 on June 4 and 7 only

▶ **Treatment of Grapes Indoors and Out**
7/6/00-22/11/00
Demonstrations of summer treatment on June 6 and winter treatment on Nov 22, both at 10.30.

▶ **Growing Vegetables**
19/6/00-19/6/00
Runs from 10.00-16.00. Please call for more details

▶ **Wisley's Birds**
20/6/00-20/6/00
10.00-16.30. Please call for extra information

▶ **Pruning of Shrubs**
21/6/00-25/6/00
Demonstrations at 14.00 on June 21 and 10.30 on June 25

▶ **Herb Day**
26/6/00-26/6/00
10.30-16.30. Call for more details

▶ **Budding of Fruit Trees**
5/7/00-5/7/00
A demonstration at 10.30

▶ **Garden Pests and Diseases**
12/7/00-12/7/00
From 10.00-16.00. Please call for extra information

▶ **Pruning of Fruit Trees and Bushes**
12/7/00-19/11/00
Demonstrations at 10.30 on July 12, 16, Nov 15, 17 and 19 only

▶ **Hedges and Screens**
14/7/00-14/7/00
Course runs from 10.00-16.00. Call for further information

▶ **Summer Borders**
16/7/00-19/7/00
Walks at 10.30 on July 16 and 19 only

▶ **Plant Propagation for Beginners and Beyond**
21/7/00-21/7/00
Runs from 10.00-16.00. Please call for further information

▶ **Paper Making**
22/7/00-23/7/00
From 10.00-16.30. For further details, please call

▶ **Family Fortnight**
29/7/00-13/8/00
Family fun with educational and garden-based activities for children such as art and pot-painting workshops and creepy crawly lectures

▶ **Photography Masterclass (RHS Members only)**
30/7/00-30/7/00
Join our special guest photographer for a relaxed and informative photographic day. Call for details

▶ **Painting in the Garden**
5/8/00-6/8/00
Capture Wisley on paper from 10.00-16.30. Please call for details

▶ **Drought-Resistant Plants**
9/8/00-9/8/00
Walk to be held at 10.30

▶ **Sculpture Trail**
1/9/00-27/9/00
The garden trail will feature work created from a range of materials and covering a diversity of subject matter

▶ **Lawn Maintenance**
20/9/00-24/9/00
Demonstrations at 14.00 on Sept 20 and 10.30 on Sept 24

▶ **Autumn Colour**
8/10/00-11/10/00
Walks at 10.30 on Oct 8 and 11 only

▶ **Apple Days**
19/10/00-22/10/00
A programme of demonstrations, walks and tasting in celebration of Britain's favourite fruit.

▶ **Two-day Botanical Drawing Course**
21/10/00-22/10/00
Drawing with special guest tutor from 10.00-16.30. Please call for further details

▶ **Soil Management for Gardeners**
25/10/00-25/10/00
Demonstration commencing at 14.00

▶ **The Charm of Wisley Under Glass**
1/11/00-1/11/00
A walk starting at 10.30

▶ **Christmas at Wisley**
18/11/00-26/11/00
Demonstrations and workshops inspired by the festive season

Surrey

Valley Gardens in Windsor Great Park

Wick Road Englefield Green Egham Surrey SL4 2HS

[J13 M25, then off A30, approached via Wick Rd, parking in Valley Gardens will avoid a 2m round walk. Otherwise a walk from Savill Garden Car Park]

Tel: 01753 860222 Fax: 01753 859617

400 acre gardens are situated on the north bank of Virginia Water Lake. Probably one of the finest woodlands gardens in the world and contains an unrivalled collection of rhododendrons, azaleas, camellias, magnolias and countless other spring flowering tress and shrubs An outstanding display of acres of native wild daffodil during March and April. Adjoining the woodland garden is the 10 acre heather garden which provides much colour during winter and summer. A new development of dwarf and slow growing conifer collection cover several acres. Autumn is becoming better and better in the Valley Gardens with numerous Japanese maples, red oaks, cherries, liquidambars and much more, all producing a magnificent display of colour throughout the Fall.

All year daily 08.00-19.00 or sunset if sooner
Pay barrier for parking £3.00 per car (10p, 50p and £1 coins only) Coaches by prior appointment during weekdays only £20.00

Winkworth Arboretum

Hascombe Road Nr Godalming Surrey GU8 4AD

[2m NW on B2130]

Tel: 01483 208477 Fax: 01483 208252
www.cornuswwweb.co.uk

This lovely woodland covers a hillside of nearly 100 acres, with fine views over the North Downs. The best time to visit is April, for the azaleas, bluebells and other flowers, and October for the autumn colours. There is a newly-renovated boathouse - a tranquil resting place with balcony view over the lake. Please note, disabled and pushchair access is limited.

All year daily during daylight hours may close during bad weather (high winds)
Last Admission: Dusk
A£3.00 C£1.50 Family Ticket £6.75

↓*special events*
► **National Gardnes Scheme Open Day: Tours of the Arboretum**
16/4/00-16/4/00
Meet at the information kiosk near the tearoom. Some challenging steps for the less able, £2.00 plus usual admission, 14.30-16.30
► **National Garden Scheme Open Day: Tour of the Arboretum**
15/10/00-15/10/00

See entry for 16 April

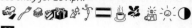

Historical

Albury Park

Albury Park Albury Guildford Surrey GU5 9BB

[1.5m E of Albury off A25 Guildford to Dorking road BR: Chilworth-2m Gomshall-2m Clandon-3m Bus Route-Tillingbourne No25 Guildford-Cranleigh]

Tel: 01483 202964

Country mansion remodeled by Pugin.
May-Sep Wed & Thur 14.00-17.00
Last Admission: 16.30
A£2.50 C£1.00

Clandon Park

West Clandon Guildford Surrey GU4 7RQ

[at West Clandon on the A247 near A246, 3m E of Guildford, 5m SW M25, 3m S of A3. Parking 300m]

Tel: 01483 224912 Fax: 01483 223479
www.nationaltrust.org.uk

A splendid 18th-century house, built by Leoni and notable for its magnificent two-storeyed Marble Hall. The house is filled with a superb collection of furniture, porcelain and textiles acquired in the 1920s by the connoisseur Mrs. Gubbay. The attractive gardens contain a parterre, grotto, sunken Dutch garden and Maori House. Home also to the Queens Royal Surrey Regimental Museum. NT Shop. Licenced restaurant open same days as house from 11.00 for coffee, lunches, teas (tel: 01483 222502). Wheelchair access to ground floor, gardens, shop and restaurant.

2 Apr-31 Oct Tue, Wed, Thur & Sun, Good Fri, Easter Sat & all Bank Hol Mon 11.30-16.30, Garden daily 09.00-dusk
Last Admission: 16.00
House & Garden: A£4.40 C£2.25 Family Ticket £11.00. Combined ticket with Hatchlands Park: A£6.40 Special group rate weekdays only: £3.80

↓*special events*
► **Dress Sale**
10/4/00-10/4/00
10.30-16.00... Details from 01372 453401
► **Connoisseurs at Clandon: How to Spot a Fake**
15/5/00-15/5/00
From model trains to trainers: today everything is collected. Tickets from Southern Region Box Office on 01372 451596, £6.00, opens 18.00 for 19.00. Disabled visitors please telephone 01483 222482 for information. Optional dinner with Georgian menu available from 20.00, booking essential on 01483 222502

► **Connoisseurs at Clandon: Tomorrow's Antiques**
16/5/00-16/5/00
See entry for 15 May
► **Connoisseurs at Clandon: The Victorians**
17/5/00-17/5/00
See entry for 15 May
► **Connoisseurs at Clandon: My Pick of Clandon**
18/5/00-18/5/00
See entry for 15 May
► **An Evening with Julian Bream**
8/9/00-8/9/00
A varied programme of classical and popular guitar favourites by this soloist of world-wide reputation. Tickets from Southern Region Box Office on 01372 451596, £16.00, 19.30 for 20.00
► **Connoisseurs at Clandon: A Ceramic 'Seven Ages of Man'**
9/10/00-9/10/00
See entry for 15 May
► **Connoisseurs at Clandon: A Stich in Time**
10/10/00-10/10/00
See entry for 15 May
► **Connoisseurs at Clandon: 'Fabergé Hearts and Coronets'**
11/10/00-11/10/00
See entry for 15 May
► **Connorsseurs at Clandon: Grand Tour - Taste to Tat?**
12/10/00-12/10/00
See entry for 15 May
► **You're the Top - A tribute to Cole Porter**
25/10/00-27/10/00
A dramatised revue featuring classic songs from his musicals, including Anything Goes, Kiss me Kate, Can Can and High Society. Tickets from Southern Region Box Office on 01372 451596. £12.00, 19.30 for 20.00
► **Dress Sale**
30/10/00-30/10/00
See entry for 10 April
► **Putting the House to Bed**
2/11/00-3/11/00
Tickets from Southern Region Box Office on 01372 451596, A£9.00 incl refreshments, 09.45 for 10.00. Optional lunch available 13.00, booking essential on 01483 222502
► **Old Tyme Music Hall**
9/11/00-10/11/00
Come suitably attired and with full lungs to join in the evening's fun! Tickets from Southern Region Box Office on 01372 451596, £15.00, 19.30 for 20.00. Optional dinner available before, booking essential on 01483 222502

Claremont House
The Claremont Fan Court Foundation Ltd
Claremont Drive Esher Surrey KT10 9LY

[0.5m SW of Esher on A307, Esher-Cobham road]
Tel: 01372 467841 Fax: 01372 471109
Excellent example of Palladian style built 1772 by Capability Brown for Clive of India; Henry Holland and John Soane responsible for the interior decoration. It is now a co-educational school run by Christian Scientists.
Feb-Nov first complete weekend Sat & Sun in each month 14.00-17.00
Last Admission: 16.30
A£3.00 C&OAPs£2.00 reduced rates for parties

Coombe Conduit
Kingston-Upon-Thames Surrey *[Buses frequent from surrounding areas. BR: Kingston-upon-Thames 0.25m]*
Tel: 020 8892 5115
Built by Henry V111 to supply water to Hampton Court Palace, three miles away, Coombe Conduit consists of two small buildings (one now a ruin) connected by an underground passage.
Managed by the Kingston Society. Entrance by appointment only contact Marble Hill House Richmond Road Twickenham TW1 2NL Tel 0181 892 5115
Admission Free by appointment

Farnham Castle Keep
Castle Hill Farnham Surrey GU6 OAG
[0.5m N onA287]
Tel: 01252 713393 Fax: 01252 711283
The castle was started in the 11th century by Henry of Blois, Bishop of Winchester, at a convenient point on the way to London; his tower stood on the mound of the keep, which was later encased in high walls. Around the keep are a ditch and bank topped by a wall.
27 Mar-31 Oct daily 10.00-18.00
Last Admission: 17.30
A£2.00 C£1.00 Concessions£1.50. Admission price includes a free Personal Stereo Guided Tour

↓*special events*
► **Farnham Caslte, 1643**
23/4/00-24/4/00
Civil War living history with the famous Farnham Greencoat soldiers. Plus musket-firing
► **Recruiting for Wellington**
1/7/00-2/7/00
Redcoat soldiers in camp, with living history displays, drill and musket-firing
► **Children's Fun Day**
2/8/00-2/8/00
Clowns, juggling, magic, face-painting and games to play
► **Children's Fun Workshop**
23/8/00-23/8/00

Hands on fun for all children. Bring a picnic and stay all day!

Goddards
Abinger Common Dorking Surrey RH5 6TH
[4.5m SW of Dorking in Abinger Common]
Tel: 01628 825920
Edwardian country house by Sir Edwin Lutyens, with Gertrude Jekyll garden, in beautiful setting on slopes of Leith Hill. Given to the Lutyens Trust in 1991 and now managed and maintained by The Landmark Trust.
August 1997 following restoration Wed pm only from beg August
A£3.00 Please telephone for further details

Greathed Manor
Ford Manor Road Dormansland Lingfield Surrey RH7 6PA
[2.5m SE of Lingfield on B2028 Edenbridge road. Take Ford Manor road beside Plough Inn Dormansland for final 1m. BR: Dormans 1.5m]
Tel: 01342 832577
Victorian Manor house.
May-Sept Wed-Thur 14.00-17.00
Last Admission: 16.30
A£2.50 C£1.00

Guildford Castle and Grounds
Castle Grounds Castle Street Guildford Surrey GU1 3TU
[A3 signposted in Guildford town centre]
Tel: 01483 444702 Fax: 01483 444444
Just a few minutes walk from Guildford High Street set in the beautiful Castle Grounds, stands the ruins of Guildford Castle. The striking Keep was probably built by Henry II as a fortress and gives fine views of the surrounding countryside. The gardens are at their best in the spring and summer when the flower beds are a riot of colour. Band concerts are held in the bandstand during the summer months and open-air theatre is a feature in the gardens during July.
Grounds daily 08.00-dusk Closed 25 Dec Keep Apr-Sept 10.00-18.00
A£0.80 C£0.35

Guildford House Gallery
155 High Street Guildford Surrey GU1 3AJ
[N side of High St opposite Sainsbury's]
Tel: 01483 444740 Fax: 01483 444742
Important features of the fascinating building are the finely decorated plaster ceilings, panelled rooms, wrought iron balcony and window catches, together with the richly carved oak and elm staircase. Guildford House dates from 1660 and has been Guildford's art gallery since 1957.
Tue-Sat 10.00-16.45
Admission Free

Hatchlands Park
East Clandon Guildford Surrey GU4 7RT
[E of E Clandon, N of A246 Guildford to Leatherhead Road, 5m E of Guildford. Plenty of on site parking available]
Tel: 01483 222482 Fax: 01483 223176
A handsome House built in 1758 by Stiff Leadbetter for Admiral Boscawen, and set in a beautiful Repton park offering a variety of park and woodland walks. Hatchlands contains splendid interiors by Robert Adam. It houses the Cobbe collection, the world's largest group of early keyboard instruments associated with famous composers e.g. Purcell, JC Bach, Chopin, Mahler and Elgar. Audio Guide. There is a small garden by Gertrude Jekyll (flowering late May to early June). Licenced restaurant, for lunches and teas open same days as house (booking advisable tel: 01483 211120). Wheelchair access to show rooms, restaurant, shop and part of the garden.
House & Grounds: 2 Apr-31 Oct Tue, Wed, Thur, Sun. Also Fri in Aug & Bank Hol Mon 14.00-17.30. Park walks: Apr-Oct daily 11.30-18.00
Last Admission: 30mins before closing
House & Grounds: A£4.40 C(5-18)£2.20. Family Ticket £11.00. Combined Ticket with Clandon Park £6 40. Park Walks & Garden only: A£1.80 C£0.90. Special group rate weekdays only: £3.60

↓*special events*

▶ **Hatchlands Hat Trick - #1 Rhythm and Blues Night**
7/7/00-7/7/00
The Blues Band plus local support band 'The Skidmarks'. Bring a picnic and enjoy this open air concert. Tickets from Southern Region Box Office on 01372 451596, £12.50, 18.30 for 19.30. Hat Trick savings: Book for 2 or 3 productions at reduced rates: 2 = £22.50, 3 = £34.00
▶ **Hatchlands Hat Trick - #2 George Melly and Helen Shapiro**
8/7/00-8/7/00
George Melly & John Chilton's Feetwarmers plus Helen Shapiro & her Quintet. See entry for 7 July
▶ **Hatchlands Hat Rick - #3 The Music of the Night**
9/7/00-9/7/00
Medleys and songs from the world's greatest musicals with a cast of stars from the West End shows and the Kingsmead String Quartet. See entry for 7 July

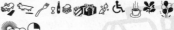

Loseley Park

Estate Offices Loseley Park Guildford Surrey GU3 1HS
[leave A3 at Compton on B3000 signposted. BR: Guildford 2m. Bus: 1.25m. Plenty of parking on site]
Tel: 01483 304440 Fax: 01483 302036
Loseley Park has been the home of the More-Molyneux family for over 400 years. The Elizabethan Mansion is set amid 1,400 acres of glorious parkland and rolling pastures grazed by the famous Jersey herd. Built in 1562 by an ancestor of the present owner, the House features many fine works of art, including paintings, tapestries and panelling from Henry VIII's Nonsuch Palace. The Walled Garden has been carefully restored over the past six years and includes an award winning rose garden, as well as herb, flower, vegetable and fountain gardens, and an idyllic moat walk. Member of the Historic Houses Association.
Garden, Gift Shop & Courtyard Tea Room: beginning May-end Sept Wed-Sat & Bank Hol. Sun in June, July & Aug 11.00-17.00. House: end May-end Aug Wed-Sun & Bank Hol 14.00-17.00. At other times by arrangement.
Last Admission: Last Tour: 16.30
House & Gardens: A£5.00 C£3.00 Concessions£4.00. Gardens only:A£2.50 C£1.50 Concessions£2.00. Discounted Group rates available

↓*special events*
▶ **Home Design Exhibition**
25/2/00-27/2/00
Ideas for the Home and Garden
▶ **Surrey Advertiser Motor Show**
6/5/00-7/5/00
Stands displaying and selling new cars and hands-on 4x4
▶ **Craft Fair**
25/5/00-28/5/00
Stalls selling and demonstrating Arts and Crafts
▶ **Open Air Opera**
23/6/00-23/6/00
▶ **WI Flower Show**
27/6/00-28/6/00
Stalls selling W1 produce and a display of flower arrangements

▶ **Great Gardening Show**
21/7/00-23/7/00
Show gardens, demonstrations, plants and garden accessories for sale
▶ **Open Air Concert and Fireworks**
13/8/00-13/8/00
Classical music and magnificent fireworks, call for further details and how to book

Polesden Lacey

Great Bookham Dorking Surrey RH5 6BD
[2m S off A246]
Tel: 01372 458203/452048 Fax: 01372 452023
In Edwardian times, this attractive Regency house was owned by a celebrated society hostess, Mrs Ronald Greville. King George VI and Queen Elizabeth The Queen Mother spent part of their honeymoon here. The house is handsomely furnished with the Greville collection of tapestries, porcelain, Old Master paintings and other works of art.
Garden all year daily 10.00-18.00, House: 29 Mar-29 Oct Wed-Sun 13.00-17.00, Bank Hol Mon 11.00-17.30. Guided group tours of house Tue-Fri am by prior appointment
Last Admission: 30mins before closing
Gardens and landscaped walks: A£3.00 Family Ticket £7.50, House: A£3.00 extra Family Ticket £7.50 extra. Extra charge for guided tour

↓*special events*
▶ **Easter Egg Hunt**
24/4/00-24/4/00
A trail around the grounds leading to an edible prize, £1.50 plus usual admission, 11.00-15.00
▶ **Stormwood '87**
28/4/00-7/5/00
Works of art made from trees lost in recent storms. Exhibits on sale and donations to the Trust, usual admission, 11.00-17.00
▶ **Valuation Day**
10/5/00-10/5/00
Phillips' professional valuers looking at items of silver, jewellery, porcelain and objet d'art, £5.00, to include the valuation of two items. Additional items £3.00 each, 11.00-16.00
▶ **London to Brighton Classic Car Run**
4/6/00-4/6/00
The London to Brighton Classic Car Run stops at the property, 09.30-13.30, usual admission
▶ **11th London to Brighton Classic Car Run**
4/6/00-4/6/00
Polesden Lacey is the 1st Check Point with Check Point 2 at Leonardslee Gardens, Sussex. Starting at Syon Park, Brentford, Middx and Finishing at Maderia Drive, Brighton
▶ **The Brass Band Millennium**
16/6/00-16/6/00
Surrey Massed Bands of more than 80 musi-

Surrey

cians conducted by Darren Wolfendale. Tickets:
Southern Region Box Office on 01372 451596,
£12.00-£35.00, 18.30 for 20.00

▶ **A Tribute to the Legends of Jazz**
17/6/00-17/6/00

*The best of today's musicians pay homage to
the legends who inspired them. Tickets:
Southern Region Box Office on 01372 451596,
£14.00-£35.00, 18.30 for 20.00*

▶ **Sunday Night is Music Night**
18/6/00-18/6/00

*An evening of popular light classics and famous
themes from film and television. Tickets:
Southern Region Box Office on 01372 451596,
£16.00-£35.00, 18.30 for 20.00*

▶ **Sunday Lunchtime Concert**
18/6/00-18/6/00

*Polesden Pops Orchestra conducted by Jonathan
Butcher. Tickets: Southern Region Box Office on
01372 451596, A£8.00-£14.00C£4.00-£10.00
Family (A2+C3)£16.00-£35.00, 10.30 for 12.00*

▶ **Guys and Dolls**
22/6/00-25/6/00

*Performed by Epsom Light Operatic Society.
Tickets: Southern Region Box Office on 01372
451596, A£8.00-£35.00 C£6.00-£18.00, 10% discount for groups of 15+, on Thursday, Friday
and Saturday matinee. All seats are reserved,
grass unreserved, 20.00 (Sat matinee 14.30)*

▶ **A Midsummer Night's Dream**
29/6/00-1/7/00

*Performed by Guildford School of Acting. Tickets
from the Southern Region Box Office on 01372
451596, A£8.00-£25.00 C£6.00-£14.00, 10% discount for groups of 15+, on Thursday, Friday
and Saturday matinee. All seats are reserved,
grass unreserved, 20.00 (Sat matinee 14.30)*

▶ **Surrey Hills Country Fair**
2/7/00-2/7/00

*A wonderful day out for the family. Includes
demonstrations, pig roast, crafts, music and traditional dancing, A£4.00 C(5-16)£2.00 C(under
5's)£Free, 11.00-17.00*

▶ **Sounds of the 60s**
2/7/00-2/7/00

*A concert featuring legendary artists from the
60s. Tickets: Southern Region Box Office on
01372 451596, A£10.00-£35.00 C£8.00-£14.00,
18.30 for 19.30*

▶ **Greville Day**
20/8/00-20/8/00

*Games and activities, suitable for all ages, usual
admission, 11.00-17.00*

▶ **A Day in the Life of a Gardener**
28/9/00-28/9/00

*Pre-booked tours throughout the day, sorry no
dogs, usual admission, 11.00-17.00*

Military & Defence Museums

Royal Logistic Corps Museum

Deepcut Camberley Surrey GU16 6RW

[signposted from B3015]

Tel: 01252 340871

Exciting displays, which use the collections of
The RLC's predecessors, explain how soldiers
have been armed, transported, fed and kept in
touch with families over the centuries.

*All year Mon-Fri 10.00-16.00, Sat 10.00-15.00.
Closed Bank Hol & Sun*

Admission Free

The Queen's Royal Surrey Regiment Museum

Clandon Park West Clandon Guildford Surrey
GU4 7RQ

*[Just off A246 Guildford - Leatherhead road
Signposted to Clandon Park (NT)]*

Tel: 01483 223419

Historical items of the former Queen's Royal
Regiment, The East Surrey Regiment and The
Queen's Royal Surrey Regiment. Research facilities available by arrangement with the curator.

*Easter-end Oct Tues-Thur, Sun & Bank Hol
12.00-17.00*

Admission Free

Mills - Water & Wind

Shalford Mill

Shalford Guildford Surrey GU4 8BS

*[1.5m S of Guildford on A281 opposite Sea
Horse Inn, BR: Shalford 0.5m Guildford 1.5m]*

Tel: 01483 561617

A large 18th-century water-mill on the River
Tillingbourne, given in 1932 by a group of
anonymous NT benefactors calling themselves
'Ferguson's Gang'. Note: Owing to fire regulations, it is not possible for visitors to go higher
than the first floor.

All year daily 10.00-17.00

*Admission Free but donations in the box wel-
come. Children must be accompanied by an
adult*

The Old Mill

Outwood Common Outwood Redhill Surrey RH1 5PW
[Outwood Common 3m S of Bletchingley off A25]
Tel: 01342 843458 Fax: 01342 843458
www.cix.co.uk/~jimnutt
The award-winning post-mill built in 1665 is the oldest working windmill in England. Surrounded by common land and National Trust woodland where nature walks and picnicking may be enjoyed. Wander freely around the Windmill with its many friendly animals, small Museum with a fine collection of bygones and old farm tools.
Easter Sun-last Sun in Oct Sun & Bank Hol Mon only 14.00-18.00. Other days and evening tours by arrangement. School parties for educational visits welcome
A£2.00 C£1.00

Natural History Museums

Haslemere Educational Museum

High Street Haslemere Surrey GU27 2LA
[off A3 London / Portsmouth road]
Tel: 01428 642112 Fax: 01428 645234
ourworld.compuserve.com/homepages/ha slemeremuseum/
Traditional & information galleries covering geology, botany, zoology, archaeology and history. The Museum is well known for the wildflower table, stuffed bear, Egyptian Mummy & observation beehive. Special events programme and visitor information centre.
All year Tue-Sat 10.00-17.00
Admission Free

Nature & Conservation Parks

Bockett's Farm Park

Young Street Fetcham Surrey KT22 9BS
[A246 south of Leatherhead]
Tel: 01372 363764 Fax: 01372 361764
Bockett's is a working farm with more than 500 sheep. They also have water buffalo, Llamas and all the usual farm animals. There is a big childrens play area with swings, slides and a straw bale mountain.
visitor comments: Thoroughly recommended for under 5's. Fantastically educational, good weather trip preferable.
All year daily 10.00-18.00 closed 25-27 Dec 31-1 2000
A£3.45 (3-17)C£2.95 OAPs £2.95 2yrs £2.05 under 2 free

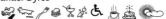

Frensham Common

Frensham Little Pond Frensham Surrey GU10 3BT
Tel: 01252 792483
↓*special events*
► **Treasure Hunt**
15/7/00-15/7/00
Sponsored by Birmingham Midshires. Price and times to be announced. Contact Sharon Zeta on 01428 683207

Holmwood Common

Dorking Surrey **Tel: 01306 741711**
Any reasonable time
Admission Free
↓*special events*
► **Spring Flowers and Masses of Jelly**
12/3/00-12/3/00
Enjoy an early spring walk. Meet the Warden at Inholms Lane car park (TQ170470) for this 2-mile walk, donations welcome, 10.30-12.30
► **New Leaves and Blossoms, Bluebells Too!**
23/4/00-23/4/00
Meet your guide at Scammels car park, Blackbrook Road (TQ182464) for this 2-mile walk, donations welcome, 14.30-16.30
► **What's Happening on the Common?**
21/5/00-21/5/00
Meet your guide at Mill Road car park (just off A24) (TQ172452) for this 2-mile walk, 14.30-16.30
► **A Summer Walk**
18/6/00-18/6/00
Meet your guide at Fourwents Pond car park, Blackbrook Road (TQ184454) for this 2-mile walk, donations 14.30-16.30
► **Holmwood Common Millennium Evening Walk**

19/7/00-19/7/00
Join us for an evening walk around the common. Meet the Warden and your guide at Fourwents Pond Car Park, Blackbrook Road (TQ184454) for this 2-mile walk, donations welcome. 19.00-21.00

► **Broadleaves and Butterflies**
23/7/00-23/7/00
Meet the Warden at Mill Road car park (just off A24) (TQ172452) for this 2-mile walk, donations welcome, 10.30-12.30

► **Children's Fun Afternoon**
9/8/00-9/8/00
Parachute games, bugs, grubs and beetles. For all the family. Meet the Warden at Fourwents Pond Car Park, Blackbrook Road (TQ184454), sorry, no dogs, C£2.50 14.00-16.00

► **Take a Look at Fungi**
24/9/00-24/9/00
Do something different. Meet at Mill Road car park (just off A24) (TQ172452) for this 1/2-mile walk, donations welcome, 14.30-16.30

► **Autumn Tints and Toadstools**
1/10/00-1/10/00
Enjoy the early Autumn tints. Meet your guide at Fourwents Pond car park, Blackbrook Road (TQ184454) for this 1/2-mile walk, donations welcome. 14.30-16.30

► **Discovering Late Fungi**
22/10/00-22/10/00
Meet at Scammels car park, Blackbrook Road (TQ182464) for this 1/2-mile walk, donations welcome, 14.30-16.30

► **Late Autumn on the Common**
19/11/00-19/11/00
Meet your guide at Mill Road car park (just off A24) (TQ172452) for this 2-mile walk, donations welcome. 14.30-16.30

► **Christmas Walk**
27/12/00-27/12/00
Come along and blow off the cobwebs. Hot drinks and cake. Meet the Warden at Mill Road car park (off A24) (TQ172452) for this 1/2-mile walk, donations, 14.00-16.00

Spencer Road Wetlands
Wood Street Sutton Surrey *[entrance on the junction of Wood St / Spencer Rd, Sutton. BR: Hackbridge]*
Tel: 020 7278 6612
Once a commercial watercress bed, this reserve is now a haven for wetland plants and willows.
Access by arrangement, telephone for details
Admission Free

Witley Common Information Centre
Witley Centre Haslemere Road Witley Godalming Surrey GU8 5QA
[7m SW of Guildford between London /

Portsmouth A3 / A286 roads, 1m SW of Milford. Bus: Stagecoach Hants / Surrey / Coastline 260 / X60. BR: Milford 2m]
Tel: 01428 683207 Fax: 01428 683207
A purpose built nature information centre set in pine woods on the edge of the common. There is an exhibition showing the history, natural history and management of th West Weald. Dogs kept under control please. Limited access for wheelchairs. Children's outdoor activities are organised during school holidays, please telephone for details.
1 Apr-31 Oct Tues-Fri 11.00-16.00. Sat, Sun & Bank Hol Mon 11.00-17.00. Closed Mon. Car park 09.00-18.00
Admission Free

↓**special events**
► **Easter Egg Trail**
21/4/00-24/4/00
£1.50, 11.00-17.00, call for details

World Wildlife Fund - UK
Panda House Weyside Park Godalming Surrey GU7 1XR
Tel: 01483 426444 Fax: 01483 426409
www.wwf-uk.org/
WWF - the global force for nature conservation. From its earliest days back in 1961, WWF has been committed to saving threatened wildlife species and their habitats. The fundamental principle is still one of the great driving forces behind the organisation - though our remit at home and abroad has broadened considerably in the 36 years since our inauguration. WWF conserves nature by protecting wild species in wild places, by promoting and practising the sustainable use of biological resources, and helping people become more aware of the environment so that they can take enlightened decisions about lifestyles and consumption. As we head towards the new millennium, WWF will pursue these fundamental tasks as part of its ultimate goal - to stop the accelerating degradation of the natural environment, and to build a future in which people live in harmony with nature. Members receive regular information on how your money is being spent, a copy of WWF News every quarter and a full-colour poster of the Bengal tiger 210 x 297mm (also available for those donating £20 or more).
All year Mon-Fri 09.00-17.00
Membership: Benefactor with a gift of £10.00 per month by Direct Debit; A Companion with a gift of £5.00 a month by Direct Debit; A Member with a gift of £2.00 per month by Direct Debit or A Member at £20.00 per year.

Surrey

Palaces

Hampton Court Palace and Gardens

Hampton Court Palace East Molesey Surrey KT8 9AU

[M25 exit J12 M3 towards central London exit at J1 Sunbury signposts follow for 4m. A308 towards Kingston. From Central London take A4 W towards Hammersmith then A316 / M3 then exit at J1 Sunbury as above. Tube: Richmond, then R68 bus. Rail: Hampton Court Station]

Tel: 020 8781 9500 Fax: 020 8781 9669
www.hrp.org.uk

With its 500 years of royal history Hampton Court Palace has something to offer everyone. Set in sixty acres of world famous gardens the palace is a living tapestry of history from Henry VIII to George II. From the elegance of the recently restored Privy Garden to the domestic reality of the Tudor Kitchens, visitors are taken back throughout the centuries to experience the palace as it was when royalty was in residence. Enjoy the splendour of the royal apartments, and look out for the ghost of Catherine Howard in the Haunted Gallery. Costumed guides and audio tours bring the palace to life and provide an insight into how life in the palace would have been in the time of Henry VIII and William III, and free family trails encourage a closer look at the Palace with the chance to win a prize. The Palace also has an exciting programme of holiday and half-term activities to entertain all the family.

Mid Mar-mid Oct Mon 10.15-18.00, Tue-Sun 09.30-18.00. Mid Oct-mid Mar Mon 10.15-16.30, Tue-Sun 09.30-16.30. Gardens: all year daily 07.00-dusk

Last Admission: 60mins before closing (Palace)
A£10.50 C(5-16)£7.00 Family Ticket (A2+C3)£31.40 Concessions£8.00. Season Tickets available

↓ *special events*

► **All the King's Creatures**
19/2/00-27/2/00
Discover the creatures of the royal court past and present. Visitors can enjoy beastly family trails and explore the theme of animals and heraldry

► **Florimania - The Queen's Flowers**
31/3/00-4/4/00
The scent of flowers is in the air as Queen Mary II's Apartments are adorned with 17th century floral bouquets and arrangements.

► **Royal Sport at Hampton Court**
22/4/00-30/4/00
Discover the sports and games enjoyed by the royal residents. Costumed tours and demonstrations

► **The Rise and Fall of Catherine Howard**
27/5/00-4/6/00
A week of activities reveals the life of Henry VIII's fifth wife

► **Privy Garden Celebration**
1/7/00-2/7/00
Join in the fifth birthday of the restoration of William III and Mary II's Privy Garden. Dates to be confirmed

► **Hampton Court Flower Festival**
6/7/00-9/7/00
The annual show returns to Hampton Court Palace,

► **Great Vine Harvest**
15/8/00-15/9/00
The harvest of the largest and oldest known vine in Europe usually takes place at the end of August and lasts for around two weeks. Dates to be confirmed

► **The Cavalier King**
21/10/00-29/10/00
A variety of activities for all ages explores the life and times of this memorable monarch

► **Lantern Lit Tours**
20/11/00-20/12/00
Lantern lit tours of Henry VIII's vast kitchens and apartments with tales of rich history and famous inhabitants. Booking essential on 020 8781 9540. Not suitable for young children. Dates to be confirmed

► **A Tudor Christmas**
27/12/00-3/1/01
Combine history with festivities and discover the very essence of a Tudor Christmas including entertainment and festive food. Dates to be confirmed

Performing Arts

Polesden Lacey Open Air Theatre

Great Bookham Dorking Surrey RH5 6BD

[M25 3.5m from J9]

Tel: 01372 451596/457223

This Open Air Theatre is situated on high rolling ground less than 25 miles from the centre of London. This 1300 acre National Trust Estate has some of the finest views in Surrey and provides a memorable location for our Open Air Theatre performances. 1400 seats in the auditorium, 300 grass enclosure places, special facilities for the disabled, hot and cold snacks available from 18.00. Free car parking, information tent, grounds open for picnicking at all events, licensed bar with wines, beers, spirits, mulled wine and soft drinks. Interval drinks may be booked in advance. Bookings to be made via: The National Trust Southern Region Box Office, PO Box 10, Dorking, Surrey RH5 6FH.

1998 Season: 20 June-5 July
Mardi Gras: A£12.00 C£6.00 Groups 10+ 10% discount. Children's Concert: A£8.00 C£5.00 C(0-5)£Free Groups 10+ 10% discount. Polesden Prom: A£12.00 C£7.00. King Lear & The Merry Widow: from £6.00-£13.00 concessions and discounts avilable for some performances. The Pasadena Roof Orchestra: from £9.00-£11.00 no concessions or discount avialable

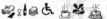

Spectator Sports

Craigie Taylor
Albury House The Street Albury Gilford Surrey GU5 NAE

Epsom Racecourse
Epsom Downs Epsom Surrey KT18 5LQ
[2m S of Epsom on B290, J8 & J9 M25. BR: Epsom Downs or Tattenham Corner]
Tel: 01372 726311 Fax: 01372 748253
www.demon.co.uk/racenews.epsom
Major races run: The Vodafone Derby; The Vodafone Oaks; Vodafone Diomed S; Vodafone Coronation Cup; Moet & Chandon Silver Magnum
Call for fixture list
Dependent on event
↓ *special events*
► **Derby Day**
10/6/00-10/6/00

Lingfield Park Racecourse
Lingfield Surrey RH7 6PQ
[M25 J6, S on A22 signposted. BR: Lingfield, London Bridge & Victoria. Helicopter landing by prior arrangement]
Tel: 01342 834800 Fax: 01342 835874
www.lingfieldpark.co.uk
The busiest racecourse in the country. 71 meetings on turf and all weather tracks. Major races run: Derby Trial; Oaks Trial; Silver Trophy; Summit Junior Hurdle. There is a 18 hole golf course, training permitted on All-Weather Track; special party rates available on application. Pavilion Suite also available for conference and exhibition centres.
All year for 58 publicised race meetings, see below

Members: A£15.00 C(under 16)£Free OAPs£2.00 voucher off food. Grandstand £11.00. Group rates available on application

discount offer: £2.00 discount per person, on production of coupon
↓ *special events*
► **February Fixtures**
2/2/00-26/2/00
Flat Winter Racing on Feb 2, 5, 9, 12, 16, 19, 23, and 26 which is Clowns and Magic Day
► **March Fixtures**
1/3/00-29/3/00
Flat Winter racing on Mar 1, 4, 8 and 29. Mixed Winter Derby on Mar 18
► **April Fixtures**
7/4/00-12/4/00
Flat Winter Racing on Apr 7 and 12
► **May Fixtures**
12/5/00-27/5/00
Flat Racing on May 12, 13 (Derby Trial Group 3 and Oaks Trial Listed Race), 20 (Cockney Night) and 27 (60s and 70s Night)
► **June Fixtures**
3/6/00-27/6/00
Flat Racing on June 3 (Victory Day), 6, 14, 25 (Country and Western Day), and 27
► **July Fixtures**
1/7/00-19/7/00
Flat Racing on July 1 (Australian Night), 12, 14 and 19
► **August Fixtures**
11/8/00-31/8/00
Flat Racing on Aug 11 (Family Fun Day), 19 (Ladies Night), 23 and 31
► **September Fixtures**
5/9/00-29/9/00
Flat Racing on Sept 5, 22 and 29
► **October Fixtures**
4/10/00-23/10/00
Flat Racing on Oct 4, 11 and 23 (Family Fun Day)
► **November Fixtures**
7/11/00-28/11/00
Flat Winter Racing on Nov 7, 9, 14, 18, 22 and 28
► **December Fixtures**
6/12/00-28/12/00
Flat Winter Racing on Dec 6, 13, 16, 20 and 28. National Hunt on Dec 9

Surrey

Surrey

Sandown Park Racecourse

Portsmouth Road Esher Surrey KT10 9AJ
[M25 J10, A3, A224 to Esher. BR: Esher from Waterloo. Helicopter landing with prior arrangement]

Tel: 01372 463072 465205

Racecourse of the Year for five consecutive years. On non-racing days , excellent facilities for exhibitions, banqueting, conferences, caravan rallies etc.

Call for list of fixtures
Feature Days: £7.00-16.00, Premier Days: £9.00-£17.00, Classic Days: £10.00-£26.00. Parking Classic: £6.00 Other: £5.00. Advanced bookings must not be made later than 3 clear working days before date of meeting for discount rates to apply

↓ *special events*

► **Pre Christmas Craft and Gift Fayre**
21/10/00-22/10/00
Speciality quality gifts for the Christmas season including entertainment, 10.00-18.00, tickets £1.00-£5.00

Sport & Recreation

Aquarius Sailing Club

c/o 21 Manor Drive North New Malden Surrey KT3 5PB
[on the river Thames just upstream from Hampton Court. Access is through a key system]

Tel: 020 8337 9000

The lively club has been going since 1948 and sails a range of small dinghies. The emphasis is on good fun cruising with a smattering of competitive - but not too serious racing. The club does compete locally and enjoys a good reputation amongst the river based clubs. Bar in the club house, with kitchen for members use, but no catering facilities.

Easter-1 Nov every Sun, Wed evenings in summer. Individual access at any time
New members welcome, annual membership A£48.00 C£11.00 one off entry fee for new members

🍺🥤

Theme & Adventure Parks

Chessington World of Adventures

Leatherhead Road Chessington Surrey KT9 2NE
[situated on the A243. Approximately 2m from both the A3 and J9/10 M25. BR: 30mins from Waterloo to Chessington Station on South West trains]

Tel: 01372 727227 Info Line Fax: 01372 725050

www.chessington.co.uk

Chessington World of Adventures, the South's No. 1 theme park and animal experience is filled with fantastic family adventures. Watch out for amazing new crazy cartoon land, opening in April 2000 featuring a world famous cartoon character in a multi-million pound investment. Also at Chessington the mighty Samurai ride, the swirling Rameses Revenge, plunging Dragon falls and wild encounters with exotic animals, you'll have an unbeatable day out.

visitor comments: All rides are free - you can ride as many times as you want. Good quality gifts. Staff are polite and friendly. Limited rides for very young children, but there's still loads to see and do, making it a great day.

5 April-29 Oct 10.00-17.00. 15 July-3 Sept Extra Happy Hours (open till 21.00). Family Fright Nights (open till 21.00) 21, 22, 27, 28 & 29 Oct Last Admission: 15.00
Queuing Times: Possible in peak season and weekends
A£19.50 C(under 4)£Free C(4-13)£15.50 OAPs£10.50 Disabled£9.50
Family Ticket £59.00 Group rates available for 12+ for details call: 01372 729560 (prices subject to change)

Thorpe Park

Staines Lane Chertsey Surrey KT16 8PN

[J11 or 13 M25 on A320 between Chertsy / Staines]
Tel: 01932 562633 Fax: 01932 566367
www.thorpepark.co.uk
The Great Thorpe Park offers thrills, excitement and a great day out for all the family. New for 1999 Pirates 4-D: you may have experienced 3-D and you may have been stunned by the visual effects, but for the first time in the UK and only at Thorpe Park you can experieince the 'fourth dimension', an experenice so new, so intense you'll never trust your senses again! Recoil as the edvanture comes alive before your eyes and not only see and hear, but also feel the action. Thorpe Park is also the UK's wettest theme park, you'll get Wet Wet Wet! whatever the weather on the 3 torpedo tubes that twist and turn in all directions before spilling you out into the pool below, or take the plunge on an inflatable raft down a 40ft slide as you Depth Charge. If you want to get wetter still, try white water rafting on Thunder River, or the world famous Loggers Leap, a water flume that's wet, wild, wonderful and the highest in the UK! And don't forget the little ones who have a water ride of their very own, Dino Bumper Boats, where they can get bumper to bumper in motorised rubber tyres in this watery version of dodgems. Of course Thorpe Park still has everything you could need for a perfect day out, whatever your age or shoe size! Adrenaline-seekers can scream in fear as they realise there is X:\ No Way Out - the world's first and only pitch-black backwards rollercoaster - whilst younger 'pink knuckle' riders will enjoy the Flying Fish rollercoaster. Little ones can make friends with the animals on Thorpe Farm, climb aboard one of the rides in Octopus Garden, enjoy the lives shows and music or explore Slides by SLides, a slide and climb playground in a tropical setting. And with the excellent catering facilities on park you need never run out of energy!
visitor comments: Editor's Choice. Great for children of all ages (and adults!). Plenty of space to run around. Beach area with waterslides. An excellent day out!
Feb-Nov daily. Midnight weekend & Bank Holiday opening in August
Queuing Times: varies
A£16.50 C(0.9m)£Free C(1.4m)£13.00 C(1.4m+)£15.95 OAPs&Disabled£13.00 Carers/Helpers£15.95. New this year the Family Ticket (valid for 4 people, minimum 1 adult) for only £52.00. All you have to do is call the credit card hotline on 0990 880 880 before 17.00 on the day prior to your visit. Alternatively buy one on the day for £56.00.
↓*special events*
▶ **Christmas Craft Festival**
10/11/00-12/11/00
Ideal for those unusual Christmas gift ideas.

Commences 10.00-18.00. Tickets £1.00-£5.00

Farnham Tourist Information Centre
Council Offices South Street Farnham Surrey GU9 7RN
Tel: 01252 715109 Fax: 01252 725083
www.waverley.gov.uk
Mon-Thur 09.30-17.15 Fri 09.00-16.45 Sat 09.00 -12.00

Guildford Tourist Information Centre
14 Tunsgate Guildford Surrey GU1 3QT
[M25, A3 Guildford town centre]
Tel: 01483 444333
Tourist Information Centre supplying: Accommodation Booking; Post Office For Local Events; Town Guides.
Jan-30 Apr Mon-Sat 09.30-17.00, 1 May-30 Sept Mon-Sat 09.00-17.30 Sun 10.00-17.00, 1 Oct-31 Dec Mon-Sat 09.30-17.00

Transport Museums

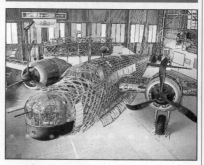

Brooklands Museum
Brooklands Road Weybridge Surrey KT13 7QN
[J10/11 A3 & M25]
Tel: 01932 857381 Fax: 01932 855465
www.motor-software.co.uk
Brooklands racing circuit was the birthplace of British motorsport and of British aviation. From 1907 when it opened, to 1987 when the British Aerospace factory closed, it was a world-renowned centre of engineering excellence. The Museum opened in 1991 on 30 acres of the original 1907 motor racing circuit and features Brookland racing cars and vintage aircraft as well as historic buildings. Home to John Cobb's 24 litre Napier-Railton. The Campell Shed in the restored motoring vil-

Surrey

lage is now open with a new display telling the story of Brooklands Track from 1907. 'Percy' is supposed to haunt the Banking by the Members Bridge, he died on Hallowe'en!
All year Tue-Sun, Summer: 10.00-17.00. Winter: 10.00-16.00, closed Good Fri & Christmas week Last Admission: 16.00
A£6.00 OAPs&Students£5.00 C(5-16)£4.00
discount offer: One Child Free With Each Adult Paying Full Admission

↓ *special events*
► **Morris and Austin Day**
12/3/00-12/3/00
► **Napier Railton Demonstration Runs**
26/3/00-14/5/00
Held on Mar 26 and May 14 only
► **Mazda Rx7 Meeting**
2/4/00-2/4/00
► **"Aircool 2000"**
9/4/00-9/4/00
► **MG Day - The MG Era**
16/4/00-16/4/00
► **London Douglas Motorcycle Club**
23/4/00-23/4/00
► **Alternative Power Day**
24/4/00-24/4/00
► **20 Ghost Club Annual Driving Tests**
30/4/00-30/4/00
► **'May-Day' - Emergency Vehicle Gathering**
1/5/00-1/5/00
All manner of vintage and classic emergency vehicles with demonstrations
► **Citroen Specials and STD Interregister**
7/5/00-7/5/00
► **Classic Camper Club and Kougar Owners Club**
14/5/00-14/5/00
► **Jaguar Drivers Club International Spring Rally**
21/5/00-21/5/00
► **Axa Classic Rally Start**
28/5/00-28/5/00
► **British Sportscar Day**
4/6/00-4/6/00
The Past- The Present-The Future
► **The Indian Motorcycle Club of Great Britain**
11/6/00-11/6/00
► **Napier Motor Carriage Centenary**
18/6/00-18/6/00
With Esher Model Flying Club Display also
► **Brooklands Society Reunion**
2/7/00-2/7/00
► **Brooklands Italian Festival**
8/7/00-9/7/00
Normal admission plus additional charge
► **Brooklands to Beaulieu Run**
23/7/00-23/7/00
With Panther Car Club also
► **Norton Owners Club**
29/7/00-29/7/00
► **BMW Car Club 02 Register**

6/8/00-6/8/00
► **Stag Owners Club National Day**
13/8/00-13/8/00
► **Jensen Club**
20/8/00-20/8/00
► **Bristol Owners Club Annual Concours**
27/8/00-27/8/00
► **South East Alvis Day**
3/9/00-3/9/00
► **Brooklands Relived - VMCC**
10/9/00-10/9/00
► **The TVR Brooklands Gathering**
17/9/00-17/9/00
► **Rover SD1**
24/9/00-24/9/00
► **Railton Owners Club Meeting**
30/9/00-30/9/00
► **Midget and Sprite Club Meeting**
1/10/00-1/10/00
► **Dudley Gahagan Memorial Sprint**
7/10/00-7/10/00
► **Autumn Italian Car Day**
8/10/00-8/10/00
► **750 Motor Club Autumn Festival**
21/10/00-21/10/00

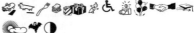

Dapdune Wharf
Wharf Road Guildford Surrey GU1 4RR
[just off A320 in Guildford Town centre behind Surrey Sports Ground]
Tel: 01483 561389 Fax: 01483 561389
The Wey was one of the first British rivers to be made navigable, and opened to barge traffic in 1653. This 15.5 mile waterway linked Guildford to Weybridge on the Thames, and thence to London. The Godalming Navigation, opened in 1764, enabled barges to work a further 4 mile up river. Dapdune Wharf in Guildford is the home of Reliance, a restored Wey barge, as well as models and an interactive exhibition telling the story of the waterway, the people who lived and worked on it, and the barges built there. New for 1998 is a tea room and ice-creams normally available at Dapdune Wharf and electric launch river bus service - from Dapdune Wharf to Guildford, operating during opening hours; additional charge (including NT members).
1 Apr-1 Nov Wed 12.00-17.00, Weekends & Bank Hol 11.00-17.00. Pre-booked groups and school parties welcome throughout the year.
A£2.50 Family Ticket £6.00. Pre-booked groups £1.50

↓ *special events*
► **Working Waterways Week**
15/4/00-16/4/00
A weekend of guided walks along the towpath, with demonstrations, displays and boat trips to mark the start of Woking Waterways Week. Call

Surrey

for details. Donations welcome

► Easter Egg Hunts
20/4/00-24/4/00

Follow a trail around Dapdune Wharf and Island. Two trails available, suitable for 3-6 and 7-13 year olds, C£1.00 plus usual admission, 11.00-17.00

► Lock Up Your Kids!
27/5/00-4/6/00

A week of activities including boat trips to the lock, £2 per boat trip plus usual admission, 11.00-17.00 on 27-29 May, 1-3 June

► Down Your Wey
18/6/00-18/6/00

Pond dipping, hurdle making, nature trails, river walks and boat trips are just some of the things you can see and do on this family day out, usual admission, 11.00-17.00

► Coracle Making
24/6/00-25/6/00

Discover how these unique boats are made and see how they are handled in the water, usual admission, 11.00-17.00

► Guildford Boat Gathering
1/7/00-1/7/00

Annual gathering of boats. Follow the Raft Race from Millmead Lock at 14.30 and watch the Decorated Boat Pageant in the Meadows at 18.00, donations welcome

► Get Knotted
1/7/00-2/7/00

Try your hand at tying up a boat or learn how to make a rope fender or keyring. Cost of materials plus usual admission, 11.00-17.00

► Walk this Wey!
9/7/00-9/7/00

Meet the Lengthsman at Millmead Lock (SU996992) for this 4-mile walk, £1.00, 14.30-16.00

► Walk this Wey!
16/7/00-16/7/00

A wildlife activity walk for adults with younger children. Meet your guide at Millmead Lock (SU996992) for this 1-mile walk. The walk will end at Dapdune Wharf, £1.00 donation, 14.30-16.00

► Walk this Wey!
23/7/00-23/7/00

Stoke Lock, Guildford, Surrey - A walk along the towpath and adjoining Riverside Park. Meet the Lengthsman at Stoke Lock (TQ002516) for this 3.5-mile walk, £1.00 donation, 14.30-16.00

► Treasure Hunts
27/7/00-30/7/00

Follow a map of Dapdune Wharf and Island, collecting clues which will lead you to the hidden treasure. Trails for 3-6 and 7-13 year olds, £1.00 plus usual admission, 11.00-17.00

► Treasure Hunts
1/8/00-31/8/00

See entry for 29 July, except on each Thur, Sat, Sun and Bank Hol in August

► Treasure Hunts
2/9/00-3/9/00

See entry for 27 July

► National Heritage Open Day
9/9/00-10/9/00

Free entry to Dapdune Wharf and other buildings along the Navigations. Free guided walks also, donations welcome

► Guided Walk
10/9/00-10/9/00

Discover about the varied past of Coxes Mill. Meet the Lengthsman, Kevin Morgan, at Coxes Mill Pond (TQ061641), £1.00 donation, 14.30-16.00

► Guided Walk
10/9/00-10/9/00

This walk will look at the clues to the Wey's industrial past which still survive today. Meet the Lengthsman at Stoke Lock (TQ002516) for this 3.5-mile walk, £1.00 donation, 14.00-15.30

► Pirate Party / Treasure Trail
30/7/00-30/7/00

Fancy dress competition for best dressed pirate, treasure hunts and other activities, £1.00 plus usual admission, 11.00-17.00

Land Rover Museum

Alfold Road Dunsfold Godalming Surrey GU8 4NP

Tel: 01483 200567 Fax: 01483 200738

Zoos

Gatwick Zoo

Russ Hill Glovers Road Charlwood Horley Surrey RH6 0EG

[Signposted off A23]

Tel: 01293 862312 Fax: 01293 862550

The zoo covers almost 10 acres and has hundreds of birds and mammals. The monkey island has spider and squirrel monkeys and other animals and birds can be seen in large naturalised settings.

visitor comments: The Zoo is nicely set out around Monkey Island - take along a picnic. Wonderful for small children.

All year daily Mar-Oct 10.30-18.00 Nov-Feb 10.30-dusk

Last Admission: 60 mins before closing

A£3.95 C(3-14)£2.95 C(0-3)£Free OAPs£3.45

Sussex

Sussex

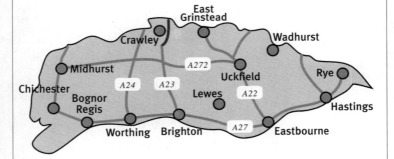

Sussex

Abbeys

South Downs

Eastbourne East Sussex *[South Downs meet at the sea at the Seven Sisters. Car parking at Crowlink and Birling Gap]*
Tel: 01892 890651 Fax: 01892 890110

The South Downs meet the sea at the Seven Sisters, just west of Eastbourne in East Sussex, forming one of the best-known and loved lengths of coast in England. There are some of the most delightful walks and unspoilt views. There are no designated wheelchair routes and visitors may wander where they wish.
All year any reasonable hour
Admission free

Animal Attractions

Fishers Farm Park

Newpound Lane Wisborough Green Billingshurst West Sussex RH14 0EG
[off A272]
Tel: 01403 700063 Fax: 01403 700823
www.fishersfarmpark.co.uk

Fishers Farm Park is a unique place to visit, mixing rural activities with up front fun and gives the whole family a wonderful day out. There is so much to do whatever the weather. The Farmyard and barns give children and adults the opportunity to see animals well cared for in a happy environment, close enough to touch - you can even enter some of the pens to say hello to the goats and lambs. The play areas are designed for varying age groups, ideally suited for toddlers to 9 year olds, with everything from toddlers swings to a giant zip slide. Have an ice-cream on the Beach, while the children paddle, then meander through the woods to the Fun-karts, tractor track and toddlers race circuit! While the grown-ups can enjoy tea and home-made cakes, the children can burn off their remaining energy racing around the 3-level playzone and drop slide.

visitor comments: Good facilities for children. Excellent playground. Plenty of farm animals and hands-on experience.
All year daily 10.00-17.00. Closed 25 & 26 Dec Mid Season: A£5.00 C&OAPs£4.50 Family Tickets (A2+C2)£17.00, (A2+C3)£21.25, (A3+C3)£25.50. High Season: A£6.00 C&OAPs£5.50 Family Tickets (A2+C2)£21.00, (A2+C3)£26.25, (A3+C3)£31.50. Nov & Jan: Low Season special weekday prices

Gumber Bothy Gumber Farm

Slindon Estate Nr Arundel Warden Arundel West Sussex BN18 0RG
[No vehicular access 1m to S of South Downs Way BR: Amberley 4m via South Downs Way]
Tel: 01243 814554/814484

Traditional West Sussex farm buildings in this peaceful and unspoilt area of the South Downs. The Bothy is one mile from the South Downs Way and 5 minutes walk from Stane Street, the old Roman road. Set in the heart of the 1417-ha Slindon Estate, the Bothy makes an ideal base for exploring the many rights-of-way.
31 Mar-end Oct. Please phone for details A£5.00 C£2.50. Reduction for parties of 12 or more Mon-Fri only. Possible price increase

Seven Sisters Sheep Centre

The Fridays East Dean Eastbourne Sussex BN20 0DG
[4m W of Eastbourne off A259. Plenty of on site parking available]
Tel: 01323 423207 Fax: 01323 423302

A family run farm for animal lovers of all ages, with over 45 British breeds of sheep and all the other farm favourites, tame enough to touch and feed. Daily bottle feeding sessions. Lambing time 4 March until 1 May then closed until 20 May. 20 May until 3 September, come and see daily shearing and sheep milking demonstrations. Tractor trailer rides, tea room, gift shop and picnic area.

visitor comments: Good value. Lambing time is a delight.
4 Mar-1 May & 20 May-3 Sept Mon-Fri 14.00-17.00. Sat & Sun and East Sussex school hol 11.00-17.00
Last Admission: 16.00
A£3.00 C(2-15)£2.00 Concessions£2.50
discount offer: Two For The Price Of One. Valid Until 3 Sept 2000

Archaeology

Worthing Museum and Art Gallery

Chapel Road Worthing West Sussex BN1 1HP
[on A24/A27]
Tel: 01903 239999 /204229 Sat Fax: 01903 236277

A particularly rich collection of archaeological finds is displayed in this museum. There are artifacts from prehistoric, Roman, Anglo-Saxon and medieval times, a downland display, toys, pottery, pictures and a large costume collection from the 18th to 20th centuries. A wheelchair is available for disabled visitors and

there are entrance ramps, toilets and a lift.
All year Mon-Sat Summer: 10.00-18.00, Winter:
10.00-17.00
Admission Free

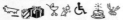

Arts, Crafts & Textiles

Brighton Museum and Art Gallery
Church Street Brighton East Sussex BN1 1UE
[M23 / A23: London A27: Lewes & Worthing
10mins from BR: Brighton]
Tel: 01273 290900 Fax: 01273 292841
Houses delightful collections of local and
national importance, highlights include Art
Nouveau and Art Deco design, fashion from
the 18th century to the 1980's, 'My Brighton,'
history at the touch of a screen, Galleries of
Non-Western Art, hands-on Archaeology
Discovery Room, history galleries with children's activities and temporary exhibitions.
The museum will undergo a major facelift
after being awarded a Lottery Heritage Grant
of £7.6 million. More space will be created to
ensure some of the museum's national collections to be displayed including the Henry
Willet Collection of Pottery and Porcelain.
There will also be new interactive displays and
photographs on the urban and social history
of Brighton and Hove. With a lift and improve-
ments for disabled visitors work has already
commences with the completion expected for
2001, the museum will remain open during
refurbishment. Disabled access to ground floor
only.
All year Mon, Tue, Thur, Fri & Sat 10.00-17.00,
Sun 14.00-17.00. Closed Good Fri 24-26 Dec
Last Admission: 17.00
Admission Free

Hastings Embroidery
White Rock Theatre White Rock Hastings East
Sussex TN34 1JX
[on the sea front opposite the Pier]
Tel: 01424 781000 Fax: 01424 781170
Housed in the White Rock Theatre the 80 yard
embroidery illustrates great events in British
history from 1066 to modern times. It was
sewn by the Royal School of Needlework using
threads, cords, metals, lace, jewels and appropriate cloths. For details of Theatre
Productions see events below or call for a
brochure.
All year 11.00-16.00 (except Mar and 25 Dec)
Last Admission: 1 hr before closing
A£2.00 Concessions£1.00 Reductions for parties
over 20
↓*special events*

► **Jim Davidson**
22/3/00-22/3/00
At 19.45, adults only, tickets £15.50 and £13.50
► **Barnum**
15/4/00-22/4/00
At 19.30 and matineè on Apr 19 and 22 only at
14.30
► **Hank Marvin**
26/4/00-26/4/00
At 19.30, tickets £15.50 and £14.50
► **The Golden Age of Hollywood**
28/4/00-28/4/00
At 19.30, tickets £10.00 and £8.00
► **The New Adventures of the Chuckle**
Brothers
6/5/00-6/5/00
Held at 14.00 and 17.00, tickets £7.50 and £6.50
► **Carmen**
12/5/00-13/5/00
Held at 19.30, tickets £13.50 and £10.00
► **Mack and Mabel**
27/5/00-3/6/00

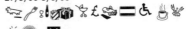

Hastings Museum and Art Gallery
Johns Place Cambridge Road Hastings East
Sussex TN34 1ET
[off A21 beside sports complex]
Tel: 01424 781155 Fax: 01424 781165
A wide variety of displays, including new
dinosaur, local wildlife, and North American
Indian galleries, also local industry and iron-
work as well as painting and ceramics. For
those special events marked with an *, a
British Sign Language interpreter is available
on request. Please give at least two weeks
notice.
All year Mon-Fri 10.00-17.00, Sat 10.00-13.00 &
14.00-17.00, Sun 15.00-17.00
Admission Free
↓*special events*
► **The Artists Journey**
8/2/00-27/2/00
► **The Sussex Archaeological Society**
3/3/00-3/3/00
*Please call for details *
► **'Ragtime, "Jelly Roll" and All That Jazz'**
10/3/00-10/3/00
An exploration of the roots of the finest truly
American music from its bawdy low-life begin-
nings to its finest hour in the 1930s and 40s,
£6.50
► **Native American Indian Crafts**
25/3/00-25/3/00
Maximum 15 places, please call for details
► **The Beginning of Recorded Sound 1876-**
1925
7/4/00-7/4/00
*Call for further details *
► **Dinosaurs and Dodos**

8/4/00-4/6/00
A hands-on exhibition following dinosaurs through time. The Dodo makes a special appearance in a display of pictures, artefacts and art works
► **Dinosaur Day**
26/4/00-26/4/00
Make a dinosaur mask, footprint or model. Children under 7 must be accompanied by an adult. £0.50 per child, no booking necessary
► **Resort Costume**
5/5/00-5/5/00
*Call for more information ***
► **New Moire Music and Improvised Duets for the Millennium.**
27/5/00-27/5/00
Hastings composer and saxophonist Trevor Watts, has composed new music for the Moire Millennium Group. Tickets A£6.50 Concessions£4.50
► **Create a Creature**
27/5/00-27/5/00
Create a mythical creature for the new Millennium. Please call for details
► **Meet Barry the Badger**
10/6/00-10/6/00
45 minute sessions starting at 11.00, 14.00 and 15.30
► **Clobber**
17/6/00-20/8/00
*An exhibition about youth, identity, image and going out, created by young people for young people. ***
► **Native American Indian Beadwork**
24/6/00-24/6/00
All day workshop for persons aged 16 and above. A£10.00 Concessions£5.00
► **Coastal Currents 2000**
2/9/00-29/10/00
*Exhibition of photographs produced by Effie Paleologou over a six month residency, exploring ideas of a sense of place and location ***
► **Patterns Through Time**
11/10/00-31/12/00
*Work from the Embroiderers' Guild Collection (Hampton Court) and contemporary pieces by members of the East Sussex Guild ***

Hove Museum and Art Gallery
19 New Church Road Hove East Sussex BN3 4AB
[BR: Hove 15mins walk. Bus: 1 / 6 / 19 / 25 / 49 / 49A]
Tel: 01273 290200 Fax: 01273 292827
Superb collection of paintings, applied arts and South East Arts Collection of Contemporary Craft. Home to 'Hove to Hollywood' film gallery and magical Childhood Room. Continuous programme of exhibitions. Wheelchair access to ground floor. Toilet adapted for wheelchair users.

All year Tue-Sat 10.00-17.00, Sun 14.00-17.00.
Café: Wed-Sun. Closed Mon, 23-26 Dec & 1 Jan
Admission Free

Pallant House Gallery
9 North Pallant Chichester West Sussex PO19 1TJ
Tel: 01243 774557 Fax: 01243 536038
This faithfully restored Queen Anne town house contains one of the finest collections of 20th century British art in the country. Permanent collections include the Hussey and Kearley bequests, the Geoffrey Freeman collection of Bow porcelain and enamels and many fine pieces of antique furniture. Exciting temporary exhibitions held throughout the year.
All year Tue-Sat 10.00-17.00, Sun & Bank Hol 12.30-17.00
Last Admission: 16.45
A£2.80 C£1.00 OAPs£2.20 Students£1.70

Rye Art Galleries
Easton Rooms 107 High Street Rye East Sussex TN31 7JE
[pass through the Landgate arch into Rye High Street and the Easton Rooms' entrance is approximately 300yds on the L]
Tel: 01797 222433/223218 Fax: 01797 225376
Rye Art Gallery has two exhibition areas: The Easton Rooms and The Stormont Studio, linked by a courtyard with a magnificent garden view over the marsh towards the sea. It's lively and ambitious programme featuring the very best of contemporary fine and applied art make it a must to visit.
All year daily 10.30-13.00 then 14.00-17.00.
Closed occasionally for re-hanging
Last Admission: 16.00
Admission £Free, purchase prices range from £3.00-£3,000

Sculpture at Goodwood
Hat Hill Copse Goodwood Chichester West Sussex PO18 0QP
[4m N of Chichester follow signs to Goodwood House from A285 located on Goodwood-East Dean Lane]
Tel: 01243 538449 Fax: 01243 531853
www.sculpture.org.uk
Contemporary British sculpture with changing displays. Works commissioned from major and emerging British artists.
5 Mar-31 Oct Thur-Sat 10.30-16.30
Last Admission: 15.30
A£10.00 C&Students£6.00 Concessions available

Sussex

The Truggery

Coopers Croft Herstmonceux Hailsham East Sussex BN27 1QL

[on A271 outskirts at Herstmonceux, 9m from Eastbourne. From A22 at Hailsham, Boship roundabout, take A271 in direction of Bexhill for 4m]

Tel: 01323 832314 Fax: 01323 832314

Local craftsmen can be seen in the workshop on weekdays demonstrating preparation of timber, use of the drawknife and assembly of a trug. Full range of trugs and English basket-ware for sale in the shop.

All year Tue-Sat 10.00-17.00. Open some Bank Hol and Sun in summer call before making a special journey
Last Admission: 17.00
Admission Free

Towner Art Gallery and Local Museum

High Street Borough Lane Old Town Eastbourne East Sussex BN20 8BB

[on A259]

Tel: 01323 411688/417961 Fax: 01323 648182

Housed in an elegant 18th century building set in delightful gardens in Eastbourne Old Town. Home to a splendid collection of 19th and 20th century British art including the SE Arts Collection of Contemporary Art and a gallery devoted to Eric Ravilious, Eastbourne's most acclaimed 20th century artist.

All Year Mar-Nov Tue-Sat 12.00-17.00, Sun & Bank Hol 14.00-17.00, Nov-Mar closing time 16.00. Closed 24-27 Dec, 1 Jan, Good Fri
Last Admission: 30mins before closing
Admission Free Parties over 15 book in advance
Charge for special exhibitions

Birds, Butterflies & Bees

Bentley Wildfowl and Motor Museum
Harveys Lane Halland Lewes East Sussex BN8 5AF

[7m NE of Lewes signposted on A22, A26 & B2192]

Tel: 01825 840573 Fax: 01825 841322

Hundreds of swans, geese and ducks from all over the world can be seen on lakes and ponds along with flamingoes and peacocks. Fine array of Veteran, Edwardian and Vintage vehicles, house has splendid antiques and wildfowl paintings. Woodland walks, nature-trail, audio-visual in the education centre, adventure playground, and miniature train running during Summer weekends and Bank Holiday Mondays. Guild of Sussex Craftsmen. Dogs only in parking area.

Grounds, Wildfowl Reserve & Motor Museum: 20 Mar-31 Oct daily 10.30-16.30 (17.00 in July & Aug) Nov & Feb & 1-19 Mar weekends only 10.30-16.00. Closed Dec-Jan. House: 1 Apr-31 Oct 12.00-17.00 closed in winter
Last Admission: 16.30
A£4.80 C(under 3)£Free C(4-15)£3.00 Family Ticket (A2+C4)£14.50 OAPs&Students£3.80.
Group rates 11+ 10% discount. Special rates for pre-booked school parties and the disabled
discount offer: Two For The Price Of One

WWT Arundel, The Wildfowl and Wetlands Trust

Mill Road Arundel West Sussex BN18 9PB

[close to the A27 & A29, at Arundel follow the brown signs, 0.75m along Mill Road on the right hand side. 1.5m from BR: Arundel]

Tel: 01903 883355 Fax: 01903 884834

Make a direct contribution to conservation. WWT Arundel is a place to visit 364 days of the year. Over 1,000 ducks, swans and geese. Take a walk in beautiful scenery overlooked by Arundel Castle, or watch birds from our superb viewing gallery, or restaurant. Guide Dogs admitted only.

All year daily, Summer: 09.30-17.30, Winter: 09.30-16.30, Closed Christmas
Last Admission: Summer 17.00 Winter 16.00
A£4.25 C(4-16)£2.25 Family Ticket(A2+C2) £10.75 OAPs£3.25 Pre-booked Party 10+ A£3.25 C£1.95 OAPs£2.60

Country Parks & Estates

Woods Mill Countryside Centre

Sussex Wildlife Trust Woods Mill Henfield West Sussex BN5 9SD

[1.5m S of Henfield on A2037]

Tel: 01273 492630 Fax: 01273 494500

The centre consists of a wildlife and country-

Sussex

side exhibition in an 18th-century watermill, and a trail through varied habitats. Partial access for the disabled.
Reserve: Apr-Sept daily 11.00-17.00.
Countryside Centre: Sun 11.00-17.00
A£1.00 C£0.50

Festivals & Shows

Airbourne 2000
Seafront and Western Lawns Eastbourne East Sussex [A22 from London, A259 from Hastings, A27 from Brighton. BR: Trains from London & Gatwick hourly]
Fax: 01323 638686
www.eastbourne.org/events
Four day airshow. Vast range of flying displays, arena displays, trade stands, Red Arrows, RAF exhibition, helicopter rides and grand finale fireworks.
Aug 17-20 2000 10.00-18.00
Admission Free

Battle Festival 2000
Sussex TN39 5HY
[Battle is located in the centre of 1066 country and is well signposted from all local directions]
Tel: 01424 773322 Fax: 01424 773436
Battle Festival 2000 sees the 40th Battle Arts Festival & the Millennium theme is "Back to the Future." The emphasis is on YOUTH and EXPERIENCE & some events are being specially devised for older age groups. At the same time there will be Youth Bands & Youth Street Theatre as well as the usual mix of Literature, Classical Music, Drama, Town Walks, Live music in Pubs and Open Air Art Exhibitions. Some events take place at Battle Abbey, others at hotels around the town, some in Battle Memorial Hall and the youth performances will tour the local villages. For further details a FREE Festival Brochure is available from April at your local T.I.C or call the Battle T.I.C on 01424 773721 for accommodation deals also. Visit East Sussex's Oldest Arts Festival and step BACK TO THE FUTURE!
July 1-14 2000
A£2.50-£15.00 C£1.00 Some free events, group rates by arrangement.

Bexhill 100 Festival of Motoring
The Seafront De La Warr Parade Bexhill-on-Sea Sussex TN40 1LS
[Between Hastings and Eastbourne on A259 coast road. From London A22, A21 and M23]
Tel: 01424 730564 Fax: 01424 730564
www.bexhill100.co.uk
This unique Festival (sponsored by Hastings Direct Insurance) celebrates Bexhill-on-Sea as the birthplace of British Motor Racing in 1902 and takes place on the May Bank Holiday Weekend each year, displaying hundreds of veteran, vintage, classic, custom, racing, American and military vehicles on an elegant Edwardian seafront, the original track. One of the largest, most popular family events in the South of England with stands, shops, stalls, funfair, aerobatics, kid's rides, marching bands, an entertainment marquee and yachts bobbing out at sea - something for everyone.
Apr 29-May 1 2000 10.00-18.00 (evening only on Apr 29) See events below
Admission Free

↓ *special events*

► **Bexhill 100 Festival of Motoring**
29/4/00-29/4/00
The evening of April 29 sees a Classic Vehicle town parade with street entertainment and fireworks to follow.
► **Bexhill 100 Festival of Motoring**
30/4/00-1/5/00

Brighton Festival 2000
Brighton Sussex BN1 1EL
[events take place at various venues throughout Brighton]
Tel: 01273 700747 Fax: 01273 707505
www.brighton-festival.org.uk
England's biggest arts festival takes place every May in Brighton. Families will enjoy our opening Children's Parade, circus, funfair and special children's theatre shows. With some 900 events over 3 weeks, there is plenty to see and do in Brighton at Festival time. Our free festival programme will be available in March.
May 6-28 2000
Prices are dependant on the choice of event

Brighton Kite Festival
The Sheepfold Peacehaven East Sussex BN10 8EG
[on A27 near Uni of Sussex.]
Tel: 01273 582309
Held on the 8th and 9th of July this exciting festival includes Kites of all shapes and sizes, children's workshops and competitions.
July 8-9 2000
Admission Free

Chiddingly Festival 1999
Various venues Chiddingly East Sussex *[off A22 at Golden Cross between Uckfield / Hailsham]*
Tel: 01825 872338
www.chiddingly.co.uk

Sussex

Chiddingly Festival is a small mixed rural Arts Festival extending over two weeks. Celebrating it's 22nd anniversary in 2000, this small rural community, and award winning Festival, have attracted artists from all over the world. Providing a platform where both amateur and professionals can share their talent and abilities the Festival has managed, with the help of its sponsors, to come in within budget each year.
Sept 2000 at various times, dates to be confirmed
Various prices

Corpus Christi Carpet of Flowers 2000

Cathedral of Our Lady and St. Philip Howard Arundel Sussex BN18 9AY
[A27 midway between Worthing / Chichester. Car and coach parking in Mill Road by the main Castle entrance]
Tel: 01903 882297 Fax: 01903 885335
Corpus Christi is celebrated each year 60 days after Easter and has become a very special event for the people of Arundel and its many visitors. A unique event in this country, with a carpet of fresh flowers 93ft long is lain down the centre aisle of the Cathedral which was first established by the Duke of Norfolk in 1877.
June 21-22 2000, 21st 09.30-21.00, 22nd 10.45-17.00
Admission Free

Crawley Festival and Folk Festival

The Hawth Hawth Avenue Crawley West Sussex RH10 6YZ
[M23 J10, follow the Theatre signs]
Tel: 01293 553636 Box Office Fax: 01293 533362
www.hawth.co.uk
Festival: Events throughout the town from a High Street Fair to open air concerts. Folk Festival: A two-day spectacular featuring performances from top British and Irsh bands and American music, plus dance groups, stalls, workshops, food, bars, camping facilities and free parking. Plus concerts Friday and Saturday featuring top named bands. Full programme available from the end of May 2000.
Festival: June 24-July 8, Folk Fstival: June 30-July 2
Prices vary from approx: A£5.00-£25.00, C£Free-£14.00, Concessions£3.50-£20.00

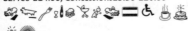

Direct Line International Ladies Tennis Championships 2000

International Lawn Tennis Centre Devonshire Park College Road Eastbourne Sussex BN21 4JJ
[A22 from London, A259 from Hastings, A27 from Brighton. Trains from London & Gatwick hourly]
Tel: 01323 415442 Fax: 01323 638686
www.eastbourne.org/events
A Wimbledon warm-up featuring professional players from all over the world. Traditional English Garden Party atmosphere and surroundings.
June 17-24 2000 09.00-close of play
Prices range from £2.00 for ground tickets and £22.00 for centre court tickets. Call box office 01323 412000

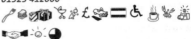

Downs Steam Show

office Dean Management P O Box 12 Chichester West Sussex PO20 7PH
[venue: Weald and Downland Open Air Museum - Singleton - Chichester. On the A286 N of Chichester. Follow Brown sings for Open Air Museum]
Tel: 01243 641284 Fax: 01243 641284
The 9th annual Downs Steam Show at the Weald and Downland Open Air Museum, is located at one our finest museums, having a fascinating collection of over 40 regional historic buildings which have been restored and rebuilt to their original form. The Steam Show is a working event for traction engines, one of the major steam events in the south. With timber sawing and hauling, road rolling and a vintage fair, plus a range of vintage machinery, models and rural bygones, the event and the Museum present a superb day out.
Aug 2000, dates to be confirmed, 10.00-17.00 both days
A£5.20 C£2.50 Family Tickets ££14.00. Group rates direct from Weald and Downland Open Air Museum

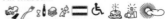

East Preston Festival

Village Hall Sea Road East Preston Littlehampton Sussex BN16
[Off A259 between Rustington and Goring]
Tel: 01903 771161
Over 70 events take place during the week including an antiques market, exhibitions, craft market day, dance, drama, music and carnival parade.
Enjoy the varied programmes of events.
June 10-18 2000 10.00-19.30
Various

Eastbourne Millenium Dance Festival

Bishop Bell Secondary School Priory Road Eastbourne Sussex *[A22 from London, A27* from Brighton, A259 from Hastings. BR: from London and Gatwick hourly]

Daytime workshops consisting of American, English and International folk dancing. Four varieties of evening dances including French. Advisable to book in advance, call Box Office on 01323 895680.

Apr 28-May 1 2000 Times vary according to events

A£5.00 per workshop and approx. £35.00 for weekend season ticket.

Eastbourne Millennium Horse Show

Gildredge Park Saffrons Road Eastbourne Sussex [A22 from London, A27 from Brighton, A259 from Hastings. Trains from London & Gatwick hourly]

Tel: 01323 415000 Fax: 01323 410322

Show Jumping, Gymkhana, pony rides, dog show and children's attractions.

Aug 12-13 2000

A£3.00 C£Free Concessions to be confirmed

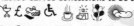

Eastbourne Women Millennium Celebration

Winter Garden Floral Hall Compton Road Eastbourne Sussex [A22 from London A27 from Brighton A259 from Hastings. BR: from London and Gatwick hourly]

Animate and inanimate display of changes to womens lives, showing crafts past and present and Millennium Masterchef competition final. Day will include static displays of changing decorative styles, links with local female artists and a demonstration on the development of cuisine.

July 1 2000 10.00-17.00

Free admission

Emergency 2000 "999 Display"

Western Lawns Eastbourne Seafront Eastbourne Sussex [A22 from London, A259 from Hastings, A27 from Brighton. Train from London and Gatwick hourly]

Tel: 01323 646600

A display of all 999 services and recovery services. Displays, demonstrations, stalls and attractions for children.

July 22-23 2000

Admission Free

Goodwood Motor Racing Circuit

Goodwood Chichester West Sussex PO18 0PX [from: J10 M25, take A3 to Milford, then A283 to Petworth, from Petworth take the A285 to Halnaker then follow signs to Goodwood. From: Southampton, Portsmouth, Worthing and Brighton take the A27 to Chichester and follow signs to Goodwood from the by-pass. From: Petersfield, Haslemere and A3 take A286 to

Singleton. From: Pulborough and Horsham, take A29 to meet A27, then as from Brighton]

Tel: 01243 755055 Fax: 01243 755058

www.goodwood.co.uk

Goodwood Circuit is the only completely original racetrack to have survived the pressures of the modern world, a classic circuit in the great tradition of post-war motor sport. The Goodwood Motor circuit first opened for racing in 1948. The brainchild of the ninth Duke of Richmond, better known to the motor racing fraternity as Freddie March. An integral part of Britain's post-war sporting heritage, Goodwood became the battle ground for such motor racing legends as Stirling Moss, Mike Hawthorn, Jim Clark and Graham Hill. Even today the lap record stands to Jim Clark and Jackie Stewart after an epic battle in 1965. Raised viewing platform for those in wheelchairs available. Access by disabled parking pass which must be applied for in advance.

Goodwood Revival Meeting: 15-17 Sept
Fri 15th Sept: Advance £10.00 On the Day £15.00 Sat 16th Sept: Advance £20.00 On the Day £25.00 Sun 17st Sept Advance £30.00 On the Day £35.00. Circuit Weekend (Fri, Sat & Sun) Advance Only £50.00. Grandstands (per seat) Fri Advance £10.00 On the Day £15.00 Sat Advance £15.00 On the Day £20.00 Sun Advance £25.00 On the Day £30.00

↓ *special events*

▶ **Goodwood Festival Of Speed**
23/6/00-25/6/00

World's biggest historic motor racing festival. Star drivers and rare cars. From 06.00-18.00

Herstmonceux Castle Medieval Festival

Herstmonceux Castle Hailsham Sussex BN27 1RP

[Rail: Polegate, bus every 30mins. Off the A271 signposted]

Tel: 01273 723249 Fax: 01273 723249

www.herstmonceux.com

Herstmonceux Castle Medieval Festival, now in its eighth year is Britain's largest three-day celebration of the colourful Middle Ages. In this magical setting, history will come to life. Hundreds of combatants with cannon support will siege the castle walls. Mounted Knights will joust and Europe's finest archers will compete. Activities and entertainment for the whole family, fire-eaters, falconry puppeteers, strolling minstrels, period craft stalls, living history village and kid's kingdom. 24hr recorded information: 0891 172902.

Aug 26-28 2000 10.00-18.00

A£10.00 C(3-13)£5.00 Concessions£9.00 Family Ticket £20.00 Group rates and advance tickets available: 01273 723249. 24hr recorded information 0891 172902.

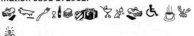

Hickstead Showground (All England Jumping Course)

London Road Hickstead Haywards Heath West Sussex RH17 5NU

[10m north of Brighton off A23. Bus: Brighton & Hove 01273 886200; London & Country Buses 01293 414081 / 0990 747777. An express coach service runs daily from Victoria Coach Station in Central London to Hickstead and return 0990 808080. Taxis operate to the showground from all Railway Stations. Ringside parking available on a first come first served basis, arrive early.]

Tel: 01273 834315 Fax: 01273 834452
www.hickstead.co.uk

Hickstead hosts The Royal International Horse Show, The European Showjumping Championships and The British Jumping Derby as well as the spectacular Summer Concert Season. The complete family day out. 150 Trade Stands, Children's Fun Fair, bars and restaurants.

All year depending on event
Admission to the two public grandstands is FREE and on a first come first served basis. Event prices are detailed in the events section. Coach parties 30+ attract 20% reduction

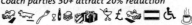

Horsham Town Centre Festival

Festival Office: Carfax North Street Horsham West Sussex RH12 1RL

[A24 to Horsham]

Tel: 01403 215265 Fax: 01403 215268

Three days of fantastic festival fun. Live music, dance spectacular, Battle of the Bands, Street entertainment and old time stree fayre with steam engines, carousel, big wheel and chair-o-planes.

Oct 2000, dates to be confirmed 10.00-22.00 each day
Admission Free, Fayre rides are charged

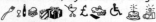

LTA Tennis Tournaments

ITLC Devonshire Park Eastbourne Sussex *[A22 from London, A259 from Hastings, A27 from Brighton. BR: trains hourly from London and Gatwick]*

A series of tournaments, the details of which can be found in the following special events.
July 24- Sept 10 2000. 11.00-close of play unless otherwise specified.
Free admission
↓ *special events*

► **LTA County Cup Tennis**
24/7/00-28/7/00
Six top counties compete for the LTA County Cup. All doubles matches, both ladies and mens competitions

► **LTA Family Festival of Tennis**
7/8/00-12/8/00
Competitive family fun tennis for ages 16 and below. 10.00-close of play

► **LTA Men's Inter-County 35+ Tennis Championship**
25/8/00-27/8/00
Inter-county lawn tennis championship for over 35's featuring 36 counties playing singles and doubles matches

► **LTA South of England Tennis Championship**
28/8/00-2/9/00
A tennis tournament for veterans attracting top players in singles and doubles matches

► **LTA Ladies Inter-County 35+ Tennis Championships**
8/9/00-10/9/00
Inter-county tennis fixture for over 35's featuring 28 counties playing singles and doubles

McKeevers Movers Fitness Fiesta 2000

Winter Garden Compton Road Eastbourne Sussex BN21

[A22 from London, A259 from Hastings, A27 from Brighton. Train from London and Gatwick hourly]

Tel: 01323 768530

Take part in sessions, workshops and watch displays. There will be keep fit, aerobics, salsa, rock 'n' roll, tap, line & belly dancing and gymnastics. There will be line dancing in the evening. Monies collected will support Osteoporosis and Blind Society.

July 2 2000, 10.00-17.00, 19.30-21.30
Daytime: nominal charge. Evening £4.00 for line dancing (booking required)

Millennium MG Rally

Western Lawns Grand Parade Eastbourne East Sussex *[A22 from London; A27 from Brighton; A259 from Hastings. Trains hourly from London and Gatwick]*

Tel: 01903 693915

A Rally starting in Petersfield with MG's ranging from 1920's to present day. Finishing in Eastbourne with an exhibition and live band.
Sept 3 2000 8.00-10.30 rally start 17.00 end of event
Admission Free

Rallye Entente Cordiale 2000

Sovereign Harbour Eastbourne Sussex *[A22 from London; A27 from Brighton; A259 from Hastings. Trains from Gatwick and London*

hourly. Plenty of on site parking.]
Fax: 01323 638686
www.eastbourne.org/events
A maritime festival in partnership with France.
Flotilla of yachts and motor boats, quay-side
entertainment, old Gaffers, water sports and
fireworks.
July 8-16 2000
Admission Free

Rye Medieval Festival 2000
Rye Sussex TN31 7NY
*[A259 Dover to Rye. A21(M) London to
Tonbridge to Rye]*
Tel: 01797 226696 Fax: 01797 223460
A medieval festival including battle re-enact-
ments, a grand procession, medieval music,
crafts and jousting. There will also be a long-
bow tournament, juggling convention and liv-
ing history. All for free!
Aug 5-6 2000, 10.00-17.00
Admission Free

Skate 2000
Princes Park and Parade Eastbourne Sussex
*[A22 from London, A259 from Hastings, A27
from Brighton. Trains every hour from London
and Gatwick.]*
Fax: 01323 638686
www.eastbourne.org/events
Speed skating, artistic demonstrations,
instructions, free participation, skating ramps
and roller disco.
July 30 2000 10.00-19.00
Admission Free

The Great South Downs Run (Jaguars)
Western Lawns Eastbourne Sussex *[A22 from
London, A27 from Brighton, A259 from
Hastings. BR: trains hourly from London and
Gatwick]*
Run starts from Petersfield in Hampshire with
1959-1999 Jaguar models taking part. Run
finishes in Eastbourne in full exhibition.
*May 14 2000 Rally start 08.30 then 12.00-17.00
on lawns*
Free admission

visions2000 - The Festival of
International Animated Theatre
Brighton Sussex *[University of Brighton on
Grand Parade, central Brighton]*
Tel: 01273 643012 Fax: 01273 643038
October 2000 see Brighton and the UK get ani-
mated with visions2000, Britain's largest festi-

val of international animated theatre.
visions2000 shows off extraordinary contemporary theatre which uses puppetry and props
in innovative ways. As well as performances
for adults and children, there are exhibitions
and film. Dramatic, daring and downright
entertaining!
*Oct 18-29 2000 performances and Oct 7-29
exhibitions*
Prices vary according to event.

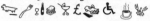

Walk 'n' Wheels
Sovereign Centre Royal Parade Eastbourne
Sussex *[A22 from London, A27 from Brighton,
A259 from Hastings. BR: from London and
Gatwick hourly]*
Part of the National event "Ride the Net" to
promote green methods of transport and the
cycle network. Includes a series of routed
walks, cycling taster sessions, historical and
modern bicycle displays and cycle rides.
*June 25 2000 10.00-17.00 (times to be con-
firmed)*
Reduced prices for early booking.

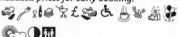

Folk & Local History
Museums

Battle and District Historical Society
Museum Trust
Memorial Hall High Street Battle Sussex TN33
0AQ
[opposite Abbey Green car park in Battle]
Tel: 01424 775955
The focal point is a diorama of the Battle of
Hastings and a reproduction of the Bayeux
Tapestry. There are also local history exhibits. A
Summer Arts Festival is held, and the Battle
Festival takes place in June/July. Special dis-
plays of old photographs, toys etc. are
arranged throughout the season.
*Easter-Sept Mon-Sat 10.00-16.30, Sun 14.00-
17.00*
Last Admission: 15mins before closing
A£1.00 C(accompanied)£Free otherwise £0.20
discount offer: Two For The Price Of One.

Castle and Museum of Sussex
Archaeology
Barbican House 169 High Street Lewes East
Sussex BN7 1YE
[located centrally in Lewes off the High Street.]
Tel: 01273 486290 Fax: 01273 486990
The imposing ruins of Lewes castle dominate
the town. Original Norman it shows signs of
rebuilding in the 13th and 14th centuries, and

Sussex

Sussex

again under Thomas Read Kemp MP and others. The 16th-18th century Barbican House has a museum with displays on prehistoric, Roman, Saxon and medieval Sussex. Features 25 minute audio-visual presentation. Lewes Living History model and audio-visual show.
All year Castle & Museum Mon-Sat 10.00-17.30, Sun and Bank Hol 11.00-17.30. Closed Christmas
Last Admission: 30 mins before closing
A£3.70 C£1.90 Family Ticket £10.50 OAPs&Students£3.20

Chichester District Museum
29 Little London Chichester West Sussex PO19 1PB
[from Portsmouth on the A27, Museum is on E side of the City, turning opposite MacDonalds]
Tel: 01243 784683 Fax: 01243 776766
Find out about the people who lived around Chichester in the past, from pre-history through to Roman and Medieval times. Other displays include Civil War, Victorian Chichester and 'Chichester since 1900.' See our changing exhibitions. In 1998 our Exhibitions include 'What! No Romans' which looks at life before the Romans, and 'Roll out the Barrel' the history of local pubs and breweries.
All year Tue-Sat 10.00-17.30 Closed Bank Hol, Good Fri, 25-26 Dec & 1 Jan
Admission Free

Ditchling Museum
Church Lane Ditchling Hassocks West Sussex BN6 8TB
[on the B2116 off the High Street in the old village school]
Tel: 01273 844744
The Sussex Village of Ditchling, beneath the South Downs, has long been the home and workplace of many famous artists including Eric Gill - sculptor and engraver and Edward Johnston - calligrapher. Their work and that of other Ditchling craftsmen is on permanent display in the museum. Housed in the Victorian village school the museum also displays period rooms and costumes, cottage parlour, farm tools and special exhibitions.
Apr-Oct Tue-Sat & Bank Hol Mon 10.30-17.00, Sun 14.00-17.00. Nov-Mar weekends only
A£2.00 C£0.50 OAPs£1.50. Prices subject to alteration. Group rates available

Henfield Museum
Village Hall High Street Henfield West Sussex BN5 9DB
[on A281 Horsham to Brighton Road]
Tel: 01273 492546
Local history including domestic objects, costume, agricultural tools, archaeology and geology. Local paintings and photographs.
All year Mon, Tue, Thur & Sat 10.00-12.00. Wed & Sat 14.30-16.30, other times by appointment
Admission Free

Horsham Museum
9 The Causeway Horsham West Sussex RH12 1HE
[3m walk from town centre]
Tel: 01403 254959
Set in a timber-framed Tudor house, Horsham Museum is like no other in the country. With its unique collection of prehistoric life including the Rudgwick polacanthus dinosaur and dragonflies, the Museum will delight children and adults alike. With over 100 years of collecting, the Museum has a wealth of objects on display in the extensively refurbished galleries, including ceramics, toys, bicycles, local trades, farming, domestic life, paintings, furniture etc. If you come on the hour you can hear the grandfather clocks chime!
All year Mon-Sat 10.00-17.00
Admission Free

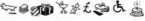

Marlipins Museum
High Street Shoreham-By-Sea West Sussex BN43 5DA
[on the A259]
Tel: 01273 462994
The Marlipins Museum has a wide range of exhibits relating to local history and archaeology. There is also a maritime gallery displaying a fine collection of ship portraits, ship models, and other items of local maritime interest. The building in which the museum is housed may have been built as a customs house.
1 May-30 Sept Tue-Sat 10.00-13.00 & 14.00-16.30, Sun 14.00-16.30
A£1.50 C(5-15)£0.75 Students & OAPs £1.00

Old Town Hall Museum of Local History
High Street Hastings East Sussex TN34 3EW
[in Hastings, signposted]
Tel: 01424 781166
Situated in the heart of Hastings Old Town, the museum was originally a Georgian Town Hall built in 1823. Displays include the history of Hastings, the Battle of Hastings, the Cinque Ports and maritime history - smuggling, shipwrecks and fishing. Famous local personalities including John Logie Baird, inventor of television, are also featured.
Apr-Sept Tue-Sun 10.00-13.00 & 14.00-17.00. Oct-Dec & Mar 14.00-16.00
Admission Free

Priest House

North Lane West Hoathly East Grinstead West Sussex RH19 4PP
[off B2028]

Tel: 01342 810479

The 15th-century house has been converted into a small folk museum with a variety of interesting exhibits including samplers, needlework, furniture, kitchen and agricultural implements. The house is set in a traditional English cottage garden, at its best during the summer months, and a formal herb garden is now well established on the site.

1 Mar-31 Oct Mon-Sat 11.00-17.30, Sun 14.00-17.30
A£2.30 C(5-15)£1.10 OAPs&Students£2.10.
Group: A£2.10 C£1.00 (min 20)

Steyning Museum

Church Street Steyning West Sussex BN44 3YB
[in Steyning]

Tel: 01903 813333

A lively local history museum bringing to life a beautiful and fascinating town with its roots in Saxon England. Plus regular special exhibitions.

All year Tue Wed Fri & Sat 10.30-12.30 plus Tue Wed Sat & Sun 14.00-16.30 (Summer) 14.30-16.00 (Winter)
Admission Free

Weald and Downland Open Air Museum

Singleton Chichester West Sussex PO18 0EU
[on A286 between Midhurst and Chichester. Discounted combined ticket on Stagecoach Coastline Bus. Plenty of parking on site]

Tel: 01243 811348 Fax: 01243 811475
www.wealddown.co.uk

Situated in a beautiful downland setting, this museum displays more than 40 rescued historic buildings from south-east England. The buildings range from early medieval houses to a 19th-century schoolhouse and Victorian labourers cottages. There is a medieval farmstead complete with animals, gardens and fields, a lakeside cafe, a working watermill and lots more of interest.

All year Mar-Oct daily 10.30-18.00 Nov-Feb Wed Sat & Sun 10.30-16.00 26 Dec-1 Jan 10.30-16.00
Last Admission: Main Season 18.00 Winter 16.00
A£6.00 C(5+)&Students£3.00 Family Ticket (A2+C3)£15.00

discount offer: One Child Free With Two Full Paying Adults. Valid Until 31 Oct 2000

↓*special events*

▶ **The Fire Event**
26/3/00-26/3/00
A brand new, one day event built around the fascinating, mesmeric and practical qualities of fire and the uses people have made of it through history

▶ **Mothering Sunday**
2/4/00-2/4/00
Free entry and a bunch of daffodils for mothers and grandmothers. Pram concours, traditional children's games and lots of fun.

▶ **Traditional Food Fair - Easter**
23/4/00-24/4/00
Producers set up shop to offer you a taste and the chance to buy quality food and drink not available in the supermarkets

▶ **Museums' & Galleries Moth**
1/5/00-31/5/00
A variety of interesting exhibitions and residencies all enhancing the museums core activities

▶ **Jaguar Car Club**
19/5/00-19/5/00
Entente Cordiale European Tour. See the flamboyant and glamorous Jaguar cars from the 1929 Standard Swallow to the latest S-Types and XJ220.

▶ **Half Term Activities**
29/5/00-2/6/00
Join in with lots of unusual and interesting traditionally based activities for children.

▶ **Heavy Horse Summer Spectacular**
4/6/00-4/6/00
A wonderful and continuous display of the grace, skill and power of these magnificent beasts

▶ **The Copper Family...**
19/7/00-19/7/00
... perform songs and tell tales of Sussex past by candlelight in one of the medieval hall houses of the museum. Commencing at 20.00, separate charge

▶ **Rare and Traditional Breeds Show**
23/7/00-23/7/00
Over 500 farmyard animals. Busy rural show loved for its personal and friendly atmosphere.

▶ **South Downs Harness Club Show**
6/8/00-6/8/00
Horses and ponies showing off their driving skills in full show finery. Classes for beginners through to experienced whips and grooms.

▶ **Romeo and Juliet**

Sussex

10/8/00-10/8/00

Open air Shakespeare performed by Illyria.
Recall the delighted of being young and in love.
Tickets and details available on 01243 811348

► **Children's Activity Weekend**

12/8/00-13/8/00

Children, (and their parents and carers!) can try
their hand at an astonishing range of things..
far too many to mention

► **Emperor's New Clothes**

18/8/00-18/8/00

Hans Christian Anderson's well loved tale per-
formed by Illyria. Rollicking good fun for all

► **Rural History Re-enactment**

24/8/00-29/8/00

An authentic reconstruction of English domestic
history.

► **Autumn Countryside Collection**

21/10/00-22/10/00

A celebration of how the countryside used to be

► **Half Term Activities**

23/10/00-27/10/00

Many and various activities for children includ-
ing music, storytelling and lots to make and do.

► **Tree Dressing**

3/12/00-3/12/00

A festival of trees rooted in the Green Man leg-
ends of ancient times and the importance of
natural objects to man

Winchelsea Museum

High Street Winchelsea East Sussex TN36 4EA
Tel: 01797 224395
The Court Hall, one of the oldest buildings in
Winchelsea, now houses the museum with the
old prison cells underneath. Dating back to the
13th century, it was restored in the 16th and
later centuries. There is a model of the town as
it was in 1292, collections of clay pipes, bottles
and other exhibits of local interest.
Mid May-Sept Tue-Sat 10.30-12.30 & 14.00-
17.00, Sun 14.00-17.00
A£0.50 C(0-14)£0.20

Food & Drink

Sedlescombe Vineyards

Cripp's Corner Sedlescombe Robertsbridge
Sussex TN32 5SA
[situated on the B2244, 8m N of Hastings and
1.5m N of the village of Sedlescombe. Plenty of
on site parking]
Tel: 01580 830715 Fax: 01580 830122
www.tor.co.uk/sedlescombe
England's premier organic vineyard (est. 1979)
offering woodland nature trail and wine tasting. Producers of quality English wines, fruit

wines, sparkling wines, fruit juices and farmhouse ciders all the Soil Association Organic
standards. Ideal location for a picnic. Shop also
stocks foreign organic wines and gifts.
All year daily 10.00-18.00. Guided tours by
arrangement.
A£3.50 C£Free OAPs£2.00

Gardens & Horticulture

Apuldram Roses

Appledram Lane South Chichester West Sussex
PO20 7EF
[1m SW of Chichester - A286 Birdham-Wittering
road from Chichester. Turn right into Dell Quay
Road then right again into Apuldram Lane]
Tel: 01243 785769 Fax: 01243 536973
Specialist Rose Nursery growing over 300 vari-
eties of Hybrid Teas, Floribundas, Climbers,
Ramblers, Ground Cover, Miniature and Patio
Roses. Also a large selection of shrub roses
both old and new. Mature Rose Garden to
view.
All year daily Mon-Sat 09.00-17.00, Sun & Bank
Hol 10.30-16.30. Parties by prior arrangement
Admission Free

Berri Court

Main Road Yapton Arundel West Sussex BN18
0ED
Tel: 01243 551663
3 acre garden of wide interest in centre of
Yapton Village.
Sun & Mon - viewing by appointment
A£1.50 in aid of National Garden Scheme
admission Free

Borde Hill Garden

Balcombe Road Haywards Heath West Sussex
RH16 1XP
[1.5m N of Haywards Heath, 3m from M23, ,
signposted from Cuckfield / Haywards Heath]
Tel: 01444 450326 Fax: 01444 440427
www.bordehill.co.uk

A botanical garden of contrasts established in the 19th century. Set in 200 acres of parkland, the garden contains a phenomenal range of rare trees, shrubs and perennials. All year colour. Recent Garden Rennaissance with Lootery grant includes Rose and Italian Gardens and Victorian Greenhouses.
All year daily 10.00-18.00 (or dusk if earlier)
Last Admission: 17.00
A£4.50 C£1.75 OAPs £3.75 Family Day Ticket £11.00 Family Season Ticket £27.50. Pre-booked groups of 20+ £4.00. Guided tours available

↓ *special events*

► **Special Camellia Days**
18/3/00-31/3/00
58th Anniversary of Camellia 'Donation' created at Borde Hill Garden. View the other 33 varieties of Camellias on show also. Talks and tours by Camellia specialists by prior arrangement

► **Sculpture Trail**
1/4/00-31/5/00
Discover at each turn, sculptures set within this romantic garden ranging from figurative to abstract, from bronze to glass

► **Garden Festival**
15/4/00-16/4/00
10th Festival with specialist nurseries, collectable plants, crafts, fine foods and wine. Free garden tours

► **Easter Special for Children**
23/4/00-24/4/00
Free Easter Egg for each child completing the Easter trail

► **Children's Animal Fair**
6/5/00-7/5/00
Wide selection of animals including penguins, meerkats, snakes, ferret racing, rare rabbits and chickens. Crafts, children's entertainers, donkey and tractor rides and trout fishing. 10.00-17.00, A£3.00 C£3.00

► **Rhododendron and Azalea Time**
13/5/00-28/5/00
Spectacular displays of Rhododendron and Azaleas - over 1000 varieties

► **Rose and Craft Days**
17/6/00-30/6/00
5th anniversary of the Rose Garden. Enjoy the Rose Garden at its peak with over 450 fragrant plants with Crafts Festival. Tours and advice available

► **Millennium Music Festival**
23/6/00-25/6/00
Music from pop to classical to celebrate the year 2000. Admission prices and times to be confirmed

► **BH Horse Trials**
1/7/00-2/7/00
7th Borde Hill Horse Trials held in Borde Hill's spectacular parkland. Cross-country, show jumping and dressage from local and international riders

► **Children's Activities**

1/8/00-31/8/00
Held every weekday afternoon in the parkland - face painting, juggling, pond dipping, children's trail and fishing. Please call to confirm dates

► **Fuchsia Show**
6/8/00-6/8/00
Fuchsia displays and sales from specialist nurseries plus information and talks on the growing and care of your fuchsias

► **L'Elisir d'Amore (The Love Potion)**
12/8/00-12/8/00
Garden Opera returns after their great success last year, with Donizetti's hilarious rustic comedy. 19.00-22.00, A£18.50 Concessions£16.50

► **Rare Plants Fair**
3/9/00-3/9/00
A feast for plant hunters - specialist nurseries selling unusual plants

► **Children's Fun Days**
23/10/00-27/10/00
Activities for children every afternoon in the adventure playground, 14.00-17.00

Cobblers Garden
Tollwood Road Mount Pleasant Crowborough East Sussex TN6 2ND
[off Crowborough Hill 100yds up Mount Pleasant above Wheatsheaf Pub]
Tel: 01892 655969
2 Acre sloping site designed by present owners since 1968 to display outstanding range of herbaceous and shrubs species and famous watergarden, giving all season colour. Subject of numerous articles and T.V. programmes. Now a very famous garden.
26 May, 11-22 June, 13 July, 3 25 Aug 14.30-17.30, 11 June Wine Party 17.30-20.00
A£3.10 include home made teas

Coke's Barn
Westburton Pulborough West Sussex RH20 1HD
[1m off A29 at Bury]
Tel: 01798 831636
0.75 acre cottage garden surrounding 17th century barn. Features interesting corners and plants.
By appointment only
A£1.00

Denmans Garden
Clockhouse Denmans Lane Fontwell Arundel West Sussex BN18 0SU
[5m E of Chichester on A27. Limited on site parking]
Tel: 01243 542808 Fax: 01243 544064
This garden has been created from land which

Sussex

was part of an estate owned by Lord Denman in the 19th century. The present three-and-a-half acre garden was begun in the 1940's by the late Mrs J H Robinson and has gradually developed over the last 50 years. A school of Garden Design is housed in the Clock House. Since 1980 the garden has been run by John Brookes and from Clock House, within the property he runs his School of Garden Design. The garden is unique in its domestic scale, and in its combination of a strong organic design which is overlaid by generous planting. Having a dry, gravelly soil - both Mediterranean and native plants are grown in profusion. There are areas of glass, for plant sales and a garden cafe for coffee, light lunches and tea.

1 Mar-31 Oct daily 09.00-17.00
A£2.90 C(4+)£1.60 C(0-4)Free OAPs£2.60
discount offer: Two Full Paying Adults For The Price Of One. Excluding Weekends and Bank Holidays. Valid 1 Mar-31 Oct 2000

↓*special events*
► Garden Design Course
24/3/00-25/3/00
The Gravel Garden. Programme: 09.15-16.30, coffee, lunch and tea included in the £51.75 per person incl vat. Call for booking details

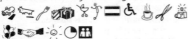

High Beeches Gardens Conservation Trust

High Beeches Lane Handcross Haywards Heath West Sussex RH17 6HQ
[10m N of Brighton, 1m E of A23 at Handcross, on B2110]
Tel: 01444 400589
Help us to preserve these twenty acres of enchanting landscaped woodland and water gardens, a favourite with Christopher Lloyd. Enjoy daffodils, Magnolias, Rhododendrons, Bluebells and Azaleas, in the Spring. In Autumn, this is one of the most brilliant gardens for leaf colour. Gentians and Primulas are naturalised here. Follow our Tree Trail and discover many rare plants. In summer, four acres of natural Wildflower Meadows are at their best. Hot and cold drinks, ice cream and biscuits in Gate Lodge. Café / Restaurant on special event days only. Non-profit making charity no 299134.

1 Apr-30 June, and 1 Sept-31 Oct Thur-Tue 13.00-17.00. July & Aug Mon & Tue only 13.00-17.00
Last Admission: 17.00
A£3.50 Accompanied C£Free. Groups by prior appointment, £15.00 surcharge for special opening. A£4.50 of 90mins guided tour

Highdown Gardens

Littlehampton Rd Ferring Worthing Sussex *[N off A259]*
Tel: 01903 501054/239999
Unique chalk garden laid out by Sir Frederick and Lady Stern in 1910. These gardens were laid out in a chalk pit on Highdown Hill. There are rock plants, flowering shrubs and daffodils, as well as excellent views.
All year Apr-Sept Mon-Fri 10.00-18.00 Sat Sun & Bank Hol Mon 10.00-18.00, Oct-Nov Mon-Fri 10.00-16.30, Dec-Jan Mon-Fri 10.00-16.00, Feb-Mar Mon-Fri 10.00-16.30
Admission Free

↓*special events*
► Wrinkles and Pipes of Highdown Hill
27/5/00-27/5/00
Bring your kite. Meet at Highdown Gardens car park (TQ098042) for this 1-mile walk, donations to the Devil's Dyke Appeal, 14.00-15.30

Holly Gate Cactus Garden and Nursery

Billingshurst Road Ashington Sussex RH20 3BB
[10m equidistant between Horsham and Worthing on A24 0.5m off on the B2133. Plenty of on site parking available.]
Tel: 01903 892930
www.users.globalnet.co.uk/~tmh
A mecca for the cactus enthusiast, with more than 30,000 succulent cactus plants, including many rare types. They come from both arid and tropical parts of the world, and are housed in over 10,000 square feet of greenhouses.
All year daily 09.00-17.00. Closed 25-26 Dec
A£2.00 C&OAPs£1.50. Group rates 20+ A£1.50 C£1.00
discount offer: Two For The Price Of One

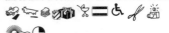

Leonardslee Gardens

Lower Beeding Horsham West Sussex RH13 6PP
[4m SW of Handcross via B2110 at bottom of M23. BR: Horsham 5m. Bus: 107. Plenty of on site parking]
Tel: 01403 891212 Fax: 01403 891305
Spectacular rhododendrons and azaleas in a peaceful 240 acre valley garden with 7 beautiful lakes. Enjoy the Rock Garden, fascinating Bonsai exhibition, Alpine house, Exhibition of Victorian Motorcars (1895-1900), and NEW for 1999 is the 'Behind the Dolls House' exhibition. Visit the Wallabies, wildfowl and deer. There is a restaurant, souvenirs and plants for sale. No dogs whatsoever admitted.
Apr-Oct daily 09.30-18.00, May daily 09.30-20.00

Last Admission: 17.00
May weekends: A£6.00 weekdays: A£5.00, Apr
& June-Oct: A£4.00, C£2.50 (at all times) Season
Ticket: £12.00

↓ *special events*

► **Bonsai Weekend**
6/5/00-7/5/00
Demonstrations and advice on the art of growing Bonsai

► **11th London to Brighton Classic Car Run**
4/6/00-4/6/00
Leonardslee Gardens is the 2nd Check Point with
Polesden Lacey, Surrey being Check Point 1.
Starting at Syon Park, Brentford, Middx and
Finishing at Maderia Drive, Brighton

► **West Sussex Country Craft Fair**
24/6/00-25/6/00
Craft Fair with stalls and demonstrations.

Nymans Garden
Handcross Haywards Heath Sussex RH17 6EB
[B2114]
Tel: 01444 400321 Fax: 01444 400253
www.nationaltrust.org.uk
Set in the Sussex Weald, Nymans has flowering shrubs and roses, a flower garden in the
old walled orchard, and a secret sunken garden. Lady Rosse's drawing room, library and
walled gardens, now open, provide an insight
into the Messel family's creative character.
There are some fine and rare trees and wonderful woodland walks.
Gardens: 1 Mar-29 Oct Wed-Sun & Bank Hol
Mon 11.00-18.00 or sunset if sooner. House: 29
Mar-29 Oct Wed-Sun & Bank Hol Mon 12.00-
16.00. For details about new winter weekend
opening and special events, call 01444 400321
Last Admission: Garden: 17.30
A£5.00 C£2.50 Family Ticket £12.50 RHS members free
discount offer: Two For The Price Of One. Not
Valid on Bank Holidays

↓ *special events*

► **Guided Woodland Walk**
26/4/00-27/4/00
Meet at the temple the Pinetum in garden (ask
at reception for directions) for this 2-3-mile
walk, sorry, no dogs, booking essential, £6.50,
including cream tea (Friends of Nymans £6.00)
14.00-17.00

► **Jazz Nights in the Garden**
14/7/00-16/7/00
Featuring Campbell Burnap and the All-Stars.
Tickets from Southern Region Box Office on
01372 451596, £14.00, 18.00 for 19.00-22.00 on
14 and 16 only

► **Teddy Bears' Picnic**
22/7/00-22/7/00
Pirate-themed fancy-dress teddy bears' picnic,
Punch & Judy, side shows, story-telling. Call for
prices, 12.00-17.00

► **Craft Fair**
5/8/00-6/8/00
Local craftspeople, usual admission, 11.00-
17.00

► **Opera in the Garden**
11/8/00-11/8/00
Opera Brava perform popular classics, from
Mozart to Gilbert & Sullivan. Tickets: Southern
Region Box Office on 01372 451596, £17.50,
18.30 for 19.30

► **Barber of Seville**
12/8/00-12/8/00
Rossini's masterpiece performed by Opera Brava.
Tickets from Southern Region box office on
01372 451596, £17.50, 18.30 for 19.00

► **Guided Woodland Walk**
26/10/00-26/10/00
See entry for 26 April

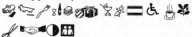

Pashley Manor Gardens
Pashley Road Ticehurst Wadhurst Sussex TN5
7HE
[on B2099 off A21 follow brown signposts.
Plenty of parking on site]
Tel: 01580 200888 Fax: 01580 200102
www.pashleymanorgardens.com
Pashley Manor Gardens offer a sumptuous
blend of romantic landscaping, imaginative
plantings and fine old trees, fountains, springs
and large ponds. This is a quintessentially
English Garden of a very individual character
with exceptional views to the surrounding
valleyed fields. Many eras of English history
are reflected here, typifying the tradition of
the English Country House and its garden.
Member of the Historic Houses Association.
Garden & Tea Rooms: 8 Apr-30 Sept Tue, Wed,
Thur, Sat and Bank Hol Mon 11.00-17.00.
Gardens also open Oct Mon-Fri 11.00-16.00
A£5.00 Concessions£4.50

↓ *special events*

► **Tulip Festival**
27/4/00-1/5/00
With Bloms Bulbs

► **Sculpture Week**
13/5/00-19/5/00

► **Spring Plant Fair**
21/5/00-21/5/00

► **Spring Plant Fair**
15/6/00-18/6/00

► **'Marriage of Figaro'**
29/7/00-29/7/00
Opera in the Garden, an evening performance
by Opera 2000

► **Summer Plant Fair**
13/8/00-13/8/00

Sussex

Sheffield Park Garden

Uckfield Sussex TN22 3QX

[midway between East Grinstead / Lewes, 5m NW of Uckfield]

Tel: 01825 790231 Fax: 01825 791264

A magnificent 40-ha landscaped garden, with 5 lakes linked by cascades and waterfalls, laid out in the 18th century by Capability Brown. Carpeted with daffodils and bluebells in spring, its rhododendrons, azaleas and stream garden are spectacular in early summer. In autumn the gardens are ablaze with colour. *Jan & Feb Sat-Sun 10.30-16.00. Mar Tue-Sun 10.30-16.00. 1 Apr-31 Oct Tue-Sun & Bank Hol Mon 10.30-18.00 or dusk if earlier. 2 Nov-23 Dec Tue-Sun 10.30-16.00*

Last Admission: 1 hour before closing
A£4.20 C£2.10 Family Ticket £10.50. Group rates £3.20. RHS members free

↓ special events

▶ **Easter Egg Trail**
21/4/00-21/4/00
Normal opening times, £1.50 extra charge

▶ **Bird Walk**
27/4/00-27/4/00
Tickets £5.00, commences at 07.00

▶ **Gardeners Tour**
19/5/00-19/5/00
See the gardens through the eyes of the people who know it best, starts at 18.30, tickets £6.00

▶ **Bat Walk**
24/7/00-24/7/00
Tickets £6.00, walk begins at 20.30

▶ **Teddy Bears' Picnic**
7/8/00-7/8/00
Held between 12.00-16.00, A£3.00 C£1.50

▶ **Victorian Weekend**
9/8/00-20/8/00
Aug 9 and 20 only. Normal opening times and prices

▶ **Fungi Workshop and Walk**
9/10/00-9/10/00
Workshop 11.00-12.30, walk 13.30-15.30. Bring packed lunch, tickets £6.00

▶ **Autumn Colour**
16/10/00-16/10/00
Experience the rich colours of the Garden in autumn. Begins at 14.00, tickets £6.00

▶ **Christmas Carols in the Garden**
13/12/00-13/12/00
Event commences at 18.30

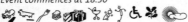

Wakehurst Place

Selsfield Road Ardingly Haywards Heath Sussex RH17 6TN

[J10 M23, A264 towards East Grinstead. 1.5m NW on B2028. BR: Haywards Heath. Bus Nos: 482 / 772 on Sundays. Plenty of on site parking available]

Tel: 01444 894066 Fax: 01444 894069

www.rbgkew.org.uk

Managed by the Royal Botanic Gardens, Kew; Wakehurst Place is set in over 180 acres. Vibrant ornamental plantings, providing year round colour and interest, blend into the beautiful natural landscape. Footpaths lead through sweeping woodlands of native and exotic trees. Set around a striking Elizabethan mansion containing a gift shop and a nearby restaurant.

visitor comments: Excellent gardens, well worth a long visit, particularly long walk to lower ponds.

All year daily from 10.00, closing times vary according to season, please call if making a special journey. Closed 25 Dec & 1 Jan

Last Admission: 30mins before closing

A£5.00 C(0-5)£Free C(5+)£2.50 Family Ticket (A2+C4)£13.00 Concessions£3.50

↓ special events

▶ **Spring Weekend**

6/5/00-7/5/00

Guided walks and vehicular tours departing throughout the day, usual admission, 10.00

▶ **Woodland Skills**

9/7/00-9/7/00

Traditional woodland skills, usual admission, 10.00

▶ **Countryside Craft Fayre**

26/8/00-28/8/00

A fair with a theme of 100 years ago with over 150 crafts stands, A£4.00 C£1.50 OAPs£3.50, 10.00-18.00

▶ **West Sussex Millennium Cycle Ride**

17/9/00-17/9/00

One of four cycle rides - from 9-36 miles. Visit the new Millennium Seed Bank project at Wakehurst Place - the start and finish point for the cycle rides, open free to cyclists participating. Cycling Support Services on 01273 230822, £5.00 discounts available for early bookers and family groups. (Times to be confirmed).

▶ **Autumn Colour Weekend**

14/10/00-15/10/00

See entry for 6 May

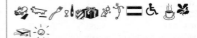

Sussex

West Dean Gardens
Estate Office West Dean Chichester West
Sussex PO18 8QZ
*[signposted off A286. Plenty of on site parking
available.]*
**Tel: 01243 818210/811301 Fax: 01243
811342**
www.westdean.org.uk/
An historic garden of 35 acres in a tranquil
downland setting. Noted for its 300ft long pergola, mixed and herbaceous borders, rustic
summerhouses, water garden and specimen
trees. The recently restored walled garden contains a fruit collection, Victorian glasshouses,
an apple store and a large working kitchen
garden, restaurant and shop. Member of the
Historic Houses Association. Photography of
the gardens only is permitted.
*11-5 Mar, Apr & Oct daily 11.00-17.00, May-
Sept daily 10.30-17.00*
Last Admission: 16.30
*A£4.00 C£2.00 Family Ticket (A2+C2)£10.00
OAPs£3.50*

↓*special events*
▶ **The Garden Event**
24/6/00-25/6/00
*Sundials to Salvias. The best specialist nurseries
from around the south-east selling all types of
rare and unusual plants*
▶ **The Pergola Open Air Theatre**
10/7/00-22/7/00
*Programme to be announced. Please call for fur-
ther information*
▶ **Chilli Fiesta Weekend**
12/8/00-13/8/00
*'Natures Napalm' - a calorific celebration of
peppers with a punch!*
▶ **The Totally Tomato Show**
9/9/00-10/9/00
*Scarlet, shiny and slightly sinful - a toast to the
tempting Tomato*

▶ **Apple Day**
15/10/00-15/10/00
Adam's Apple - in praise of the fruit of Paradise.

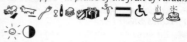

Heritage & Industrial

Amberley Museum
Station Road Amberley Arundel West Sussex
BN18 9LT
[B2139]
Tel: 01798 831370 Fax: 01798 831831
www.fastnet.co.uk/amberley.museum/
This exciting working museum reflects the
industrial history of the south east of England.
Here you can visit the craftsmen - the black-
smith, potter, printer or boat builder, and
experience the sights, sounds and smells of
their workshops. Allow at least 3 hours for a
visit.
*Daily 8 Mar-2 Nov Wed-Sun 10.00-18.00. Open
daily during local school holidays: 1-19 Apr; 20-
31 May; 15 July-6 Sept & 21 Oct-1 Nov*
A£6.00 C£3.00 Family Ticket£16.00 OAPs£5.30

**British Engineerium Museum of Steam
and Mechanical Antiquities**
off Nevill Road Hove East Sussex BN3 7QA
*[adjacent to the Greyhound / Co-op complex.
Signposted off A27]*
Tel: 01273 559583 Fax: 01273 566403
This restored Victorian water pumping station
has an original working beam engine of 1876
and a French Corliss horizontal engine which
won first prize at the Paris International
Exhibition of 1889. There are also traction
engines, fire engines and many other fun-size
and model engines. New interactive exhibition
for children. Boilers are fired up and in steam
first Sun in month and Bank Hols. 'Giants
Toolbox' - curriculum based activity.
*All year daily 10.00-17.00. Closed week prior to
Christmas*
Last Admission: 16.00
*A£3.50 C&Concessions£2.50 Family Ticket
£10.00*

Story of Rye
Rye Heritage Centre Strand Quay Rye East
Sussex TN31 7AY
[at the Strand Quay in Rye, follow TIC signposts]
Tel: 01797 226696 Fax: 01797 223460
A complete sound and light show bringing the
history of Rye alive! Follow the smugglers'
footsteps and experience the medieval life and
times of Rye as it was in bygone ages.
Mar-Oct daily 09.00-17.30. Nov-Feb daily 10.00-

Sussex

16.00
Last Admission: 15mins before closing
Centre or Personal Stereo Tour: A£2.00 C£1.00
Concessions£1.50. Group rates 10+ £1.00. All
leaders and drivers £Free
discount offer: Two For The Price Of One For
Either The Story of Rye Or The Personal Stereo
Tour

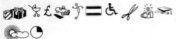

Historical

1066 Story in Hastings Castle
Castle Hill Road West Hill Hastings Sussex
TN34 3RG
[A259 or A21 into Hastings signposted]
Tel: 01424 781111 Fax: 01424 781186
Visit Britain's first Norman Castle built by
William the Conqueror in 1067, after the
Battle of Hastings. Enter the medieval siege
tent and enjoy an exciting audio-visual experi-
ence 'The 1066 Story' which covers the
Conquest and the history of the Castle through
the centuries.
Easter-Sept daily 10.00-17.00, Oct-Easter daily
11.00-last show 15.30
A£3.00 C£2.00
discount offer: Two For The Price Of One
↓ *special events*
▶ **Hastings & St Leonards Millennium Festival**
20/4/00-1/5/00
*Featuring Jack in the Green Morris Dancing
Festival, a dinosaur day, opera South East, jazz
breakfasts, millennium ceilidh and a Mayday
marathon walk*

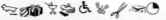

Alfriston Clergy House
The Tye Alfriston Polegate Sussex BN26 5TL
*[4m NE of Seaford just E of B2108. BR: Berwick
2.5m]*
Tel: 01323 870001
The 14th century Wealdon hall house was the
first building to be acquired by the Trust, in
1896. The building is half-timbered and
thatched, and contains a medieval hall, exhibition room and two other rooms open to the
public. The charming garden is filled with traditional cottage favourites, some grown since
Roman times and now almost lost to cultiva-
tion.
*27 Apr-31 Oct Mon, Wed, Thur, Sat & Sun, Bank
Hol Mon & Good Fri 10.00-17.00.*
Last Admission: 16.30 or dusk if sooner
*A£2.50 C£1.25 Family Ticket £6.25 Group Rate
15+ £2.00*
↓ *special events*
▶ **Garden Tour**
15/6/00-15/6/00
Led by the gardeners at 18.00, £5.00
▶ **Garden Surgery**
6/7/00-6/7/00
▶ **Alfriston Village Fair**
28/8/00-28/8/00
▶ **Apple and Woodcraft Day**
7/10/00-7/10/00

Anne of Cleves House Museum
52 Southover High Street Lewes East Sussex
BN7 1JA
*[5min walk from train station. 10min from
town centre on foot.]*
Tel: 01273 474610
This 16th century town house was given to
Anne of Cleves by Henry VIII as part of her
divorce settlement. Now devoted to arts and
crafts, agriculture, industrial and domestic life,
with a notable collection of Sussex ironwork
including early gun-founding material. There
is a medieval herb garden outside. In the summer guided tours take place to nearby Lewes
Priory.
*1 Jan-14 Feb & 1-31 Dec Tue, Thur & Sat 10.00-
17.00. 15 Feb-30 Nov Mon-Sat 10.00-17.30, Sun
12.00-17.30*
Last Admission: 30 mins before closing
*A£2.30 C£1.10 Family Ticket (A2+C2)£6.20
OAPs&Students£2.10. Groups (min 20): A£2.10
C£1.00 OAPs&Students£2.00. Combined ticket
with Lewes Castle & Barbican House: A£4.80
C£2.50 Family Ticket (A2+C2)£12.00
OAPs&Students £4.00. Group Combined: A£4.20
C£2.40 OAPs&Students£3.30*

Arundel Castle
Arundel West Sussex BN18 9AB

[A27 signposted. Coach park is opposite Castle entrance]

Tel: 01903 882173 Fax: 01903 884581

This great castle, home of the Dukes of Norfolk, dates from the Norman Conquest. Containing a very fine collection of furniture and paintings, it is still a family home reflecting the changes of nearly a thousand years.

1 Apr-29 Oct Sun-Fri 12.00-17.00. Closed Sat & Good Fri. Speical openings by prior arrangement only.

Last Admission: 16.00

A£6.70 C(5-15)£4.20 Family Ticket £A2+C2)£18.00 OAPs£5.70. Group rates 20+ A£6.20 C£5-15)£3.70 OAPs£5.20. Special Opening Rates: Mornings £8.00 per person, minimum fee £400.00, Evenings, Sat & Sun £9.00 per person, minimum fee £450.00

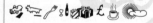

Bateman's

Burwash Etchingham Sussex TN19 7DS

[5m S of Burwash A265. BR: Etchingham 3m]

Tel: 01435 882302 Fax: 01435 882811

Home of Rudyard Kipling from 1902-36. Kipling's rooms and study are as they were during his lifetime. A watermill grinds corn for flour (Sat pm only) at the bottom of a beautiful garden. Alongside is one of the oldest working water-driven turbines in the world, installed by Kipling to generate electricity for the house. Dog creche available!

4 Apr-1 Nov Sat-Wed, Good Fri & Bank Hol Mon 11.00-17.30. Corn milled on Sat 14.00

Last Admission: 16.30

A£5.00 C£2.50 Family Ticket £12.50. Group rates £4.00

↓ *special events*

► **Family Fun Day**

30/5/00-30/5/00

► **Last Night of the Proms with Fireworks**

5/8/00-5/8/00

Starts at 19.30, £15.00 per ticket

► **The Counterfeit Stones and the Tremeloes**

6/8/00-6/8/00

Starts 19.30, £15.00 per ticket

Battle Abbey

High Street Battle Sussex TN33 0AD
[leave A21 onto A2100 abbey at end of Battle High Street]
Tel: 01424 773792
www.english-heritage.org.uk
One date in English history that everyone can remember is 1066, the Battle of Hastings, when the Anglo Saxon army was defeated by the invading troops of William the Conqueror. Visit this famous site and experience the height of the battle at it's fiercest, through unique interactive displays. Also see the atmospheric ruins of the Abbey.
All year daily 1 Apr-30 Sept 10.00-18.00. 1 Oct-31 Oct 10.00-17.00. 1 Nov-31 Mar 10.00-16.00. Closed 24-26 Dec & 1 Jan
A£4.00 C£2.00 Family Ticket (A2+C3) £10.00 Concessions£3.00 All prices include introductory video and interactive battlefield audio tour

↓ *special events*

► **Medieval Living History**
28/5/00-29/5/00
From Noon. A military encampment with men-at-arms training with weapons, plus cookery and herbs
► **Children's Fun Day**
31/5/00-3/8/00
Clowns, juggling, magic, face-painting and games to play on 31 May-1 June and 2 & 3 Aug only
► **American Civil War Battle**
10/6/00-11/6/00
From Noon. Meet soldiers of the 1860's and watch a spectacular battle
► **Classic Car Show and Country Fayre**
16/7/00-16/7/00
From 11.00. Superb cars, with cavalcade at 15.00 and supporting family attractions

Sussex

► **Warriors of Hastings**
22/7/00-8/10/00
Meet a mounted Norman knight and a Saxon warrior   fron noon on 22/23, 29/30 July, 5/6, 12/13, 19/20 27/28 Aug, 2/3, 9/10, 16/17, 23/24 30 Sept/1 Oct, 7/8 Oct
► **The French and Indian Wars**
19/8/00-20/8/00
From Noon. 1750's Indian encampment, colonial living history and savage skirmish.
► **The Battle of Hastings Spectacular**
14/10/00-15/10/00
From Noon. Re-enactment of the most famous battle in English history, on the original site.

Bodiam Castle
Bodiam Robertsbridge Sussex TN32 5UA
[3m S of Hawkhurst, 2m E of A21 Hurst Green. BR: Robertsbridge 5m]
Tel: 01580 830436 Fax: 01580 830398
Built in 1385 against a French invasion which never came, and as a comfortable dwelling for a rich nobleman. Voted one of the most popular and exciting castles for children to explore with spiral staircases and battlements. There is an audio-visual presentation on life in a medieval castle, and a small museum.
All year 13 Feb-31 Oct daily 10.00-18.00. Nov-3 Jan Tue-Sun 10.00-16.00. Closed 24-26 Dec. Last Admission : Feb-Oct 17.00 or dusk. Nov-Jan dusk Last Admission: Feb-Nov 17.00 or dusk. Nov-Jan dusk
A£3.50 C£1.75 Family Ticket £8.75 Group rates £3.00. Car Parking £1.00.
↓ *special events*
► **The Emperor's New Clothes**
25/6/00-25/6/00
Open air theatre for families. Starts 18.30, tickets A£8.00 C£4.00
► **Romeo and Juliet**
16/7/00-16/7/00
Open air theatre starting at 18.30, tickets £9.00.
► **Magic**
22/7/00-22/7/00
A tribute to Freddie Mercury and Queen, 19.30, tickets £13.00
► **Book Day and Family Fun**
9/8/00-9/8/00
► **Treasure Hunt**
27/10/00-29/10/00
Normal opening times, £2.00 extra charge

Boxgrove Priory
Church Lane Boxgrove Chichester Sussex PO18 0ED
[N of Boxgrove 4m E of Chichester on minor road off A27 BR: Chichester-Littlehampton]
Tel: 01243 774045

Remains of the Guest House, Chapter House and church of a 12th century priory.
All year any reasonable time
Admission Free

Bramber Castle
Castle Lane Bramber Steyning West Sussex BN44 3FB
[on W side of Bramber village off A283]
A former home of the Dukes of Norfolk, this ruined Norman stronghold lies on a ridge of the South Downs and gives wonderful views.
Any reasonable time
Admission Free

Bricwall House and Gardens
Rye Road Northiam Rye East Sussex TN31 6NL
[7m NW of Rye on B2088]
Tel: 01797 252494 Fax: 01797 252567
Home of the Frewen family since 1666. 17th century drawing room, superb plaster ceilings and family portraits. Grand staircase. The grounds contain a formal wall garden, topiary and an arboretum.
Apr-Sept Sat & Bank Hol Mon 14.00-17.00 at other times by prior arrangement with the curator 01797 223329
A£2.50

Camber Castle
Rye Sussex TN
[access across fields off the A259 1m S of Rye off harbour road. BR: Rye 1.25m. Bus: 01273 474747]
Tel: 01797 223862
A rare example of an Henrician fort surviving in its original plan. Monthly guided walks of Rye Harbour Nature Reserve. Under local management of Rye Harbour Nature Reserve
1 July-30 Sept Sat 14.00-17.00. Monthly guided walks of Rye Harbour Nature Reserve including Camber Castle. Please telephone the Reserve Manager 01797 223862 for further information.
A£2.00 C£1.00 Concessions£1.50

Charleston
Firle Lewes East Sussex BN8 6LL
[6m E of Lewes on A27 between Firle and Selmeston]
Tel: 01323 811626 Fax: 01323 811628
The home of Vanessa Bell and Duncan Grant (painters), which became the country retreat of the group known as Bloomsbury. Decorated walls, furniture, textiles and ceramics, influenced by the post-impressionists, fresco painting and Italian and French interior decoration.

Sussex

visitor comments: The guided tour is worthwhile.

23 Mar-30 June & 1 Sep-31 Oct Wed-Sun &
Bank Hol Mon 14.00-17.00, 1 July-31 Aug Wed
Sun 11.00-17.00
Last Admission: 17.00
A£5.00 C£3.00 Connoisseur Days £6.00
S&OAP&UB40&Concessions Wed & Thur

Danny House

New Way Lane Hurstpierpoint Hassocks West
Sussex BN6 9BB
[Between Hassocks and Hurstpierpoint B2116 -
off New Way Lane BR: Hassocks-1m]
Tel: 01273 833000
Elizabethan E-shaped house, dating from
1593.
May-Sept Wed & Thur 14.00-17.00
Last Admission: 16.30
A£2.50 C£1.00

Firle Place

Firle Lewes East Sussex BN8 6LP
[off A27 Eastbourne to Brighton road]
Tel: 01273 858335 Fax: 01273 858188
Home of the Gage family for over 500 years
the house has a Tudor core but was remodelled in the 18th century. Its treasures include
important European and English Old Master
paintings, fine English and French furniture
and porcelain, including notable examples
from Sèvres and English factories. There are
family monuments and brasses in St. Peter's
Church, Firle. Member of the Historic Houses
Association.
June-Sept Sun, Wed, Thur & Bank Hol Mon
14.00-17.00, Group bookings May-end Sept
Last Admission: 16.30
Queuing Times: 30mins for Guided Tour
A£4.00 C£2.00

Glynde Place

The Street Glynde Lewes East Sussex BN8 6SX
[off A27 between Lewes and Eastbourne]
Tel: 01273 858224
A lovely Elizabethan manor with 18th century
additions, in a beautiful downland setting. It
is still a family home, lived in by descendents
of the original owner.
June-Sept Wed-Thur & Sun & May Bank Hol
Sun-Mon 14.00-17.00
A£4.00 C£2.00 Group rates available

Goodwood House

Goodwood Chichester West Sussex PO18 0PX
[3 miles north east of Chichester, signposted
from the A27]

Tel: 01243 755000 Fax: 01243 755005
Goodwood House has taken on new life. After
two years of intensive restoration the Regency
splendor of the Egyptian State Dining Room is
guaranteed to make visitors catch their
breath. The grand Yellow Drawing Room forms
a glowing heart to the house with it's
ottomans, sofas and chairs. The richness of the
state rooms provides a perfect setting for the
magnificent art collections including paintings by Canaletto, Stubbs, Reynolds and Van
Dyck, porcelain, furniture and tapestries.
Goodwood is also the home of the famous
Goodwood motor racing circuit and racecourse. Many special events are held throughout the year. Member of the Historic Houses
Association.
Mid Apr-end Sept Sun & Mon,Aug Sun-Thur
13.00-17.00. Closed event days.
A£6.00 C12-18£3.00 C(Under 12)£Free Groups
25+ £4.50
discount offer: £1.00 Off Entry Price For
Adults And Children

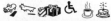

Great Dixter House and Gardens

Northiam Rye East Sussex TN31 6PH
[A28]
Tel: 01797 252878 Fax: 01797 252879
Great Dixter is the family home of gardening
writer Christopher Lloyd. Built c1460 and
restored and extended by Lutyens in 1910, it
boasts the largest surviving timber-framed
hall in the country. Christopher has devoted
his lifetime to creating one of the most experimental gardens including topiary, flower
meadows and the famous Long Border and
Exotic Garden.
1 Apr-29 Oct Tue-Sun & Bank Hol Mon 14.00-
17.00
House & Gardens: A£6.00 C£1.50. Gardens only:
A£4.50 C£1.00.

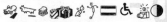

Hammerwood Park

Hammerwood East Grinstead Sussex RH19
3QE
[3.5m E of East Grinstead on A264 Tunbridge

Wells 1m W of Holtye. BR: East Grinstead then by taxi for £6.00. plenty of on site parking available]

Tel: 01342 850594 Fax: 01342 850864
www.name.is/hammerwood

Said by visitors to be the most interesting house in Sussex. Built in 1792 as a temple of Apollo, the house was the first work of Latrobex, the architect of the White House and The Capitol Building in Washington DC, USA. Family members conduct visitors on a colourful tour of the building and its grounds, ending in tea with a fine collection of lucious cakes and scones, served beneath a replica of the Parthenon frieze in the Elgin Room.

Easter Mon-end Sept Wed, Sat & Bank Hol Mon 14.00-17.30. Guided tour starts 14.05. Coach (21 seats or more) only by appointment. School groups welcome
A£4.50 C£1.50

discount offer: Three For The Price of Two

Herstmonceux Castle, Gardens and Grounds

Herstmonceux Hailsham Sussex BN27 1RN
[located just outside the village of Herstmonceux on the A271, the entrance is on Wartling road. Plenty of free on site parking]
Tel: 01323 833816 Fax: 01323 834499
www.seetb.org.uk/herstmonceux

Experience the peace and tranquility of 550 acres of glorious woodland and Elizabethan gardens surrounding a 15th century moated castle. Visitor's Centre, Children's Woodland play area, Tearoom and Nature trail.

15 Apr-29 Oct daily 10.00-18.00
Last Admission: 17.00 (16.00 in Oct)
A£3.50 C&Concessions£2.70. Joint ticket available with the Science Centre. Group booking rates for 15+ call 01323 834457

↓ *special events*

► **Easter Egg Hunt**
23/4/00-23/4/00
Find the eggs hidden in the grounds of the Castle

► **Summer Proms**
24/6/00-24/6/00
Popular classics and firework finalé with Royal Philharmonic Orchestra. Commences 20.00, grounds open 16.00. Tickets from White Rock Theatre 01242 78100

► **Kite Festival and Fun Day**
30/7/00-30/7/00
A day out for all the family

► **Medieval Festival**
26/8/00-26/8/00
300 men and women in period costume attacking and counter-attacking will full cannon sup-

port in an effort to storm the castle and lay siege

Lamb House

West Street Rye East Sussex TN31 7ES
Tel: 01892 890651 Fax: 01892 890110

This 18th century house was the home of novelist Henry James from 1898 until his death in 1916, and was later occupied by E. F. Benson writer of the Lucia books, who was at one time mayor of Rye. The house is surrounded by an attractive garden. The fax number given is for the National Trust Regional Office.

1 Apr-31 Oct Wed & Sat 14.00-18.00. 1999 Times: 27 Mar-30 Oct Wed & Sat 14.00-18.00 Last Admission: 17.30
A£2.50 C£1.25

Lewes Castle and Barbican House Museum

169 High Street Lewes East Sussex BN7 1YE
[Lewes Castle is located centrally in Lewes off the High Street, a few minutes walk from the bus and railway stations. Lewes is accessed from A27, A26 and A275, drivers using the A27 should enter the town from the eastern end of the Lewes by-pass via Guilfail Tunnel, Lewes.]
Tel: 01273 486290

The Lewes properties provide a wide range of possibilities for educational activities including artifact handling sessions, gallery tours activity sheet and practical workshops. The Museum at Barbican House traces the development of local people and features the Normans and their Castles, Medieval Realms and the history of Lewes, complimented by the Lewes Town Model.

visitor comments: Excellent video history. Opportunity to study the scale model making view from the top more relevant. Bookshop is well worth a visit.

All year Mon-Sat 10.00-17.30, Sun & Bank Hol 11.00-17.30. Closed 25-26 Dec. Castle closes at dusk in winter
Last Admission: Dusk during Winter
A£3.50 C(5-15)£1.80 OAPs&Students£3.00 Family Ticket (A2+C2)£10.00. Group: A£3.10 C£1.50 OAPs&Students£2.70 (min 20). Combined ticket with Anne of Cleves House: A£4.80 C£2.50 OAPs&Students£4.00 Family ticket(A2+C2)£12.00

Monk's House

Rodmell Lewes East Sussex BN7 3HF
[4m SE of Lewes in Rodmell village near the church, off former A275 (now unclassified). NO access from A26]
Tel: 01892 890651 Fax: 01892 890110

A small village house and garden, and the

home of Leonard and Virginia Woolf from 1919 until Leonard's death in 1969. The house and garden are administered and largely maintained by the tenant on the Trust's behalf. Maximum of 15 people in the house at a time. The fax number given is for the National Trust Regional Office.

1 Apr-31 Oct Wed & Sat 14.00-17.30. 1999 Times: 27 Mar-30 Oct Wed & Sat 14.00-17.30 Last Admission: 17.00

A£2.50 C£1.25, no reduction for Groups which should be booked in advance with tenant, coaches to set down at maid road and park elsewhere as street too narrow

Newtimber Place

Newtimber Place Newtimber Hassocks West Sussex BN6 9BU

[From London: A23 towards Brighton, Pyecombe Exit (Signposted Hassocks), right at T Junction and first left over bridge over A23. Right at T Junction and rejoin the A23 N. Turn off at junction A281 Henfield. Over next roundabout, right at signpost for Newtimber Church, house is at end of lane. From Brighton: A23 N exit onto A281 signposted Henfield. Over roundabout, at first crossroads turn right signposted Newtimber Church, house is at end of lane]

Tel: 01273 833104 Fax: 01273 833298 www.newtimber.demon.co.uk

Newtimber Place is a Sussex moated house, built of flint and brick with a roof of Horsham Stone. The manor is mentioned in the Domesday Book. The current house is mainly late 17th century. A special feature of the house if the 18th century Etruscan style wall paintings in the hall, which were derived from the plates in "Greek and Roman Antiquities" written for Sir William Hamilton and published in folio at Naples 1766-1767. The moat is fed by natural springs and is 50 foot wide in places with rushes, waterlillies and other water plants. There is also an octagonal Georgian dovecote in the grounds. Some areas of the property may be inaccessible for wheelchairs.

May-Aug Thur 14.00-17.00 by appointment only. Groups at other times by arrangement A£2.00 C£0.50

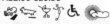

Parham House and Gardens

Parham Pulborough West Sussex RH20 4HS

[3m SE of A29 main gate on A283 Pulborough / Storring road signposted]

Tel: 01903 744888 Fax: 01903 746557

Surrounded by a deer park, fine gardens and 18th-century pleasure grounds in a beautiful downland setting, this Elizabethan family home contains a good collection of paintings, furniture, carpets and rare needlework. The garden at Parham won the prestigious Christie's Garden of the Year Award in 1990. Open to visitors for 50 years, Parham is now offering light lunches served in our 15th century Big Kitchen from 12 noon each open day.

1 Apr-end Oct Wed, Thur, Sun & Bank Hol, Gardens: 12.00-18.00 House: 14.00-18.00 Last Admission: 17.00

A£5.00 C(5-15)£1.00 Family Ticket £10.00 OAPs£4.00 Groups on application

Petworth House and Park

Petworth Sussex GU28 0AE

[A272 / A283 centre of Petworth. Plenty of on site parking available]

Tel: 01798 342207/343929 Fax: 01798 342963

Magnificent House in 700 acre deer park landscaped by 'Capability' Brown. Showrooms contain fine collection of paintings by Turner, Van Dyck and Gainsborough. Fine furniture, Grinling Gibbons carvings, Laguerre murals, ancient and Neo-classical sculpture. Old Kitchens and ancillary rooms newly restored. Guided tours by prior arrangement, picnic allowed - no special seating or covered area. Photography allowed of exterior-interior only by prior arrangement.

House: 1 Apr-1 Nov Sat-Wed, Good Fri & Fri in July & Aug 13.00-17.30. Car Park, Pleasure Ground, Shop & Tea Room: 18,19, 25 & 26 Mar 12.00-16.00, then as house, 12.00-18.00. Park: daily 08.00-dusk (closed from 12.00 on 23-25 June for Open Air Concerts)

Last Admission: House: 16.30 Old Kitchens: 17.00

Queuing Times: Bank Hol approx 30mins House & Kitchens: A£6.00 C(5-17)£3.00 Family Ticket(A2+C2)£15.00. Group Rate £5.50 per person for booked parties of 15+. Pleasure Grounds only: £1.50. Park: £Free. National Trust Members £Free. Private Guided Tours for booked groups

discount offer: 50p Group Rate Reduction

↓ special events

▶ **Easter Egg Trail**
22/4/00-24/4/00
Treasure trail leading to edible prize, for children 3-8 & 9-12, £1.50 plus usual admission, 12.00-15.30

▶ **Visual Arts Exhibition**
29/4/00-17/5/00
Mixed media exhibition by local artists, usual admission for the grounds, 13.00-17.00, with the exception of Thur & Fri

▶ **Murder Mystery**
7/5/00-7/5/00
Can you solve the murder? Charge plus usual admission, 13.00-16.00

Sussex

► **Danse Royale**
14/5/00-14/5/00
*18th century dance and music, A£6.00 C£3.00
plus usual admission, 13.30 & 15.00*

► **Active Archaeology**
21/5/00-21/5/00
Hands on activities, charge plus usual admission, 13.00-16.00

► **Concert of English Music**
26/5/00-26/5/00
*Music from late 17th century, tickets in advance
from property (incl refreshment), 19.30*

► **Embroiders' Guild Exhibition**
27/5/00-27/5/00
Touring exhibition of 2,000 embroidered cushions, usual admission for the grounds, 13.00-17.00, not Thur & Fri

► **Craft Festival**
27/5/00-29/5/00
*Craftspeople and artists exhibiting and selling
their work, A£4.00 (non-member), £3.00 (NT
member C£1.00, 10.30-18.00*

► **Murder Mystery**
4/6/00-4/6/00
See entry for 7 May

► **Active Archaeology**
18/6/00-18/6/00
See entry for 21 May

► **An Evening With Bryan Ferry - to be confirmed**
23/6/00-23/6/00
Call venue for details

► **Party in the Park**
24/6/00-24/6/00
*Double the music, treble the fun, plus great fireworks. Tickets: Southern Region box office 01372
451596, A£18.00 C£10.00, 16.30 for 18.00*

► **Petworth Proms**
25/6/00-25/6/00
*The Royal Philharmonic Orchestra, the London
Philharmonic Choir. Tickets: Southern Region
box office 01372 451596, A18.00 C£10.00. 10%
discount groups of 15+, 15% coach parties 30,
18.30 for 20.00*

► **Silk Painting**
7/7/00-7/7/00
*Create an item from silk, working from your
own unique design. Tickets in advance from the
property, charge plus usual admission, 13.00-
16.00*

► **Textiles**
14/7/00-14/7/00
*Make something and take it home. Tickets in
advance from the property, charge plus usual
admission, 13.00-16.00*

► **Petworth Festival Exhibition**
15/7/00-30/7/00
*Usual grounds admission , 13.00-17.00 not on
Thur*

► **Kite Festival**
16/7/00-16/7/00
Bring a kite or buy one and try one.

*Entertainment for all the family, pedestrians
free, car £5.00, 11.00-17.00*

► **Petworth Festival Events**
20/7/00-27/7/00
*Concerts and open air theatre Call 01798
342207 for times and prices*

► **Painted Glass**
21/7/00-21/7/00
*Tickets in advance from the property. Charge
plus usual admission, 13.00-16.00*

► **Active Archaeology**
23/7/00-23/7/00
See entry for 21 May

► **Treasure Trail**
28/7/00-28/7/00
*C£1.00, other activities for small additional
charge, 12.00-16.00*

► **Silk Painting**
4/8/00-4/8/00
See entry for 7 July

► **Textiles**
11/8/00-11/8/00
See entry for 14 July

► **Treasure Trail**
18/8/00-18/8/00
See entry for 28 July

► **Jan Roddick Watercolours Exhibiton**
19/8/00-30/8/00
Usual grounds admission, 13.00-17.00

► **Danse Royale**
3/9/00-3/9/00
See entry for 14 May

► **Historic Interiors of the Country House**
7/10/00-18/10/00
*Paintings by Vanessa Walstaff of National Trust
Properties, usual admission, 13.00-17.00*

► **Swords and Shields**
25/8/00-25/8/00
*Make, and decorate, a sword and shield. Tickets
in advance, charge plus usual admission, 13.00-
16.00*

Preston Manor
Preston Road Brighton East Sussex BN1 6SD
[M23 / A23. BR: Brighton.]
Tel: 01273 292770 Fax: 01273 292871
This charming Edwardian Manor House and
gardens is beautifully furnished with notable
collections of silver, furniture and paintings
and presents a unique opportunity to see an
Edwardian home both 'Upstairs' and
'Downstairs.' The servants's quarters can also
be seen, featuring kitchen, butler's pantry and
boot hall. Guided Tours by prior arrangement.
Disabled access to gardens only.
*All year Tue-Sat 10.00-17.00, Sun 14.00-17.00,
Mon 13.00-17.00, Bank Hol Mon 10.00-17.00.
Closed Mon 10.00-13.00, Good Fri & 25-26 Dec
Last Admission: 17.00*

A£3.10 C(0-16)£1.95 Family Tickets:
(A2+C4)£8.15 (A1+C4)£5.05 Concessions£2.60.
Group 20+ £2.60 (tour leader and driver admitted free when accompanying a group).
Brighton & Hove School parties FREE, 1 adult
free for every 10-20 children/students, 2 for
every 21-40 & 3 for every 41-60. Winter
Concessionary Rates: School parties Oct-Feb
only £1.60. Joint ticket with Royal Pavilion
£6.50. Guided tours: up to 20 £30.00, per person thereafter £1.50

Royal Pavilion Art Gallery and Museum

4-5 Pavillion Buildings Brighton East Sussex
BN1 1EE
*[A23, M23 central Brighton. BR: Brighton
(10mins)]*
Tel: 01273 290900 Fax: 01273 292871
Justifiably termed 'the most extraordinary
palace in Europe,' this former seaside resi-
dence of King George IV is a sight no visitor to
Brighton should miss. Decorated in the
Chinese taste with an Indian exterior, this
Regency Palace is quite breathtaking. Guided
tours by prior arrangement, gift shop and tea
rooms. Wheelchair access on ground floor only.
*All year 1 June-30 Sept daily 10.00-18.00, 1 Oct-
31 May daily 10.00-17.00. Closed 25-26 Dec*
A£4.50 C£2.75 Family Tickets £7.25-£11.75
Concessions£3.25. Group rates 20+ £3.75. Joint
ticket with Preston Manor £6.50. Winter
Concession rates: School parties Oct-Feb only
£2.00. Guided tours up to 20 £20.00, per person
thereafter £1.00, UK School Parties £0.50 per
person

Rye Castle Museum

Rye Castle Gungarden Rye East Sussex TN31
7HH
*[in Rye town centre, signposted as either Ypres
Tower, Museum and East Street]*
Tel: 01797 226728
Housed in stone tower built as a fortification
in 1249 later used for three hundred years as
the town prison - the cells remain. The
Museum is now on TWO SITES, there is a new
exhibition at East Street which opens Easter
1999.
*Easter-31 Oct daily 10.30-17.30. Winter: Sat &
Sun only 10.30-17.30*
Last Admission: 17.00
A£1.50 C£0.50 OAPs&Students£1.00. Pre-
booked Groups rates available

Sackville College

Church Lane East Grinstead West Sussex RH19

3AZ
[off A22]
Tel: 01342 321930/326561
Jacobean Almhouse, founded in 1609 by
Robert Sackville, 2nd Earl of Dorset, and still in
use. Visit the Common Room, Great hall,
Chapel and Warden's Study (where the carol,
"Good King Wenceslas" was written). Original
furniture.
*June & July Wed-Sat 14.00-17.00, Aug daily
14.00-17.00*
A£1.50 C£0.75. Parties by arrangement Apr-
Oct. 1999 Prices: A£2.00 C1.00. Parties by
arrangement Apr-Oct

Saint Hill Manor

Saint Hill Road East Grinstead Sussex RH19 4JY
*[2m SW of East Grinstead on Saint Hill Road
BR East Grinstead Follow A22 down Imberhorne
Lane and over into SaintHill Road]*
Tel: 01342 326711
Fine Sussex sandstone house built in 1792 and
situated near the breathtaking Ashdown
Forest. Saint Hill Manor's final owner,
acclaimed author and humanitarian, L Ron
Hubbard lived for many years with his family.
*All year daily tours 14.00-17.00 on the hour or
by appointment*
Admission Free

St Mary's House and Gardens

The Street Bramber Steyning West Sussex
BN44 3WE
*[10m NW of Brighton in village of Bramber off
A283]*
Tel: 01903 816205
Famous historic house in the downland village
of Bramber. Built in 1470 by William
Waynflete, Bishop of Winchester, founder of
Magdalen College, Oxford. Classified as 'the
best example of late 15th century timber-
framing in Sussex.' Charming gardens with
amusing animal topiary. Exceptional example
of the prehistoric living Fossil Tree, Ginkgo
Biloba. Mysterious Ivy clad 'Monks' Walk.' Fine
panelled rooms including unique Elizabethan
'Painted Room,' and interesting exhibitions.
New attraction: visit the rediscovered lost
Victorian Gardens now under restoration.
Home-Made teas available for group bookings
and open afternoons.
*Easter-end Sept Sun Thur & Bank Hol Mon
14.00-18.00, Party bookings by prior arrangement*
A£4.00 OAPs£3.70 C£2.00, pre-booked groups
25+ £3.70. 1999 Prices: A4.00 C£2.00. Pre-
booked Groups 25+ £3.80

Sussex

Standen

East Grinstead Sussex RH19 4NE
*[2m S of East Grinstead, signposted from
B2110. Plenty of on site parking available]*
Tel: 01342 323029 Fax: 01342 316424
**www.nationaltrust.org.uk/regions/south-
ern**
Standen is a showpiece of the 19th century
Arts & Crafts movement. It was designed for
the Beale family by Philip Webb, a close friend
of William Morris, the artist and reformer,
whose textiles and wallpapers adorn the inte-
rior. Informal hillside gardens with superb
views over the Sussex countryside.
*29 Mar-5 Nov Wed-Sun & Bank Hol Mon.
House: 12.30-16.00. Shop: 12.30-17.00.
Restaurant: 11.30-17.00. Gardens: 12.30-18.00.
Picnic Area & Woodland Walk: 10 Nov-17 Dec.
Gardens and Shop: Fri-Sun 13.00-16.00
Last Admission: House: 16.00, Property: 17.00
House & Garden: A£5.00 C£2.50. Garden:
A£3.00 C£1.50 Family Ticket £12.50*

↓*special events*
▶ **Behind the Scenes**
20/6/00-20/6/00
*See parts of this beautiful home not normally
open to the public, A£5.00 C£2.50 (non-members), A£2.50 C£1.25 (members, 11.00-16.00 last
entry 15.00*
▶ **Behind the Scenes**
26/9/00-26/9/00
See entry for 20 June
▶ **Putting the House to Bed**
1/11/00-5/11/00
*Closing up the house for winter, usual admis-
sion, 12.30 for 14.00-15.00*

Wish Tower Puppet Museum

Martello Tower 73 King Edwards Parade
Eastbourne East Sussex BN21 4BY
*[on Seafront near Western Lawn opposite the
Grand Hotel]*
Tel: 01323 417776 Fax: 01323 644440
www.puppets.co.uk
The Wish Tower exhibition is housed in
Martello Tower 73, completed in 1806 and
intended as a defence fortification against
Napoleon. Now houses a puppet museum
including a history of puppets museum.
*Easter-Oct daily 11.00-17.00, Nov-Easter Closed
A£1.80 C&OAPs£1.25. Residents 10% discount
Concessions£0.65*

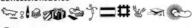

Maritime

Brighton Fishing Museum

201 Kings Road Arches Brighton East Sussex
BN1 1NB
Tel: 01273 723064
At the centre of Brighton's fishing quarter on
Old Ship Beach. Fishermen work in adjacent
arches and on the Hard. Exhibition includes
boats, artifacts, pictures and archive film.
All year daily 10.00-17.00
Admission Free

Eastbourne Lifeboat Station

Eastbourne East Sussex BN
(1822) Mersey, Sovereign Marina, Langney
Point, Inflatable 'D', Foreshore, Royal Parade, Nr
Princess Park. Visits not possible to Mersey
lifeboat for the foreseeable future due to
restricted harbour access during continuing
construction.
All year to Inflatable 'D' Parties
Admission Free

Fisherman's Museum

Rock-A-Nore Road Hastings East Sussex TN34
3DW
[E end of Hasting Old Town]
Tel: 01424 461446
This was once the fishermen's church, and now
houses such exhibits as paintings, photographs, model craft and the last of Hasting's
luggers built for sail. Display of photographs
and artifacts relating to Hastings fishing
industry and the Old Town of Hastings.
*All Year usually Easter-Sept daily 10.00-17.00,
Oct-Easter daily 11.00-16.00. Closed 25 Dec*
Admission Free

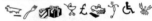

Hastings Lifeboat Station

Hastings East Sussex TN
(1858) Mersey and Inflatable 'D', 'Old Town'
next to fishing fleet. Lift, viewing gantry, class-
room/lecture room, guided tours by reserva-
tion.
All year daily. Closed Christmas
Admission Free

Lifeboat Museum and Boathouse

Inshore Boathouse Kingsway East Beach Selsey
West Sussex PO20
[B2145]
**Tel: 01243 602833 / 605601 Fax: 01243
605601**
Pictorial display of RNLI nationally and history
of the Selsey lifeboat station. Models of
lifeboats and video film showing lifeboats. 47'
Tyne Class lifeboat "City of London" also 'D'
class Lifeboat.
*Easter-Oct daily. Other times by arrangement
for parties*
Admission Free

Littlehampton Museum
Manor House Church Street Littlehampton West Sussex BN17 5EP
[off A259]
Tel: 01903 715149 Fax: 01903 734784
A small, friendly museum close to the High Street of this port and seaside resort. There are displays of local history, art, archaeology and a lively programme of temporary exhibitions, including SPACE: The REAL Frontier exhibition, July-Oct 1998, about the past and present of space exploration.
All year Tue-Sat incl Summer Bank Hol 10.30-16.30
Admission Free

Museum of Local History
High Street Hastings East Sussex TN34 3EW
Tel: 01424 781166
Displays on maritime history, the Cinque Ports, smuggling, fishing, local personalities such as John Logie Barid.
Easter-end Sep Tue-Sun 10.00-13.00 & 14.00-17.00
Admission Free

Newhaven Local and Maritime Museum
Paradise Family Leisure Park Avis Road Newhaven East Sussex BN9 0D4
[A26 to B2238 and A259 to B2238 follow Brown Museum signs]
Tel: 01273 514760/612530
New comfortable building alongside the Leisure complex which itself features all services. The Museum has unique pictorial displays and video cinema featuring local, maritime and general interest items. Show cases of artefacts, ship wreck finds, and models, sit and browse through 70 photo albums. Restaurant adjoining.
28 Mar-26 Oct Wed 14.00-17.00, Weekends & Bank Hol 11.00-17.00, 27 Oct-27 Mar Weekends 14.00-17.00
Last Admission: 30mins before closing
A£1.00 Accompanied C£Free

Royal National Lifeboat Institution Museum
King Edwards Parade Eastbourne East Sussex BN21 4BY
[off King Edward Parade on sea front]
Tel: 01825 761466
Many types of lifeboats from the earliest date to present time. Exhibits include pictorial displays of recent rescues and lifeboats artefacts.
24 Mar-1 July daily 10.00-16.00, 2 July-30 Sept daily 10.00-17.00, 1 Oct-5 Jan 98 daily 10.00-16.00

Admission Free

Shipwreck Heritage Centre
Rock-A-Nore Road Hastings East Sussex TN34 3DW
Tel: 01424 437452 Fax: 01424 437452
A museum devoted entirely to the history of wrecked ships. Weather satellite, radar, audio-visual show. Loop system for deaf in theatre.
Easter-Oct daily 10.30-17.00, Summer months 10.30-18.00
Last Admission: 16.15
A£1.95 C£1.75 Family Ticket £5.50 OAPs£1.50 Group rates call

Smugglers Adventure
St. Clements Caves Cobourg Place West Hill Hastings East Sussex TN34 3HY
[J5 M25 A21]
Tel: 01424 422964 Fax: 01424 717747
A themed experience housed in a labyrinth of caverns and passages deep below the West Hill. Visitors first tour a comprehensive exhibition and museum including video presentation, before embarking on the Adventure Walk - a trip through several acres of caves with life-size tableaux, push-button automated models and dramatic scenic effects depicting life in the days of 18th century smuggling.
Easter-Sept daily 10.00-17.30, Oct-Easter daily 11.00-16.30. Closed 25-26 Dec
A£4.50 C£2.95 OAPs&Students£3.75 Family Ticket £12.95

Military & Defence Museums

Royal Military Police Museum
Roussillon Barracks Broyle Road Chichester West Sussex PO19 4BN
[on A286 N of Chichester]
Tel: 01243 534225 Fax: 01243 534288
Fully refurbished in 1985, tracing military police history from Tudor times to date - along with cleverly presented aspects of the RMP role in the modern professional army. Features include historic uniforms, a new medal room, nostalgic 'National Service' kit lay out and Barrack Room. North Africa diorama of desert mine field c1942 and videos.
Apr-Sept Tues-Fri 10.30-12.30 & 13.30-16.30, Sat & Sun 14.00-17.00, Oct-Mar Tues-Fri 10.30-12.30 and 1.30-16.30, closed Jan
Admission Free

Sussex

Tangmere Military Aviation Museum Trust

Tangmere Chichester West Sussex PO20 6ES
[off A27. Plenty of parking on site]
Tel: 01243 775223 Fax: 01243 789490
Based at a former airfield, which played an important role during World War II, this museum spans 80 years of military aviation and has a wide-ranging collection of relics relating to Tangmere and air warfare in the south-east of England. A hangar houses record breaking aircraft Meteor and Hunter, plus a rare Supermarine Swift. Actual size replicas of Spitfire MK5, Hurricane and Spitfire prototype K5054. There are various simulators including one of a Spitfire for young visitors to 'fly'.
Mar-Oct daily 10.00-17.30. Feb & Nov daily 10.00-16.30
Last Admission: 1 hour before closure
A£3.00 C£1.50 OAPs£2.50
discount offer: Two For The Price Of One
↓*special events*
▶ **D Day Luncheon**
10/6/00-10/6/00
With a Guest Speaker, call for further details
▶ **Battle of Britain Luncheon**
16/9/00-16/9/00
A special day celebrating 60th anniversary
▶ **Armistice Day Service**
11/11/00-11/11/00
▶ **Open Day**
28/11/00-28/11/00

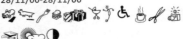

The Military Museum of Sussex

Redoubt Fortress Royal Parade Eastbourne East Sussex BN22 7AQ
[on Eastbourne seafront]
Tel: 01323 410300 Fax: 01323 732240
The Military Museum of Sussex within the Napoleonic Redoubt Fortress traces the history of the three armed services from 1700 to the Gulf War. Collections on show include The Royal Sussex Regiment, The Queen's Royal Irish Hussars, Royal Navy and RAF as well as the British Model Soldier Society. 1812 Military band concerts with fireworks weekly July-

September.
Easter-5 Nov daily 09.30-17.30
Last Admission: 16.45
A£2.20 C(0-16)&OAPs£1.10 Group rates 10+ £1.10

Mills - Water & Wind

West Blatchington Windmill

97 Holmes Avenue Hove East Sussex BN3 7LE
[easily accessible from A27 Brighton Bypass. Bus: 5B / 27]
Tel: 01273 776017
A hexagonal smock windmill built circa 1820 and sketched by John Constable in 1825. Fine museum of milling and agricultural history and exhibits. Discover how grain is turned into flour in a traditional windmill. Disabled access is limited to ground floor only.
May-Sept Sun & Bank Hol 14.30-17.00. Groups by prior arrangement other days
A£0.70 C£0.30. Parties by arrangement

Music & Theatre Museums

Mechanical Music and Doll Collection

Church Road Chichester West Sussex PO19 4HN
[1m E off A27 signposted]
Tel: 01243 785421/372646 Fax: 01243 370299
A unique opportunity to see and hear barrel organs, polyphons, musical boxes, fair organs etc - all fully restored and playing for your pleasure. A magical musical tour to fascinate and entertain all ages. The doll collection contains fine examples of Victorian china and wax dolls, also felt and velvet dolls of the 1920's.
All year Easter-Sept Sun-Fri 13.00-17.00. Oct-Easter Sun only 13.00-17.00. Closed in Dec. Evening bookings by arrangement
Last Admission: 16.00
A£2.00 C£0.75

Natural History Museums

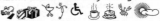

Booth Museum of Natural History

194 Dyke Road Brighton East Sussex BN1 5AA
[M23 & A23. 1.5m NW of town centre on Dyke Road, opposite Dyke Road Park. Bus: 10 / 11]
Tel: 01273 292777 Fax: 01273 292778
The museum was built in 1874 to house the bird collection of Edward Thomas Booth (1840-

1890). His collection is still on display, but the museum has expanded considerably since Booth's day and now includes thousands of butterfly and insect specimens, geology galleries with fossils, rocks and local dinosaur bones and a magnificent collection of animal skeletons. Wheelchair access via rear door. No adapted toilet for disabled visitors.

All year Mon-Wed Fri-Sat 10.00-17.00, Sun 14.00-17.00. Closed Good Fri, 25-26 Dec & 1 Jan
Admission Free

Nature & Conservation Parks

Devil's Dyke

Pond Cottage Wick Farm Albourne Sussex BN6 9DY

[off the A23. Brighton & Hove bus service from 24 May-27 Sept Route 77 on Sun and Bank Hol: Rottingdean - Sea Front (hail and ride service only) - Palace Pier Brighton - King Alfred, Hove - Hove Street - King George V Avenue - Devil's Dyke. Running hourly and when weather permitting the bus may be open top. NB: It will NOT stop a Brighton or Hove railway stations]

Tel: 01273 834830

The Devil's Dyke Estate is contained within the Sussex Downs area of outstanding natural beauty with extensive views over the whole of the western Weald to the north and the English Channel to the south. The wall of the downland ridge which dominates the local landscape is cut by a succession of undulations while the dip slope rolls gently down to the coast. The other major landscape feature is the enigmatic Devil's Dyke itself, carved deeply into the escarpment. Devil's Dyke itself offers a wide range of recreational activities, from cycling to hang-gliding; just a few hundred yards from the car park, however, it is possible to experience solitude, sharing the landscape with skylarks, the wind in the grass and the drowsy buzz of insects.

Any reasonable times
Admission Free. Activities charged

↓*special events*

▶ **Easter Egg Hunt**
22/4/00-24/4/00
Egg-citing fun for all the family at the Devil's Dyke Egg Hunt. Meet at the Stone Seat, Devil's Dyke car park (TQ258110) for this 1.5-mile walk, C£1.50 (non-member), C£1.00 (member) A£Free, 11.00-15.00

▶ **Easter Egg Rolling Competition**
24/4/00-24/4/00
Bring your own hand-decorated hard-boiled egg, and try your hand at this traditional Easter custom. Prizes! C£1.50 (non-member) £1.00

(member) A£Free - unless they enter the competition too! 11.30-13.00. Meeting point as for entry 22 April

▶ **Pedal to the Pub**
29/4/00-29/4/00
An all-day bike ride along byways and bridleways in search of railways and a pub lunch. Don't forget to bring money for lunch. Meet at Aldrington Railway Station, Hove (TQ280057) for this 20-mile bike ride. Sorry, no dogs, donations to the Devil's Dyke Appeal, 10.30-16.30

▶ **Three Hills Half Marathon**
14/5/00-14/5/00
Bring money for a pub lunch. Meet at Hassocks Railway Station (TQ304155) for this 15-mile walk, donations to the Devil's Dyke Appeal, 10.30-16.30

▶ **The Knee High Jungle**
20/5/00-20/5/00
Meet at the Stone Seat, Devil's Dyke car park (TQ258110) for this 2-mile walk , donations to the Devil's Dyke Appeal, 14.00-15.30

▶ **Ugly Bug Safari**
28/5/00-28/5/00
Bring bug boxes if you have them. Meet at the Stone Seat, Devil's Dyke car park (TQ258110) for this half-mile walk, sorry, no dogs, donations to the Devil's Dyke Appeal, 14.00-15.30

▶ **Pedal to the Pub**
10/6/00-10/6/00
See entry for 29 April

▶ **Ugly Bug Safari**
22/6/00-22/6/00
See entry for 28 May

▶ **Victorian Innovation, Pleasure and Scandal**
9/7/00-9/7/00
Meet at the Stone Seat, Devil's Dyke car park (TQ258110), for this 1-mile walk, donations to the Devil's Dyke Appeal, 14.00-15.30

▶ **Knee High Jungle**
16/7/00-16/7/00
See entry for 20 May

▶ **Devil's Dyke Detective**
27/7/00-27/7/00
Meet at the Stone Seat, Devil's Dyke car park (TQ258110), donations to the Devil's Dyke Appeal, 14.00-15.30

▶ **Ugly Bug Safari**
2/8/00-2/8/00
See entry for 28 May

▶ **Ugly Bug Safari**
20/8/00-20/8/00
See entry for 28 May

▶ **Devil's Dyke - Butterfly Bonanza**
26/8/00-26/8/00
The Downs are renowned for their rare and beautiful butterflies. Meet at the Stone Seat, Devil's Dyke Car Park (TQ258110) for this 3-mile walk, donations to the Devil's Dyke Appeal, 14.00-16.30

▶ **Pedal to the Pub**
2/9/00-2/9/00

See entry for 29 April

▶ **What the Devil's Happening at the Dyke?**
8/10/00-8/10/00
*Meet a work party in action and have a taste of
conservation work. Tea provided. Meet at the
Stone Seat, Devil's Dyke car park (TQ258110) for
this 3-mile walk, donations to the Devil's Dyke
Appeal, 14.00-16.30*

▶ **Devil's Dyke - The Devilish Dyke**
31/10/00-31/10/00
*Dare you walk with the Warden when ghosts
and ghouls are out and about? Bring a lantern,
boots and a bulb of garlic. Meet at the Stone
Seat, Devil's Dyke Car Park (TQ258110) for this 3-
mile walk, donations to the Devil's Dyke Appeal,
19.30-21.30*

🦋

Pulborough Brooks RSPB Nature Reserve
Upperton's Barn Visitor Centre Wiggonholt
Pulborough West Sussex RH20 2EL
[A283 brown tourist signs from Pulborough]
Tel: 01798 875851 Fax: 01798 873816
Set in the Arun Valley and reached via the
Visitor Centre on A283 at Wiggonholt,
Pulborough Brooks is an excellent reserve for
family visits. A two mile nature trail leads
through hedged-lined lanes to viewpoints
overlooking restored wet meadows.
*All year daily. Nature Trail: 09.00-21.00 or dusk
if sooner. Closed 25 Dec. Visitor Centre: daily
10.00-17.00. Closed 25 & 26 Dec
A£3.00 C£1.00 Family Ticket(2A&4C) £6.00
Concessions£2.00*

🦆🦢✏️🎁🍴🎁 ♿🚶🏃♿☕

On the Water

Chichester Harbour Water Tours
9 Cawley Road Chichester Sussex PO19 1UZ
*[signposted off A27 bypass and the A286, follow
signposts to Chichester Harbour Water Tours.
Ample parking in the public car park at
Itchenor.]*
Tel: 01243 786418 Fax: 01243 786418
See much of the unspoilt area from the water,
from the narrow harbour mouth to the Dell
Quay, Bosham and Thorney Island Channels.
Warm clothing is recommended. Dogs on leads
are welcome.
*All year, talking timetable available on the
above number
A£5.00 C£2.00, Charter bookings for 25+ £4.50
each*

🍴🎁🚶£🛥♿☕🌿🚂⏰🏠🚻🚹

Places of Worship incl Cathedrals

Chichester Cathedral

West Street Chichester West Sussex PO19 1PX
[city centre]
Tel: 01243 782595 Fax: 01243 536190
In the heart of the city, this fine Cathedral has
been a centre of Christian worship and com-
munity life for 900 years and is the site of the
Shrine of St Richard. Its treasures range from
Romanesque stone carvings to 20th century
works by Feibusch, Benker-Schirmer, Chagall,
Piper, Procktor, Skelton and Sutherland. Loop
system during Cathedral services; touch and
hearing centre and braille guide for the blind.
Guide dogs only.
*Easter Mon-end Oct daily 07.30-19.00. End Oct-
Easter Sun 07.30-17.00
Admission Free - Donations invited*

↓*special events*
▶ **Millennium Festival of Flowers**
1/6/00-3/6/00
*'Tidings of Great Joy'. Details and tickets from
Chichester Cathedral Restoration Trust on 01243
776922*

Micheltham Priory
Upper Dicker Hailsham Sussex BN27 3QS
[2.5m W of Hailsham off A22 and A27]
Tel: 01323 844224 Fax: 01323 844030
Set on a tranquil moated island surrounded by
spacious gardens. Founded in 1229 for
Augustine Canons the Priory is approached
through a 14th century gatehouse spanning
the country's longest medieval moat. The
buildings which escaped the Dissolution were
incorporated into a Tudor Farm and became a
splendid country. Features a working watermill, physic garden, smithy, rope museum and
the Elizabethan Great Barn. Member of the
Historic Houses Association.
*15 Mar-31 Oct Wed-Sun Apr-July & Sept 10.30-
16.00; Mar & Oct 10.30-16.00; Aug daily 10.30-
17.30
Last Admission: 45mins before closing
A£4.20 C(5-15)£2.20 OAPs&Students£3.50.
Registered Disabled / Carer £2.10 Family Ticket
(A2+C2)£10.80. Group: A£3.30 C£2.00 (min 20)*
↓*special events*
▶ **11th London to Brighton Classic Car Run**
4/6/00-4/6/00
*Route Two: Starts Crystal Place, London. Check
point 1. Groombridge Gardens, Kent, Check
Point 2. Michelham Priory, Sussex. Finishing at
Maderia Drive, Brighton. No charge to visitors at
the Start and Finish points*

🦆🦢✏️🍴🎁♿🚶🏃♿☕

St Mary's Church
Lion Street Rye Sussex TN31 7LB
[located in Rye town centre]

Tel: 01797 224935
Much visited church at the centre of Rye. Large and welcoming atmosphere. Excellent all-round views from the top of the tower.
All year daily 09.00-18.00 or dusk if earlier
Tower: A£2.00 C£1.00

Railways

Bluebell Railway
Sheffield Park Station Uckfield East Sussex TN22 3QL
[4.5m E of Haywards Heath, off A272 on A275 BR: Haywards Heath, East Grinstead]
Tel: 01825 722370/723777 Fax: 01825 724139
The Bluebell Railway operates steam trains through nine miles of Sussex countryside. Sheffield Park is the main station. Here you will find the locomotive sheds, shop, museum and restaurant. Trains run between Sheffield Park, Horsted Keynes and Kingscote. Due to planning restrictions, there is no parking at Kingscote station. Passengers wishing to board here must catch the bus (service 473) which connects Kingscote and East Grinstead. Pullman dining trains run Saturday evenings and Sunday lunchtimes, and can be chartered - please call 01825 722008 for details. In December 'Santa Special' Christmas trains operate.
visitor comments: In a lovely setting. My 2 year old loved the train journey!
Open every weekend, daily May-Sept & during School Hol. Call 01825 722370 for Talking Timetable
3rd Class Return Fare: A£7.40 C(3-15)£3.70 Family Ticket £19.90. Museum & Locomotive sheds only: A£1.60 C£0.80. Discounts for pre-booked groups of 20+

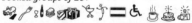

Science - Earth & Planetary

Foredown Tower
Foredown Road Portslade Brighton East Sussex BN41 2EW
[Bus: 1a / 6]
Tel: 01273 292092 Fax: 01273 292092
A beautifully converted Edwardian water tower is home to the Countryside Centre on the Sussex Downs and the only operational camera obscura in the South East. The viewing gallery gives outstanding views over the surrounding countryside and across the Channel. Plus weather station, interactive computers, countryside data, astronomy events.
All year Thur-Sun & Bank Hol 10.00-17.00 and

other days by appointment. Closed Mon-Wed inc.
A£2.00 C£1.25. Groups £1.50

Herstmonceux Science Centre
Hailsham East Sussex BN27 1RP
[BR: Polegate, bus every 30mins. Off the A271 signposted]
Tel: 01323 832731 Fax: 01323 832741
www.science-project.org
Located in the grounds of Herstmonceux, the Science Centre has more than 60 exciting exhibits. Shake-hands with yourself in the Optics Dome or investigate the Orbit Well in the Forces of Gravity Corridor. The Science Centre has a hands-on approach and children can learn how much fun science can be by using mirrors, magnets, lasers and illusions. There is also an Astronomy Exhibition, shop, café and picnic areas.
Mar-Oct daily 10.00-17.00
A£3.30 C(under 5)£Free C(5-15)£2.70 Family Ticket £9.50

Sealife Centres & Aquariums

Brighton Sea Life Centre
Marine Parade Brighton East Sussex BN2 1TB
[A23, M23]
Tel: 01273 604233/604234 Fax: 01273 681840
www.sealife.co.uk
The magnificent Brighton Sea Life centre combines the timeless elegance of fantastic Victorian architecture with the most up-to-date marine life habitats. The spectacular underwater tunnel - the longest in England - winds its way through an enormous seabed, alive with sharks, rays and conger eels. Newly restored Victorian displays are now home to over 60 varieties of marine wildlife - including many unusual native and tropical species, and the mystical Kingdom of the Seahorse lets you discover all about these beautiful creatures and their complex behaviour.
visitor comments: Experienced some difficulty with parking. Suitable for all ages - quite spectacular.
All year daily 10.00-18.00. Additionally later in summer and school hol. Closed 25 Dec
Last Admission: 17.00
A£5.95 C(0-3)£Free C(4-14)£3.95 Students&UB40s£4.25 Concessions available

Hastings Sea Life Centre
Rock-A-Nore Road Hastings East Sussex TN34 3DW
[A21 from London A259 from Eastbourne and

Sussex

Folkestone signposted in Hastings]
Tel: 01424 718776 Fax: 01424 718757
Steeped in maritime history, Hastings provides the ideal setting for a Sea Life Centre...and ancient Rock-A-Nore Road, with its curious fishermen's huts and pebbly beach, is the ideal location within the resort. New in '97 - Neptune's Nursery - follow the incredible early life-cycles of sharks, rays, cuttlefish, seahorses and other mini-marine marvels from newly-hatched eggs and larvae to tiny babies and half-grown juveniles.
All year daily 10.00-18.00
Last Admission: 17.00
Queuing Times: Max 20mins
A£4.95 C£3.50 OAPs£3.75

Social History Museums

Buckleys Yesterdays' World
Next to Battle Abbey 80-90 High Street Battle East Sussex TN33 0AQ
[J5 M25, A2100 off A21]
Tel: 01424 775378 Fax: 01424 775174
www.yesterdaysworld.co.uk
Experience a 'day in a bygone age' at one of the most unusual attractions in South East England. In a charming medieval house you'll see over thirty shop and room displays with thousands of authentic exhibits dating from 1850-1950. A new Kitchen Exhibition details kitchen equipment from 1900s-1960s. To help you discover the past there are push button commentaries, moving figures and evocative smells.
visitor comments: Highly recommended! A brilliant day out, with lovely gardens and a tea garden to relax in. Nice shop with bits and bobs!
All year daily Mar-Oct 10.00-18.00, Oct-Mar daily, hours vary call for details. Closed 25-26 Dec & 1 Jan
Last Admission: Summer: 16.45 Winter: 16.00
A£4.50 C(under 4)£Free C£2.99 OAPs£3.99
Disabled £2.00 Family Ticket(2A+2C) £13.95
discount offer: Two For The Price of One

How We Lived Then Museum of Shops and Social History
20 Cornfield Terrace Eastbourne East Sussex BN21 4NS
[between seafront and town centre BR: Eastbourne 10mins]
Tel: 01323 737143
Over the last 40 years, Jan and Graham Upton have collected over 100,000 items which are now displayed on four floors of authentic old shops and room-settings, transporting visitors back to the age of their grandparents. Grocers, chemists, sweet shops, iron-mongers, tailors, cobblers, photographers, jewellers, music and toy shops are all respresented in fascinating detail.
1999: Feb-Dec daily 10.00-17.30. 2000: All year daily 10.00-17.30
Last Admission: 17.00
1999: A£2.75 C(5-15)£1.50 OAPs£2.25. 2000: A£3.00 C(5-15)£2.00 OAPs£2.50

Spectator Sports

Brighton Racecourse
Freshfield Road Brighton Sussex BN2 2XZ
[A23 to Brighton, take A27 to Lewes and follow signs to Woodingdean]
Tel: 01273 603580 Fax: 01273 673267
Brighton Racecourse overlooks the sea and downs. There are 20 meetings between April and October. Major races run: Brighton Mile; Brighton Challenge Cup; Brighton Sprint H'cap; Brighton Summer Challenge. The racecourse is also available for non racing events, please call for further information.
Racing Apr-Oct
A£4.00-£12.00 C£Free

Fontwell Park Racecourse
Fontwell Park Arundel West Sussex BN18 0SX
[next to A27 between Chichester & Arundel. BR: Barnham. Plenty on free on site parking.]
Tel: 01243 543335 Fax: 01243 543904

Beautifully located within the ground of Fontwell Park, racing has taken place at this easily accessible Sussex venue for 75 years. Conference and Special Event facilities available.

Race meetings Aug-May 11.30-18.00
Daily Member £14.00 Tattersalls £10.00 Silver Ring £6.00 OAPs£3.00 C(0-16)£Free. Discounted pre-booked group rates available

↓ *special events*

► **Fontwell Fixture**
6/3/00-6/3/00
1st Race at 14.20

► **Fontwell Fixture**
21/3/00-21/3/00
1st Race at 14.20

► **Fontwell Fixture**
27/4/00-27/4/00
1st Race at 14.00

► **Bank Holiday Meeting**
1/5/00-1/5/00
Bank Holiday fun for all the family

► **Bank Holiday Meeting**
29/5/00-29/5/00
Family entertainment with face painting and bouncy castle for children

► **Fontwell Fixture**
25/8/00-25/8/00
1st Race at 14.10

► **Fontwell Fixture**
28/8/00-28/8/00
1st Race at 14.30

► **Fontwell Fixture**
19/9/00-19/9/00
1st Race at 14.15

► **Fontwell Fixture**
1/10/00-1/10/00
1st Race at 14.30

► **Fontwell Fixture**
25/10/00-25/10/00
1st Race at 14.10

► **Fontwell Park**
6/11/00-6/11/00
1st Race at 13.10

► **Fontwell Fixture**
5/12/00-5/12/00
1st Race at 13.10

► **Fontwell Fixture**
30/12/00-31/12/00
1st Race at 12.35

Goodwood Racecourse
Goodwood Chichester West Sussex PO18 0PS
[on the A286 N of Chichester. BR: Chichester]
Tel: 01243 755022 Fax: 01243 755025
www.gloriousgoodwood.co.uk
Set high up on the Sussex Downs with dramatic views to the Solent, Goodwood is one of the most beautiful racecourse in the world. The high quality racing together with the elegance and style of Goodwood makes this the perfect place for groups or individuals. The racing starts in the middle of May, closely followed by the Friday evening meetings in June. July race week is a major fixture in the English racing season. It attracts the most successful owners, top jockeys and leading trainers from around the world. The late August and early September race meetings are featured around the weekends.

Racing May-Sept
£5.00-£20.00 dependant on meeting and enclosure. Pre-booked group rates available

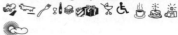

Sport & Recreation

Knockhatch Adventure Park
Hempstead Lane Hailsham Sussex BN27 3PR
[A22 at Hailsham. 9m N of Eastbourne]
Tel: 01323 442051 Fax: 01323 843878
Exciting, yet relaxing - the most varied day out around. Bird of prey centre, children's farm, crazy golf, boating lake, soft play, an indoor play area of 2000 sq ft, adventure playground, nature trail, free fall slides, grass karting, laser game, laser clays, picnic areas and restaurant, and for groups/corporate events: archery, paintball, clay shooting and karting.

1 Apr-30 Sept weekends and school holidays 10.00-17.30. At other times (except Jan) open to pre-booked groups
A£5.25 C£4.25 Family Ticket £16.95
OAPs&Concessions£3.45

Salts Park
Marine Parade Seaford East Sussex BN25 2PY
[A259 on the sea front]
Tel: 01323 490727
A park containing children's adventure playground, skating ramp, 7 tennis courts and pitch & putt golf.

1 Apr-30 Oct daily 10.00-dusk. 1 Nov-31 Mar Sat & Sun only 10.00-dusk
Admission Free

Theme & Adventure Parks

Paradise Park
Avis Road Newhaven East Sussex BN9 0DH
[signposted off A26 & A259. Just 30mins from

Sussex

Brighton and 20mins from Eastbourne. Plenty of on site parking available]

Tel: 01273 512123 Fax: 01273 616005
www.paradisepark.co.uk

Discover one of Britain's best Indoor Botanic Gardens and Paradise Water Gardens, an inspiration for garden lovers. Situated in 9 acres of grounds all of which are flat and disabled friendly. The gardens are designed with themed areas illustrating different habitats from around the world. Attractions include an extensive Planet Earth Exhibition, Garden Centre and Pleasure Gardens with children's rides and amusements, an extensive coffee shop offering delicious meals all adding up to the perfect day out for everyone.

visitor comments: Editors Choice: Children enjoyed every aspect. A thoroughly excellent day out. Easy to get round for little legs, plenty of animals to pet, no indoor picnic area.

All year daily 10.00-18.00. Closed 25-26 Dec.
Alternative phone number 01273 616006
Combined Ticket to all 3 attractions: A£4.25
C&OAPs£3.99 Family Ticket (A2+C2)£15.99

discount offer: Two For The Price Of One

Stade Family Fun Park

East Beach Street Hastings Sussex TN34 3AR
[located on A259, Hastings seafront]

Tel: 01424 716068 Fax: 01424 719609

The Stade is a unique amusement park offering excellent family value. Super kids rides, dodgems, ghost train, roller coaster and boating lake. NEW for Easter 2000: The Oh!Zone indoor entertainment centre offering ten pin bowling, dodgems, interactive venture play area, Big Screen Sport, amusements and a range of catering.

Oh!Zone: daily from 15 April 2000. Park: 15 Apr-4 Sept, 19-27 Feb & 21-29 Oct daily, Mar-Oct weekends only from 10.00
Ride tokens: £0.50p each; Wristbands from £5.00

Tourist & Visitor Information Centres

Arundel Tourist Information Centre

61 High Street Arundel West Sussex BN18 9AJ
[A27 near junction of A284]

Tel: 01903 882268 Fax: 01903 882419

Tourist Information Centre supplies:
Accommodation Bookings Nationwide;
Holiday Information Service; Information on

Events and Places to Visit; Audio Tour of Arundel.

All year daily Winter: Nov-end Mar 10.00-15.00; Summer: 09.30-17.00 Closed for lunch
Admission Free

Battle Tourist Information Centre

88 High Street Battle East Sussex TN33 0AQ
Tel: 01424 773721 Fax: 01424 773436
www.battletown.co.uk

Tourist Information Centre supplying:
Accommodation Booking; Leaflets; Maps; Guides; Information on Events and Booking Service; Maps for 1066 Walk; Gift Shop; Multi-Lingual Leaflets; Travel and Theatre Bookings including Cross-Channel Crossing Tickets and National Express; Complete Holiday Information Service. Eurotunnel Bookings, Eurostar Bookings, Battle Theatre Club and Rainbow Holidays Bookings.

Daily Nov-Feb10.00-16.00, Mar-June 09.00 - 17.00, July-Aug 9.30-17.30, Sept-Oct 09.00-17.00
Admission Free

Bexhill-on-Sea Tourist Information Centre

51 Marina Bexhill-On-Sea Sussex TN40 1BQ
[on the seafront opposite Bexhill Sailing Club]
Tel: 01424 732208

Tourist Information Centre supplying:
Accommodation Booking; National Express Tickets; Cross-Channel Ferry and Eurostar Tickets; Day Excursions and Coach Tours; Guides, Maps & Books.

Jan-Apr & Oct-Dec Mon-Fri 0.930-17.00, Sat 10.00-16.00 & Sun 11.00-15.00, May-Sept Mon-Fri 09.30-18.00, Sat 09.30-17.00 & Sun 10.00-16.00, Bank Hol 10.00-16.00
Admission Free

Bognor Regis Tourist Information Centre

Belmont Street Bognor Regis West Sussex PO21 1BJ
Tel: 01243 823140

Feb-Mar Mon-Fri 09.30-16.00, Sat 10.00-16.00, Feb-Apr Sun 10.00-15.00, Apr-July Mon-Fri 10.00-17.00, 1 Apr-2 May Sat 10.00-17.00, 3 May-20 July Sat & Sun 10.00-17.00, 21 July-7 Sept Mon-Fri 09.30-17.30 Weekends 10.00-17.30, 8 Sept-2 Nov Mon-Fri 09.30-17.00 Sat 10.00-17.00 & Sun 10.00-16.00, 3 Nov-31 Dec Mon-Fri 09.30-16.00 Sat 10.00-15.00

Boship Tourist Information Centre

Boship Roundabout A22 Lower Dicker Hailsham East Sussex BN27 4DP

Tel: 01323 442667
*Jan-23 Mar 23 & Nov-Dec Mon-Fri 09.15-15.30,
Jan-Dec Weekends 10.00-17.00, Apr-Oct Mon-Fri
09.15-17.15*

Brighton Tourist Information Centre
10 Bartholomew Square Brighton East Sussex
BN1 1JS
Tel: 01273 292599
www.tourism.brighton.co.uk
*Sept-June Mon-Fri 09.00-17.00 Sat 10.00-17.00,
July-Aug 09.00-18.15 Sat 10.00-18.00, Sun Mar-
June 10.00-16.00, July-Aug 10.00-17.00 Sept-
Oct 10.00-16.00 Nov-Feb closed*

Chichester Tourist Information Centre
29a South Street Chichester West Sussex PO19
1AH
Tel: 01243 775888 Fax: 01243 5394499
www.chichester.gov.uk
*2 Jan-31 Dec Mon-Sat 09.15-17.15, 1 Apr-30
Sept Sun 10.00-16.00, Bank Hol 10.00-16.00*

Eastbourne Tourist Information Centre
3 Cornfield Road Eastbourne East Sussex BN21
4QL
Tel: 01323 411400
*2 Jan-31 Dec Mon-Sat 09.30-17.30, 15 June-28
Sept Sun 10.00-13.00, Bank Hol 10.00-16.00*

Fontwell Tourist Information Centre
Little Chef Complex Fontwell West Sussex
BN18 0SD
Tel: 01243 543269
*Jan-31 Mar Mon-Fri 09.00-17.00 Sat 10.00-
17.00, 1 Apr-28 Sept Mon-Fri 09.00-18.00
Weekends 10.00-18.00, 29 Sept-31 Dec Mon-Fri
09.00-17.00, 29 Sept-2 Nov Weekends 10.00-
17.00, 3 Nov-31 Dec Sat 10.00-17.00*

Hastings Old Town Tourist Information Centre
The Stade Hastings Sussex TN34 1EQ
*[A21 or A259, follow signs to the Old Town,
located opposite the coach park]*
**Tel: 01424 781111/781120 Fax: 01424
781186**
Tourist Information Centre supplies:
Accommodation Booking; P&O, Hoverspeed,
Sea France Le Shuttle Agencies; Guide Friday;
Sale of Souvenirs, Books, Guides, Stamps and
Phone Cards.
*Summer: Tue-Fri 09.30-17.00, Sat & Sun 09.30-
17.30, July & Aug daily 09.30-18.00 Oct-Easter
Sat & Sun 10.00-16.00*
Admission Free

Hastings Tourist Information Centre
Queens Square Priory Meadow Hastings
Sussex TN34 1TL
*[A21 or A259, follow signs to the town centre
and Priory Meadow shopping centre, located in
town hall]*
Tel: 01424 781111 Fax: 01424 781133
www.hastings.gov.uk
Tourist Information Centre supplies:
Souvenirs; Books; White Rock Theatre Tickets;
Coach Bookings/Tours; National Express, P&O,
Le Shuttle and Hoverspeed Agent;
Computerised Rail Journey Planner and Car
Route Planning Service.
*Daily Summer 09.30-18.00, Winter10.00-17.00
Sun 10.00-16.00*
Admission Free

↓ *special events*
► **Hastings Music Festival**
28/2/00-25/3/00
*Competitive musical festival with classes for
mime, singing, instrumental, speech, drama
and dance*
► **Hastings Half Marathon**
19/3/00-19/3/00
*The top Half Marathon in the UK held around
the outskirts of the town*
► **Hastings and St Leonards Millennium
Festival**
20/4/00-1/5/00
► **Hastings Easter Indoor Bowls Tournament**
21/4/00-24/4/00
*At Falaise Indoor Bowls Centre, a bowls tourna-
ment with prize money*
► **Castle Cycle Challenge Hastings**
23/4/00-23/4/00
*A cycle event for local charities. Prizes for differ-
ent classes and age groups*
► **Jack in the Green Morris Dance Festival**
28/4/00-1/5/00
*Procession on Bank Hol Mon with Jack in the
Green weekend of music, dance, singing and
street entertainment*
► **Vintage Bus and Transport Rally**
14/5/00-14/5/00
*Held at the Oval, vintage buses and trolley buses
of the Hastings fleet including classic cars and
commercial vehicles*
► **Walking the Fish Festival**
26/5/00-26/5/00
*A spectacular costumed carnival parade by
schools and community groups with artists*
► **The Robert Tressell Festival**
27/5/00-29/5/00
*Bourne Arts Centre. Events centred around
Robert Tressell's "The Ragged Trousered
Philanthropists"*
► **Open Air Band Concerts**
28/5/00-27/8/00

Sussex

Sussex

Held every Sunday from May 28-Aug 27
► **1066 Country Randonnee**
4/6/00-4/6/00
Randonee Les Belles D'Europe challenge over a distance of 106.6 km
► **Sea Angling Boat Festival**
16/6/00-18/6/00
The 97th Festival to be held on the seafront with prizes and trophies to be won
► **Hastings Beer Festival**
6/7/00-8/7/00
Live music, more than 50 different ales and Saturday afternoon family entertainment
► **Hastings Old Town Week**
5/8/00-13/8/00
Open houses, concerts, art exhibitions, drama, coffee mornings, cream teas, folk music and more
► **Hastings Old Town Carnival**
11/8/00-11/8/00
Part of Old Town Week with judging, procession (approx 17.30) and more
► **1066 Soccer Tournament**
26/8/00-28/8/00
Non stop soccer tournament for under 7 to under 16 age groups at Bulverhythe Playing Fields from 09.30-18.00 daily
► **Hastings Week**
7/10/00-15/10/00
Various events to celebrate the anniversary of the Battle of hastings, Oct 14 1066

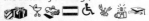

Horsham Tourist Information Centre
9 Causeway Horsham Sussex RH12 1HE
Tel: 01403 211661 Fax: 01403 215268
2 Jan-31 Dec Mon-Sat 10.00-17.00
Last Admission: 17.00

Hove Tourist Information Centre
Town Hall Church Road Hove Sussex BN3 3BQ
[from A27 follow signs for Hove, then TIC signs]
Tel: 01273 292589 Fax: 01273 293027
www.tourism@brighton-hove.gov.uk
Tourist Information Centre supplying: BABA's; Bookings for Coach Excursions; Local Bus Tickets; Maps; Guides; Stamps; Phonecards; Souvenirs; Information on Local and National Events; Tickets for Town Hall Functions and Local Functions.
Jan 4-Dec 24 Mon Tue Thur Fri 09.00-13.00 & 14.15-17.00 Wed 10.30-13.00 & 14.15-17.00
Admission Free

Hove Tourist Information Centre
King Alfred Leisure Centre Kingsway Hove Sussex BN3 2WW
Tel: 01273 746100 / 720371
2 Jan-24 Dec Mon-Fri 09.00-17.00, 28 Mar-25

Aug Weekends 09.00-17.00
↓*special events*
► **South Coast Dolls House and Miniatures Fair**
8/4/00-12/11/00
April 8-9 and Nov 12 only at Hove Town Hall. 150 stands of miniatures. Refreshments, huge car park and FREE prize draw. A£3.00 Accompanied C£Free OAPs£2.00

Lewes Tourist Information Centre
187 High Street Lewes East Sussex BN7 2DE
Tel: 01273 483448
2 Jan-28 Sept Mon-Fri 09.00-17.00 Sat 10.00-14.00, 1 Apr-28 Sept Sat 10.00-17.00 Sun 10.00-14.00, 1 Oct-31 Dec Mon-Fri 10.00-17.00 Sat 10.00-14.00
↓*special events*
► **Fourth Southdown Real Ale and Cider Festival**
23/6/00-24/6/00
Held at Lewes Town Hall, with over 50 real ales plus traditional ciders, perrys, country wines, food and entertainment

Littlehampton Tourist Information Centre
Windmill Complex Coastguard Road Littlehampton West Sussex BN17 5LH
Tel: 01903 713480
28 Apr-25 May Thur-Fri 12.00-16.00 Sat & Sun 10.00-16.00, 26 May-20 July daily 10.00-17.00, 21 July-7 Sept daily 10.00-17.30, 8 Sept- 28 Sept Thur-Fri 12.00-16.00 Sat & Sun 10.00-17.00

Midhurst Tourist Information Centre
North Street Midhurst West Sussex GU29 9DW
Tel: 01730 817322 Fax: 01730 817120
1 Apr-30 Sept Mon-Sat 09.30-17.30, 1 Apr-30 Sept Sun 11.00-16.00, 1 Oct-31 Mar Mon-Sat 10.00-17.00

Peacehaven Tourist Information Centre
Meridian Centre Roderick Avenue Peacehaven Sussex BN10 8BB
Tel: 01273 582668

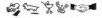

Petworth Tourist Information Centre
Market Square Petworth West Sussex GU28 0AF
Tel: 01798 343523
2 Jan-31 Mar Mon-Sat 10.00-16.00, 1 Apr-30 Sept Mon-Sat 09.30-17.30 Sun 11.00-16.00, 1 Oct-31 Dec Mon-Sat 10.00-16.00

Rye Tourist Information Centre

The Heritage Centre Strand Quay Rye Sussex
TN31 7AY

[on A259 between Hastings / Folkstone]

Tel: 01797 226696 Fax: 01797 223460

www.rye.org.uk/heritage.htm

Tourist Information Centre supplies:
Accommodation Local and National; Theatre
Tickets; Hoverspeed Tickets; Rye Town Model
Show; Rye Audio Tours; Free Heritage Centre
Exhibition; Gift Shop; Disabled Access.

*All year daily Mar-Oct 09.00-17.30, Nov-Feb
10.00-16.00*

Admission Free

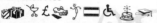

Seaford Tourist Information Centre

25 Clinton Place Seaford Sussex BN25 1NP

Tel: 01323 897426

*All year Mon-Fri 09.00-5.00, Easter-Oct Sat
10.00-17.00*

Worthing Tourist Information Centre

Marine Parade Worthing Sussex BN11 3PX

Tel: 01903 210022

Seasonal

Worthing Tourist Information Centre

Chapel Road Worthing Sussex BN11 1HL

Tel: 01903 210022 Fax: 01903 236277

All year 09.30-17.00

Toy & Childhood Museums

Arundel Toy and Military Museum

23 High Street Arundel West Sussex BN18 9AD

*[Arundel is on the A27, situated in the town
centre]*

Tel: 01903 882908/507446

A Georgian cottage in the heart of town displaying a vast and unique collection of interesting old toys, games, dolls, dolls' houses,
teddy bears and model toy soldiers. There are
also Royal commemoratives, boats, 'Goss' china
models, 'Britains' farmyards, puppets,
pocillovy (egg-cups), small militaria and
curiosities collected from all over the world,
and fascinating for all the family.

*All year Weekends, School & Bank Hol 12.00-
17.00, June-Sept daily 10.30-17.00. Most days
in Spring & Oct*

*A£1.25 C(0-15) Family Ticket £4.00
Students&OAPs£1.00. Pre-booked groups 20+*

Museum and Heritage Centre

61 High Street Arundel West Sussex BN18 9AJ

Tel: 01903 882908

Vast intriguing collection of family toys and
dolls.

*Easter-Oct weekends & Bank Hol. Mon-Fri
11.00-17.00 in high season*

A£1.00 C£0.50p

Zoos

Drusillas Park

Alfriston Sussex BN26 5QS

*[off A27 between Brighton / Eastbourne, 7m
from Seaford beach]*

Tel: 01323 870234 Fax: 01323 870846

www.drusillas.co.uk

Drusillas Park is widely regarded as the Best
Small Zoo in England with a wide variety of
animals along the pretty, well planned zoo
walk. Beautiful gardens, Explorers Restaurant,
Playland, Indoor Toddler Village, Petworld,
Train, Panning for Gold, Wacky Workshop,
Maasai exhibition, Animal Encounter sessions
and five shops including Teddy's Jungle Safari.
New for 2000: Millennium Bugs and the mysterious Saki Monkeys. Wheelchair access
throughout. Situated near historic Alfriston
and next door to the English Wine Centre.
Indoor and Outdoor picnic areas. Our
Challenge Days for Beaver Scouts, Brownies,
Cubs and Rainbows consist of a simple, informative Quiz which helps children to observe
and understand their environment. Dates follow in the special events section.

visitor comments: A complete day out at reasonable cost. Very informative and educational. Excellent play area.

*All year Summer: daily 10.00-18.00, Winter:
daily 10.00-17.00. Closed 24-26 Dec
Last Admission: 60mins before closing
A£7.60 C(0-3)£Free C(3-12)£6.50 OAPs, Long
Term Disabled & Carers £6.00 Groups 15+:
A£6.60 C(3-12)£5.50 C(0-3)£Free OAPs, Long
Term Disabled & Carers £5.00. Please enquire
for winter discount prices*

↓*special events*

▶ Adopter Day

Sussex

25/3/00-7/10/00
Held on Mar 25 and Oct 7 only
▶ **Brownie Challenge Days**
15/4/00-16/12/00
*Held on Apr 15, May 20, June 24, July 8, Sept 16,
30 and Dec 16 only*
▶ **Julian Ford and his Birds of Prey**
19/4/00-30/8/00
*Fabulous display of these majestic birds with
talks and small flying displays. Held on Apr 19,
26, July 26, Aug 2, 9, 16, 23 and 30 only*
▶ **Charlie the Clown**
20/4/00-31/8/00
*Held on April 20, 27, June 1, Aug 3, 10, 17, 24
and 31 only*
▶ **Easter Egg Challenge**
21/4/00-24/4/00
▶ **Beaver Challenge Day**
29/4/00-9/12/00
*Held on Apr 29, May 27, June 17, July 1, 15, Sept
23, Oct 14 and Dec 9 only*
▶ **Reptile Weekend**
6/5/00-10/9/00
Held on May 6-7 and Sept 9-10 only
▶ **Rainbow Challenge Day**
6/5/00-9/12/00
Held on May 6, June 3, Oct 7 and Dec 9 only
▶ **Cub Challenge Day**
13/5/00-16/12/00
*Held on May 13, June 10, Oct 21 and Dec 16
only*
▶ **East Sussex Morris Minor Owners Club Rally**
14/5/00-14/5/00
▶ **Primate Weekend**
27/5/00-4/6/00
▶ **Waterworld**
25/7/00-15/8/00
Held on July 25 and Aug 15 only
▶ **Clowns Day**
27/7/00-27/7/00
▶ **Fur, Feathers and Fins**
1/8/00-22/8/00
Held on Aug 1 and 22 only
▶ **Animal Wars**
8/8/00-8/8/00
▶ **Animal Wars**
29/8/00-29/8/00
▶ **Creepy Crawlies Day**
24/9/00-24/9/00
▶ **Boo's Haunted Cottage**
21/10/00-29/10/00
▶ **Santa's Christmas Cottage**
1/12/00-23/12/00
▶ **What does Santa do after Christmas?**
27/12/00-7/1/01
*Come along and you might just see Santa relax-
ing in his secret Drusillas hide away*

236

South of England Rare Breeds Centre
Ashford

Up to Two Adults At Group Rate (£2.75)

not to be used in conjunction with any other offer, one coupon per party not valid on Bank Hols and event weekends.

Discount Coupon   **Valid until end Feb 2001**

Wingham Wildlife Park
Canterbury

One Free Child With Two Full Paying Adults

not to be used in conjunction with any other offer, one coupon per party not valid on Bank Hols and event weekends.

Discount Coupon   **Valid until end Feb 2001**

Dover Museum
Dover

Two For The Price Of One

not to be used in conjunction with any other offer, one coupon per party not valid on Bank Hols and event weekends.

Discount Coupon   **Valid until end Feb 2001**

Old Town Hall Museum
Margate

One Child Free With A Full Paying Adult

not to be used in conjunction with any other offer, one coupon per party not valid on Bank Hols and event weekends.

Discount Coupon   **Valid until end Feb 2001**

Biddenden Vineyards
Biddenden

10% Discount On All Shop Purchases

not to be used in conjunction with any other offer, one coupon per party not valid on Bank Hols and event weekends.

Discount Coupon   **Valid until end Feb 2001**

Mount Ephraim Gardens
Faversham

£1.00 Off Entrance For Adults

not to be used in conjunction with any other offer, one coupon per party not valid on Bank Hols and event weekends.

Discount Coupon   **Valid until 30 Sept 2000**

DAYS OUT UK
The Leading Days Out Guide
P O Box 427
Northampton
NN2 7YJ

This coupon entitles the holder to the discount offer
shown on the reverse side. To claim your discount
please present this coupon when paying for your entry.

Customer care line number *free* phone 0800 316 8900

This coupon entitles the holder to the discount offer
shown on the reverse side. To claim your discount
please present this coupon when paying for your entry.

Customer care line number *free* phone 0800 316 8900

This coupon entitles the holder to the discount offer
shown on the reverse side. To claim your discount
please present this coupon when paying for your entry.

Customer care line number *free* phone 0800 316 8900

This coupon entitles the holder to the discount offer
shown on the reverse side. To claim your discount
please present this coupon when paying for your entry.

Customer care line number *free* phone 0800 316 8900

This coupon entitles the holder to the discount offer
shown on the reverse side. To claim your discount
please present this coupon when paying for your entry.

Customer care line number *free* phone 0800 316 8900

This coupon entitles the holder to the discount offer
shown on the reverse side. To claim your discount
please present this coupon when paying for your entry.

Customer care line number *free* phone 0800 316 8900

Fleur de Lis Heritage Centre

Faversham

Two For The Price Of One (Excludes Tour)

not to be used in conjunction with any other offer, one coupon per party not valid on Bank Hols and event weekends.

Page 19

DAYS OUT UK
The Leading Days Out Guide
P O Box 427
Northampton
NN2 7YJ

Discount Coupon — Valid until end Feb 2001

Cobham Hall

Gravesend

£1.00 Off Admission to House/Garden

not to be used in conjunction with any other offer, one coupon per party not valid on Bank Hols and event weekends.

Page 20

DAYS OUT UK
The Leading Days Out Guide
P O Box 427
Northampton
NN2 7YJ

Discount Coupon — Valid until 29 Aug 2000

Dover Old Town Gaol

Dover

Two For The Price Of One

not to be used in conjunction with any other offer, one coupon per party not valid on Bank Hols and event weekends.

Page 22

DAYS OUT UK
The Leading Days Out Guide
P O Box 427
Northampton
NN2 7YJ

Discount Coupon — Valid until end Feb 2001

Squerryes Court

Westerham

Two For The Price Of One

not to be used in conjunction with any other offer, one coupon per party not valid on Bank Hols and event weekends.

Page 30

DAYS OUT UK
The Leading Days Out Guide
P O Box 427
Northampton
NN2 7YJ

Discount Coupon — Valid 1 Apr-30 Sept 2000

Canterbury Tales

Canterbury

One Child Free With Each Full Paying Adult

not to be used in conjunction with any other offer, one coupon per party not valid on Bank Hols and event weekends.

Page 33

DAYS OUT UK
The Leading Days Out Guide
P O Box 427
Northampton
NN2 7YJ

Discount Coupon — Valid until end Feb 2001

Maritime Museum

Ramsgate

One Child Free With A Full Paying Adult

not to be used in conjunction with any other offer, one coupon per party not valid on Bank Hols and event weekends.

Page 33

DAYS OUT UK
The Leading Days Out Guide
P O Box 427
Northampton
NN2 7YJ

Discount Coupon — Valid until end Feb 2001

This coupon entitles the holder to the discount offer
shown on the reverse side. To claim your discount
please present this coupon when paying for your entry.

Customer care line number *free* phone 0800 316 8900

This coupon entitles the holder to the discount offer
shown on the reverse side. To claim your discount
please present this coupon when paying for your entry.

Customer care line number *free* phone 0800 316 8900

This coupon entitles the holder to the discount offer
shown on the reverse side. To claim your discount
please present this coupon when paying for your entry.

Customer care line number *free* phone 0800 316 8900

This coupon entitles the holder to the discount offer
shown on the reverse side. To claim your discount
please present this coupon when paying for your entry.

Customer care line number *free* phone 0800 316 8900

This coupon entitles the holder to the discount offer
shown on the reverse side. To claim your discount
please present this coupon when paying for your entry.

Customer care line number *free* phone 0800 316 8900

This coupon entitles the holder to the discount offer
shown on the reverse side. To claim your discount
please present this coupon when paying for your entry.

Customer care line number *free* phone 0800 316 8900

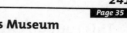

DAYS OUT UK
The Leading Days Out Guide

P O Box 427
Northampton
NN2 7YJ

Royal Engineers Museum
Gillingham

One Child Free With One Full Paying Adult

not to be used in conjunction with any other offer, one coupon per party not valid on Bank Hols and event weekends.

Discount Coupon · Valid until end Feb 2001

DAYS OUT UK
The Leading Days Out Guide

P O Box 427
Northampton
NN2 7YJ

Page 36

Crabble Corn Mill
Dover

50p Off Adult Ticket or £1.00 Off Family Ticket

not to be used in conjunction with any other offer, one coupon per party not valid on Bank Hols and event weekends.

Discount Coupon · Valid until end Feb 2001

DAYS OUT UK
The Leading Days Out Guide

P O Box 427
Northampton
NN2 7YJ

Page 39

Romney Hythe & Dymchurch Railway
New Romney

One Person Free With A Full Paying Adult, all Stations Return Ticket. One Coupon Per Day

not to be used in conjunction with any other offer, one coupon per party not valid on Bank Hols and event weekends.

Discount Coupon · Valid until end Feb 2001

DAYS OUT UK
The Leading Days Out Guide

P O Box 427
Northampton
NN2 7YJ

Page 42

Folkestone Racecourse
Folkestone
£2.00 Discount Per Person

not to be used in conjunction with any other offer, one coupon per party not valid on Bank Hols and event weekends.

Discount Coupon · Valid until end Feb 2001

DAYS OUT UK
The Leading Days Out Guide

P O Box 427
Northampton
NN2 7YJ

Page 42

Dreamland Fun Park
Margate

One Child Wristband Free With Every Full Paying Adult Wristband

not to be used in conjunction with any other offer, one coupon per party not valid on Bank Hols and event weekends.

Discount Coupon · Valid until end Feb 2001

DAYS OUT UK
The Leading Days Out Guide

P O Box 427
Northampton
NN2 7YJ

Page 43

White Cliffs Experience
Dover

One Child Free With One Full Paying Adult

not to be used in conjunction with any other offer, one coupon per party not valid on Bank Hols and event weekends.

Discount Coupon · Valid until end Feb 2001

This coupon entitles the holder to the discount offer shown on the reverse side. To claim your discount please present this coupon when paying for your entry.

Customer care line number *free* phone 0800 316 8900

This coupon entitles the holder to the discount offer shown on the reverse side. To claim your discount please present this coupon when paying for your entry.

Customer care line number *free* phone 0800 316 8900

This coupon entitles the holder to the discount offer shown on the reverse side. To claim your discount please present this coupon when paying for your entry.

Customer care line number *free* phone 0800 316 8900

This coupon entitles the holder to the discount offer shown on the reverse side. To claim your discount please present this coupon when paying for your entry.

Customer care line number *free* phone 0800 316 8900

This coupon entitles the holder to the discount offer shown on the reverse side. To claim your discount please present this coupon when paying for your entry.

Customer care line number *free* phone 0800 316 8900

This coupon entitles the holder to the discount offer shown on the reverse side. To claim your discount please present this coupon when paying for your entry.

Customer care line number *free* phone 0800 316 8900

DAYS OUT UK
The Leading Days Out Guide

P O Box 427
Northampton
NN2 7YJ

Page 46

Eurotunnel Education Service
Folkestone

10% Discount On All Group Bookings

not to be used in conjunction with any other offer, one coupon per party not valid on Bank Hols and event weekends.

Discount Coupon   Valid until end Feb 2001

DAYS OUT UK
The Leading Days Out Guide

P O Box 427
Northampton
NN2 7YJ

Page 47

Druidstone Wildlife Park
Canterbury

Two For The Price Of One

not to be used in conjunction with any other offer, one coupon per party not valid on Bank Hols and event weekends.

Discount Coupon   Valid until 30 Nov 2000

DAYS OUT UK
The Leading Days Out Guide

P O Box 427
Northampton
NN2 7YJ

Page 48

Howletts Wild Animal Park
Canterbury

£2.00 Off Adult or Child Admission With A Full Paying Adult

not to be used in conjunction with any other offer, one coupon per party not valid on Bank Hols and event weekends.

Discount Coupon   Valid until end Feb 2001

DAYS OUT UK
The Leading Days Out Guide

P O Box 427
Northampton
NN2 7YJ

Page 53

Apsley House, The Wellington Museum
London

Two For The Price Of One

not to be used in conjunction with any other offer, one coupon per party not valid on Bank Hols and event weekends.

Discount Coupon   Valid until end Feb 2001

DAYS OUT UK
The Leading Days Out Guide

P O Box 427
Northampton
NN2 7YJ

Page 57

Design Museum
London

One Child Free With Each Full Paying Adult

not to be used in conjunction with any other offer, one coupon per party not valid on Bank Hols and event weekends.

Discount Coupon   Valid until end Feb 2001

DAYS OUT UK
The Leading Days Out Guide

P O Box 427
Northampton
NN2 7YJ

Page 57

Estorick Collection of Modern Italian Art
London

Two For The Price Of One

not to be used in conjunction with any other offer, one coupon per party not valid on Bank Hols and event weekends.

Discount Coupon   Valid until end Feb 2001

This coupon entitles the holder to the discount offer shown on the reverse side. To claim your discount please present this coupon when paying for your entry.

Customer care line number *free* phone 0800 316 8900

This coupon entitles the holder to the discount offer shown on the reverse side. To claim your discount please present this coupon when paying for your entry.

Customer care line number *free* phone 0800 316 8900

This coupon entitles the holder to the discount offer shown on the reverse side. To claim your discount please present this coupon when paying for your entry.

Customer care line number *free* phone 0800 316 8900

This coupon entitles the holder to the discount offer shown on the reverse side. To claim your discount please present this coupon when paying for your entry.

Customer care line number *free* phone 0800 316 8900

This coupon entitles the holder to the discount offer shown on the reverse side. To claim your discount please present this coupon when paying for your entry.

Customer care line number *free* phone 0800 316 8900

This coupon entitles the holder to the discount offer shown on the reverse side. To claim your discount please present this coupon when paying for your entry.

Customer care line number *free* phone 0800 316 8900

Page 66

Soviet Carpet and Art Gallery
London
5% Discount Off All Rugs;
15% Discount Off All Art

not to be used in conjunction with any other offer, one coupon per party not valid on Bank Hols and event weekends.

DAYS OUT UK
The Leading Days Out Guide
P O Box 427
Northampton
NN2 7YJ

Discount Coupon   Valid until end Feb 2001

Page 68

Victoria and Albert Museum
London
Two For The Price Of One on Std Admission (£5)
Not Valid for Exhibitions

not to be used in conjunction with any other offer, one coupon per party not valid on Bank Hols and event weekends.

DAYS OUT UK
The Leading Days Out Guide
P O Box 427
Northampton
NN2 7YJ

Discount Coupon   Valid until end Feb 2001

Page 70

Chislehurst Caves
Chislehurst
One Free With A Second Of Equal Or Greater Value
Is Purchased

not to be used in conjunction with any other offer, one coupon per party not valid on Bank Hols and event weekends.

DAYS OUT UK
The Leading Days Out Guide
P O Box 427
Northampton
NN2 7YJ

Discount Coupon   Valid until end Feb 2001

Page 80

Honeywood Heritage Centre
Carshalton

Two For The Price Of One

not to be used in conjunction with any other offer, one coupon per party not valid on Bank Hols and event weekends.

DAYS OUT UK
The Leading Days Out Guide
P O Box 427
Northampton
NN2 7YJ

Discount Coupon   Valid until end Feb 2001

Page 84

Chelsea Physic Garden
London

Two For The Price Of One

not to be used in conjunction with any other offer, one coupon per party not valid on Bank Hols and event weekends.

DAYS OUT UK
The Leading Days Out Guide
P O Box 427
Northampton
NN2 7YJ

Discount Coupon   Valid until 29 Oct 2000

Page 90

Royal Mint Sovereign Gallery
London

10% off ANY product displayed

not to be used in conjunction with any other offer, one coupon per party not valid on Bank Hols and event weekends.

DAYS OUT UK
The Leading Days Out Guide
P O Box 427
Northampton
NN2 7YJ

Discount Coupon   Valid until end Feb 2001

This coupon entitles the holder to the discount offer shown on the reverse side. To claim your discount please present this coupon when paying for your entry.

Customer care line number *free* phone 0800 316 8900

This coupon entitles the holder to the discount offer shown on the reverse side. To claim your discount please present this coupon when paying for your entry.

Customer care line number *free* phone 0800 316 8900

This coupon entitles the holder to the discount offer shown on the reverse side. To claim your discount please present this coupon when paying for your entry.

Customer care line number *free* phone 0800 316 8900

This coupon entitles the holder to the discount offer shown on the reverse side. To claim your discount please present this coupon when paying for your entry.

Customer care line number *free* phone 0800 316 8900

This coupon entitles the holder to the discount offer shown on the reverse side. To claim your discount please present this coupon when paying for your entry.

Customer care line number *free* phone 0800 316 8900

This coupon entitles the holder to the discount offer shown on the reverse side. To claim your discount please present this coupon when paying for your entry.

Customer care line number *free* phone 0800 316 8900

247

Alexandra Palace
London

Two For The Price Of One For Ice Rink

not to be used in conjunction with any other offer, one coupon per party not valid on Bank Hols and event weekends.

Discount Coupon — Valid until end Feb 2001

DAYS OUT UK
The Leading Days Out Guide
P O Box 427
Northampton
NN2 7YJ

Page 90

Page 101

Queen Elizabeth's Hunting Lodge
London

Two Adults For The Price Of One

not to be used in conjunction with any other offer, one coupon per party not valid on Bank Hols and event weekends.

Discount Coupon — Valid until end Feb 2001

The Leading Days Out Guide
P O Box 427
Northampton
NN2 7YJ

Page 102

Rose Theatre Exhibition
London

Two For The Price Of One

not to be used in conjunction with any other offer, one coupon per party not valid on Bank Hols and event weekends.

Discount Coupon — Valid until end Feb 2001

The Leading Days Out Guide
P O Box 427
Northampton
NN2 7YJ

Page 104

Syon House and Gardens
Brentford

Two For The Price Of One Full Paying Adult For Combined Ticket Only

not to be used in conjunction with any other offer, one coupon per party not valid on Bank Hols and event weekends.

Discount Coupon — Valid until end Feb 2001

The Leading Days Out Guide
P O Box 427
Northampton
NN2 7YJ

Page 106

Whitehall
Sutton

Two For The Price Of One

not to be used in conjunction with any other offer, one coupon per party not valid on Bank Hols and event weekends.

Discount Coupon — Valid until end Feb 2001

The Leading Days Out Guide
P O Box 427
Northampton
NN2 7YJ

Page 110

Dickens House Museum
London

Two For The Price Of One

not to be used in conjunction with any other offer, one coupon per party not valid on Bank Hols and event weekends.

Discount Coupon — Valid until end Feb 2001

The Leading Days Out Guide
P O Box 427
Northampton
NN2 7YJ

This coupon entitles the holder to the discount offer shown on the reverse side. To claim your discount please present this coupon when paying for your entry.

Customer care line number *free* phone 0800 316 8900

This coupon entitles the holder to the discount offer shown on the reverse side. To claim your discount please present this coupon when paying for your entry.

Customer care line number *free* phone 0800 316 8900

This coupon entitles the holder to the discount offer shown on the reverse side. To claim your discount please present this coupon when paying for your entry.

Customer care line number *free* phone 0800 316 8900

This coupon entitles the holder to the discount offer shown on the reverse side. To claim your discount please present this coupon when paying for your entry.

Customer care line number *free* phone 0800 316 8900

This coupon entitles the holder to the discount offer shown on the reverse side. To claim your discount please present this coupon when paying for your entry.

Customer care line number *free* phone 0800 316 8900

This coupon entitles the holder to the discount offer shown on the reverse side. To claim your discount please present this coupon when paying for your entry.

Customer care line number *free* phone 0800 316 8900

This coupon entitles the holder to the discount offer shown on the reverse side. To claim your discount please present this coupon when paying for your entry.

Customer care line number *free* phone 0800 316 8900

This coupon entitles the holder to the discount offer shown on the reverse side. To claim your discount please present this coupon when paying for your entry.

Customer care line number *free* phone 0800 316 8900

This coupon entitles the holder to the discount offer shown on the reverse side. To claim your discount please present this coupon when paying for your entry.

Customer care line number *free* phone 0800 316 8900

This coupon entitles the holder to the discount offer shown on the reverse side. To claim your discount please present this coupon when paying for your entry.

Customer care line number *free* phone 0800 316 8900

This coupon entitles the holder to the discount offer shown on the reverse side. To claim your discount please present this coupon when paying for your entry.

Customer care line number *free* phone 0800 316 8900

This coupon entitles the holder to the discount offer shown on the reverse side. To claim your discount please present this coupon when paying for your entry.

Customer care line number *free* phone 0800 316 8900

Cabaret Mechanical Theatre
London

£1.00 Off Family Ticket

not to be used in conjunction with any other offer, one coupon per party not valid on Bank Hols and event weekends.

Discount Coupon   Valid until end Feb 2001

Musical Museum
Brentford

Two For The Price Of One

not to be used in conjunction with any other offer, one coupon per party not valid on Bank Hols and event weekends.

Discount Coupon   Valid until 31 Oct 2000

Puppet Theatre Barge
London

One Ticket Free With Every Four Seats Booked

not to be used in conjunction with any other offer, one coupon per party not valid on Bank Hols and event weekends.

Discount Coupon   Valid until end Feb 2001

Polka Theatre for Children
London
Two For The Price Of One
For Saturday 2nd Main House Performance

not to be used in conjunction with any other offer, one coupon per party not valid on Bank Hols and event weekends.

Discount Coupon   Valid until end Feb 2001

Royal Observatory Greenwich
London

One Free With Adult Ticket
Ref: DOG

not to be used in conjunction with any other offer, one coupon per party not valid on Bank Hols and event weekends.

Discount Coupon   Valid until end Feb 2001

London Aquarium
London

£2.00 Off Published Admission Price

not to be used in conjunction with any other offer, one coupon per party not valid on Bank Hols and event weekends.

Discount Coupon   Valid until end Feb 2001

This coupon entitles the holder to the discount offer
shown on the reverse side. To claim your discount
please present this coupon when paying for your entry.

Customer care line number *free* phone 0800 316 8900

This coupon entitles the holder to the discount offer
shown on the reverse side. To claim your discount
please present this coupon when paying for your entry.

Customer care line number *free* phone 0800 316 8900

This coupon entitles the holder to the discount offer
shown on the reverse side. To claim your discount
please present this coupon when paying for your entry.

Customer care line number *free* phone 0800 316 8900

This coupon entitles the holder to the discount offer
shown on the reverse side. To claim your discount
please present this coupon when paying for your entry.

Customer care line number *free* phone 0800 316 8900

This coupon entitles the holder to the discount offer
shown on the reverse side. To claim your discount
please present this coupon when paying for your entry.

Customer care line number *free* phone 0800 316 8900

This coupon entitles the holder to the discount offer
shown on the reverse side. To claim your discount
please present this coupon when paying for your entry.

Customer care line number *free* phone 0800 316 8900

Page 151

Gunnersbury Park Museum
London

Any Three Postcards Free

not to be used in conjunction with any other offer, one coupon per party not valid on Bank Hols and event weekends.

Discount Coupon **Valid until end Feb 2001**

Page 152

Chelsea Football Club
London

4th Child Free When Family Ticket Purchased

not to be used in conjunction with any other offer, one coupon per party not valid on Bank Hols and event weekends.

Discount Coupon **Valid until end Feb 2001**

Page 156

UK Bungee Club
London

One Person Jumps Free - The Other Pays Full Price
(All Jumpers MUST Pay The £15 Membership and Insurance)

not to be used in conjunction with any other offer, one coupon per party not valid on Bank Hols and event weekends.

Discount Coupon **Valid until end Feb 2001**

Page 157

M.C.C. Museum and Tour of Lord's
London

Two For The Price Of One

not to be used in conjunction with any other offer, one coupon per party not valid on Bank Hols and event weekends.

Discount Coupon **Valid until end Feb 2001**

Page 157

Museum of Rugby & Twickenham Stadium Tours
Twickenham

One Child Free With A Full Paying Adult

not to be used in conjunction with any other offer, one coupon per party not valid on Bank Hols and event weekends.

Discount Coupon **Valid until end Feb 2001**

Page 157

Wimbledon Lawn Tennis Museum
London

£1.00 Off Adult Admission

not to be used in conjunction with any other offer, one coupon per party not valid on Bank Hols and event weekends.

Discount Coupon **Valid until end Feb 2001**

The Leading Days Out Guide

P O Box 427
Northampton
NN2 7YJ

This coupon entitles the holder to the discount offer shown on the reverse side. To claim your discount please present this coupon when paying for your entry.

Customer care line number *free* phone 0800 316 8900

This coupon entitles the holder to the discount offer shown on the reverse side. To claim your discount please present this coupon when paying for your entry.

Customer care line number *free* phone 0800 316 8900

This coupon entitles the holder to the discount offer shown on the reverse side. To claim your discount please present this coupon when paying for your entry.

Customer care line number *free* phone 0800 316 8900

This coupon entitles the holder to the discount offer shown on the reverse side. To claim your discount please present this coupon when paying for your entry.

Customer care line number *free* phone 0800 316 8900

This coupon entitles the holder to the discount offer shown on the reverse side. To claim your discount please present this coupon when paying for your entry.

Customer care line number *free* phone 0800 316 8900

This coupon entitles the holder to the discount offer shown on the reverse side. To claim your discount please present this coupon when paying for your entry.

Customer care line number *free* phone 0800 316 8900

Page 158

Segaworld

London

Two Multi-Ride Tickets For The Price Of One

not to be used in conjunction with any other offer, one coupon per party not valid on Bank Hols and event weekends.

Discount Coupon   Valid until end Feb 2001

Page 162

London Transport Museum

London

£1.00 Off Adult, 50p Off Child Admissions OR

£2.00 Off Family Ticket(A2+C2)

not to be used in conjunction with any other offer, one coupon per party not valid on Bank Hols and event weekends.

Discount Coupon   Valid until end Feb 2001

Page 163

London Zoo

London

One Child Free With A Full Paying Adult

not to be used in conjunction with any other offer, one coupon per party not valid on Bank Hols and event weekends.

Discount Coupon   Valid until end Feb 2001

Page 166

Rural Life Centre

Farnham

Two For The Price Of One

not to be used in conjunction with any other offer, one coupon per party not valid on Bank Hols and event weekends.

Discount Coupon   Valid until end Feb 2001

Page 173

RHS Garden Wisley

Woking

Two For The Price Of One. Mon-Sat only

not to be used in conjunction with any other offer, one coupon per party not valid on Bank Hols and event weekends.

Discount Coupon   Valid Oct 2000-Mar 2001

Page 183

Lingfield Park Racecourse

Lingfield

£2.00 Off Per Person

not to be used in conjunction with any other offer, one coupon per party not valid on Bank Hols and event weekends.

Discount Coupon   Valid until end Feb 2001

P O Box 427 Northampton NN2 7YJ — The Leading Days Out Guide

This coupon entitles the holder to the discount offer shown on the reverse side. To claim your discount please present this coupon when paying for your entry.

Customer care line number *free* phone 0800 316 8900

This coupon entitles the holder to the discount offer shown on the reverse side. To claim your discount please present this coupon when paying for your entry.

Customer care line number *free* phone 0800 316 8900

This coupon entitles the holder to the discount offer shown on the reverse side. To claim your discount please present this coupon when paying for your entry.

Customer care line number *free* phone 0800 316 8900

This coupon entitles the holder to the discount offer shown on the reverse side. To claim your discount please present this coupon when paying for your entry.

Customer care line number *free* phone 0800 316 8900

This coupon entitles the holder to the discount offer shown on the reverse side. To claim your discount please present this coupon when paying for your entry.

Customer care line number *free* phone 0800 316 8900

This coupon entitles the holder to the discount offer shown on the reverse side. To claim your discount please present this coupon when paying for your entry.

Customer care line number *free* phone 0800 316 8900